"The world desperately needs greater wisdom on the nature and purpose of work. Guitián contributes to this need giving us the collective insights of an impressive group of theologians drawing upon a 2000-year-old wisdom tradition. All scholars and practitioners would greatly benefit from its insights".

Michael J. Naughton, *University of St. Thomas, USA*

"The fruit of an impressive multi-year scholarly collaboration at the University of Navarra, this volume makes a distinctive and valuable contribution to contemporary Catholic discussions on work. Offering 'new perspectives' that foreground the theological, scholars draw fresh, tradition-anchored insights from scripture, patristics, liturgy, dogma, ethics, and more. Ecumenical and international voices further enrich this noteworthy book".

Christine Firer Hinze, *Fordham University, USA*

Theology of Work

Theology of Work: New Perspectives emerges from the necessity to continue theological reflection on work in light of the challenges posed by our contemporary world. The contributions offer a global perspective of the meaning of work, drawing from Trinitarian theology, theology of creation, eschatology, theological anthropology, and Christology. They shed light from the perspective of faith on the integration of different work dimensions, and consider how the theology of work is called to challenge social structures in light of revelation. The volume mostly develops the theology of work from a Catholic perspective, but Protestant and Orthodox approaches are also explicitly explored. The chapters cover different theological areas, such as biblical, dogmatic, patristic, and moral theology, to provide enriching and complementary perspectives. Offering fresh and valuable theological insights on work, this book will be of particular interest to scholars of theology and religious studies.

Gregorio Guitián is Associate Professor of Moral Theology and Dean of the School of Theology at the University of Navarra, Spain.

Routledge New Critical Thinking in Religion, Theology and Biblical Studies

The *Routledge New Critical Thinking in Religion, Theology and Biblical Studies* series brings high-quality research monograph publishing back into focus for authors, international libraries, and student, academic, and research readers. This open-ended monograph series presents cutting-edge research from both established and new authors in the field. With specialist focus yet clear contextual presentation of contemporary research, books in the series take research into important new directions and open the field to new critical debate within the discipline, in areas of related study, and in key areas for contemporary society.

Anglican Confirmation 1820–1945
From 'Renewing the Baptismal Covenant' to 'The Sacramental Principle'
Phillip Tovey

Divine Presence as Activity and the Incarnation
Revisiting Chalcedonian Christology
Alexander S. Jensen

Natural Final Causality and Scholastic Theology
Corey Barnes

Conflict and Catholic Social Ethics
An Interdisciplinary Approach
Taylor J. Ott

Divine Revelation and the Sciences
Essays in the History and Philosophy of Revelation
Edited by Balázs M. Mezei

For more information about this series, please visit: https://www.routledge.com/religion/series/RCRITREL

Theology of Work
New Perspectives

Edited by
Gregorio Guitián

LONDON AND NEW YORK

First published 2025
by Routledge
4 Park Square, Milton Park, Abingdon, Oxon OX14 4RN

and by Routledge
605 Third Avenue, New York, NY 10158

Routledge is an imprint of the Taylor & Francis Group, an informa business

© 2025 selection and editorial matter, Gregorio Guitián; individual chapters, the contributors

The right of Gregorio Guitián to be identified as the author of the editorial material, and of the authors for their individual chapters, has been asserted in accordance with sections 77 and 78 of the Copyright, Designs and Patents Act 1988.

All rights reserved. No part of this book may be reprinted or reproduced or utilised in any form or by any electronic, mechanical, or other means, now known or hereafter invented, including photocopying and recording, or in any information storage or retrieval system, without permission in writing from the publishers.

Trademark notice: Product or corporate names may be trademarks or registered trademarks, and are used only for identification and explanation without intent to infringe.

British Library Cataloguing-in-Publication Data
A catalogue record for this book is available from the British Library

Library of Congress Cataloging-in-Publication Data
Names: Guitián, Gregorio, editor.
Title: Theology of work : new perspectives /
edited by Gregorio Guitián.
Description: Abingdon, Oxon ; New York, NY : Routledge, 2025. |
Series: New critical thinking in religion, theology and biblical studies |
Includes bibliographical references and index.
Identifiers: LCCN 2024028993 (print) | LCCN 2024028994 (ebook) |
ISBN 9781032821375 (hbk) | ISBN 9781032831961 (pbk) |
ISBN 9781003508212 (ebk)
Subjects: LCSH: Work—Religious aspects—Catholic Church. |
Work—Religious aspects—Christianity.
Classification: LCC BX1795.W67 T43 2025 (print) |
LCC BX1795.W67 (ebook) | DDC 261.8/5—dc23/eng/20240807
LC record available at https://lccn.loc.gov/2024028993
LC ebook record available at https://lccn.loc.gov/2024028994

ISBN: 978-1-032-82137-5 (hbk)
ISBN: 978-1-032-83196-1 (pbk)
ISBN: 978-1-003-50821-2 (ebk)

DOI: 10.4324/9781003508212

Typeset in Sabon
by codeMantra

To Professor José Luis Illanes

Contents

List of contributors	*xi*
Preface	*xv*
GREGORIO GUITIÁN	
Acknowledgments	*xvii*

1 Theology of work: context, integration, challenge   1
GREGORIO GUITIÁN

PART I
Context   17

2 Does God work? Shall we work in heaven? In search of a
theological foundation for human work   19
SANTIAGO SANZ SÁNCHEZ

3 Laboring for rest: rudiments of an Orthodox theology of work   39
ALEXIS TORRANCE

4 Human–divine synergy. Human labor and the
transformation of the cosmos in Russian thinkers of the
early twentieth century   59
ANDRZEJ PERSIDOK

5 Creative art and theology of work: contributions from
St. Bonaventure   77
ISABEL M. LEÓN-SANZ

6 Daily life and work in the light of the mystery of Christ   95
ANTONIO ARANDA

7 Work, οἰκοδομή and πνεῦμα. A view from the Pauline categories   112
JUAN LUIS CABALLERO

x *Contents*

PART II
Integration   129

8 The value of work in the Book of Ecclesiastes (*Qoheleth*). Is
       an optimistic view possible given the onerous experience of
       many jobs?   131
       DIEGO PÉREZ GONDAR

9 Rethinking work from the Book of Leviticus   150
       FRANCISCO VARO

10 From *homo faber* to *homo liturgicus*. Toward a theology
        of work in liturgical perspective   169
        FÉLIX MARÍA AROCENA

11 The personal good of work. A comprehensive reading of the
        subjective dimension of work   187
        HÉLIO LUCIANO

12 Contemplation at work. Social contemplation and mysticism
        for an integral ecology of work   203
        MARTIN SCHLAG

PART III
Challenge   225

13 Work in Protestant perspective: a not so unintended Reformation 227
        D. STEPHEN LONG

14 Labor of love: the meaning of work in the household   247
        MARY L. HIRSCHFELD

15 Embracing better work: a reply to Jeremy Posadas   267
        DAVID CLOUTIER

16 Work, hope, and secularity   285
        ANA MARTA GONZÁLEZ

       Index   *301*

Contributors

Antonio Aranda (1942–2023) was Professor of Dogmatic Theology in the School of Theology of the University of Navarra, Spain. His most recent monograph is *A imagen de Dios en Cristo: cuestiones de antropología teológica* (Eunsa, 2023, 411pp.).

Félix María Arocena is Professor of Liturgical Theology in the School of Theology of the University of Navarra, Spain. He is the author of *Las colectas del Misal romano. Domingos y Solemnidades del Señor* (Centro Liturgico Vincenziano [CLV], 2021, 500pp).

Juan Luis Caballero is Associate Professor of New Testament in the School of Theology of the University of Navarra, Spain. He has recently published "Elementos para una teología paulina del trabajo" (*Scripta Theologica*) and "Freedom and Dependence in Pauline Writings. A theological Approach according to Colossians and Ephesians" (*Θεολογία*).

David Cloutier is Professor of Moral Theology in the Department of Theology with a concurrent appointment in the Business Ethics and Society Program of the Mendoza College of Business, at the University of Notre Dame, USA. He is the author of two award-winning books, *The Vice of Luxury* (Georgetown University Press, 2015) and *Walking God's Earth: The Environment and Catholic Faith* (Liturgical, 2014).

Ana Marta González is Professor of Philosophy at the University of Navarra, Spain, and Director of the Department of Philosophy. She recently authored *Trabajo, sentido y desarrollo. Inflexiones de la cultura moderna* (Dykinson, 2023), and "Culture and Hope. Reflections on Bellah's Unfinished Project" (In: *Challenging Modernity*, Columbia University Press, 2024).

Gregorio Guitián is Associate Professor of Moral Theology and Dean of the School of Theology of the University of Navarra, Spain. His research focuses on Catholic Social Teaching on Economics and has published several books and journal articles. He is leading the project "The meaning of work in recent theology".

xii *Contributors*

Mary L. Hirschfeld is John T. Ryan Jr. Associate Professor of Theology and Business Ethics and Academic Director of the Business Ethics and Society Program at the University of Notre Dame, USA. Her book *Aquinas and the Market: Toward a Humane Economy* was published by Harvard University Press in 2018.

Isabel M. León-Sanz is Associate Professor in the School of Theology of the University of Navarra, Spain. She received the "Marco Arosio Award" 2017 (Cattedra Marco Arosio di Alti Studi Medievali, APRA, Roma) for her book *El arte creador en san Buenaventura. Fundamentos para una teología de la belleza* (Eunsa, 2016).

D. Stephen Long is Cary M. Maguire University Professor of Ethics at Southern Methodist University, USA. He recently published *On Teaching and Learning Christian Ethics* (Georgetown University, 2024).

Hélio Luciano is Assistant Professor of Moral Theology in the School of Theology, University of Navarra, Spain, where he also earned his Ph.D. He focuses on fundamental moral theology and morality applied to bioethics, seeking to contribute to the development and understanding of contemporary ethical issues.

Diego Pérez Gondar is Associate Professor in the School of Theology of the University of Navarra, Spain. He specializes in Old Testament texts in the New Testament through intertestamental literature. His publications focus on the use of Psalms in NT texts, emphasizing dialogism within the Judeo-Christian tradition.

Andrzej Persidok is Assistant Professor of Fundamental Theology at the Catholic Academy in Warsaw, Poland. He pursued his studies at the University of Navarra (Pamplona, Spain), where he completed his doctoral degree in theology in 2016 with a dissertation on Christology and anthropology in the works of Henri de Lubac.

Santiago Sanz Sánchez is Professor in the School of Theology of the Pontifical University Santa Croce in Rome, Italy. He recently authored *Alfa e omega. Breve manuale di protologia ed escatologia* (Fede & Cultura, 2021). He is currently working with M. Ramage on a monograph on the Lectures of J. Ratzinger on the Doctrine of Creation.

Martin Schlag is Alan W. Moss endowed Chair for Catholic Social Thought at the University of St. Thomas in Minnesota, USA, where he is the Co-Director of the Terrence J. Murphy Institute for Catholic thought, law, and business. His research is focused on the intersection of theology and business in society.

Alexis Torrance is Archbishop Demetrios Associate Professor of Byzantine Theology at the University of Notre Dame, USA. He recently authored

Human Perfection in Byzantine Theology: Attaining the Fullness of Christ (Oxford University Press, 2020)

Francisco Varo is Professor of Biblical Studies in the School of Theology of the University of Navarra, Spain. He has recently authored "Anthropological and ethical elements in the criminal law of the Hebrew Bible" (REHJ 42) and "The sociological background of the semantic field of the foreigner in the Pentateuch" (RSPT 103).

Preface

Gregorio Guitián

In early 2020, amidst the pandemic, and conscious of the relevance of work for the human person and the contemporary challenges it presents, a group of professors in the School of Theology of the University of Navarra embarked on a research project on the theology of work.

Beginning with an extensive review of literature on theology of work from recent decades, the project aims to explore useful approaches to current challenges surrounding work. A distinctive element of the project is its intentional inclusion of participants from diverse theological areas (scripture, dogmatics, patristics, and morals), thus providing enriching and complementary perspectives. As a result, the project PIUNA Strategic Line: "The Meaning of Work in Recent Theology" was born. Its primary objective is to detect new categories or perspectives from the existing theological literature on work to enhance our understanding of human work in the present context.

Over two years, the team held monthly seminars leading to several publications. After that time, the participants, along with other invited scholars, convened for a two-day workshop titled *Theology of Work: New Perspectives*, at the University of Navarra (May 30–31, 2023). During this event, these scholars presented and discussed their research findings. This volume captures a portion of the outcomes from the project and aims to offer valuable theological perspectives for those who recognize the urgency of reflecting on work within the contemporary landscape.

The contributions of the book mostly develop the theology of work from a Catholic perspective; yet the Protestant and Orthodox approaches are also explicitly explored. Indeed, a distinctive feature of the book is that it offers further development of the theology of work through Catholic lenses, thus contributing to an existing conversation, which, at least in recent years, seemed to be a more prevalent concern among Protestant authors. Compared to similar works and in searching for different approaches, the contributors in this volume have deliberately selected other books of the *Bible*, engaged with different authors, paid attention to a broader spectrum of dimensions related to work, or sought to challenge the current understanding of work.

xvi *Gregorio Guitián*

As theologians, we are aware that finding specific solutions to the current situation requires an interdisciplinary approach, but we can definitely contribute with a wisdom perspective. Similarly, the complexity of today's world demands a vast array of theological views. While this book does not intend to be exhaustive, it will stimulate readers to develop the theological viewpoints offered and to inspire fresh approaches within their own discipline that may illuminate the challenges of human work.

In fact, the research project in which this book is framed embraces an interdisciplinary vision, encompassing two phases. The initial phase, as explained, is strictly dedicated to establishing theological foundations. But beginning in September 2023, the subsequent phase is interdisciplinary and involves a series of research projects addressing various contemporary work challenges, such as "Work as a Human Vector of Sustainable Development", "Vocational Professions and the Organization of Work", "Rest, Work, and Leisure", among others. Professor Ana Marta González (School of Philosophy, University of Navarra) co-directs the theological project with me and is in charge of the establishment and supervision of the interdisciplinary phase. This comprehensive endeavor includes the involvement of approximately 50 scholars from different disciplines and institutions, constituting the Strategic Research Line of the University of Navarra: "Work, Care, and Development". The participants conduct research in the fields of theology, medicine, nursing, philosophy, economics, sociology, philology, literature, history, arts, education, psychology, law, communication, architecture, ecology, demography, and engineering.

In our lives, we do not only invest considerable time in work but also engage in frequent conversation about it. Work serves as both occupation and preoccupation. Yet, given its central role in human existence, work merits profound reflection rather than being assumed or taken for granted. It is time to delve deeply into this essential aspect of human experience, and theology, like many other disciplines, has much to contribute.

Acknowledgments

This book has been made possible through the generous collaboration and support of many. First and foremost, I extend my gratitude to the University of Navarra for recognizing the relevance of the topic and providing support throughout the project. I am deeply appreciative of Professor Ana Marta González and all participants for their commitment and dedication. I must also acknowledge the invaluable contributions of my colleagues at the School of Theology of the University of Navarra. Their enthusiastic engagement has been crucial in advancing this research. I am also thankful to scholars from various countries whose insights, reviews, and suggestions have enriched both the content of this book and the project behind it. Special recognition goes to Professors César Izquierdo, Rafael Domingo, and Miguel Brugarolas for their encouraging support and advice, as well as to Professor William Mattison, the Department of Theology, and the Mendoza College of Business at the University of Notre Dame for hosting me during the editing of the book. In addition, I wish to pay tribute to the late Professor Antonio Aranda (1942–2023). He foresaw the importance of a project on the theology of work from the very beginning, immediately agreed to take part in it, but unfortunately passed away shortly after reviewing his contribution for this volume. Lastly, I extend my appreciation to Rocio de Lange and Carola Maomed for their diligent editorial assistance.

1 Theology of work: context, integration, challenge

Gregorio Guitián

Enlightened by faith, theology offers unique insights on realities that matter and concern humanity, and nowadays, the subject of work is certainly one of them. Throughout history, theological reflection has addressed the topic of work in various ways, sometimes explicitly but partially.[1] However, it was the momentous transformation brought about by the first industrialization that triggered the so-called "social question", thrusting work into the limelight and bringing forth significant philosophical and theological reflection on the matter. Over the years, the first allusions to a "theology of work" appeared in France[2] though the subsequent evolution of our world has considerably altered the landscape.

We are now witnessing a rapid evolution marked by a variety of manifestations, some of them dramatic. High unemployment rates in numerous countries afflict millions of individuals, both young and middle-aged, with the dire struggle of seeking employment but finding none. Simultaneously, in many developing countries, numerous individuals toil under harsh conditions in the service of our developed world in what are referred to as "sweatshops"[3]—conditions that, in the words of Pope Leo XIII in 1891, can again be described as "little better than that of slavery itself".[4]

On the other hand, people increasingly give more importance to the subjective experience of work, viewing it as a means of individual fulfillment, social integration, and a source of psychological stability, freedom, and autonomy.[5] Consequently, there has been a growing academic literature in the social sciences exploring the concept of "meaningful work".[6] However, it is noteworthy that in the quest for meaningful work, some individuals become "workaholics" elevating work to an almost religious status, i.e., "the belief that work is not only necessary to economic production, but also the centerpiece of one's identity and life's purpose".[7] Moreover, the prevalent long working hours and frenetic rhythms characteristic of contemporary societies often lead many workers into a spiral of stress and anxiety, eventually resulting in burnout. This fact contributes to a sense of apprehension among young individuals entering the labor market. An illuminating example is a student who obtained the first place in Spain's national exam for medical specialization. Since the student would be the first to choose a specialization, she sought advice from veteran

DOI: 10.4324/9781003508212-1

2 Gregorio Guitián

doctors: "many of them—she recalls—were burned out, and others told me that the days and nights on-call had increased their pay 'but had taken years off their lives'". Faced with this reality, she chose dermatology "to be happy and not get burned out".[8] In this context, it is not surprising that disenchantment led millions of workers in developed countries to voluntarily quit their jobs during the pandemic (at least temporarily) due to reasons such as low pay, lack of opportunities for professional advancement, or feeling undervalued—a phenomenon now known as "the great resignation".[9]

Finally, a few years ago, the International Labour Organization envisaged a horizon characterized by "flexibilization" and precariousness.[10] Due to technological advances, work is expected to become less stable, more informal, employers more indirect, and workplaces becoming more "fissured" due to the outsourcing of numerous services, often redirected to developing countries. Consequently, jobs that are easier to automate will disappear, while those requiring greater interpersonal skills and creativity will increase. As a result, inequality is predicted to rise, and the complexity of this scenario will make it more challenging to ensure the protection of workers on a global scale. The truth, however, is that this future is already here.

This quick description serves to explain why work is again an area of interest to theology. Consequently, this book arises from the necessity to continue theological reflection on work in light of the challenges posed by our world. As explained in the Preface, the framework of this book is the project "The Meaning of Work in Recent Theology", at the School of Theology of the University of Navarra.[11] A group of scholars from diverse theological areas (scripture, dogmatics, patristics, morals), have held regular seminars over the past years, enabling each participant to delve into their respective themes and resulting in several publications.[12] Ultimately, this volume is the culmination of an enriching dialogue.

In this context, the review of the recent bibliography on the theology of work[13] and the studies carried out so far in the project lead us to identify what I believe are the four key contributions that the theology of work can make at the present time: the definition of work, the contextualization of work, the integration of its dimensions, and the challenging of the current understanding and organization of work. Leaving aside the first theme, which is a preliminary question, the contributions in this volume are concentrated around the other three cores, which I summarize as "context", "integration", and "challenge". These key points frame and allow us to understand the themes addressed in this volume. Therefore, in what remains of the introduction, I will first deal with the definition of work and then present the other three themes and the contributions of the authors of the volume.

The theology of work

The first question that stands out in the literature is the very definition of work. As early as 1957, Otto Piper asserted that "it is only on the basis of

Theology of work: context, integration, challenge 3

a comprehensive analysis of the nature and function of work that the attempt can be made to formulate a Christian theology of work".[14] However, there have been frequent complaints regarding this issue. For Joseph Thomas, for instance, the difficulty is found in "the very imprecision of the object to which it refers", since work itself "has undergone a rapid evolution that renders many writings obsolete".[15] In a similar vein, authors like Joseph Comblin refrain from providing a fixed definition, understanding work as a dynamic reality shaped by the circumstances of each era.[16] Thus it is unsurprising that John Paul II, in his 1981 encyclical *Laborem Exercens*, defined work as "any human activity that can and must be recognized as work, amid all the many activities of which man is capable and to which he is predisposed by his very nature".[17]

Even scholars outside the field of theology encounter difficulties in offering a complete and comprehensive definition of work, or in explaining what makes it meaningful. Professor Joanne Ciulla reports that only in the *Oxford English Dictionary*, there are nine pages including definitions of work; *The Random House Dictionary* brings 54 definitions and *Webster's New Unabridged Dictionary* provides 45.[18] Having written a book on the meaning of human work and returned to the subject 17 years later, Ciulla began by stating that "there is little that is self-evident about the concept of meaningful work" (p. 198). Apparently, meaningful work is

> in the eye of the beholder. We know it when we have it, because it has a way of lighting up our lives or making the time that we spend working good in a certain way. If this sounds fuzzy, it's because it is. Given the variety of people and what they find meaningful, I was not ready to proclaim what meaningful work is for everyone.
>
> (p. 197)

The reader, however, should not be intimidated by the complexity of defining work. In 1971, Yves Simon started his book *Work, society, and culture* by noting that "the daily life of man is composed of things whose meaning is hidden in the mystery of their familiarity. Work is one of these".[19] The French philosopher devoted the first chapter of his book to the concept of work. Simon holds that the difficulty with providing a definition of work stems from a lack of essential unity, for work is a complex whose components make it hard to comprise it in one essence. However, he was able to offer some clear ideas: (a) work cannot be defined only in metaphysical terms; its social dimension is decisive; (b) work is a socially useful activity; it implies a service to society; (c) work is not, and it can never be, an activity of "free expansion" or development (as opposed to activities done out of necessity and in ways largely predetermined, i.e., governed by laws which the worker has no power to change); and (d) the irksomeness of work is not an essential characteristic of it.[20]

Without a deep analytical insight, it is not surprising that definitions of work vary between those that are too broad, encompassing almost all human

4   *Gregorio Guitián*

activity, and those that are too narrow. For example, Hanson points out that some definitions focus solely on work as an activity to transform the environment, overlooking its impact on the worker's self-transformation.[21] Others, often unconsciously, reduce work to paid employment. In my view, apart from the perspective bias that influences any definition of work, its complexity also stems from the necessity for an in-depth understanding of human beings, as work is intricately tied to the fact that man and woman are created in the image and likeness of God, who is a profound mystery. Work serves as a metaphor for the human being, and there is an inherent mystery surrounding man.

This is where theology can make valuable contributions. As Joseph Thomas underscores, the theology of work is a coherent reflection that situates human work within the broader context of God's plan, known through divine revelation.[22] It provides a comprehensive perspective founded on reason and enlightened by faith, placing the meaning of work within the framework of creation's purpose and humanity's role in it.

Darrell Cosden, the author of one of the two most outstanding monographs on the theology of work in recent years, offers a definition worth mentioning as it provides a useful reference for further discussion.[23] Cosden not only seeks a complete definition of work but also emphasizes its intrinsic ontological value, willing to avoid any hierarchical arrangement of its dimensions to ensure each aspect is equally recognized. In his view, hierarchizing would imply downplaying the importance of some dimension of work.[24] For Cosden, the fundamental mistake made by John Paul II in *Laborem Exercens* is the subordination of the objective dimension of work to its subjective dimension. This mistake, according to Cosden, is also present in Volf's work, as he gives precedence to the instrumental aspect of work (as a means of sustenance). One can observe that the idea of hierarchy is sensitive to Cosden, but rejecting it leads him to blur the very concept of the image and likeness, and thus of human dignity. In fact, Cosden emphasizes the ontological dimension of work in view of the new creation so strongly that

> objective work (matter) ceases to be an object in the sense that Pope John Paul II describes it. It becomes also and equally a subject. In this scenario, humans and things can be placed beside each other and theoretically both can be valued equally and non-hierarchically.
>
> (p. 35)

On this basis, work is defined as

> a transformative activity essentially consisting of dynamically interrelated instrumental, relational, and ontological dimensions; whereby, along with work being an end in itself, the worker's and others' needs are providentially met; believers' sanctification is occasioned; and workers express, explore and develop their humanness while building

Theology of work: context, integration, challenge 5

up their natural, social and cultural environments thereby contributing protectively and productively to the order of this world and the one to come.

(pp. 178–179)

The definition is, perhaps, too articulate and complex. It is not possible to analyze each of the dimensions identified by Cosden—a thorough examination of which takes up the entirety of his monograph. For our purpose, however, it is sufficient to point out that the definition includes the elements of necessity and sociability elucidated by Yves Simon, together with the emphasis on the intrinsic value of work for the future world. Nevertheless, it is not clear whether the insistence on the intrinsic value of work to the point that "believer's sanctification is occasioned" could be interpreted in terms of a secularization of sanctification, as if every work somehow, providentially, sanctifies.[25]

This question leads us to hold that any attempt at a theological definition of work necessarily implies a normative or moral dimension. This is because the theological perspective is rooted in the purpose and potential intended for our nature and defines work in terms of its relationship to that divine order. It is clear that just as not every response of men and women to God's call is consistent with the purpose for which God has created them (we may consider the existence of sin), so not every kind of work or mode of working adequately responds to the divine design.

To spare the reader from a lengthy review of various theological definitions of work, I will directly present the theological definition of work developed within the context of this project, following a thorough review of the relevant literature:

> Work is a type of human action oriented towards supporting one's own life (or that of others) in response to God's call to personal perfection and collaboration in the development of creation. It is carried out within a social context, serving the needs of the human community to which one belongs.[26]

The elements pointed out by Yves Simon are present here too along with the moral dimension implied by the calling to personal perfection. Thus the definition includes the fundamental concepts of intentional human action, necessity, vocation to personal perfection (including sanctification), the social and service-oriented dimension,[27] and the contribution to the development of the cosmos according to the purpose intended by God (which points at eschatology).

In his chapter, Alexis Torrance objects that this definition excludes those works that do not: (a) contribute to the perfection of the person—or even may hinder it—; (b) develop creation, or (c) serve the needs of the human community. In this sense, it appears that many jobs today would not qualify as true

6 *Gregorio Guitián*

work. This remark deserves comment. All activities commonly considered as "work" participate in some aspects of the definition of work that we propose, such as being a means of earning a living. In that sense, they are work. However, as explained earlier, a theological definition of work should include a moral dimension. Insofar as those activities might not align with other dimensions of work in conformity with God's call, such as genuinely contributing to a person's perfecting, they cannot be considered work in the proper, full, or completely true sense. In other words, if work is not integrated into the broader context of the purpose and potential intended for our nature, it runs the risk of losing its true meaning. Theology is called upon to provoke a thoughtful consideration in this regard so that work can effectively align with what God intended it to be.

This last aspect broadens the understanding of work and leads us to the second crucial element that the theology of work brings to the contemporary approach: contextualizing work.

Context

Some years ago, a much experienced professor of theology shared a story that had a lasting impact on his academic work. One day, an elderly woman told him, in tears, the story of her life: she and her husband had devoted the best efforts of their lives to working in a company. They worked really hard even though this implied often giving up time for relaxation, hobbies, cultural activities, etc. They had an only son who secured a good job after graduation. They then gave him a motorcycle with which, one day, he tragically lost his life in an accident. Shattered, they blamed each other for having come up with the idea of that fatal gift. However, what tormented her most was not that, but the realization that their life's highest achievement had been solely their contributing to the company's economic value, resulting in a higher retirement pension than their co-workers. While her co-workers seemed fulfilled, surrounded by their children and grandchildren, she and her husband were left alone, having missed out on many enriching experiences due to work. Grief-stricken, she concluded that if she could go back in time, she would approach her life very differently and ended up begging him, since he was a professor, to write books to help young people not to make the same mistake.

This real story shows that the genuine meaning of work is not guaranteed even if all the objective conditions (remuneration, work hours, health, safety, efficiency, effectiveness, technical excellence, etc.) or subjective conditions (social recognition, self-esteem, skills, self-fulfillment, service, etc.), as described in the literature on meaningful work, are met. Work needs a context. We always make our decisions in pursuit of what we consider the greater good for ourselves. We make our decisions according to a hierarchy of goods, whether consciously or not. Therefore, it is vital to understand work not in isolation but in the broader context of the good of human life as a whole.[28]

Theology of work: context, integration, challenge 7

However, the "context" implied by this story is not the whole picture because there is an additional layer in the theological understanding of "context": transcendence. Experience shows that there are plenty of people who perceive and live their work as a calling, as part of their response to the divine invitation to participate in God's purpose for this world. This context involves an orientation toward transcendent horizons beyond mere economic and personal fulfillment or prestige. When work lacks such a transcendent horizon, it falls short as a human ideal. Just as rivers flow into the sea, human work must open itself to the immensity of transcendence. In this sense, revelation, culminating in Jesus Christ, offers a global perspective that can be invaluable in properly understanding the context of human work.

The theological definition of work is rooted in the nature and purpose that God has bestowed upon human beings and creation as a whole. Divine revelation, coupled with human experience, provides valuable insights into the meaning of mankind and the world. At the core, man and woman are created in the image and likeness of God, imbued with a unique mission within creation.[29] The blessing-mission they receive (cf. Gen 1:23) and their actions in the world, including work, are influenced by this distinct way of being. Nature and mission are intertwined. Moreover, humans are a unity of dualities: created in duality of sexes, human beings are material and spiritual, individual and social, rational and free, tied to matter and in a transcendent relationship with God, who is spirit. Thus, understanding the context of work—the mystery of man and his ultimate purpose—is crucial for work to achieve its full meaning.

The first part of this book, "context", aims to provide a comprehensive global perspective, drawing from Trinitarian theology, theology of creation, eschatology, theological anthropology, and Christology. While the reflection ascends to higher realms, it also offers inspiring insights for understanding human work.

The theology of work has made significant efforts to contextualize work within the framework of the end of creation. Recently, some contemporary Protestant theologians[30] have emphasized an eschatological understanding of work, building on discussions of the theology of earthly realities. In Chapter 2, Santiago Sanz critically analyzes recent positions, addressing the question of whether God's actions in creation can be considered work, which holds importance in relation to the doctrine of image and likeness.

Alexis Torrance and Andrezj Persidok approach work from the perspective of Orthodox theology. This is already novel because, as Torrance points out, there is very little theological literature on the subject within the realm of Orthodoxy. In Chapter 3, Torrance situates work in the context of humanity's journey toward its ultimate end, which is the blessed repose of the saints in union with Christ. This orientation, integrating the power of the incarnation and the eschatological destiny of humanity, not only imbues work with meaning but also underscores a set of principles. Rather than focusing on the type of work that is done, what matters is how work is oriented toward

8   *Gregorio Guitián*

Christ and guided by His commandments. Moreover, the contribution of work to communion is also emphasized, where each individual contributes through their own work and shares in the work of others. On his part, in Chapter 4, Andrezj Persidok explores the lesser-known views on work of some Russian Orthodox theologians and philosophers, including Bulgakov, Berdyaev, and their predecessors Fyodorov and Solovyov. They view labor and economy through an eschatological lens, perceiving work as a struggle against death until the universal resurrection. Human labor is seen as the "sophinization" or humanization of the world, aiming to transform it into a work of art. In this context, Man's vocation is seen as creative work, while sin frustrates this endeavor, causing work to potentially confine this world to its own finiteness and mortality.

Isabel León delves suggestively into the mystery of the Trinity to approach human work in Chapter 5. She draws from St. Bonaventure's doctrine of Trinitarian creative art, which, interconnected with the concept of image and likeness, highlights the uniqueness of human being: the only creature that acts artistically (i.e. that works) by carrying out a mediating function in the universe. Man is ordered to God, with all of nature guiding him or her toward knowing and loving God. Through their work, men and women imbue their actions with truth and significance, unveiling hidden aspects of God's glory. St. Bonaventure's thought allows us to consider the relationship between nature and human work in a balanced way, to deepen the foundation of creativity, and to understand the interplay between ability, intelligence, and love in labor. Thus, work becomes not only a testimony of rational lordship but, above all, a gift and a service.

Another often overlooked aspect in recent literature is the work of Christ. Despite the scarcity of references to work in the Gospels, a theological reflection that identifies as Christian cannot ignore the totality of Christ's life—not only his public life or the paschal mystery—as the key to the Christian conception of work. In Chapter 6, Antonio Aranda† explores the implications of the incarnation for a theological consideration of work, presenting a perspective marked by Christ's filial condition, and its impact on daily work life.

Finally, in Chapter 7, Juan Luis Caballero places work in the context of Pauline ecclesiology. Through a study of the letters of the Apostle Paul, the author shows how the images of the family, the home, and the body that Paul uses to describe the Church can also be useful for considering work. Indeed, work has a relational dimension and a dimension of contribution to the whole, of building up, which can be illuminated by faith. Drawing from the thought of St. Paul, Caballero proposes some "laws of edification" that can help individuals engaged in work to deepen the meaning of this activity.

Integration

The context, however, does not cancel the tensions experienced in everyday work. In real life—as in the story reported earlier—work, being a profound

Theology of work: context, integration challenge 9

expression of the mystery of humanity, is characterized by apparently opposing poles due to the complications introduced by sin into the human condition. These poles include the objective and the subjective dimensions of work; work and worship; work and faith; work and family; work and rest, to till and to keep (Gen 2:15); work and contemplation; personal project and the common good, and so on. Cosden rejects any hierarchy in considering the different dimensions of work (ontological, instrumental, and relational), but at the end of his book, he does acknowledge the need for hierarchy in certain circumstances.[31] Indeed, when confronted with real-life problems, it is impossible to escape priorities, albeit temporarily. Despite work having an intrinsic consistency and goodness, it is inserted in a context at the service of an ultimate end, which is not work itself but the purpose bestowed by God upon human nature. Yet this purpose takes on a concrete orientation: "If then you were raised with Christ, seek what is above, where Christ is seated at the right hand of God" (Col 3:1).

What Cosden is actually seeking when he rejects the hierarchy among the dimensions of work is a holistic vision that considers all of its dimensions at the same time. He speaks of "ethical equilibrium" or "harmonious balance" (p. 181), but it seems to me that the concept that perfectly captures the main thrust of recent theological reflection on work is "integration".[32] Indeed, in order to properly contextualize work within the whole of life, it is necessary to integrate the various aspects that come together in work, which is a total fact. In this regard, Michael Naughton's sharp observation in his book on work and leisure is very pertinent: the aim is not to achieve a balance or the elimination of one of these aspects, but to go further, to seek an integration in which each aspect informs, corrects, and complements the other.[33]

To be sure, the best service a theology of work can make lies in contributing to the discovery and pursuit of the path to work's integration into people's lives, and the transformation of social structures. In this regard, the Christian—and particularly the Catholic—worldview is strongly familiar with the idea of integration, as exemplified in the *paradoxical double affirmation* that runs through the Christian faith: God is one and triune, not one thing or the other (aut-aut), but both at once (et-et); Jesus Christ is true God and true man; in the Eucharist there is at once the real presence of Christ and the appearances of bread and wine; Mary is virgin and mother; the Church is human and divine; the human being is bodily and spiritual, individual and social, and so on. It is not a matter of balance but integration.

The contributions in the second part of this book share the common goal of shedding light from the perspective of faith on the integration of different work dimensions. In Chapter 8, Diego Pérez Gondar builds on a previous work that shows how the category of spousal covenant in the Genesis account of creation integrates work and family.[34] He addresses the clash between this optimistic vision of work and the onerous, tiring, or desperate experience of many jobs. For this task, he revisits the book of Ecclesiastes—whose vision of work seems ambiguous—in light of the

10   *Gregorio Guitián*

account of the fall (Gen 3). In Chapter 9, Francisco Varo takes an original approach to examine the integration between work and worship through the Book of Leviticus, which apparently says nothing about work. Varo discovers the close relationship between work and worship in this book and draws out interesting insights and consequences to be considered in contemporary work. Félix María Arocena addresses in Chapter 10 the separation between faith and work—a major concern in recent literature on the theology of work—by examining liturgical theology and the incorporation of work into the sacramental mystery, particularly the Eucharist. The grace of redemption accomplished by Jesus Christ, actualized in the Eucharist, plays a pivotal role in advancing the integration of diverse work dimensions into a cohesive whole.

One of the major contributions of John Paul II's Encyclical *Laborem Exercens* is the distinction and relationship between the objective and subjective dimensions of work, i.e., between the result of work (including technological and economic aspects) and the inner transformation of the working subject.[35] This topic has received considerable attention by the literature.[36] Yet, conscious of the tensions existing between these two aspects, Hélio Luciano explores in Chapter 11 a more unified view of human work from the perspective of fundamental moral theology, which has long discussed the objective and subjective aspects of moral action. On the basis of the work done by Daniel Granada, in which he highlights the recurring tension between the objective and subjective aspects of work, and suggests that the categories of virtue and love–affection–charity may serve to unify the action of work,[37] Luciano aims to integrate the objective elements into the subjective relationship. This integration is built on an understanding of moral life in which objective elements influence the individual and play a role in their free response. Elements such as just retribution, personal identity, solidarity, and inner freedom hold moral relevance and enrich the concept of work in both individual and social life. In a sense, this chapter addresses Cosden's critique of the hierarchical approach of the two dimensions of work, as highlighted by *Laborem Exercens*.

Still regarding the subjective dimension, the connection between work and contemplation remains a classic theme in practical (spiritual) theology. While engaged in work, the person is also called to contemplation. In Chapter 12, Martin Schlag looks to a different perspective for integrating work and contemplation by focusing on eco-theology. In fact, according to God's design, man and woman were placed in the garden to till it but also to keep it. Schlag draws upon the Catholic Social Teaching, Aquinas' thought, and the teachings of St. Josemaría Escrivá.

It might seem that the task of integrating work within the context of a comprehensive conception of the meaning of human life relies only on individual freedom, with the Christian also counting on divine grace, ordinarily channeled through the sacraments. Yet, there is another crucial dimension to be considered and the third part of the book turns to it.

Challenge

A theology of work cannot ignore or take for granted the structural context that significantly influences people's responses and efforts to integrate work into their lives as a whole.[38] In fact, many of the difficulties people experience today are largely due to the social and cultural context—including the economic system, legislation, work organization, technology—which implies a view of the value and meaning of human work and development. Where necessary, theology is also called to challenge this context in light of revelation. This is the direction taken by the contributions in the last part of the volume.

Some of the phenomena of the contemporary labor landscape described at the beginning of this introduction are related to the capitalist economic system. In Chapter 13, Duane Stephen Long approaches this situation from a Protestant perspective. On the one hand, he challenges Weber's "Protestant work ethic" and, on the other, presents an alternative inspired by a reformed Christian socialism. In contrast to a system that often offers jobs that don't support workers, isolates and prohibits basic social intercourse, consumes time as if it were a commodity, lacks any meaning or purpose, etc., Long proposes forms of cooperation and mutual love in companies that can transform structures.

An important part of the difficulty in integrating work and family lies in ideas deeply rooted in prevailing economic thinking, much of which is based on "rational choice" theories. The result is an economic system that is no longer able to see the colorfulness of human work; it sees work only in black and white, that is, only in terms of the commercial value attached to it. In Chapter 14, Mary Hirschfeld challenges this logic precisely because it prevents the virtues (and especially prudence) that are one of the keys to integrating the various dimensions of work in the service of a broader project. Drawing on studies by some women economists on work in the home, she questions the erosion of community caused by mainstream economic logic.

In confronting the current economic system, some scholars in the field of theology of work have put forward a thought-provoking proposal known as the "anti-work ethic".[39] This ethical stance challenges the inherent goodness of human work advocating for its outright elimination or diminishment. In Chapter 15, David Cloutier engages with this proposition critically, analyzing its underlying motivations and identifying its valuable aspects. As an alternative, he proposes a way to improve work by placing it in a vital context where notions of gift and service contribute to the development of both the person and society.

Finally, in Chapter 16, Ana Marta Gonzalez draws attention to the impact of secularization on contemporary society, wherein the crisis of work becomes evident through phenomena like the "great resignation". She posits that at its core, the crisis of work is intricately linked to a profound lack of hope and a disconnect between individual aspirations for personal growth and the broader contribution to the common good of society. To address

12   *Gregorio Guitián*

this disheartening perspective and instill a renewed sense of hope, Gonzalez proposes a transformative solution: the re-thinking of work and development through the lens of care and service, grounded in the redemption brought forth by Christ.

* * *

In concluding this introduction, I wish to emphasize this last point. Integrating human work within the context of God's divine plan demands the assistance of grace, which flows to us through the redemption of Jesus Christ. Through the transformative power of baptism, Christians are reborn as children of God in Christ. This fact influences every aspect of their lives, including their vocation to work. Empowered by infused theological virtues, Christians gain access to a profound context that provides meaning to their existence, with the risen Christ at its center, inspiring a path to integration and structural reform.

In this regard, it is worth recalling a mystical event that profoundly shaped the understanding of work for St. Josemaría Escrivá.[40] As will be noted throughout this book, several contributions implicitly or explicitly draw inspiration from his teachings. However, one intuition stands out prominently, stemming from a fresh interpretation of the words of Jesus as reported in the Gospel of John (12:32–33): "And when I am lifted up from the earth, I will draw everyone to myself. He said this indicating the kind of death he would die". The experience took place on August 7, 1931, while Escrivá was celebrating Mass. He documented the event in his personal notes:

> August 7, 1931: Today this diocese celebrates the feast of the Transfiguration of Our Lord Jesus Christ. When making my Mass intentions, I noted the interior change that God has made in me during these years (…). The time for the Consecration arrived. At the very moment when I elevated the Sacred Host, without my losing the necessary recollection, without my becoming distracted (for I had just made, mentally, the Offering to the Merciful Love), there came to my mind, with extraordinary force and clarity, that passage of Scripture, *Et ego, si exaltatus fuero a terra, omnia traham ad me ipsum* [Jn 12:32]. (Ordinarily, before the supernatural, I feel afraid. Later comes the "Do not be afraid, it is I.") And I understood that there will be men and women of God who will lift the cross, with the teachings of Christ, to the pinnacle of all human activities….And I saw our Lord triumph, attracting to himself all things.[41]

Human work, often marked by suffering, gains its ultimate meaning when drawn toward Christ on the Cross—a symbol of His infinite love for humanity. This attraction to Christ serves as the inspiration and key to integrating the various dimensions of work and to striving for the improvement of social structures within God's purpose for humanity. As emphasized by the

Second Vatican Council, "only in the mystery of the incarnate Word does the mystery of man take on light. (...) Christ, the final Adam, by the revelation of the mystery of the Father and His love, fully reveals man to man himself and makes his supreme calling clear".[42]

Notes

1 For a synthetic and brief overview of the attitude of Christian antiquity toward work, see Manuel Mira, "Influjo del Cristianismo en el concepto antiguo de trabajo," *Franciscanum* 66 (2024): 1–48 (on the Influence of Christianity on the ancient concept of work). On the other hand, it should be noted that the scope of theological reflection on work during periods that are often evaluated pejoratively has recently begun to be reconsidered. For example, "the religious of the High Middle Ages did far more than any other group to establish the foundation of Western civilization. In no small part is this due to their development of and adherence to Christian work theology" (cf. Patricia Ranft, "Work Theology in the High Middle Ages," in *Holiness Through Work. Commemorating the Encyclical Laborem Exercens*, ed. Martin Schlag (South Bend: St. Augustine Press, 2022): 34–59, 59.

2 Cf. Eugène Masure, "La théologie du travail," *Le supplément de la vie spirituelle* 52 (1937): 65–79; Marie–Dominique Chenu, *Pour une théologie du travail* (Paris: Editions du Seuil, 1955); Henrie Rondet, "Élements pour une théologie du travail," *Nouvelle revue théologique* 77 (1955): 123–143.

3 Cf. Gregorio Guitián and Alejo J. G. Sison, "Offshore Outsourcing from a Catholic Social Teaching Perspective," *Journal of Business Ethics* 185 (2023): 595–609, https://doi.org/10.1007/s10551-022-05209-8.

4 Leo XIII, Encyclical *"Rerum Novarum,"* (On Capital and Labor), May 15, 1891, https://www.vatican.va/content/leo-xiii/en/encyclicals/documents/hf_l-xiii_enc_15051891_rerum-novarum.html.

5 International Labour Organization, *The Future of Work We Want. A Global Dialogue* (Geneva, 2017).

6 For a panoramic view, cf.: *The Oxford Handbook of Meaningful Work*, eds. Ruth Yeoman et al. (Oxford University Press, 2019); Catherine Bailey, et al., "A Review of the Empirical Literature on Meaningful Work: Progress and Research Agenda," *Human Resource Development Review* 18, no. 1 (2018): 83–113; Christopher Michaelson, "A Normative Meaning of Meaningful Work," *Journal of Business Ethics* 170 (2021): 413–428, https://doi.org/10.1007/s10551-019-04389-0; Brent D. Rosso et al., "On the Meaning of Work: A Theoretical Integration and Review," *Research in Organizational Behavior* 30 (2010): 91–127, https://doi.org/10.1016/j.riob.2010.09.001.

7 Derek Thomson, "Workism Is Making Americans Miserable," *The Atlantic*, February 24, 2019, https://www.theatlantic.com/ideas/archive/2019/02/religion-workism-making-americans-miserable/583441/.

8 Cf. "Número uno del MIR: 'He elegido dermatología para ser feliz y no quemarme'," *ABC*, Miércoles, 15 de febrero de 2023, 34.

9 Cf. https://www.washingtonpost.com/business/2022/02/01/job-quits-resignations-december-2021/. Regarding the reasons for abandonment, see: https://www.pewresearch.org/fact-tank/2022/03/09/majority-of-workers-who-quit-a-job-in-2021-cite-low-pay-no-opportunities-for-advancement-feeling-disrespected/.

10 Cf. International Labour Organization, *The Future of Work We Want. A Global Dialogue* (Geneva, 2017). For an Overview of EU Labor law Through the Lenses of the Catholic Social Teaching see: Mark Bell, *Catholic Social Teaching and*

14 *Gregorio Guitián*

Labour Law. An Ethical Perspective on Work (Oxford: Oxford University Press 2023). As for the USA, see: Christine Firer Hinze, *Radical Sufficiency: Work, Livelihood, and a US Catholic Economic Ethic* (Washington, DC: Georgetown University Press, 2021).

11 Cf. Gregorio Guitián and Ana Marta González, "Theology of Work: New Perspectives," *Scripta Theologica* 54 (2022): 757–787, https://doi.org/10.15581/006.54.3.757-787. This article is the starting point of the project. It offers a state of research on the theology of work and the proposal of the project.

12 Cf. Diego Perez Gondar, "The Anthropology of Work from Biblical Theology. A New Consideration of Gen 2:4b-25," *Scripta Theologica* 55 (2023): 9–37, https://doi.org/10.15581/006.55.1.9-37; Hélio Luciano, "La Comprensión de la noción de trabajo en la teología brasileña del Siglo XX," *Veritas* 54 (2023): 147–171, http://dx.doi.org/10.4067/S0718-92732023000100147; Gregorio Guitián and Alejo J. G. Sison, "Offshore Outsourcing from a Catholic Social Teaching Perspective," *Journal of Business Ethics* 185 (2023): 595–609, https://doi.org/10.1007/s10551-022-05209-8; Pablo Blanco, "The Idea of Work: from Luther to Pentecostals in Recent Protestant Authors," *Teologia I Moralność* 17 (2022): 189–203; Juan Luis Caballero, "Freedom and Dependence in the Pauline Writings. A Theological Approach According to Colossians and Ephesians," *ΘΕΟΛΟΓΙΑ* 93 (2022): 7–33; César Izquierdo, "El Trabajo en la filosofía de la acción de Maurice Blondel," in *Libellus quasi speculum. studi offerti a Bernard Ardura* A cura di Piernantonio Piatti (Cittá del Vaticano: Libreria Editrice Vaticana, 2022): 1003–1015; Juan Luis Caballero, "Elementos para una teología paulina del trabajo. Sobre el documento '¿Qué es el hombre?'" *Scripta Theologica* 53 (2021): 169–190; Gregorio Guitián, "How Financial Institutions can Serve the Common Good of Society. Insights from Catholic Social Teaching," *Business Ethics, the Environment & Responsibility* 32, no.S2 (2023): 84–95, https://doi.org/10.1111/beer.12376; Ana Marta González, *Trabajo, Sentido y Desarrollo* (Madrid: Dykinson 2023).

13 For a bibliography, see Gregorio Guitián and Ana Marta González, "Theology of Work: New Perspectives," *Scripta Theologica* 54 (2022): 757–787, https://doi.org/10.15581/006.54.3.757-787.

14 Otto Piper, "The Meaning of Work," *Theology Today* 14 (1957): 174–194, 180.

15 Joseph Thomas, "Estado de la cuestión sobre el sentido teológico del trabajo," *Revista Fomento Social* 76 (1964): 391–400, 392.

16 Luciano, "La Comprensión de la noción de trabajo en la teología brasileña del siglo XX," 156.

17 John Paul II, Encyclical letter "*Laborem Exercens*" (On human work), September 14, 1981, Introduction, https://www.vatican.va/content/john-paul-ii/es/encyclicals/documents/hf_jp-ii_enc_14091981_laborem-exercens.html.

18 Cf. Joanne Ciulla, *The Search for Ethics in Leadership, Business and Beyond* (Cham: Springer Nature Switzerland, 2020), 197–209. The pages correspond to the chapter entitled "The moral conditions of work".

19 Yves R. Simon, *Work, Society, and Culture* (New York: Fordham University Press, 1971), 1.

20 Yves R. Simon, *Work, Society, and Culture* (New York: Fordham University Press, 1971), 2–56.

21 Cf. Jeffrey Hanson, *Philosophies of Work in the Platonic Tradition. A History of Labor and Human Flourishing* (London-New York-Dublin: Bloomsbury, 2022), 3.

22 Cf. Joseph Thomas, "Estado de la cuestión sobre el sentido teológico del trabajo," *Revista Fomento Social* 76 (1964): 391. According to Miroslav Volf, the theology of work "is a dogmatic reflection on the nature and consequences of human work.

Theology of work: context, integration, challenge   15

It does not make ethical theological reflection on human work superfluous but provides it with an indispensable theological framework" (Miroslav Volf, *Work in the Spirit: Toward a Theology of Work* [Eugene, OR: Wipf and Stock, 2001; Oxford University Press, 1991], 74). However, this view seems to leave moral theology, which would come later, at the margins of the theology of work, whereas Thomas' definition accommodates theological endeavor as a whole.

23 Darrell Cosden, *A Theology of Work: Work and the New Creation* (Carlisle: Paternoster, 2004). The other, and more important in my opinion, is Miroslav Volf, *Work in the Spirit: Toward a Theology of Work* (Eugene, OR: Wipf and Stock, 2001; Oxford University Press, 1991), 74.

24 Cf. Darrell Cosden, *A Theology of Work: Work and the New Creation* (Carlisle: Paternoster, 2004), 180.

25 I owe prof. Steve Long for raising this question.

26 Gregorio Guitián and Ana Marta González, "Theology of Work: New Perspectives," *Scripta Theologica* 54 (2022): 761, https://doi.org/10.15581/006.54.3.757-787.

27 On the relationship between work and service, see: Gregorio Guitián, "Service as a Bridge between Ethical Principles and Business Practice: A Catholic Social Teaching Perspective," *Journal of Business Ethics* 128 (2015): 59–72, https://doi.org/10.1007/s10551-014-2077-z.

28 In this regard, the approach to moral theology elaborated by Ángel Rodríguez Luño is very enlightening. See Enrique Colom and Ángel Rodríguez Luño, *Chosen in Christ to Be Saints. I: Fundamental Moral Theology* (Rome: Edizioni Santa Croce, 2016).

29 Cf. Gerhard Von Rad, *Genesis: A Commentary* (Philadelphia: The Westminster Press, 1961), 58; J. Alberto Soggin, "To Rule," in *Theological Lexicon of the Old Testament*, Vol 2, eds. Ernst Jenni and Claus Westermann (Peabody, MA: Hendrickson Publishers, 1997), 689–691, 690.

30 Primarily Miroslav Volf, *Work in the Spirit: Toward a Theology of Work* (Eugene, OR: Wipf and Stock, 2001; Oxford University Press, 1991), and Darrell Cosden, *A Theology of Work: Work and the New Creation* (Carlisle: Paternoster, 2004).

31 Darrell Cosden, *A Theology of Work: Work and the New Creation* (Carlisle: Paternoster, 2004), 179–180.

32 Cosden Himself States: "I am Convinced that her task [of the Church] must Increasingly be to Guide all of her Children into a Deeper Integrative Understanding of the Nature and Meaning of Human Work" (Darrell Cosden, *A Theology of Work: Work and the New Creation* (Carlisle: Paternoster, 2004), 187).

33 Cf. Michael J. Naughton, *Getting Work Right. Labour and Leisure in a Fragmented World* (Steubenville: Emmaus Road, 2019).

34 Cf. Diego Perez Gondar, "The Anthropology of Work from Biblical Theology. A New Consideration of Gen 2:4b-25," *Scripta Theologica* 55 (2023): 9–37, https://doi.org/10.15581/006.55.1.9-37.

35 Cf. John Paul II, Encyclical letter "*Laborem Exercens*" *(on Human Work)*, September 14, 1981, Introduction, https://www.vatican.va/content/john-paul-ii/es/encyclicals/documents/hf_jp-ii_enc_14091981_laborem-exercens.html, #5–6. According to Volf, this encyclical is "one of the most remarkable ecclesiastical documents on the question of work ever written" (Miroslav Volf, *Work in the Spirit: Toward a Theology of Work* [Eugene, OR: Wipf and Stock], 2001; Oxford University Press, 1991, 5).

36 Most recently, cf. *Holiness through Work. Commemorating the Encyclical Laborem Exercens*, ed. Martin Schlag, (South Bend: St. Augustine Press, 2022).

37 Cf. Daniel Granada, "Consideración unitaria del trabajo como acción en la historia de la teología del trabajo," *Scripta Theologica* 56, no. 2 (2024): 377–406, https://doi.org/10.15581/006.56.2.377-406.

16   *Gregorio Guitián*

38 Cf. Élio Estanislau Gasda, *Fe cristiana y sentido del trabajo* (Madrid: San Pablo – Universidad Pontificia de Comillas, 2011).
39 Cf. Jeremy Posadas, "The Refusal of Work in Christian Ethics and Theology: Interpreting Work from an Anti-work Perspective," *Journal of Religious Ethics* 45, no. 2 (2017): 330–361, https://doi.org/10.1111/jore.12180; Kathi Weeks, *The Problem with Work: Feminism, Marxism, Antiwork Politics, and Postwork Imaginaries* (Durham, NC: Duke University Press, 2011).
40 Founder of Opus Dei, an institution of the Catholic Church whose mission is precisely to spread the call to holiness through ordinary life and especially through work.
41 Josemaría Escrivá, *Apuntes*, nn. 217–218; quoted in Andrés Vazquez de Prada, *The Founder of Opus Dei. The Life of Josemaría Escrivá*, vol. I (Princeton, NJ: Scepter Publishers, 2001), 287–288.
42 Vatican Council II, *Pastoral Constitution "Gaudium et Spes" (on the Church in the Modern World)*, December 7, 1965, #22, https://www.vatican.va/archive/hist_councils/ii_vatican_council/documents/vat-ii_const_19651207_gaudium-et-spes_en.html.

Part I
Context

2 Does God work? Shall we work in heaven? In search of a theological foundation for human work

Santiago Sanz Sánchez

Introduction

In the last decades much effort has been dedicated, both in Protestant and Catholic theology, to building what has been called a "theology of work", in order to find the profound meaning of that kind of activity which consumes most of the efforts, minds, hearts, and time of human being.[1] It was recognized, especially in the Catholic tradition, that there was a gap to be filled,[2] rediscovering aspects that were present in the divine Revelation and that had not generally been developed or taken into serious consideration in the past centuries.

As far as the Protestant sphere is concerned, there have been notable studies that have set out to develop a theology of work capable of tuning in to the social, political, and cultural issues that are currently manifested in the vast and complex world of work. Both Volf and Cosden,[3] among others, dedicate a significant part of their studies to dialogue with the contemporary world, offering a phenomenological and philosophical analysis that illustrates the roots of the current situation of the world of work, which, for many, offers more shadows than lights. Precisely for this reason, in the task of searching for meaning in an activity that, despite occupying a good part of our time, seems to have lost its most existential significance, these authors set out to develop an ontology of work that can offer meaning and hope to our contemporaries. These works highlight the need to go back from the phenomenological and philosophical level to the theological dimension in the strict sense, in order to find in Revelation lights that can illuminate the complexity of our situation. This last perspective, strictly theological, will be the focus of this contribution, which presupposes the need for and importance of developing other perspectives, as is done in other chapters of this book.

In this sense, work has been seen as a calling, rooted in the divine project of God the Father's creation, as a participation in the divine work of the Son of God's redemption (which he himself assumed as incarnate man during his Nazareth years) as well as a charism given by the Holy Spirit, to be developed in view of the eschatological new creation toward which all of us walk.

DOI: 10.4324/9781003508212-3

20   *Santiago Sanz Sánchez*

It seems that, by rooting the dignity and meaning of work in the divine plan of creation, redemption, and eschatological fulfillment, we can solidly build a theological view of human work. Nevertheless, there is a point deserving particular attention, which normally is merely mentioned, without a real discussion of it. As it was clearly established by the Church Fathers, the history of salvation (*economia*) is embedded in the divine being itself (*theologia*);[4] therefore, the question unavoidably arises, whether God himself works, meaning, whether creation and redemption can be viewed as God's work.

Closely connected, another question appears: if work belongs to the divine project of creation from the times of the Garden of Eden, considering the link between the beginning and the end, so characteristic of Christian economy, should we postulate that, at the end of times, in the new creation, there will be human work?

These thoughts come in a significant degree from the Protestant traditions. They open the space to discuss the role of human collaboration in the divine project: human beings, created in the image of God, are called to cooperate with God in the coming of his Kingdom. Therefore, it will be useful from the beginning to ponder the relationship between the two ways in which humans are called to help the divine creative activity, that is, procreation and production, to use Taylor's terminology[5]: family and work are the main spheres of human realization and, at the same time, cooperation with the creative power, wisdom, and love of God.

I shall try to synthetize what others have said on these issues, so as to determine whether it is necessary, in order to get an adequate theological foundation of human work, to affirm both that God works and that there will be work in heaven. In my view, the answer should be analogical (*quodammodo*), that is, yes in a certain sense, and no in another sense. I shall explain my position, analyzing in this order the two questions. Firstly, whether God works and in what sense we can sustain such affirmation; and secondly, if this means that work belongs not only to the divine economy of salvation, but that it is rooted in the very being of God forever, and therefore we will participate in this constant activity in eternal life.

God as worker in the Bible and in some recent theological proposals

Guitián and González highlight how recently "some authors stress the intrinsic meaning of work as a reflection of God's work in creation and redemption".[6] In fact, Jensen identifies several times in which the Bible speaks of God as a worker: metalworker, farmer, potter, gardener, forester, etc.[7] He uses the expression "God the Worker", as he thinks that God is always at work with his creatures. Quoting Aquinas on analogy, he uses the similarity of work as a way of describing divine activity *ad extra*: creation, redemption, and new creation. He refers to the trinitarian relationships in which Father, Son, and Spirit are always at work equally as a key to understand

Does God work? Shall we work in heaven?   21

any created human work as needed and made always in relation with others. This is a way to emphasize the primacy of the person, the worker, over the work to be done.

This view has been contrasted by those authors, aligned with phenomena such as "the great resignation",[8] who challenge the intrinsic goodness of work, considering it rather as an evil to be avoided. According to Posadas, Christian theology has assumed, without sufficient foundation, that what God does in creation is work.[9] Regarding the New Testament, even Volf, an author who considers human work in positive terms, says that in no way can a "Gospel of work" be found in the New Testament, despite John Paul II's claims in *Laborem exercens*,[10] as Jesus himself abandoned his work at the beginning of his public life and took his disciples out of their occupations when he called them.[11]

The first point to make here is to recognize the uniqueness of the biblical account of human labor when contrasted with other ancient Near Eastern myths. Bergsma has explained that *Enuma Elish*, *Atrahasis Epic*, and other texts narrate how the mother goddess Mami created humanity from the clay of the earth and the blood of a slain god as a race of slaves to do the work of the gods on their behalf, as they complained to her about the burden of obtaining their own food.[12] In contrast, the Hebrew Bible presents the one creator as a God who himself works. Although the account of the six days of creation (Gen 1:1–2:1) never uses the word "work" (*ʿăbôdâ*) or "labor" (*mĕlāʾkâ*) for the divine activity, the sacred author does regard the Lord as having performed "labor" retrospectively in his description of the seventh day:

> And on the seventh day God finished his labor (mĕlāʾe) which he had done, and he rested on the seventh day from all his labor (mĕlāʾch) which he had done. So, God blessed the seventh day and hallowed it, because God rested from all his labor (mĕlāʾch) which he had done in creating.
>
> (Gen 2:2–3)[13]

We see, then, that

> unlike the Mesopotamian gods, the Lord God of Israel does not shrink from "labor". Rather, the divine labor of six days followed by the day of rest establishes the rhythm of human labor, such that the weekly productivity of human beings punctuated by the Sabbath is not an expression of their slave status but of their likeness to God.[14]

The recent document from the Pontifical Biblical Commission on Biblical Anthropology contains a detailed analysis of work in the Bible.[15] While comparing God's creating action to that of an artisan, it shows also the differences between divine and human work.[16] In any case, there is no doubt that human activity, if done in collaboration with God,[17] in a certain way imitates divine activity in its features of wisdom, love, and creativity.[18]

> The Sabbath is the day on which the faithful imitate their God [...]. In six days, God made the universe (Ex 20:11a) and on the seventh day "he rested" (Ex 20:11b). Human beings will do the same: in their work they will make present the divine work, and on the Sabbath, they will experience the peaceful enjoyment of all that has been "accomplished" by the Creator (Gen 2:1–2) and by themselves.[19]

In order to highlight the continuous active presence of God in the world, the Bible applies the metaphor of the variety of human professions to the divine action.

> In reality, as is affirmed in the rest of the biblical tradition, the Lord does not stop acting (cf. Jn 5:17) [...]. It is above all the prophets who testify to the active presence of God in human affairs (Is 43,13), thus inspiring also the other sacred writers. In their pronouncements they use, in an obviously analogical way, the same terminology that is used to define "work", in particular the verbs "to do" ('āśāh), "to act" (pā'al) [...]. In addition to the terminology indicated above, they have recourse to metaphors that relate to work, comparing, for example, God to a farmer who plants a vineyard and tends to it (Isa 5,1–7; 27:3; Jer 2:21; cf. also Ps 80:9–10), or to a potter who by molding gives form to objects (Isa 29:16; 43:7; 44:2; 64:7; Jer 18:6).[20]

God acts in a wonderful way at the beginning and continuously alongside the history of salvation (Isa 12:5; 25,1; Ps 77:13; 92:5; 143:5). He will act also in the final eschatological event through which his salvific work will show him as Lord of history (Isa 44:23; Am 9:12; Hab 1:5). There, the Bible once again uses metaphors coming from human work, "whereby God is compared to a refiner (Mal 3:2), a builder (Isa 44:26; Jer 18:9; 31:4), a farmer (Isa 60:21; Jer 24:6), etc., symbols that indicate the restoration of everything, a kind of new creation (Isa 43:19; 66:22)".[21]

In this sense, when considering the New Testament and the fact that Jesus, being an artisan, abandoned his work and asked his disciples to do the same, the document interprets this fact not as a contempt, but as a change which implies a positive valuation of what is abandoned for a higher activity.

> This information suggests an appreciation for manual activities [...]. As happened with Moses (Ex 3:1) and David (1 Sam 16:11; 17:34), who were called from shepherding to be leaders of Israel (Ex 3:10; 2 Sam 7:8), as with Gideon, Elisha and Amos, farmers or breeders (Judg 6:11; 1 Kings 19:19; Am 7:15), the first of whom became a leader and judge (Judg 6:14), and the others prophets (1 Kings 19:21; Am 7:14–15),

Does God work? Shall we work in heaven? 23

so the Apostles changed their way of life because of their encounter with Christ.[22]

The document shows how in the gospels, especially in the parables, we can see several working activities mentioned: "that of the sower (Mt 13:3), the labourer (Mt 20:1), the merchant of pearls (Mt 13:45), the steward (Mt 24:45), the manager (Lk 16:1), as well as that of the housewife who kneads the flour (Mt 13:33)".[23] It also highlights

the interpretation of the "ministry" of teaching and healing carried out by Jesus and his disciples in terms of "work" (Mt 9:37–38; Jn 5:17; 9:4) [...]. This work "is like" (cf. Mt 13:24.31.33.44–45.47) that of the ploughman (Lk 9:62), the sower (Mt 13:3), the reaper (Mt 9:37–38; Jn 4:38), the shepherd (Jn 10:14), the fisherman (Mt 4:19; 13:47–48).[24]

The reference to God's action in terms of working is not addressed in detail by recent authors who have written theologies of work. As is well known, Volf has proposed a shift from a vocational view of work founded in the theology of creation, and then considered as "static", to a more "dynamic" pneumatological outlook, founded in eschatology and based in the notion of charism.[25] If we see human work in light of creation, then we will speak of cooperation with God in his *creatio continua*. In this framework, "no human work corresponds to *creatio ex nihilo* (*bara*). At the same time, it draws an analogy between divine making (*asa*) and human work",[26] in the sense that God "makes human work a means of accomplishing his work in the world. As Luther said, human work is God's mask behind which he hides himself and rules everything magnificently in the world".[27] If we follow the recent tradition that bases "theology of work on human proleptic cooperation in God's eschatological *transformatio mundi*",[28] then human beings in their daily work are seen as "co-workers in God's kingdom".[29]

Recognizing the complementarity between both understandings,[30] Volf observes that traditionally the work of the Spirit was limited to salvation, and then to salvation in the individual spirit. Instead, the Spirit really is "not only *spiritus redemptor*, he is also *spiritus creator*".[31] This way, he criticizes Luther's reduction of the anthropological locus of salvation to the inner man. "The outward man and the whole material reality remain outside the sphere of the salvific activity of God".[32] The pneumatological understanding of work leads then to affirm that "human beings were created to live on earth as God's coworkers in anticipation of the new creation",[33] and for this very reason, the Spirit imparted to them various gifts (charisms) to accomplish that task. "The charismatic nature of all Christian activity is the theological basis for a pneumatological understanding of work".[34]

The goal of the Holy Spirit in the church and in the world is the same: the Spirit strives to lead both the realm of nature (regnum naturae)

24 *Santiago Sanz Sánchez*

and the realm of grace (regnum gratiae) toward their final glorification in the new creation (regnum gloriae).[35]

Cosden has explicitly described the divine action as work in his proposal of an ontology of work. "I understand work's essential nature to be derived ontologically from its having been built into the fabric of creation by God. The person is a worker, not as an accident of nature but because God first is a worker and persons are created in his image".[36] At the same time, Cosden shares the eschatological switch, given by Moltmann and Volf to the theology of work, from the vocational model based in the initial creation to the eschatological model based in the concept of new creation.

> Their eschatological orientation means that from protology work is perceived as teleologically directed and oriented forward the future new creation rather than backward toward the restoration of the initial creation. It is an eschatological mandate rather than simply a creation mandate.[37]

This implies a new perspective in seeing God's activity as work.

> Moltmann rather develops the idea by appealing to the concept of the work of redemption, the theology of the cross. God is a worker, but this is not seen primarily in the fact that God created the universe. More prominently it is seen in redemption.[38]

"Work is not simply about human development, ultimately work is about God and God's eschatological renewal of heaven and earth. Work is ontological. Work is participation in God's history".[39] To speak about "ontology" does not mean that we realize ourselves through work, as it would imply to affirm a kind of justification by works.[40] Moltmann does not use the traditional Protestant language of obedience and service. "His appeal is that our human work should correspond to God's".[41]

Catholic teaching has adopted most of these insights. In his encyclical Letter *Laborem Exercens*, John Paul II refers also to work as a sharing in the activity of the Creator:

> We find this truth at the very beginning of Sacred Scripture, in the Book of Genesis, where the creation activity itself is presented in the form of "work" done by God during "six days" (cf. Gen 2:2; Ex 20:8, 11; Deut 5:12–14), "resting" on the seventh day (cf. Gen 2:3). Besides, the last book of Sacred Scripture echoes the same respect for what God has done through his creative "work" when it proclaims: "Great and wonderful are your deeds, O Lord God the Almighty" (Rev 15:3).[42]

The Pope went on calling this truth *the first Gospel of work*,

> for it shows what the dignity of work consists of: it teaches that man ought to imitate God, his Creator, in working, because man alone has the unique characteristic of likeness to God. Man ought to imitate God both in working and also in resting, since God himself wished to present his own creative activity under the form of work and rest. This activity by God in the world always continues, as the words of Christ attest: "My Father is working still..." (Jn 5:17): he works with creative power by sustaining in existence the world that he called into being from nothing, and he works with salvific power in the hearts of those whom from the beginning he has destined for "rest" (cf. Heb 4:1, 9–10) in union with himself in his "Father's house". (Jn 14:2)[43]

John Paul II highlights how this aspect has been made evident in the life of Jesus, who has assumed human work giving to it new perspectives,[44] along the lines of what the Second Vatican Council had taught some years before: "we hold that through labor offered to God man is associated with the redemptive work of Jesus Christ, Who conferred an eminent dignity on labor when at Nazareth He worked with His own hands".[45]

Some years before, the Belgian theologian Gustave Thils dedicated the entire last chapter of his theology of terrestrial realities to human work.[46] Affirming that man is like God when he works as he cooperates in the creative action, Thils recognizes implicitly the fact of divine work. He refers to Pseudo-Dionysius the Areopagite's sentence: "what is more Divine than all, becoming a fellow worker with God".[47] Precisely because of this, after sin, man can be seduced beyond any reasonable measure by the dignity of his work, therefore Thils reminds us with Aquinas that to collaborate with God in time occurs at the level of secondary causes, which do not ever reach the level of the prime causality of God. A creature has nothing which is not created.[48] The same can be said regarding the redemptive aspect of human work that can be just a cooperation in the work of salvation headed only by Christ.[49]

Shall we work in heaven?

A theology of work must investigate the relation of work to the future destiny of the whole creation, including human beings as individual and social beings, and the non-human environment. The appropriate theological framework for developing a theology of work is not anthropology, but an all-encompassing eschatology.[50]

As we saw before, the eschatological shift recently proposed by Volf implies a reading of protology in light of eschatology. "The significance of secular work depends on the value of creation, and the value of creation

26   *Santiago Sanz Sánchez*

depends on its final destiny".[51] According to this outlook, it is not enough to interpret human cooperation with God in light of the doctrine of creation, seeing "work as cooperation with God in the *creatio continua*". This rests as a valid, although partial, approach that should be completed conceiving "work as cooperation with God in the anticipation of God's eschatological *transformatio mundi*".[52] God does not only call people to become his children, but also gives charisms so that they can accomplish his will anticipating the new creation. "All Christians have several gifts of the spirit. Since most of these gifts can be exercised only through work, work must be considered a central aspect of Christian living".[53]

This view considers work as fundamental to human existence, "belonging to the very purpose for which God originally made human beings".[54] In this pneumatological approach, "charisms include both liturgical activities and activities in the world [...]. God's Spirit inspires people both to work and to worship".[55] This fact has an important consequence.

> If work is a fundamental dimension of human existence, then work cannot have only an instrumental value. If I am created to work, then I must treat work as something I am created to do and hence treat it as an end in itself.[56]

This way, "when one considers work as an end in itself, one will believe that God is pleased not only when human beings work, but also when they delight in their work".[57] No doubt that "it is a strength of the vocational understanding of work that it conceives of work as service to fellow human beings".[58] But, while in this perspective "one can be called to do a particular work irrespective of one's inclinations [...] in the pneumatological understanding [...] one discovers what work God is calling one to do by reflecting on the gifts one has received".[59]

Volf does not push these insights to the extreme, so as to arrive at the question of whether, given that work is essential to human beings, we shall work in heaven. This will be the step accomplished by Cosden in his proposal of an ontology of work. Let us delve into his reasoning.

Cosden shares with McIntyre the need to restore the category of teleology in the anthropological thought. However, following O'Donovan, he thinks that "the basis for teleology, is not Aristotelian philosophy but creation and eschatology in the light of resurrection".[60] In Christian theology "a teleology must primarily be grounded within the reality of Christ",[61] as his "resurrection vindicates created order [...] backward to creation [...] forward to eschatology".[62] We should realize with Moltmann that the "initial creation is only properly understood eschatologically" and that "nature's eschatological goal is redemption".[63]

Applying these ideas from Moltmann to our subject, Cosden states that "a theology of human purpose is essential to a theological anthropology and an ontology of work".[64] If "Christology is understood as the fulfillment of anthropology, and the anthropology becomes the preparation for Christology",

Does God work? Shall we work in heaven? 27

then "to be in God's image through Christ includes, if not directly at least by implication and application, work [...]. Work is not simply an instrumental activity [...], it is a fundamental condition of human created existence. It is ontological".[65] And then, due to the essential eschatological character of Christian theology, we should conclude that this "ontology of work is not a limited ontology in the present creation [...], it is also a fundamental condition of being human in the new creation".[66] In other words, trying to describe the eschatological state of the redeemed, in light of discontinuity and at the same time continuity, we could say that "human purpose will be transformed and freed from sin, mortality, suffering and grief, but it will still be the same human purpose that we currently experience".[67] Then, if "our *Gestalt* will be preserved and transformed [...] thus work understood as an ontological foundation of human purpose will also be preserved and transformed".[58]

Clearly established, according to Cosden, "there will be glorified work in the new creation", and "this can be shown with the help of Moltmann's reflection on *sabbath* and *shekinah*".[69] On the one side, we have the temporal aspect of the *sabbath*. While on this earth, there is a temporal work–rest cycle founded on the biblical *sabbath*, in the new creation that cycle will pass away, and so "the distinction between work and rest will disappear".[70] Cosden reiterates then that "the reason for positing glorified work lies in its being ontologically a part of our humanness and livingness which will be preserved and transformed in eternal life".[71] On the other side, we have the spatial dimension of *shekinah*, that is, the consideration of the images of the city of God and the crystal temple, which lead us to assume that

> here the question of glorified work shows its plausibility [...]; human products and projects (here a city) are appropriate to the new creation [...]; there will be genuine community and continued but new human livingness.[72]

The conclusion is already clear: "Ontologically work is so fundamental to created and human existence that it is necessarily a part of both this life and the life to come".[73]

We should admit that it is difficult to find a categorical statement regarding work in heaven in the Catholic magisterial teaching. As is already well known, the question was posited in the decades before the Second Vatican Council, in terms of what value should we recognize human work in this world in order to build or prepare the world to come. Given the different approaches, the so-called incarnationist and eschatologist, the Constitution *Gaudium et spes* tried to mediate by teaching that

> while earthly progress must be carefully distinguished from the growth of Christ's kingdom, to the extent that the former can contribute to the better ordering of human society, it is of vital concern to the Kingdom of God (cf. Pius XI, *Quadragesimo Anno*: AAS 23 [1931], p. 207). For after we have obeyed the Lord, and in His Spirit nurtured on earth the

28 *Santiago Sanz Sánchez*

values of human dignity, brotherhood and freedom, and indeed all the good fruits of our nature and enterprise, we will find them again, but freed of stain, burnished and transfigured, when Christ hands over to the Father: "a kingdom eternal and universal, a kingdom of truth and life, of holiness and grace, of justice, love and peace" (Preface of the Feast of Christ the King). On this earth that Kingdom is already present in mystery. When the Lord returns it will be brought into full flower.[74]

In any case, there is no trace here of an affirmation regarding human work in the new creation.

The same can be said when we analyze some contributions from the Catholic side to the theology of work. Whenever the eschatological aspect of work is mentioned, it is normally seen as referred to how our working in this world serves to prepare the coming of the new creation.[75] But there seems to be no special interest in describing our lives in heaven as characterized by working. The more explicit affirmation can be found in F. J. Nocke, who says that "although we don't know in which way the fulfilment will be verified, Christian hope is certainly sure of the relationship between the present action and the future world".[76] If our humanizing activity contributes to the Kingdom of God, while it cannot be identified with it, we could say something similar regarding heaven, although we ignore the mode in which it will be realized. Referring to the biblical image of the city of God, Nocke adds that

> we are called to collaborate in its construction. We cannot predict with certainty how this building work will proceed to the end. Perhaps something or even all of what we build will collapse. But our effort will not have been in vain. The city will rise. God himself undertakes this. We don't even know exactly the final construction plan. Perhaps, when we finally see the completed city, its streets, squares, houses and gates, we will wonder ourselves how everything turned out so differently from what we had imagined. But we will realize that the products of our work have not simply been removed by God, to be replaced by his initiative. In the city built by God we will recognize the stones (and perhaps also the structures) on which we ourselves have worked.[77]

In Lubac's words, "human work builds along the centuries the house which God will transfigure to make it his home".[78]

As we see in these references, it is more frequent to highlight the influence of sin in human activities and then that the final transfiguration of the world will be also a purification. At the same time, in his study of Christian eschatology, Schmaus speaks of some kind of activity in heaven:

> the resting in God is not a passive resting from labor, as when we try to relax after a tiring day's work. The rest of heaven allows man to be active in a measure fitted to his nature and in a way he desires: it is

Does God work? Shall we work in heaven? 29

ordered towards love [...]. Heaven is at once the most intense activity and the highest form of rest [...]; the happiness of heaven cannot be understood as a blissful idleness.[79]

Concluding remarks

After having analyzed what different authors, Protestant and Catholic, have to say about the questions posed at the beginning of this paper, I have no definitive answers to them. I conclude simply by summarizing the main ideas, pointing at some positive elements and some criticisms.

It is important not to forget that the ultimate aim of what I am about to say is to shed the light of theology on the situation of work in the contemporary world. This moves between the human desire for cooperation and its character for solving problems and difficulties. There is an inevitable component of wear, fragility, and contingency, which affects everything created in the present condition. From there, man longs to reach a definitive situation of salvation in which these limits will cease to be present.

First, we should welcome as a theological progress the attempt to build an ontology of work, especially when it comes from the Protestant area, where traditionally metaphysics and ontology were not well considered. Moreover, speaking of an ontology of work implies recognizing the role of human cooperation with God in the realization of the new creation. Nevertheless, the question remains, where to put the center of this ontology. The possibilities can be found in the different phases of the history of salvation creation, Christology, or eschatology.

As we have seen, both Volf and Cosden try to focus on eschatology, giving valid reasons for doing so. In my view, this is not without limitations. The most evident to me is the question of human cooperation with God, which is a clear element of debate between Protestants and Catholics. In the explanations that we have analyzed, there is a place for it, but one can legitimately wonder about its real value. In fact, in Moltmann's view, which inspires both the proposals of Volf and especially Cosden, the primacy of grace leads one to think that "judgment cannot consist of the consequences of evil action. God does not judge us according to what we have done".[80] We can agree with him that being is more important than doing and having, but at the same time we cannot forget that free beings determine themselves through their actions, and Jesus' words are very clear on this regard:

> whatever you did for one of the least of these brothers and sisters of mine, you did for me [...]; whatever you did not do for one of the least of these brothers and sisters of mine, you did not do for me.
>
> (Mt 25:40.45)

Among Protestants, it is said that through our work, we can anticipate the new creation. Among Catholics, the point is that through work we help God

30 *Santiago Sanz Sánchez*

to build the new creation, that is, we collaborate with his providence in the coming of the Kingdom. An example of this is the recent study of Gautier who, from a Thomistic outlook, proposes a theology of work from the point of view of divine providence,[81] in continuity with the pioneer suggestions given by Chenu.[82] From this perspective, if work is a participation in divine providence, and considering this as the divine guide to the end of everything, then once the end is achieved, it seems that there is no need of any more work.

Others, from a Catholic perspective, see human work as a way to exercise and grow in the virtues, a standpoint that seems, by and large, absent in a Protestant view, which prefers to see work fundamentally as an occasion to manifest the divine action. Certainly, we must delve into the question of the relationship between divine causality and human causality, and the way in which the latter can be integrated without cancelling the primacy of the former. This integration seems possible when we accept the doctrine of analogy of being and see the importance of the notion of participation. This is a different perspective from that of Volf and Cosden who, instead, use the language of anticipation[83] with the addition, in the latter case, that we will continue to work in heaven.

This last affirmation requires careful consideration, as it gives rise to several challenges. Certainly, some kind of activity is not unthinkable in paradise. But to say that we continue working there could deviate the attention from what is essential in heaven, namely the contemplation of God, which is the end of human beings.[84] Cosden rightly highlights the continuity and discontinuity between this world and the world to come, between this economy and the *pleroma*. Nevertheless, when he establishes his hypothesis of a future work in heaven, some questions arise. In fact, as we have seen, Christian tradition speaks in terms of rest and joy in paradise. Indeed, we could read Rev 14.13 ("their deeds follow them") in the sense that our works accompany us to heaven. But this cannot be seen as the beginning of a new "Origenian" history of salvation. What we have done here configures us for the eternity, we will not be subject to new changes, the vision of God completely fulfills us and cannot be lost, it fixes our will forever.

We shouldn't forget Jesus' words to the Pharisees: "they are like the angels in heaven" (Mk 12:25). As is well known, this is referred to the reality of the risen from death in relation to marriage, but there are consistent reasons to apply the same in relation to work, as both dimensions together constitute the divine project of creation for humankind, which is called to participate in the creative power of God precisely through both activities.[85] In heaven, there will be no need for marriage, as the number of the elected is already completed. It seems likewise that there will be no need to work, as we will have all our needs fulfilled. After all, Posadas would not be completely wrong in his anti-work theory. We could hardly find a logic sustaining the reasonability of many human activities that are significant only in this world, such as medical doctors, advocates, manual workers, drivers…

Does God work? Shall we work in heaven? 31

As Augustine said, commenting on Psalm 83, it seems that such human activities are meaningful in a limited and sinful world, but not in a condition where there is no more pain, hunger, suffering, and death.[86] What kind of work would remain in such condition? One could think in the creativity of artists or in playing, but then a new question arises: would this kind of activity be real work?

Let us return to the starting point. Volf and Cosden hold a pneumatological doctrine of creation mostly based on Moltmann's cabalistic view of creation as self-limitation.[87] This doctrine has received severe criticisms among Protestants, especially from Pannenberg, who nonetheless holds a strong eschatological approach to the whole Christian theology.[88] Moreover, in order to highlight the immanence of God in the world (his indwelling *shekinah*), as an attempt to fill the gap of the presence of *Spiritus Creator* in theological reflection, Moltmann banishes the idea of causality and instead invokes participation,[89] but the strength of a metaphysics of being is precisely to put together both dimensions: causality and participation, transcendence and immanence.[90] Pneumatology cannot become a kind of "Joachinite" doctrine of completion, we should see it, instead, in harmony with the work of the Father and of the Son.

Christian faith perceives everything in light of Christ. This means that there is a circularity between the beginning and the end, so that in a sense, the beginning can be seen in light of the end, but in other sense, the end can be seen in light of the beginning, and both must be seen in light of Christ, who is at the same time "the Beginning and the End" (Rev 21:6) "the First and the Last" (Rev 22:13). In my point of view, these authors grant excessive importance to eschatology as future, while they don't give the necessary prominence to the fact that the resurrection of Christ donates us already eternal life. Pneumatology should be combined with protology having Christology as their center and light.[91]

Ultimately, perhaps there are no better words than Augustine's paradoxical description:

> This rest is not a slothful inaction, but a certain ineffable tranquility caused by work in which there is no painful effort. For the repose on which one enters at the end of the toils of this life is of such a nature as consists with lively joy in the active exercises of the better life.[92]

Notes

1 Cf. Gregorio Guitián and Ana Marta González, "Theology of Work: New Perspectives," *Scripta Theologica* 54 (2022): 757–787, https://doi.org/10.15581/006.54.3.757-787.

2 Cf. Gustave Thils, *Théologie des réalités terrestres*, 2 vols. (Paris: Desclée de Brouwer, 1946–1949); Yves Marie Congar, *Jalons pour une théologie du laïcat* (Paris: Cerf 1954); Marie-Dominique Chenu, *The Theology of Work. An Exploration* (Dublin: Gill & Son, 1963).

32   Santiago Sanz Sánchez

3 Cf. Miroslav Volf, *Work in the Spirit. Toward a Theology of Work* (Eugene, OR: Wipf & Stock Publishers, 2001); Darrell Cosden, *A Theology of Work. Work and the New Creation* (Carlisle: Paternoster Press, 2004).

4 Cf. Santiago Sanz, "Lavoro, creazione e redenzione," *Verso una spiritualità del lavoro professionale. teologia, antropologia e storia a 500 anni dalla Riforma*, vol. 3, eds. Javier López Díaz e Federico Requena (Roma: EDUSC, 2018), 17–69.

5 Cf. Charles Taylor, *Sources of the Self. The Making of the Modern Identity* (Cambridge, MA: Harvard University Press, 2001, 10th edition), 211.

6 Cf. Gregorio Guitián and Ana Marta González, "Theology of Work: New Perspectives," *Scripta Theologica* 54 (2022): 770.

7 Cf. David H. Jensen, *Responsive Labor. A Theology of Work* (Louisville-London: Westminster John Knox Press, 2006), 46–49.

8 Cf. Gregorio Guitián and Ana Marta González, "Theology of Work: New Perspectives," *Scripta Theologica* 54 (2022): 770.

9 Cf. Kathi Weeks, *The Problem with Work: Feminism, Marxism, Antiwork Politics, and Postwork Imaginaries* (Durham: Duke University Press, 2011); Jeremy Posadas, "The Refusal of Work in Christian Ethics and Theology. Interpreting Work from an Anti-work Perspective," *The Journal of Religious Studies* 45 (2017): 330–361, https://doi.org/10.1111/jore.12180.

10 John Paul II, "Encyclical letter" *Laborem Exercens* (on Human Work), September 14, 1981, https://www.vatican.va/content/john-paul-ii/es/encyclicals/documents/hf_jp-ii_enc_14091981_laborem-exercens.html. Hereafter LE.

11 Cf. Gregorio Guitián and Ana Marta González, "Theology of Work: New Perspectives," *Scripta Theologica* 54 (2022): 774; Cf. Miroslav Volf, *Work in the Spirit. Toward a Theology of Work* (Eugene, OR: Wipf and Stock Publishers, 2001), 93: "We search in vain in the NT for a cultural mandate, let alone for the gospel of work. Jesus left carpenter's tools when he started public ministry, and he called his disciples away from their occupation".

12 See "Enuma Elish" 6,33–36; "Atrahasis" 1,190–197; and "Creation of Man by the Mother Goddess" (ANET³ 99–100); cf. John Bergsma, "The Creation Narratives and the Original Unity of Work and Worship in the Human Vocation," *Work: Theological Foundations and Practical Implications*, eds. R. Keith Loftin and Trey Dimsdale (London: SCM Press, 2018), 11–29, 12; see also Claus Westermann, *Creation* (Philadelphia: Fortress Press, 1974), 51.

13 "Three times in this concluding postscript reference is made to the "his labor which he [God] had done," (mĕla'ᵏtô 'ăšer 'āśâ), with variation the third time ("his labor which God had done in creating," (mĕla'ᵏtô 'ăšer-bārā' 'ĕlōhîm la'ăśôt). The noun mĕlā'ᵏâ covers a wide variety of human labor in the Hebrew Bible, both secular (Lev 13:48,51; Jer 18:3; Ps 107:23; 1 Chron 27:26) and sacred (Ex 36:2; 1 Kgs 5:30; 1 Chron 26:29; 2 Chron 29:34" (Bergsma, "The Creation Narratives," 13).

14 Bergsma, "The Creation Narratives," 13. Morales holds that "there is no term in Holy Scripture which expresses what we today mean by 'work'. But in Genesis 1, God is a creating Being who works and rests. He is not an idle God, and 'work-rest is a divine vital rhythm'" José Morales, *Creation Theology* (Dublin: Four Courts Press, 2001), 234; the internal quotation comes from Antonio Bonora, "Trabajo," in dirs. Pietro Rossano, Gianfranco Ravasi, Antonio Girlanda, *Nuevo diccionario de teología bíblica* (Madrid: Paulinas, 1990), 1897.

15 Pontifical Biblical Commission, *What Is Man? A Journey through Biblical Anthropology* (London: Darton Longman & Todd Ltd, 2021) (first published by the Vatican in Italian: 30.09.2019).

16 Pontifical Biblical Commission, *What Is Man? A Journey through Biblical Anthropology* (London: Darton Longman and Todd Ltd, 2021) (first published by the

Does God work? Shall we work in heaven? 33

Vatican in Italian: 30.09.2019), no. 104, pp. 106–107: "In Scripture, however, not only is work assigned to 'ādām before the transgression, but above all this directive is preceded by a series of actions of God, who as if he were a craftsman grappling with formless matter, brings into existence what is 'good' (Gen 1:4.10.12.18.21.25.31; 2:9.12) [...]. Of course, while the work of God is effortless, the creature grows weary and tired (Is 40:28–30); and while the Creator immediately achieves the result of his project (Isa 48:3; Ezek 12:25; Ps 33:9), the human being must accept a time delay to see the fruit of one's work (cf. Mk 4:27–29)".

17 Pontifical Biblical Commission, *What Is Man? A Journey through Biblical Anthropology* (London: Darton Longman and Todd Ltd, 2021) (first published by the Vatican in Italian: 30.09.2019), no. 108, p. 111: "'Working' and 'keeping' are therefore two joint activities. And both, as the Psalmist says, are taken on in 'collaboration' with God himself, because without God human activity is a failure, while with God it is creative and beneficial".

18 Pontifical Biblical Commission, *What Is Man? A Journey through Biblical Anthropology* (London: Darton Longman and Todd Ltd, 2021) (first published by the Vatican in Italian: 30.09.2019), no. 104, p. 107: "The imitation of Gods' work, however, must not be restricted to mere practical activity, but will take on also the components of wisdom and love which are illustrated in exemplary form in the act of creation" (Jer 10 12; 51:15; Psal 104:24; 136:5; Prov 3:19–20; 8:22–31)". Prov no. 106, p. 108: "There is no doubt that human work, in the likeness of divine action, carries within itself the character of transformative, even if not properly creative, activity; in fact, it constantly introduces innovative elements into history".

19 Pontifical Biblical Commission, *What Is Man? A Journey through Biblical Anthropology* (London: Darton Longman and Todd Ltd, 2021) (first published by the Vatican in Italian: 30.09.2019), no. 114, p. 115. After the sin, "it is no longer the garden that is his place of work, but the 'cursed' land" (Pontifical Biblical Commission, *What Is Man? A Journey through Biblical Anthropology* (London: Darton Longman and Todd Ltd, 2021) (first published by the Vatican in Italian: 30.09.2019), no. 109, p. 112).

20 Pontifical Biblical Commission, *What Is Man? A Journey through Biblical Anthropology* (London: Darton Longman and Todd Ltd, 2021) (first published by the Vatican in Italian: 30.09.2019), no. 133, pp. 127–128.

21 Pontifical Biblical Commission, *What Is Man? A Journey through Biblical Anthropology* (London: Darton Longman and Todd Ltd, 2021) (first published by the Vatican in Italian: 30.09.2019), no. 134, p. 129.

22 Pontifical Biblical Commission, *What Is Man? A Journey through Biblical Anthropology* (London: Darton Longman and Todd Ltd, 2021) (first published by the Vatican in Italian: 30.09.2019), no. 135, p. 130.

23 Pontifical Biblical Commission, *What Is Man? A Journey through Biblical Anthropology* (London: Darton Longman and Todd Ltd, 2021) (first published by the Vatican in Italian: 30.09.2019), no. 136, p. 130.

24 Pontifical Biblical Commission, *What Is Man? A Journey through Biblical Anthropology* (London: Darton Longman and Todd Ltd, 2021) (first published by the Vatican in Italian: 30.09.2019), no. 136, pp. 130–131.

25 Miroslav Volf, *Work in the Spirit. Toward a Theology of Work* (Eugene, OR: Wipf and Stock Publishers, 2001), ix: "The shift I am suggesting is from the vocational understanding of work developed within the framework of the doctrine of creation to a pneumatological line developed within the framework of the doctrine of the last things [...] based in the concept of charisma". "The broad theological framework within which I propose to develop a theology of work is

the concept of the new creation [...] following the basic insight of Moltmann's *Theology of Hope*" (Miroslav Volf, *Work in the Spirit. Toward a Theology of Work* (Eugene, OR: Wipf and Stock Publishers, 2001), 79)

26 Miroslav Volf, *Work in the Spirit. Toward a Theology of Work* (Eugene, OR: Wipf and Stock Publishers, 2001), 98.

27 Miroslav Volf, *Work in the Spirit. Toward a Theology of Work* (Eugene, OR: Wipf and Stock Publishers, 2001), 99; the internal quotation from Luther corresponds to WA 15,373.

28 Miroslav Volf, *Work in the Spirit. Toward a Theology of Work* (Eugene, OR: Wipf and Stock Publishers, 2001), 99.

29 Miroslav Volf, *Work in the Spirit. Toward a Theology of Work* (Eugene, OR: Wipf and Stock Publishers, 2001), 100.

30 Miroslav Volf, *Work in the Spirit. Toward a Theology of Work* (Eugene, OR: Wipf and Stock Publishers, 2001), 101.

31 Miroslav Volf, *Work in the Spirit. Toward a Theology of Work* (Eugene, OR: Wipf and Stock Publishers, 2001), 102.

32 Miroslav Volf, *Work in the Spirit. Toward a Theology of Work* (Eugene, OR: Wipf and Stock Publishers, 2001), 103.

33 Miroslav Volf, *Work in the Spirit. Toward a Theology of Work* (Eugene, OR: Wipf and Stock Publishers, 2001), 110. "Work in the Spirt must be understood as cooperation with God" (Miroslav Volf, *Work in the Spirit. Toward a Theology of Work* (Eugene, OR: Wipf and Stock Publishers, 2001), 114).

34 Miroslav Volf, *Work in the Spirit. Toward a Theology of Work* (Eugene, OR: Wipf and Stock Publishers, 2001), 113.

35 Miroslav Volf, *Work in the Spirit. Toward a Theology of Work* (Eugene, OR: Wipf and Stock Publishers, 2001), 119.

36 Darrell Cosden, *A Theology of Work. Work and the New Creation* (Carlisle: Paternoster Press, 2004), 17.

37 Darrell Cosden, *A Theology of Work. Work and the New Creation* (Carlisle: Paternoster Press, 2004), 46.

38 Darrell Cosden, *A Theology of Work. Work and the New Creation* (Carlisle: Paternoster Press, 2004), 57.

39 Darrell Cosden, *A Theology of Work. Work and the New Creation* (Carlisle: Paternoster Press, 2004), 60.

40 Cf. Darrell Cosden, *A Theology of Work. Work and the New Creation* (Carlisle: Paternoster Press, 2004), 61.

41 Darrell Cosden, *A Theology of Work. Work and the New Creation* (Carlisle: Paternoster Press, 2004), 71.

42 LE, no. 25.

43 LE, no. 25. cf. also *Cathechism of the Catholic Church* (Vatican City: Libreria Editrice Vaticana, 1992), 337–345; 2184–2427. https://www.vatican.va/archive/ENG0015/_INDEX.HTM.

44 LE, no. 26: "The Truth that by Means of Work man Participates in the Activity of God Himself, his Creator, was Given Particular Prominence by Jesus Christ who was Himself a man of Work [...]; the eloquence of the life of Christ is unequivocal: he belongs to the 'working world', he has appreciation and respect for human work. It can indeed be said that he looks with love upon human work". LE, no. 27: "The Christian finds in human work a small part of the Cross of Christ and accepts it in the same spirit of redemption in which Christ accepted his Cross for us. In work, thanks to the light that penetrates us from the Resurrection of Christ, we always find a glimmer of new life, of the new good, as if it were an announcement of 'the new heavens and the new earth' (cf. 2 Pt 3:13; Rev 21:1) in which man and the world participate precisely through the toil that goes with

Does God work? Shall we work in heaven?   35

work [...]. Is this new good-the fruit of human work-already a small part of that 'new earth' where justice dwells (cf. 2 Pt 3:13)? If it is true that the many forms of toil that go with man's work are a small part of the Cross of Christ, what is the relationship of this new good to the Resurrection of Christ?"

45 Vatican Council II, *Pastolar Constitution* "Gaudium et Spes" *on the Church in the Modern World*, December 7, 1965, https://www.vatican.va/archive/hist_councils/ ii_vatican_council/documents/vat-ii_const_19651207_gaudium-et-spes_en.html. Hereafter GS.

46 Cf. Gustave Thils, *Théologie des réalités terrestres*, vol. I (Paris: Desclée de Brouwer, 1946–1949), 186–194, where the author follows the classical scheme of creation and redemption, viewing the reality of work in light of this historic-salvific perspective, highlighting the fact that work is not a consequence of sin but the original vocation of human beings.

47 Pseudo-Dyonisius, *The Celestial Hierarchy*, III, 2 (London: Skeffington & Son, 1894), 22.

48 Cf. Gustave Thils, *Théologie des réalités terrestres*, vol. I (Paris: Desclée de Brouwer, 1946–1949), 189.

49 Cf. Cf. Gustave Thils, *Théologie des réalités terrestres*, vol. I (Paris: Desclée de Brouwer, 1946–1949), 192.

50 Miroslav Volf, *Work in the Spirit. Toward a Theology of Work* (Eugene, OR: Wipf and Stock Publishers, 2001), 85.

51 Miroslav Volf, *Work in the Spirit, Toward a Theology of Work* (Eugene, OR: Wipf and Stock Publishers, 2001), 93. "The goodness of the whole material creation is intrinsic, not merely instrumental. And the belief in the intrinsic goodness of creation is compatible only with the belief in the eschatological continuity" (Miroslav Volf, *Work in the Spirit, Toward a Theology of Work* (Eugene, OR: Wipf and Stock Publishers, 2001), 96).

52 Miroslav Volf, *Work in the Spirit, Toward a Theology of Work* (Eugene, OR: Wipf and Stock Publishers, 2001), 98.

53 Miroslav Volf, *Work in the Spirit, Toward a Theology of Work* (Eugene, OR: Wipf and Stock Publishers, 2001), 124.

54 Miroslav Volf, *Work in the Spirit, Toward a Theology of Work* (Eugene, OR: Wipf and Stock Publishers, 2001), 128.

55 Miroslav Volf, *Work in the Spirit, Toward a Theology of Work* (Eugene, OR: Wipf and Stock Publishers, 2001), 138.

56 Miroslav Volf, *Work in the Spirit, Toward a Theology of Work* (Eugene, OR: Wipf and Stock Publishers, 2001), 197.

57 Miroslav Volf, *Work in the Spirit, Toward a Theology of Work* (Eugene, OR: Wipf and Stock Publishers, 2001), 198.

58 Miroslav Volf, *Work in the Spirit, Toward a Theology of Work* (Eugene, OR: Wipf and Stock Publishers, 2001), 189.

59 Miroslav Volf, *Work in the Spirit, Toward a Theology of Work* (Eugene, OR: Wipf and Stock Publishers, 2001), 199.

60 Darrell Cosden, *A Theology of Work. Work and the New Creation* (Carlisle: Paternoster Press, 2004), 87.

61 Darrell Cosden, *A Theology of Work. Work and the New Creation* (Carlisle: Paternoster Press, 2004), 95.

62 Darrell Cosden, *A Theology of Work. Work and the New Creation* (Carlisle: Paternoster Press, 2004), 90.

63 Darrell Cosden, *A Theology of Work. Work and the New Creation* (Carlisle: Paternoster Press, 2004), 142.

64 Darrell Cosden, *A Theology of Work. Work and the New Creation* (Carlisle: Paternoster Press, 2004), 132.

36 *Santiago Sanz Sánchez*

65 Darrell Cosden, *A Theology of Work. Work and the New Creation* (Carlisle: Paternoster Press, 2004), 144.
66 Darrell Cosden, *A Theology of Work. Work and the New Creation* (Carlisle: Paternoster Press, 2004), 150.
67 Darrell Cosden, *A Theology of Work. Work and the New Creation* (Carlisle: Paternoster Press, 2004), 150.
68 Darrell Cosden, *A Theology of Work. Work and the New Creation* (Carlisle: Paternoster Press, 2004), 156.
69 Darrell Cosden, *A Theology of Work. Work and the New Creation* (Carlisle: Paternoster Press, 2004), 157.
70 Darrell Cosden, *A Theology of Work. Work and the New Creation* (Carlisle: Paternoster Press, 2004), 170. "Eternal rest becomes a kind of existence, as an eternal living of life characterized by perfect and harmonious relationships between God, humans and nature. Eternal rest is necessary for glorified work" (Darrell Cosden, *A Theology of Work. Work and the New Creation* (Carlisle: Paternoster Press, 2004), 170.).
71 Darrell Cosden, *A Theology of Work. Work and the New Creation* (Carlisle: Paternoster Press, 2004), 171.
72 Darrell Cosden, *A Theology of Work. Work and the New Creation* (Carlisle: Paternoster Press, 2004), 174.
73 Darrell Cosden, *A Theology of Work. Work and the New Creation* (Carlisle: Paternoster Press, 2004), 175.
74 GS no. 39.
75 At the end of his study, Illanes says that a theology of work should be developed in relationship with the doctrine of creation and with eschatology. Regarding the latter, he asks: "If man is making his way toward his last end by living his earthly existence to the full, we can ask a further question: At the end of time, what will remain of all the product of human endeavor?"; José Luis Illanes, *The Sanctification of Work* (New York: Scepter, 2003), 143–144. The author describes the extremes of a dualism that highlights the discontinuity and the opposite monism centered in the continuity, pointing at the conciliar text just referred (GS 39) as a balanced answer to the question. Morales holds that "man's vocation includes a divine commission to uncover the secrets that the Creator has hidden in the universe, to work towards the completion of his historical designs, and thereby contribute to the ultimate perfection and transformation of the cosmos [...]. Work, therefore, contains an eschatological meaning and has a mysterious but real connexion with the new heaven and the new earth"; after quoting GS no. 39, he continues: "Work does not have as its only purpose the moral perfection of the person who performs it, as if its objective result had no part to play in the make-up of the eschaton. The fruits of human work will in some way be reflected in the new heaven and the new earth, even though these are things which will be brought about solely by the will and power of God" (José Morales, *Creation Theology* (Dublin: Four Courts Press, 2001), 236–237). Sayés describes briefly the protological, Christological, and eschatological dimensions of work following and quoting GS no. 39. This author shows how the eschatological process of continuity and transformation will affect our activities and our work, clarifying that, due to the mix of good and evil in our human activities in this world, we cannot think that they become automatically definitive in heaven, as they need purification and transformation, which come only from God. At the same time, we cannot say that our humanizing actions on this earth are useless for the new world (cf. José Antonio Sayés, *Teología de la Creación* [Madrid: Palabra, 2002], 218–224).
76 Franz Joseph Nocke, *Escatologia* (Brescia: Queriniana, 1990[4]), 95.

Does God work? Shall we work in heaven? 37

77 Franz Joseph Nocke, *Escatologia* (Brescia: Queriniana, 1990), 96.
78 Henri de Lubac, *Catholicisme. Les Aspects Sociaux du Dogme,* (Paris: Éditions du Cerf, 1938), 268, no. 2.
79 Michael Schmaus, *Dogma 6: Justification and the Last Things* (Westminster: Sheed and Ward, 1984), 271. As it is well known, this English edition is not a simple translation of his *Katholische Dogmatik*, but a renewed text that considers the teachings of the Second Vatican Council. Nevertheless, in the corresponding volume of his previous dogmatic theology, there is an interesting section on activity in heaven, where Schmaus agrees with Fichte ("Anweisung zum seligen Leben, 6. Vorlesung"; in *Sämtliche Werke,* II, 299) when he affirms that man's happiness consists in activity, with an important addition, that is, man can reach this not by his own efforts, but only by sharing in the activity of God himself (cf. Schmaus, *Teología Dogmática VII. Los novísimos* [Madrid: Rialp, 1959], 607).
80 Darrell Cosden, *A Theology of Work. Work and the New Creation* (Carlisle: Paternoster Press, 2004), p. 154.
81 Cf. Christine Gautier, *Collaborateurs de Dieu. Providence et travail humaine selon Thomas d'Aquin* (Paris: Cerf 2015).
82 Cf. Marie-Dominique Chenu, *The Theology of Work. An Exploration* (Dublin: Gill and Son, 1963), 16–18.
83 I analyze the different approaches on anticipation and participation in reference to the theology of Pannenberg in Santiago Sanz, *El Futuro creador del Dios trinitario* (Valencia: Edicep, 2007), especially 163–211.
84 This is a well-known affirmation settled by the most important medieval thinkers, especially Aquinas: human beatitude, that is, our ultimate end, is to see God, and we have a natural desire for it: cf. *SCG* III, 50–51; *STh* I, q. 12, a. 1; I–II q. 3, a. 8; etc.
85 They constitute what Taylor calls 'ordinary life"; cf. Charles Taylor, *Sources of the Self. The Making of the Modern Identity* (Cambridge, MA: Harvard University Press, 2001[10]), 211. Regarding procreation and work as participation in the divine creative power, cf. Josemaría Escrivá, *Christ is Passing By. Homilies* (Strongsville, OH: Scepter Publishers, 2017), no. 24; *Friends of God. Homilies* (Strongsville, OH: Scepter Publishers, 2017), no. 57.
86 "Blessed are those who dwell in Your house. They possess the heavenly Jerusalem [...]. What will they do there? For among men it is necessity which is the mother of all employments. I have already said, in brief, brethren, run in your mind through any occupations, and see if it is not necessity alone which procuces them. Those very eminent arts which seem so powerful in giving help to others, the art of speaking in their defense or of medicine in healing, for these are the most excellent employments in this life; take away litigants, who is there for the advocate to help? Take away wounds and diseases? What is there for the physician to cure? And all those employments of ours which are required and done for our daily life, arise from necessity. To plough, to sow, to clear fallow ground, to sail; what is it which produces all these works. but necessity and want? Take away hunger, thirst, nakedness; who has need of all these things? [...]. None of those honourable actions which are common to all men will then be your employment, nor any of these good works [...]. Say now what they shall do, for I see not then any need to induce me to action [...]. They shall be always praising You. This shall be our whole duty, an unceasing Hallelujah [...]. For there shall be great endurance, and our immortal bodies shall be sustained in contemplation of God" (Augustine of Hippo, *Expositions on the Book of Psalms*, 83, 8 [New York: Christian Literature Publishing Co.], 1986), 615–616.
87 "Moltmann presents the model of the *cabala*: God's self-restricting to allow room for the other, for created time and space, within his eternity" (Darrell Cosden,

38   *Santiago Sanz Sánchez*

A Theology of Work. Work and the New Creation (Carlisle: Paternoster Press, 2004), 164).

88 Cf. Wolfhart Pannenberg, *Systematic Theology*, vol. 2, (London and New York: T and T Clark, 2004), 14–15.

89 Cf. Jürgen Moltmann, *God in Creation* (Minneapolis, MN: Fortress Press, 1993), 14.

90 Cf. Cornelio Fabro, *Participation and Causality* (Chilium, MD: IVE Press, 2020); Santiago Sanz, *Metafísica de la Creación y Teología. La racionalidad de la idea cristiana de creación a la luz de santo Tomás de Aquino*, vol. 17, Colección Cuadernos de Filosofía (Pamplona: Servicio de Publicaciones de la Universidad de Navarra, 2007), 9–105.

91 Cf. Santiago Sanz, *Alfa e omega. Breve manuale di protologia ed escatologia* (Verona: Fede & Cultura, 2021), 15–18.

92 Augustine of Hippo, *Letter to Januarius*, IX, 17.

3 Laboring for rest
Rudiments of an Orthodox theology of work

Alexis Torrance

Introduction

Despite the emergence of multiple theologies of work in the Western academy from the 1950s onwards, Orthodox theology has been rather quiet on the matter.[1] This could be attributed to multiple factors: a certain indifference, perhaps, or a different set of priorities, or simply a lack of human resources in the Orthodox theological academy through which to tackle each and every theme as it arises with the attention it deserves. Orthodoxy's reputation for offering an "other-worldly" perspective may lead us to the assumption that it can offer little by way of this-worldly engagement. But such an assumption would be rather misleading, just as it would be misleading to say that Christ himself offers no resources to engage with the world simply because he states that both he and his disciples are "not of this world" (John 17:14–16; cf. John 18:36). The purpose of this chapter is to offer some rudiments for a positive theological understanding of work from an Orthodox Christian perspective. Far from being exhaustive, or staking out specific positions on socio-political matters discussed elsewhere in this volume (such as workers' rights, economic justice, and more), it is hoped nevertheless that what is offered here can provide a helpful theological context and lens by which to think through the myriad issues related to work that affect our world.

The chapter begins with a brief discussion of the recent article "Theology of Work: New Perspectives", an article that helps give shape to much of this volume. It will be argued that the separation described there between "eschatological" and "incarnational" views of the theology of work (where the first is other-worldly and the other is this-worldly) is untenable from an Orthodox perspective. Throughout this chapter, the theology of work will be presented in terms of both eschatology and incarnation taken together and mutually implied. From here, using key resources of the Orthodox tradition, a vision of the meaning of work will be proffered. Such a vision will begin with an emphasis on the goal of human life as consisting not in work but in rest, specifically in the blessed repose of the saints in union with Christ. This emphasis on rest, far from endangering or undermining the category of work as many would suppose, actually gives it a proper grounding and

DOI: 10.4324/9781003508212-4

40 *Alexis Torrance*

purpose. The goal of rest ratifies the meaning of work. History is the arena of movement or motion, and hence also of work. From here, the nature of that work is then discussed, first in terms of spiritual work that itself serves to orient and give meaning to work understood in its more mundane sense. Once this overarching vision is sketched, several specific insights from the tradition, especially the ascetic tradition, are presented: (1) the goal of rest is diametrically opposed to the vices of idleness and despondency; (2) the question of vocation to a particular kind of job is rather secondary to the question of vocation to keep Christ's commandments (and the implications of this); (3) at the same time, the theological value of specificity is upheld, whereby a given task or job can have lasting and even eternal significance for the human being when lived out in a Christian manner; and (4) finally, the performance of our work in accordance with Christ unlocks a mystery of communion and exchange of gifts, whereby each participates in, and shares in the fruits of, the labors of the other, even while devoted to a particular task. The chapter ends by upholding the simultaneously eschatological and incarnational vision that can be gleaned from the Orthodox tradition on the question of work. This vision is one that neither idolizes the category of work, nor negates it, but places it within the larger canvas of the human thirst for eternal rest in God, a rest whose foretaste is offered within history unto all those who humbly and meekly bring their labors to Christ, the giver of rest.

Addressing the incarnational vs eschatological tension

In their pathbreaking article, "Theology of Work: New Perspectives", Guitián and González point to a number of divergent tendencies within the literature on the theology of work. Two important streams are identified, respectively, as the eschatological and incarnational perspectives. Eschatological in this context means, according to the authors, one which "relativizes the intrinsic value of temporal realities in the face of salvation and warns against naive optimism regarding development", whereas the incarnational "points out the positive value of earthly realities in light of redemption".[2] The tension seems to be, in other words, between an anti-work (eschatological) and a pro-work (incarnational) position, and an implicit preference is understandably conveyed for the latter. Yet is such a dichotomy warranted? Can there be in Christian theology an incarnational perspective on any matter that is not also eschatological, and vice versa? From an Orthodox perspective, it is inherently problematic to present these two categories as somehow at odds with one another. The incarnation is the inauguration of the eschata, the in-breaking of the kingdom of heaven in our midst. In light of the Incarnate Christ, earthly realities are indeed affirmed, but affirmed toward *an end*. It is that end "in Christ", the eschatological perspective, that itself guarantees (rather than relativizes) the intrinsic value of temporal realities. Christ did not simply come to affirm creation, but to heal it, to summon us to repentance, and to save, which means nothing less than to deify. On the question

Laboring for rest 41

of work, the theologian's task is to convincingly show how work can be interwoven into the simultaneously incarnational and eschatological vision that lies at the heart of the Christian proclamation. This should never be done, however, at the expense of, or with a view to superseding, that vision.

The definition of work offered by Guitián and González is a helpful attempt to present a relatively neutral yet nonetheless theologically informed understanding of the term. They define work as

> a type of human activity oriented to the support of one's own life (or also of others' life), which responds to God's call to the perfecting of the person and to collaborate in the development of creation, and which is carried out in a social context, that is, in service to the needs of the human community to which one belongs.[3]

Work is thus affirmed as a positive means of fulfilling human vocation (God's call), whether for the workers in question, for their neighbors, societies, and the wider world. This definition certainly has its attractions. The flip side of the definition, however, remains underdetermined if not unaddressed, for it appears to imply either that any worker, simply by virtue of the work that they do, is thereby fulfilling God's call for them, or it implies that only work that explicitly perfects the person, develops creation, and serves the needs of the human community, is truly work (and thus presumably many workers could no longer be defined as "workers" at all if their profession does not explicitly advance each of these noble goals). Both of these alternatives create problems for the articulation of a robust theology of work. In the first case, if every worker is de facto fulfilling God's will because of the work they do (i.e. if we read the definition as meaning that *all* work is the enactment of God's will for the perfection of creation), then it seems we end up with a thoroughly immanentized understanding of the God–world relationship, and the category of work has suddenly been elevated to quasi-divine status. In the second case, if we take the definition to mean that only what supports and perfects the person, their neighbor, society, and the wider world counts as work, and nothing else, then the scope for embracing a wide range of professions and types of work as fully consistent with such a grandiose definition becomes vanishingly small. In other words, on this second reading, we risk alienating the larger category of work from the theological conversation, rather than integrating it.

These two possible implications of the proposed definition might be seen as the extremes of the incarnational versus the eschatological renderings of the concept of work. If whatever work we do is simply fulfilling God's will, we are faced with a strong "incarnational" view that has all but equated human activity with divine activity and collapsed the two together. Or, alternatively, if only the divine work of perfecting persons and bringing creation to its fulfillment (i.e. to its eschatological end) qualifies as work, then who in all honesty can actually be identified as a worker? Neither of these options

42   Alexis Torrance

yields an attractive or satisfactory solution to the question of work. As I have already intimated, an insufficient integration of incarnation and eschatology will create insurmountable problems for any theology of work. It is the integration of these that allows human work to find its proper, yet distinctly circumscribed, place within Christian theology. Turning to key resources from the Orthodox tradition, an attempt will be made first to sketch out an overall canvas for such an integrated view (with special reference to St. Maximus the Confessor), followed by key principles regarding the category of work articulated in an array of influential (often ascetic) texts.

The goal of rest

In the cosmology succinctly articulated by St. Maximus the Confessor and representative of the Orthodox tradition, all created being is conditioned by three factors: its genesis or beginning (ultimately *ex nihilo*), its movement or motion, and its end or rest. The state of repose, of "eternal rest" as the Orthodox liturgical services for the departed so often repeat, is the longed-for end of the human being. As St. Maximus writes, thinking in part of the discussion of entering into God's rest in Hebrews 4: "the end of the motion of things that are moved is to rest within eternal well-being itself".[4] The human being is orientated toward finding blessed repose, and this end gives shape and meaning to all the movement or motion that precedes it. But if rest is our goal, so too is life, and "life in abundance" (cf. John 10:10).

Eternal rest must be understood as a synonym for eternal life, not as its alternative. To enter into eternal rest is to find everlasting life, and vice versa. Not only are these synonymous, however: they are also mutually illuminating. It might be tempting to think of eternal life as simply a continuation *ad infinitum* (not to say *ad nauseum*) of our current mode of existence, subject to the vicissitudes of time (but a time that lasts forever). It might also be tempting to eschew the notion of eternal rest on the basis that it sounds boring, or more sinister still, that it conjures up visions of becoming a statue frozen solid forever, buried alive in an implacable monotony. Yet both of these temptations are just that: temptations that do no justice to the terms in question. St. Maximus famously grappled with the paradox of the human goal as life-bearing rest and rest-filled life. He coined the term "ever-moving rest", for instance, as a descriptor for life in the age to come, and spoke of the "active passivity" of the saints.[5] These constitute attempts to capture something of the mystery of acquiring, as mortal beings liable to corruption, a share in the immortal and incorruptible divine life through the person of Christ.

Since it is Christ who is the source of eternal rest and eternal life for the human being, an added paradox of Christian theology is that the *telos* of human existence has already entered into the midst of history. The goal, then, is not simply at the end of this life, or at the end of time, but it is set before us as capable of participation, at least through a glass darkly, while still sojourning here below. To paraphrase the psalm, incarnation and eschaton are met together; life and rest have kissed each other. The interweaving of movement with ineffable rest has already begun within history in the life of the Church. We have, then, to summarize St. Maximus rather briefly, the following schema: first, all creation is subject to the triad of genesis–movement–rest. Next, the category of movement or motion within this triad indicates the present age and condition in which we currently find ourselves, the arena of history in which the human being adopts the path of either well-being or ill-being. The state of movement is not itself eternal, however, and finds a terminus in a one of two states of rest or *stasis*: either the blessed repose in God which he wills for all, or the freely chosen *stasis* of alienation from the source of life. Finally, since the Incarnate Christ shows us "in himself, definitively and mystically, the goal of our perfection",[6] every movement enacted in accordance with Christ in this life is a harbinger, already here and now, of the final state of rest, and brings with it a pledge of that hallowed "rest from labour" for which the human being yearns.

With this (admittedly hurried) sketch of an overarching framework in mind, we can now attempt to fill out further the role and meaning of work. It is already emerging that the category of work does not easily belong, theologically, to the ultimate goal or *telos* of human existence. But this does not thereby render it irrelevant or meaningless for human life in general (far from it). The key entry point for the concept of work lies in the middle term of Maximus' triad, i.e. *movement* or *motion*. This term is integral (indeed, central) to his whole cosmology. It is within the field of movement, after all, that we all find ourselves. The category of movement brings with it a sense of urgency, the challenge to redeem the time given to us and not squander or waste the only means we have to move salvifically from our *genesis* in creation to our *stasis* in rest. This life of movement, moreover, is inescapably connected to the life of work. Using some of the principles we have just gathered, and others which we can glean from various sources of the Orthodox tradition, we can broach the topic of work first in its more theological sense, before using this to help shed light on work and the purpose of work in its more mundane and everyday sense.

Working the works of God

The Fourth Gospel offers us the starting point for a theological understanding of work. Jesus is asked, "what shall we do, that we might work the works of God?" To which he responds: "this is the work of God, that you believe in him whom he has sent" (John 6:28–29). The primary work that concerns the Christian is the work of faith, specifically faith in Christ. Theologically, this must always remain the chief positive work of the human being: faith and all that is of faith, all that flows from it, nourishes it, and increases it. Without faith, all work tends to become barren and fruitless, an endless and thankless toil that wearies yet never truly satisfies. Faithless work may produce

44   *Alexis Torrance*

tangible results on the material plane, but its value remains by definition only ephemeral and fleeting if it has no orientation toward the things of eternity. And what are these things? "Heaven and earth shall pass away, but my words shall not pass away" (Matt. 24:35//Mark 13:31//Luke 21:33). The word of God, the teachings of Christ, provide us with access to the things of eternity, they supply us with the orientation needed for all our work. Belief in him, that foremost work of God, involves abiding in his word, and keeping that word, which is closely connected to living out his commandments: "if you love me, keep my commandments" (John 14:15).

One among those commandments, delivered just before Christ defines the work of God as faith in him, directly addresses the importance of prioritizing the work of the commandments over every other kind of labor: "Labour not for the food which perishes, but for that food which endures unto everlasting life" (John 6:26). This is a summons to work, but primarily to spiritual work, to be fed "not by bread alone, but by every word that proceeds from the mouth of God" (Matt. 4:4//Luke 4:4). It is the quest for such sustenance that must infuse and animate all Christian theology of work. And even within that quest we witness a certain hierarchy: "Martha, Martha, you are careful and troubled about many things, but one thing is needful: and Mary has chosen that good part, which shall not be taken away from her" (Luke 10:41–42). The work of Martha was true and righteous, but the work of Mary who "sat at Jesus' feet, and heard his word" (Luke 10:39) was more true and righteous still, even if to our worldly gaze she seemed to be working far less (if at all) compared to her sister. Spiritual work must take precedence over, and accompany, every other kind of work, however outwardly noble. Only then can human work as a whole find its life-giving purpose.

But what, concretely, might it mean for spiritual work to come first and journey alongside ordinary work? The manifestation of the work of faith in a given human life is, of course, multiform. But there are likewise certain constants that can be observed. One such constant is the work of prayer. The Orthodox tradition often refers to prayer as the "art of arts, and the science of sciences", that is, as the highest form of human work and human creativity.[7] It is, moreover, a universally accessible work, and one to which the faithful are permanently called: "pray always, and faint not" (cf. Luke 18:1); "pray without ceasing" (1 Thess. 5:17). Likewise, it is a work that need not exclude other employments, and although it can demand our undivided attention at certain times, it can also embrace, accompany, and give our ordinary daily work its fulfilment. We must not, however, confuse the universal accessibility of prayer with the sense that prayer is a straightforwardly easy task. As the highest kind of work, there is also a sense in which it is hardest and most strenuous. One recent Orthodox saint, a monk of unceasing prayer, meditates powerfully on this fact:

In the act of prayer, the human mind finds its noblest expression. The mental state of the scientist engaged in research, of the artist creating a work of art, of the thinker wrapped up in philosophy – even of professional

Laboring for rest   45

theologians propounding their doctrines – cannot be compared to that of the man of prayer brought face to face with the living God. Each and every kind of mental activity presents less of a strain than prayer. We may be capable of working for 10 or 12 hours on end but a few moments of prayer and we are exhausted.[8]

The author offers us a helpful and bracing corrective to the popular misconception that prayer is at best a springboard to doing some other "real work", which in practice often results in prayer being side-lined or dropping out altogether from the Christian understanding of work. Another temptation is to equate whatever work we happen to be doing with a form of prayer, such that if I am trying, for example, to do good and honest scholarship, or good and honest scientific research, then my attempts can be defined as a kind of prayer. We academics might wish to flatter ourselves into thinking that good scholarship or good science *is* prayer, but self-flattery of this sort is little more than self-deception. Such an approach completely side-steps the true demands of prayer, and rather than elevate its status, reduces and collapses it into the ways of the world. As St Sophrony writes a little later in the same work: "erudition requires long labour but prayer is incalculably harder to acquire".[9]

To construct a meaningful theology of work, one must build on the category of prayer as on a cornerstone. Whether we mean interior prayer which is "always and everywhere possible",[10] or the formalized liturgical prayer of the Church, we understand the Christian's foremost work. The Divine Liturgy, in which is celebrated the mystery of the Holy Eucharist, holds pride of place within the Orthodox understanding of prayer, and thus within the Orthodox understanding of work. The Divine Liturgy is the Lord's work, but it assimilates the faithful into that work of healing and redemption, "on behalf of all and for all".[11] It is a cosmic and supra-cosmic work, and it is the highest privilege of Christians to have their life regularly punctuated by its saving grace. As the in-breaking of the kingdom of God upon earth, the Divine Liturgy inevitably has a strong eschatological tenor, but this by no means detracts from its unmistakably incarnational quality: the Church space, the iconography, the vessels, the chanting, the readings, the bread and the wine, simultaneously point to, and gather up, the past, the present, and the future through the operation and descent of the Holy Spirit. The Divine Liturgy is not an escape from work, but its fulfilment, the ultimate juncture in which feeble human work is offered up to the Most High, and divine work attends to overshadow, hallow, and complete the meager sacrifice. Prayer thereby becomes not simply the foundation and cornerstone of human work, but its capstone too.

At this point, the reader may understandably be concerned that such an approach to the theology of work is too other-worldly, perhaps even world denying, to be at all viable ("eschatological" but not really "incarnational"). If we place faith and prayer on such a pedestal for the Christian understanding of work, where does that leave the daily labors and employments

46   *Alexis Torrance*

that consume so much of our time, the kind of work that isn't overtly or necessarily linked to either faith or prayer? Has the category of work been so spiritualized here that the material dimension is completely jettisoned? These are valid concerns, and deserve some attention. There is a tendency to assume that if one thing is prioritized in a given discussion – in this case spiritual work (faith, the commandments, prayer) in the service of eternal rest – then by implication what is not prioritized is considered useless, detrimental, or outright evil. But one does not necessarily follow from the other. When Christ orders us to "seek first the kingdom of God and his righteousness", he does not add "because everything else is of the devil" but *"and all these things shall be added unto you"* (Matt. 6:33). What is prioritized does not have to negate what is secondary. In fact, it simply puts what is secondary into a proper and healthy perspective. If work is understood primarily in terms of an economic activity, then it inevitably holds a secondary place for Orthodox theology, but secondary does not necessarily imply insignificant, still less despicable. Now that the more fundamental theological principles have been laid out for an Orthodox approach to work, we can draw on more sources to elaborate a fuller theology of work, one that speaks directly to the concept of work and labor as commonly understood.

Work as uniquely human: Laborem Exercens *and subduing the earth*

It has often been said that, properly understood, work is a uniquely human activity.[12] Indeed, the primordial commandment for human beings to "subdue the earth" (cf. Genesis 1:28) seems to indicate a constitutive role for work in the life of humanity as set apart from other creatures. This is certainly how Pope John Paul II's seminal encyclical *Laborem Exercens* takes the passage. We might even see the summons to "subdue the earth" as the Scriptural starting point and key to that encyclical's whole discussion of work, evident already in the text's opening paragraph, and repeated no less than a further 14 times thereafter. But while this commandment certainly contains a unique summons to work, there is an obvious interpretative challenge when using this text to ratify human work as such. This is the fact that "to subdue" can quite easily be taken in a contemporary context to mean something like "to enslave". Of course, John Paul II does not at all have this in mind. He wishes to use the text instead to highlight, first, the universality of work in human life. He also uses it to analyze the complex relationship between the human person as the proper subject of work, the one tasked with "subduing" and thus irreducibly dignified, and humanity's environment, including the technological and mechanized environment that now surrounds us and threatens to usurp humanity's noble role as worker.

Yet the question of what the earth's positive subjugation by human beings is supposed to look like still needs closer attention. Biblically speaking, the whole issue of work is conditioned by the fall. While the prelapsarian command to subdue the earth stands, it inevitably becomes intertwined with

Laboring for rest   47

the tragic dynamic of pleasure and pain that characterizes humanity's life of exile.[13] To "subdue the earth" in such a state is bound to be at best an ambivalent process, and the fulfilment of this commandment can hardly be straightforwardly equated with the rise of agriculture, urban development, or technological progress:

> I made great works; I built houses; I planted vineyards: I made gardens and orchards, and I planted trees in them of all kind of fruits: I made pools of water, to water therewith the wood that brings forth trees ... Then I looked on all the works that my hands had wrought, and on the labour that I had laboured to do: and, behold, all was vanity and vexation of spirit, and there was no profit under the sun.
> (Ecclesiastes 2:4–6, 11)

The cry of the Preacher cannot be lightly dismissed as simply the ravings of existential angst, to be balanced by a more positive approach. For the true fulfilment of the commandment to subdue the earth cannot in fact be enacted by a mere man, and the Preacher knows this. The human hands that reach out across the earth in order to subdue it are no ordinary hands, but the human hands of God stretched out upon the Cross; the hands of Christ. It is Jesus Christ alone who "subdues the earth" in a proper sense. The human being may be uniquely capable of work when this is understood in terms of freedom and creativity vis-à-vis his or her environment, and yet it is only Christ who uniquely accomplishes the task set before us. He does this, moreover, not through enslaving the earth with raw strength or technological prowess, but via the all-conquering and divine path of self-emptying love.[14] Having mounted the Cross, and there "tasted death for every man", all things are put in subjection under his feet (cf. Hebrews 2:8–9): it is through the Cross, in other words, that man finally subdues the earth in the person of Christ. If we wish to grapple with the notion of human work in terms of "subduing the earth", we cannot lose sight of this. It also re-enforces the notion that any theology of work cannot be fully abstracted from the driving theological concerns of the Christian faith: it must find its place in explicit relation to those concerns, and not override or eclipse them.

That said, the subjection of the earth wrought by Christ upon the Cross does not *cut off* human work from theological consideration, and in this regard, texts such as *Laborem Excercens* prove remarkably fruitful. It is incumbent upon the theologian to attempt to connect the dimension of human work to the larger canvas of redemption, neither over-exalting it, nor trivializing it. To do this, I shall propose four principles gleaned from Orthodox sources that might accompany an Orthodox theology of work, and which could add to, and further contextualize, the wider theological discussion of work. These principles are (1) rest is not the same as idleness; (2) beyond the criterion of keeping Christ's commandments, there is a certain apophaticism regarding the value of any particular kind of work; (3) at the same time, the principle

48 *Alexis Torrance*

of incarnational specificity means that a given person's work is called to bear an enduring and positive iconic quality; (4) within the context of the human being's communion with God and neighbor, there emerges the principle of the sharing of gifts, whereby the work of one is imputed to the other, and vice versa, in the bond of love and for the building up of the whole. I will look briefly at each of these principles in turn.

Idleness vs rest

An emphasis has been placed in this chapter on the priority of rest for understanding human destiny: the human being labors, but with the hope of rest, not simply in terms of having a quiet evening or a blissful retirement, but in terms of the eschatological hope of finding eternal rest in God. Such a pursuit is distinct from the work–rest dynamic that obtains in this world, which is always conditioned by movement. The human "rest" we experience now should not be conflated with our eschatological goal. At its best, such rest may point beyond to our longed-for rest in God, but it is still fundamentally intertwined with the swirl of motion that besets us. It may be good for us to "take it easy" from time to time but taking it easy is not the same as experiencing divine rest. In fact, to live our life with the sole purpose of taking it easy is a tragic inversion of the human being's proper goal and orientation. To put it briefly, true rest is not the same as idleness or laziness, but rather opposed to them. This principle is articulated with clarity by St. Basil of Caesarea, in his *Long Rules*. Although directed to monastic communities, St. Basil's discussion of work provides invaluable insights for the topic far beyond monastery walls.[15]

When he begins to discuss work, St. Basil points out that it is the laborer – not just anyone – who is "worthy of his food" (Matt. 10:10). He continues: "we must toil with diligence and not think that our goal of piety offers an escape from work or a pretext for idleness, but occasion for struggle, for ever greater endeavour, and for patience in tribulation".[16] Christians must be workers, and "the goal of piety", of communing with God, does not undermine this fact. Idleness is inimical to the way of the Gospel:

> why should we dwell upon the amount of evil there is in idleness, when the Apostle clearly prescribes that he who does not work should not eat [cf. 2 Thess. 3:10]. As daily sustenance is necessary for everyone, so labor in proportion to one's strength is also essential.[17]

The latter point regarding proportionality is important to Basil: "he who has endowed us with the ability to work demands that our labor be proportioned to our capacity".[18] Just as idleness must be avoided, so too must excessive work. And as idleness is far removed from the goal of human life, so too is obsessive and all-consuming manual labor. Basil recommends especially modes of work that do not hinder prayer, so that while our hands are busy

Laboring for rest 49

at their tasks, we may praise God sometimes with the tongue ... or, if not, with the heart, at least, in psalms, hymns, and spiritual canticles, as it is written [cf. Col. 3:16]. Thus in the midst of our work, we can fulfill the duty of prayer, giving thanks to Him who has granted strength to our hands for performing our tasks and cleverness to our minds for acquiring knowledge, and for having provided the materials, both that which is in the instruments we use and that which forms the matter of the arts in which we may be engaged, praying that the work of our hands may be directed toward its goal, the good pleasure of God.[19]

The interweaving of the work of prayer with the work of our hands is an integral component of early Christian spirituality. In the Orthodox tradition, it is especially expressed through the practice of the Jesus Prayer, a short prayer that can accompany the person's daily activities ("Lord Jesus Christ, Son of God, have mercy upon me, a sinner").[20] We see the basis for this practice already being laid out in some detail in St. Basil's *Long Rules*. It is, moreover, a means for beginning to experience divine rest in the very midst of work, the breaking-in of the immoveable kingdom while moving through the humdrum of time's daily routines. But crucially, without the God-given component of work animating human life, we do not draw closer to divine rest; we withdraw from it into a banal idleness that is good for nothing, neither for ourselves nor for our neighbor. In sum, then, idleness is an enemy of both work and true rest.

The apophatic dimension in our choice of work[21]

If work rather than idleness can help provide a passage to divine rest, what type of work should be prioritized? Are there specific jobs, theologically speaking, that need to be elevated over others? We are speaking at this point about work in its more usual sense rather than work as faith in Christ and the pursuit of his commandments, which naturally has primacy. What we find in the tradition is a distinctly apophatic approach to this question, beyond the principle that our particular job should not prevent us from enacting the commandments. We already see a measure of anxiety about reconciling one's profession with the demands of God's commandments in the New Testament, even before the beginning of Christ's public ministry, when people from a variety of professions, including tax collectors and soldiers, ask John the Baptist about how they should live (see Luke 3:10–14). The reply they each receive does not denigrate their work as such, but instead addresses the *mode* in which they should conduct themselves in their respective employments, a mode that conforms as far as possible with the commandments. Such an attitude is visible also in Christ's own ministry. He is less interested in telling people to engage in certain kinds of work and avoid others – though the elimination of certain options, like prostitution, naturally follows from his teaching – and is more interested in renewing the mode of human life as such, bringing new life to all, *regardless of their profession or lack thereof*. He does

50   *Alexis Torrance*

not advise his listeners to agonize over their job or vocation, but over the fate of their soul: "what is a man profited, if he shall gain the whole world, and lose his own soul? Or what shall a man give in exchange for his soul?" (Matt. 16:26). The subtext contains a measure of apophaticism regarding what precise job his listeners pursue. Such apophaticism also leaves open the apostolic possibility of abandoning all work in the conventional sense in order to pursue exclusively the work of the Gospel. This invitation to renounce the world inevitably makes the position of work a secondary concern in the New Testament (but, as already emphasized, secondary does not imply negligible or negative).

The apophatic dimension on the issue of what kind of work we pursue is widespread in the tradition. It is generally expressed in terms of what is expedient in particular circumstances. Thus, to return to St. Basil, even within the context of the monastery, he can argue that there is no absolute rule for what jobs should be considered as appropriate: "It is not easy to make a selection of certain trades in particular, because different ones are pursued by various persons according to the nature of localities and the opportunities offered in each region".[22] He goes on to recommend as a general guideline the kinds of work that are conducive to tranquility and an undisturbed community life, but without issuing ironclad advice. He mentions weaving, shoemaking and "the arts of building, carpentry, the smith's trade, and farming", and has a tacit preference for agricultural work "since its proper function is the procuring of necessities and farmers are not obliged to do much traveling or running about hither and thither".[23] However, his priority is not specific forms of work, since even the pursuit of the most seemingly ideal kinds of job can in some cases "cause us anxiety" and "sever our union with our brethren", in which case "we must turn away" from such work.[24]

Beyond St. Basil, we can find many examples of a similar apophatic sentiment regarding the relative value of the different types of jobs available to human beings. This is of a piece with the idea that our job is secondary to the true work of our life, which is to love God and keep his commandments. St Symeon the New Theologian (d. 1022), for instance, argues quite forcefully in this regard in his *Gnostic, Practical, and Theological Chapters*. He writes:

> Many deem the eremitical life blessed, others the common or coenobitic life, still others public service, education, teaching, or administration of churches, from each of which bodily or spiritual nourishment is procured for many. But I would not dare to express a preference for one over another, nor to say one is worthy of praise and the other of blame. For in any and every work it is the life lived on account of God and for God that is all-blessed.[25]

Once again, we find the same kind of apophaticism deployed by Symeon, where even the highly prized life of the hermit is relativized in comparison

Laboring for rest 51

with the pre-eminent human task of living for God. St. Nicholas Cabasilas, a fourteenth-century lay theologian, echoes a similar position as follows:

> The law of the Spirit is with reason a law of friendship and consequently trains us in gratitude ... [This law] makes it no less possible to exercise our skills and it places no obstacle in the way of any occupation. The general may remain in command, the farmer may till the soil, the artisan may exercise his craft, and no one will have to desist from his usual employment because of it. One need not betake oneself to a remote spot, nor eat unaccustomed food, nor even dress differently, nor ruin one's health nor venture on any reckless act. It is possible for one who stays at home and loses none of his possessions constantly to be engaged in the law of the Spirit.[26]

As a final example, and a demonstration that this approach is alive and well in the Orthodox tradition, consider the following from the twentieth-century monk St. Silouan the Athonite:

> Everyone in this world has his task to perform, be he king or patriarch, cook, blacksmith or teacher, but the Lord Whose love extends to everyone of us will give greater reward to the man whose love for God is greater. The Lord gave us the commandment to love God with all our hearts, with all our minds, with all our souls. But without prayer how can one love? The mind and heart of man, therefore, must always be free to pray.[27]

The apophatic principle, as I have termed it, is at work in all these texts. Rather than attempt to rank certain kinds of employment on a graded scale of theological suitability or God-befittingness – for how could such a process not end in a special form of elitism and hypocritical snobbery? – We find instead an apophatic distance or gap between the array of employment opportunities and vocations before us, and the person's inner relationship with God. Another way of saying this is that we are not our jobs: we are not reducible to our work, and the work we find ourselves doing, if it does not directly interfere with the possibility of prayer, is of secondary importance to our life and our identity. If we do not espouse a theology of work that keeps this apophatic principle alive (whereby we do not simply judge according to appearances about which jobs are good and which are bad), and we allow alternative criteria to completely override that apophatic principle, then we risk alienating our theology from something that is germane within the New Testament itself. We can certainly applaud the CEO of a non-profit organization for her labors in support of a righteous cause, but never at the expense of the greeter at Walmart who, according to the moral calculus of some, is somehow complicit in systemic injustice by virtue of his employment. Striving

52 Alexis Torrance

to conform job opportunities with principles of justice and equity as far as we can is one thing but using this as a guise to denigrate some workers over others, or to make definitive negative pronouncements on whole economic systems, is quite another. There is always a danger that in trying to align the Gospel with a given socio-political approach to work, we end up contradicting or pushing out the very one we ostensibly serve, whose kingdom is not from hence. It was Christ himself who rather apophatically declared that we should "render unto Caesar the things that are Caesar's" (Matt. 22:21) and who ordered his disciples, "so as not to offend", to pay their taxes with a coin from the mouth of a fish that they did not labor at all to catch (cf. Matt. 17:27). The eschatological factor, which refuses to absolutize the value of specific kinds of human work or political and economic systems in which such work occurs, cannot be ignored. The primacy of human persons over their work, a theme eloquently and repeatedly expressed in *Laborem Exercens*, must be upheld, and this means by extension the ongoing presence of an apophatic element when it comes to the question of what kind of work we do.

Incarnational specificity: the potential iconicity of our daily work

The preceding apophatic principle may appear to relativize the significance of our work to an extreme. The apophatic principle must be balanced with another, what might be called, drawing on the theology of the incarnation, the principle of enduring specificity. Such a principle is theologically underwritten by the doctrines of incarnation and resurrection, which show us the Son of God taking upon himself the properties and specificities of being human and, though subjected to an innocent death, through that death vanquishing death and corruption, raising up our nature *while preserving its natural properties and specificity intact*. This issue was discussed in much detail in Byzantium, particularly during the controversy surrounding icons. The depictability of Christ was in part philosophically ratified by the argument that human depictability is something that inheres in our nature. It is a natural property of being human to be depictable. Thus, if Christ is said to be somehow undepictable, then either he never became properly human, or if he did, then he must not have preserved his natural properties and specificity when he rose from the dead, which would be tantamount (according to the defenders of the icons) to denying the fundamental doctrines of the incarnation and resurrection.[28]

But what does this issue have to do with work? We can begin to draw a connection when we consider the theology of St. Theodore the Studite (ninth century), one of the chief defenders of icons, and also a highly influential monastic reformer. I have argued elsewhere that St. Theodore's understanding of the icon is consistent with his broader theology of Christian life, including the category of work.[29] Theodore understood that the theology of the icon contained a radical affirmation of the enduring specificity of the human

Laboring for rest 53

being, such that all our natural properties and their historical rootedness are summoned to eternal life, not some ahistorical and abstract construct of ourselves. True, what is corrupt must put on incorruption, and what is mortal must be clothed with immortality, but crucially, this does not involve the *negation* of our historical identity and specificity, but its *salvation and redemption*. Thus, our work, while of secondary importance, is not thereby excluded from the narrative of our salvation. This too is taken up in a mysterious way, not in some crude fashion where the shoemaker forever makes shoes, and the management consultant forever troubleshoots company mergers, but insofar as our work shapes our historical identity, it shapes also, for better or worse, our eschatological identity. Eschatology is not escape from history, but the fulfilment and redemption of history. St Theodore is an ardent defender of the mundane tasks of the communal monastery (gardener, cook, infirmarian, steward, etc.) over the temptation to flee to the desert and perch as a stylite upon a column.[30] This is not only a practical concern for him (as overseer of a large monastic brotherhood), but a theological one as well. Our daily work, embedded in our historical circumstances and the specificity of our life, has the potential to be iconic, to point toward the healing and redemption of our identity in Christ, and in that process, our particular work is not nullified of meaning, but invested with it. When, through the struggle to keep Christ's commandments, we align our will with his, then the work we do follows alongside, and thereby receives an eternal significance. But to make our work (whatever it may be) iconic in this sense, paradoxically, we must first acknowledge its secondary and relative significance, rejoicing in the fact that God has called each of us however many different career paths (or lack thereof) have preceded us, and in whatever walk and state of life we currently find ourselves. The fact is that our specificity, including our work life, is broken in untold ways, but the Christian believes in the God who can make the crooked straight, and who shows us in the person of Christ the redemption of our specificity. We seek not so much for a seal of approval on our particular work, but for the grace-filled *healing* of our life of work.

Personal communion: the sharing of gifts

A final principle I wish to propose from the Orthodox tradition is that of the sharing of gifts through personal communion. This follows from the idea of the potential redemptive iconicity of daily work, where work (as belonging to our specificity in history) can point toward, and be gathered up into, the mystery of salvation in the age to come. Salvation, however, is not an individualist exercise, but involves a communion of love with God and with our neighbor, the fulfilment of the two great commandments. In that communion – potently compared in the New Testament to branches on the vine and a body with its head – what belongs to one part or member is shared with all the others. In the Macarian Homilies (fifth century?), this logic of communion is explicitly applied to the category of work. Although

54   *Alexis Torrance*

the context is monastic, as with other texts we have discussed, its importance is not limited to monasticism.

Macarius upholds the ideal of brethren living together in unity and love and draws upon St. Paul's ecclesial imagery of the Body of Christ to drive his point home. In doing so, he discusses the various tasks that a given monk performs, acknowledging that "they cannot continue all day and night at one thing": some will pray for an extended time, others read, and others perform some kind of labor.[31] He continues:

> Let him who is at work say of him who is at prayer, "The treasure that my brother gets is common, and therefore mine". Let him who prays say of the reader, "The profit which he gets by reading is to my advantage". Let him who is at work say, "The service which I am doing is for the benefit of all" ... Let not him who prays judge the labouring brother because he is not at prayer. Let not him that is at work judge the one who is praying, or say, "He lies by, while I am working". Let not him who serves judge someone else, but let each one do whatever he is doing to the glory of God. Let him who reads hold him who prays in charity and cheerfulness, with the thought, "It is for me that he prays"; and let him who prays think of him who is at work, "What he is doing is done for the benefit of us all". Thus much concord and peace and unity in the bond of peace holds them all fast, and they are enabled to live together in sincerity and simplicity and the favour of God.[32]

The sharing of gifts through the communion of love is also a sharing of work, such that the work of each member is not only their own but belongs to all the members of the body. This is more than a sense of simply working toward a common good, or the thrill of being part of a team. It includes the idea that each member of the communion is a recipient of the gifts of all, that the distinct work done by each is imputed to all in a co-inherence or perichoresis of shared life and shared love. Our theology of work should include this dimension, however distant it might seem to be from our own experience.

St. Basil of Caesarea also touches on a similar intuition in a more concrete and perhaps accessible way. In his discussion of "the aim and the disposition with which workmen should perform their tasks", he repeatedly emphasizes that our work should be done for the service of our neighbor: "he who labors ought to perform his task not for the purpose of ministering to his own needs thereby, but that he may accomplish the Lord's command: 'I was hungry and you gave me to eat'" (Matt. 25:35).[33] He reminds his reader that Christ ordered us not to be solicitous for ourselves (cf. Matt. 6:25) and thus "everyone, therefore, in doing his work, should place before himself the aim of service to the needy and not his own satisfaction".[34] The path of self-giving love that he exhorts in relation to work is the same as that commended by St. Macarius, and moves us away from considering work as an individualistic endeavor, but rather as a call to communion. Basil even takes

Laboring for rest 55

up a potential challenge to this outlook, namely the words of the Apostle that "if any does not work, neither should he eat" and that the disorderly Thessalonians should "eat their own bread" (1 Thess. 3:10, 12). Doesn't this point to the idea of self-sufficiency, a sort of equation whereby our level of individual nourishment tallies with our level of individual industry and hard work? Basil pushes back against this interpretation. He sees Paul as chastising the lazy in this passage, not as enshrining an exhaustive Christian economic principle. He writes:

> Nor should anyone think that the Apostle is at variance with our words when he says: "that working they would eat their own bread" [cf. 1 Thess. 3:12]; this is addressed to the unruly and indolent, and means that it is better for each person to minister to himself at least and not be a burden to others than to live in idleness.[35]

Paul's exhortation, in other words, is for beginners, and does not capture the full Christian vision of work. As Basil goes on: "he who is striving eagerly for perfection should work night and day 'that he may have something to give to him that suffereth need' [Eph. 4:3]". It is the commandment of love that drives his theology of work, and which I believe should drive ours also.

Conclusion: laboring for rest

To think through the concept of work from a theological perspective is not a straightforward or easy task, especially in a world plagued by problems related to workers' rights, worker retention, worker exploitation, crises of vocation, the two extremes of workaholic tendencies and the questioning of the need for any and all human work, and so on. I have not pretended to directly address this dizzying and ever-shifting array of problems related to work. I have instead attempted to step back and, using the resources of the Orthodox tradition, offer a theological reading of work in relation to human life and human destiny, and several principles that might accompany a larger (and more robust) theology of work. This work of contextualization may not offer all the answers, but it can hopefully form a partial basis from which to address contemporary concerns. If there is one element of this discussion that can be taken to heart, I hope it is the importance of not severing incarnation from eschatology, history from the age to come, and the realities of daily life from the call to repent for the sake of the kingdom. A theology of work that is not orientated toward the hope of eternity, of blessed repose, and eternal life in God, would be "most miserable" (cf. 1 Cor. 15:19). But a theology of work that simply relativizes work in relation to the eschaton and turns our lived and real histories into a mere strange and tragic show upon a crumbling stage, would be equally impotent. We live in the era of movement, of motion toward an end. The source and originator of movement is not sin or the devil, but the God of love. We have been graced with this place and this time with

56 Alexis Torrance

a duty to strive for our end, to labor for rest in communion with God and our neighbor. This end is foreshadowed and hastened when the actions of our life, regardless of our particular job or station, align with the will of Christ. In meeting the Incarnate Christ, we meet our end, our eschaton. He specifically asks us in this age of hurried motion and flux to bring all our labor, all our work, to his feet, and so experience already, in him, a taste of what it's all for, a taste of eternal rest in him (cf. Matt. 11:28). By doing this, we discover the inner and lasting meaning of work itself, and our theology of work can begin to take flight.

Notes

1 There are, of course, some exceptions. See, for example, the contributions in *Christ At Work: Orthodox Christian Perspectives on Vocation*, ed. A. M. Bezzerides (Brookline, MA: Holy Cross Orthodox Press, 2006); *For the Life of the World: Toward a Social Ethos of the Orthodox Church*, eds. David B. Hart and John Chryssavgis (Brookline, MA: Holy Cross Orthodox Press, 2020), esp. Section IV; and, most especially relevant, M. Constas, "'Work while it is still light' (John 9:4). Toward an Orthodox Christian theology of work", https://holytrinitypgh. org/apc/APC-2019-National-Clergy-Retreat-Presentation-Father-Maximos-Constas.pdf.
2 G. Guitián and A. M. González, "Theology of Work: New Perspectives," *Scripta Theologica* 54 (2022): 757–787, here at 768.
3 G. Guitián and A. M. González, "Theology of Work: New Perspectives," *Scripta Theologica* 54 (2022): 761.
4 St Maximus the Confessor, *Ambiguum*, 7:10 (ed. and trans. Constas, 1: 86–87). For a fuller discussion of St Maximus' understanding of rest, see A. Torrance, *Human Perfection in Byzantine Theology: Attaining the Fullness of Christ* (Oxford: Oxford University Press, 2020), 40–81.
5 See my discussion of these terms in Maximus in Torrance, *Human Perfection in Byzantine Theology: Attaining the Fullness of Christ* (Oxford: Oxford University Press, 2020), 68–76.
6 St. Maximus the Confessor, *Ambiguum*, 42:18 (ed. and trans. Constas, 2: 156–157).
7 For instance, St. Gregory Palamas, *Triads* 2.2.2 and Sts. Kallistos and Ignatios Xanthopoulos, "On the Life of Stillness and the Monastic State", *Philokalia*, Vol. 5 (London: Faber & Faber, 2023), 32.
8 St. Sophrony the Athonite, *His Life Is Mine* (Crestwood, NY: St Vladimir's Seminary Press, 1997), 55–56.
9 St. Sophrony the Athonite, *His Life Is Mine* (Crestwood, NY: St Vladimir's Seminary Press, 1997), 65.
10 St. Sophrony, *Saint Silouan the Athonite* (Crestwood, NY: St Vladimir's Seminary Press, 2021), 294.
11 Prayer from the Anaphora of the Divine Liturgy.
12 For an Orthodox discussion of this principle, see the opening paragraphs of M. Constas, *"Work while It Is still Light" (John 9:4). Toward an Orthodox Christian Theology of Work*, https://holytrinitypgh.org/apc/APC-2019-National-Clergy-Retreat-Presentation-Father-Maximos-Constas.pdf.
13 For an in-depth discussion of the pleasure–pain dynamic introduced by the Fall, see St. Maximos the Confessor, *On Difficulties in Sacred Scripture: The Responses to Thalassios*, trans. M. Constas (Washington, DC: Catholic University of America

Laboring for rest   57

Press, 2018), 73–93 (Intro); 143–149 (Q 21); 246–248 (Q 43); 257–263 (Q 47); 402–411 (Q 58); 434–449 (Q 61).

14 On this theme, see K. Ware, "Through Creation to the Creator," in *Toward an Ecology of Transfiguration*, eds. J. Chryssavgis and B. Foltz (New York: Fordham University Press, 2013), 86–105, especially 100.

15 For further discussion of St. Basil on work, to which I am indebted, see M. Constas, "Work while It Is still Light" (John 9:4). Toward an Orthodox Christian Theology of Work, https://holytrinitypgh.org/apc/APC-2019-National-Clergy-Retreat-Presentation-Father-Maximos-Constas.pdf.

16 St. Basil, *Long Rules* 37, trans. M. Wagner in *Saint Basil: Ascetical Works* (Washington, DC: Catholic University of America Press, 1962), 306.

17 St. Basil, *Long Rules* 37, trans. M. Wagner in *Saint Basil: Ascetical Works* (Washington, DC: Catholic University of America Press, 1962), 307.

18 St. Basil, *Long Rules* 37, trans. M. Wagner in *Saint Basil: Ascetical Works* (Washington, DC: Catholic University of America Press, 1962), 307

19 St. Basil, *Long Rules* 37, trans. M. Wagner in *Saint Basil: Ascetical Works* (Washington, DC: Catholic University of America Press, 1962), 308.

20 On the Jesus Prayer, see for example, K. Ware, *The Power of the Name: The Jesus Prayer in Orthodox Spirituality* (Fairacres: SLG Press, 2014).

21 The use of the term "apophatic" and "apophaticism" in this context may be jarring to some readers, since it is often reserved in theology for the discussion of the doctrine of God proper ("negative theology"). In Orthodox theology, however, it is also sometimes deployed to describe the mystery of the human being made in the image of the incomprehensible God, as something that escapes easy rational calculus. See, for instance, D. Staniloae, *The Experience of God: Orthodox Dogmatic Theology*, Vol. 2: *The World· Creation and Deification*, trans. and ed. I. Ionita and R. Barringer (Brookline, MA: Holy Cross Orthodox Press, 2000), 94. It is in this latter sense that the term is being deployed: an apophatic approach to the question of human employment means a refusal to subject the human being to a precise calculus regarding what kind of outward work that person should be doing.

22 St. Basil, *Long Rules* 38, trans. Wagner 311.

23 St. Basil, *Long Rules* 38, trans. M. Wagner in *Saint Basil: Ascetical Works* (Washington, DC: Catholic University of America Press, 1962), 311–312.

24 St. Basil, *Long Rules* 38, trans. Wagner M. Wagner in *Saint Basil: Ascetical Works* (Washington, DC: Catholic University of America Press, 1962), 312.

25 St. Symeon the New Theologian, *Gnostic, Practical, and Theological Chapters* 3.65 (SC 51:100). See also 3.66–67, where he continues this line of thought.

26 St. Nicholas Cabasilas, *The Life in Christ* 6.9–10 (trans. de Catanzaro 173–174).

27 St. Sophrony, *Saint Silouan the Athonite* (Crestwood, NY: St Vladimir's Seminary Press, 2021), 296.

28 For more on this issue, see A. Torrance, *Human Perfection in Byzantine Theology: Attaining the Fullness of Christ* (Oxford: Oxford University Press, 2020), 82–109; 197–204 and A. Torrance, "Persons or Principles? The Meaning of the Byzantine Icon Revisited," *Image as Theology*, eds. M. McInroy, C. Strine, and A. Torrance (Turnhout: Brepols), 107–123.

29 See the chapter on St. Theodore in my Recent Monograph: A. Torrance, *Human Perfection in Byzantine Theology: Attaining the Fullness of Christ* (Oxford: Oxford University Press, 2020), 82–109.

30 Discussed in A. Torrance, *Human Perfection in Byzantine Theology: Attaining the Fullness of Christ* (Oxford: Oxford University Press, 2020), 106–107.

31 St. Macarius the Great, *Homily* 3:1: Translated in A. J. Mason (trans.), *Fifty Spiritual Homilies of St. Macarius the Egyptian* (New York: SPCK, 1921), 16.

58   *Alexis Torrance*

32 St. Macarius the Great, *Homily* 3:2–3: Translated in A. J. Mason, *Fifty Spiritual Homilies of St. Macarius the Egyptian* (New York: SPCK, 1921), 16–17.
33 St. Basil, *Long Rules* 42, trans. Wagner in *Saint Basil: Ascetical Works* (Washington, DC: Catholic University of America Press, 1962), 317.
34 St. Basil, *Long Rules* 42, trans. Wagner in *Saint Basil: Ascetical Works* (Washington, DC: Catholic University of America Press, 1962), 317.
35 St. Basil, *Long Rules* 42, trans. Wagner in *Saint Basil: Ascetical Works* (Washington, DC: Catholic University of America Press, 1962), 317.

4 Human–divine synergy. Human labor and the transformation of the cosmos in Russian thinkers of the early twentieth century

Andrzej Persidok

Wouldn't dealing with the work of Russian thinkers of the first decades of the twentieth century mean visiting exotic regions in the theological field out of the pure desire to find something original? Certainly not. Western theological thought, since the end of the twentieth century, examines the work of these thinkers with great interest, looking for the opportunity to "breathe with two lungs". But there is another reason that makes the Russian authors important witnesses: their ideas, forged in polemic with Marxist atheism, can offer clues to face the challenge of postmodern secularism.[1] This can also be applied to the issue of work.

At the turn of the nineteenth and twentieth centuries, a spiritual and intellectual phenomenon took place in Russia, which historians refer to as the "religious-philosophical revival" or "Silver Century".[2] Partially inspired by Western philosophy, partially in polemic against it, Russian thinkers belonging to this movement began to look for new ways to express the mysteries of the Christian faith and to draw from them a light to clarify problems and challenges of socio-political life. The final decades of the Czarist Empire were characterized by an all-purpose intellectual vibrancy and a great desire to find the overarching idea that would shape the future of the Russian world. It is well known that this vibrancy ended in the tragedy of the Revolution and that, ultimately, it was not religion that was to guide Russian society in the following decades. Nevertheless, from that period, there remained several original attempts to show the relevance of Christian dogma in the new cultural context. They are usually grouped into two currents. The first was the so-called "patristic revival", whose representatives – Georgy Florovsky and Vladimir Lossky, among others – sought to elaborate a synthesis of the thought of the great classics of Eastern theology, such as Pseudo-Dionysius and Maximus the Confessor. They developed their ideas within the framework of the strictest orthodoxy and concentrated on properly theological themes. The second current was characterized by a freer attitude toward theological tradition and an ardent interest in rethinking the problems of the modern world in light of Christian dogma.[3]

It is the second of the two listed currents that interests us in the present work. Its representatives, contrary to those of the "patristic revival", did not

DOI: 10.4324/9781003508212-5

60   Andrzej Persidok

limit themselves to theological themes strictly speaking, but tried to apply theological principles to the great themes of the modern worldview. Among these themes, one must certainly acknowledge the myth of progress and belief in the transformative power of human endeavors. Russian religious thinkers, forging their ideas in direct contact with communist materialism, had to address themes such as the value of human labor or the purpose of history, offering their religious interpretation. The present work attempts to bring to light what they thought about these issues, often considered as a "house specialty" of Marxism.

We will focus mainly on two of them: Sergey Bulgakov (1871–1944) and Nikolai Berdyaev (1874–1948). The former, who was primarily a theologian, situates the problem of work in the universal perspective and wonders about the significance of human work in the creative and salvific plan ordained by God. His ideas about work are found above all in his early work, "Philosophy of Economy" (1912)[4] and in what was originally to be a second part of it: "The Unfading Light" (1917).[5]

As for Berdyaev, his perspective is more personalistic and existential. Berdyaev is mainly interested in the meaning that work has in individual human existence. His reflections on human labor are scattered in several works, beginning with "The Meaning of the Creative Act" (1915) and continuing through later works. Despite adopting a different perspective from that of Bulgakov, Berdyaev sometimes enters into direct controversy with Bulgakov, especially with regard to the creative nature of work. Thanks to these elements of controversy, and also to the fact of adopting different perspectives in dealing with the same themes, it seems to us that juxtaposing the two thinkers can be a fruitful endeavor.

Before exploring the ideas of these authors, let us briefly discuss two others, who are firmly rooted in the nineteenth century. One is Nikolai Fyodorov (1827–1903), author of a bold vision of universal resurrection as the ultimate goal of the technical development of mankind. Both Bulgakov and Berdyaev engage with his ideas critically, but also strive to retain what truth remains in them. The other is Vladimir Solovyov (1853–1900), a contemporary of Fyodorov who is considered the founder of the Russian religious–philosophical revival. Both Fyodorov and Solovyov were interested in the topic of human–divine collaboration in the transformation of the world, and therefore we can present their visions as the backdrop against which the ideas of Bulgakov and Berdyaev unfold.

Fyodorov and Solovyov: pioneers

Nikolai Fyodorov, a humble Moscow librarian, was the author of a bold philosophical vision, which he himself called "the philosophy of common task".[6] What is the common task? Nothing more nor less than the victory over death and the resurrection of all the dead. At first it seems that this is simply a central idea of Christian eschatology – which is not surprising, since

Human–divine synergy 61

Fyodorov considered himself an Orthodox Christian.[7] However, the way of thinking about this subject is original: for Fyodorov, it is truly a "common task", i.e. a result of human activity. It is men who, through technical progress, have to resurrect – literally – all the dead, thus fulfilling the holy duty they have toward their fathers. The author of "The Philosophy of the Common Task" made a strong distinction between the Resurrection of Christ and the resurrection of the dead. The first took place, thanks to divine intervention. The second will be the work of men, united in universal brotherhood, who through the achievements of science and technology will bring their ancestors back to life. If the final resurrection were to take place through divine grace, Fyodorov argues, only a few would be able to enjoy eternal happiness. The majority would be exposed to God's wrath and destined for damnation.[8]

Fyodorov's vision was criticized by theologians, who saw in it a "religion of man" combined with ancestor worship. Georgy Florovsky argued that the Moscow librarian "contrasts divine and human activity, grace and labor" and that his philosophy is nothing more than "humanist activism", in which nothing would change if all references to God were removed from it.[9] Fyodorov defended himself by saying that the "common task" is not opposed to divine grace, since God brings man to maturity through his own creative experience, being a King who accomplishes everything not only for man, but also through man.[10]

The "Philosophy of the Common Task" had a strong impact on the Russian intellectual milieu, although several thinkers, aside from its acknowledging originality, also pointed out its shortcomings. Among them was Vladimir Solovyov, professor of philosophy in Moscow and Petersburg, the second of the "pioneers" of the religious–philosophical revival. At the heart of his system lies the problem of the relationship between the Creator and his creation, the union between the absolutely different. The search for the solution of this problem gave birth to "sophiology" – an important current in Russian philosophical-theological reflection.[11] The Russian philosopher speaks of a "rift" that extends between God and the world. This is due to the transcendence of God in relation to everything created. Solovyov sees it as a kind of "no man's land", which makes it possible, on the one hand, for God to emerge from his absolute transcendence and, on the other hand, for man to transcend himself, realizing the full potentiality of his human nature. There, in the "rift", the highest ideal of the collaboration of God and man and of the union between them is realized: the divine humanity, "bogochelovechestvo".[12] This ideal is realized by man, thanks to his activity. Solovyov distinguished three fields of the latter: creative activity, knowledge, and praxis. All three are necessary for him to unfold his potential, but the most important is the first. Through it, man becomes a true collaborator of God, carrying out "theurgy". This is one of the key terms of Solovyov's philosophy. Composed of two Greek words: "theos" – God, and "ergon" – work, in its original Hellenistic context, it referred to certain kinds of magical practices. However, the

62   *Andrzej Persidok*

Russian thinker understands it in a different, etymological sense, as "divine work".[13] This consists in the spiritualization of matter through culture. Man, through his creative effort, brings matter out of its hostile inertia and submits it to the spirit as to a unifying principle.[14] Thus the absolute unity of God is reflected in the union of all creation. The world returns to the prelapsarian state when it is perfected beyond what it was in the beginning.[15] Although human work is not properly creative, in the sense of a creation *ex nihilo*, by working, man actually perfects the universe. This perfection concerns matter, but has a spiritual character. Here lies the greatest divergence between Solovyov and Fyodorov. On the one hand, Solovyov agreed with the author of "The Philosophy of the Common Task" that universal resurrection is the true end of human efforts, and that it must not be imagined as purely spiritual. On the other hand, he strongly criticized him for placing excessive hope in technical progress: thus – he argued – the "common task" is more an ideology of work and social collaboration than a Christian project of transformation of the world through divine grace. Ultimately, Fyodorov's ideal appears as a manifestation of human pride, and not a realization of "divine humanity".[16]

Despite the strongly expressed dissent, we would like to highlight what the two thinkers have in common. They both examine the question of the finality and value of human activity within Christian eschatology with a clear cosmic scope. Both hold that man can fulfill God's will through his own creativity and initiative, and not only through asceticism and obedience. They both consider that the eschatological fulfillment has to do with the transformation of matter, since – as Solovyov summarizes it – we expect not only a new heaven, but also the new earth.[17] In this way, they lay the foundations for a positive view of human work, which will be taken up by the Orthodox philosophers and theologians of the next generation.

Sergey Bulgakov: the philosophy of economics seen in a "sophiological" key

Sergey Bulgakov's intellectual journey was unconventional, and all the stages he went through before reaching the mature form of his thought resonate in him. The son of an Orthodox priest, he left his faith in his youth and turned to Marxism. He studied law and political economy. Thanks to connections with thinkers of a more spiritual disposition, and to the mystical experience he had had (he recounts it in detail in "Unfading Light"),[18] he recovered his faith, and from then on his thought was increasingly impregnated by Orthodox theology.[19] In this period, he published a work entitled "The Philosophy of Economy". This is a philosophical work which seeks to bring out the meaning of man's economic activity, but without limiting itself to the purely economic perspective. Bulgakov sees human labor as a collaboration of man with divine grace, in view of a transformation of the fallen creation into a true *kosmos*, a set of created beings ordered according to God's will.

The framework of his considerations about work revolves around the issue of the union between human and divine activity. Thus, the influence of Soloviev is evident. In fact, Bulgakov takes from the latter a concept that constitutes a hallmark of his system: that of "Sophia".[20] This word, taken from the Sapiential Books, points to a mysterious realm where God and creation converge; a personal principle that, without being a fourth divine person, permeates the universe and pulls it from within into unity and communion with God. Within this cosmic drama of the "sophinization of the universe", human work, according to Bulgakov, has a considerable role.

Assuming, at first, the existential point of view, Bulgakov argues that economics is born from the need to resist death. In order to survive, man must defend himself against the silent power of inanimate nature. But defense is closely linked to attack: man transforms nature, so that it serves him instead of threatening him. This transformation consists in disrupting the order of mechanical necessity and introducing a teleological principle into it.[21] Economics is "the expression of the struggle of these two metaphysical principles: life and death, freedom and necessity, the mechanical and the organic".[22] This struggle is carried out through work, which constitutes "the foundation of life considered from the economic point of view".[23]

According to Bulgakov, labor eludes an exact definition. Citing Marx's definition of work as "expenditure of nervous and muscular energy", the Russian thinker observes that it is not truly a definition, but rather a description of the external manifestations of a certain labor.[24] To delve deeper into its inner essence, one must consider some effective will, an active going out of oneself, in which the very passion and tension of life manifests itself.[25]

Therefore, the first thing that appears is that in work, the living and active subject is opposed to nature, the latter considered in its inertia. However, seen from the other angle, labor is already included in the created order, since the subject is not an extra-worldly principle, but is part of the universe.[26] Thus, contrary to Kant, who saw the object as formed by the subject, and also to Marx, according to whom it is the object-world which shapes the subject, Bulgakov sees a reciprocal relationship in which neither extreme can be considered without the other.[27] Thus, he speaks of a certain alignment between the subject and the object of labor, which constitutes the foundational basis of economics. Only this alignment can explain how it is possible for the object to assume in itself the activity of the subject and allow itself to be transformed by it. In the process of working, the "self" and the "non-self" are the same thing; through man, nature is acting upon itself, creating itself. The instinctive work of nature becomes *through* and *in* man a conscious work.[28]

> Labor (...) is the living link between subject and object, a bridge by which the 'self' can extend into the real world and binds with it in an indivisible manner. Thanks to labor, there can be neither merely a subject (as in idealism), nor merely an object (as in materialism), but their living unity, the subject-object. It cannot be divided except by

64   *Andrzej Persidok*

examining it under one angle or another, by means of a methodological abstraction. But the polarized – unfolded – state of being is overcome only in the Absolute.[29]

Labor conceived in this way is not limited to productive activity. For Bulgakov, the accumulation of knowledge can also be labeled as such. If economics is "knowledge that becomes tangible", knowledge can be considered as the same process but in a non-sensible, ideal form.

Thanks to labor activity, the world becomes humanized. This means that nature, mute and unconscious, becomes conscious. Before the emergence of man, the transformations that occurred in nature were automatic, without any "other side" in the consciousness. Since man has existed, there has been a conscious process of recovery of the lost unity:

> The world, with its finished form summed up in Adam, with humanity at its center, was created by God, and what unfolds in time and constitutes history does nothing but reproduce the internal link and correlation between the elements of the world broken by the Fall.[30]

As can be clearly seen, Bulgakov, in discussing work, is not interested in its individual dimension: working conditions, subjective consciousness of the meaning of the work performed or the lack of it....[31] The Russian thinker sees everything in a universal perspective; in his eyes, economics is a great process by which nature, created by God, becomes itself through man considered as a single subject and not as a multitude. This is not just a metaphor: in Bulgakov's system of thought, there is a "transcendental subject" of economics. Philosophically, it is called the "Soul of the World"; theologically, the "Divine Wisdom" or "Sophia".[32] Here we address one of the central points of Bulgakov's philosophy: "sophiology". The author of "Philosophy of Economy" was one of the main exponents of this current in Orthodox theology, although he himself acknowledged his debt to the authors of the previous generation: Vladimir Solovyov and Sergey Trubetskov.[33] These authors sought to solve the problem of mediation between God and the created world.[34] They were inspired by the Sapiential Books, which in certain places speak of "divine Wisdom" in such a way as to give the impression of dealing with a personal being and not just a characteristic of God Himself. In the theological tradition, the same texts were interpreted as figures of the Word of God, the Holy Spirit, or the Virgin Mary.[35] On the other hand, the "sophiologists" read them in light of Neoplatonic speculations. Hence their conception of "Sophia" as a kind of quasi-personal being, a place of mediation between God and creation.

According to Bulgakov, there are two Sophia: the uncreated Sophia, which is the divine substance itself insofar as it is given to creation, and the created Sophia, the ensemble of all the archetypes that determine the created world, the *Anima mundi* itself.[36] The ultimate end of the history of the world is its "sophinization", which refers to the realization of the archetypes contained in the created Sophia.[37] This is carried out through economy, work understood in its broad sense. Thus, human labor, according to Bulgakov, is not creative in its own sense, since all the potentialities it develops are already contained in Sophia.[38] "Through the free and arduous historical process, man reproduces what has always existed, an ideal archetype".[39]

Thus, the humanization of the world, which the Russian thinker contemplated as the meaning of work, manifests itself as its true "sophinization". Man, who transforms the world through the labor process does not add anything artificial, does not disfigure it, does not break the fabric of nature by introducing an alien principle into it. Quite the contrary: through human labor, the world can come to its true being, hitherto hidden under layers of dark and inert matter. In reality, it is the work of Sophia itself, which restores creation through the mediation of historical humanity.[40] The means of this restoration is work. Thus, "the end of economics lies outside its limits"; it is nothing more than a path by which the world is led toward the "realized Sophia".[41] The origin of economic labor also lies beyond economics and history: both are "hierarchically and economically preceded by another economy, by another labor". In these words, Bulgakov refers to the prelapsarian state, to the paradisiacal economy, in which labor was a "disinterested and loving activity with respect to nature in order to know it, to perfect it, and to unfold its sophianity".[42] In the present state, there is only one type of human activity that preserves in itself the archetype of the prelapsarian economy. For Bulgakov, art constitutes "the end and the limit of economy, which must return to its archetype, transforming itself into art".[43] In a certain sense, by re-establishing the unity between subject and object – between Sophia and matter – man transforms the whole world into a work of art. Thus, "the whole world becomes *cosmos*, chaos conquered, tamed and illuminated. Thus the victory of economy represents a cosmic victory of beauty".[44]

Despite his great optimism regarding human progress, the author of the "Philosophy of Economy" was aware of the ambiguity of human work upon the world. In that work, he observed that apart from the economy that develops the archetypes contained in the divine plan, there is another "satanic" type of activity. Its origin is man's desire to "become like the gods". His main ambition is to create in an absolute sense, disregarding any reference to God and the divine order.[45] This is a true "metaphysical usurpation".[46] Its achievements are as astonishing as the false miracles of the Antichrist, but in reality, they are nothing more than a phantom. Beneath the surface lies a void, a non-being, a false likeness of one's own subjectivity.[47] However, although this activity has nothing in common with true "sophianic" creativity, understood as re-creation, its seductive power is enormous. This lends an ambiguous character to all economic activity.[48] Later, Bulgakov observed that what claims to be the full humanization of the world ends up being its "beastialization", since it subjugates divine creation to the animal principle in man, who asserts himself as the supreme and only power.[49]

66 *Andrzej Persidok*

Bulgakov promised to develop the latter theme in the second volume of his work, devoted to the "eschatology of economy".[50] This second volume never saw the light of day. However, when the Moscow theologian published "Unfading Light" in 1917, he subtitled it "Scholia to the Philosophy of Economy".[51] Although in this book the subject of labor and economy is not central, it contains some considerations relevant to our topic.

First, it can be seen that Bulgakov's optimism about labor and economy is waning. The author compares economy with "gray magic", which in its attempts to master the world mixes light and dark elements: on the one hand, it constitutes a creative activity, but, on the other hand, it obeys the order of necessity, of slavery to the causal order.[52] The impulse to surpass oneself does not always make man discover what is above him, but it also makes him intensify his own economic activity, in such a way that he sees all of reality in terms of work, transformation, and profit. Thus "economism" was born, a view toward life that was already common in Bulgakov's time, at the dawn of the Communist Revolution.[53] According to Bulgakov, even such a sublime spirit as Nikolai Fyodorov was not exempt from this way of thinking. Its conception, although born of a religious impulse, in the end "unilaterally exalts the human element, which ends up replacing and displacing the divine power".[54] While Fyodorov sees in human labor the key principle for the eschatological fulfillment of the universe, Bulgakov concludes that the economy has no eschatology as such, since it is too closely linked to the "curse of the earth".[55]

In Bulgakov, a certain disillusionment with labor activity coexists with an exaltation of artistic creation. If in the former man often falls into the temptation of establishing himself as the ultimate end, in the latter, he always preserves the desire to let some rays of the light of Tabor into the world.[56] There is, however, another side to this contrast between work and art. The latter can only be a symbol, a call, a promise, which, in the end, turns out to be impotent. Art carries within itself a yearning for "cosmourgia". It strives to be an instrument of the salvation of the world, but, contrary to economic activity, it has no real influence.[57] Thus, the Russian thinker contemplates the tragic nature of human activity:

> If the tragedy of an economy that understands its limits lies in the awareness of its prosaic nature, of its slavery, of its heaviness, the tragedy of art lies in the awareness of its impotence, of the terrible gap between the true splendor of the world revealed in it and its present ugliness. Art does not save, does not alleviate the sadness of earthly existence; it only consoles, but are impotent consolations appropriate and necessary?[58]

Nikolai Berdyaev: creative work as man's vocation

Nikolai Berdyaev belonged to the same generation as Bulgakov and had a similar life journey. A Marxist at the beginning of his intellectual career, he

Human–divine synergy 67

later became part of the "religious-philosophical revival". Exiled from Soviet Russia in 1922 (along with Bulgakov and others, aboard the famous "ship of philosophers"), he developed his philosophy as an emigrant in France.[59] With regard to the topic of work, he did not devote any particular comprehensive study to it. His opinions on this subject are contained in several of his works. It is worth noting that Berdyaev sometimes deals with labor with direct reference to the views of Solovyov, Fyodorov, and, above all, Bulgakov. Here we will address his ideas without following a chronological order, but rather dealing with recurring themes in several works of his, from "The Meaning of the Creative Act" (1916)[60] and "The Philosophy of Inequality" (1922)[61] to "The New Middle Ages" (1924)[62] and "The Destiny of Man" (1931).[63]

Before starting the journey through the above-mentioned works, it is worth making some general remarks. First, Berdyaev's ideas about work and economy are formed in clear controversy with Marxism and socialism. However, a no less important factor is the feeling of deep cultural crisis in the world at that time. The dehumanization of social relations, the triumphant advance of technology, the issue of unemployment, and the lack of meaning in life – all of these phenomena strike the Russian thinker and make him reflect on how to overcome them. Second, in his answers, Berdyaev is not as concerned with their orthodoxy as Bulgakov is, so his thinking develops more in the philosophical than in the theological field. The third important difference between the two authors is that, instead of the theological–cosmic perspective present in Bulgakov, Berdyaev adopts a more existential perspective. When questioning the meaning of human labor, he is interested in understanding what kind of labor is experienced as meaningful by the man who performs it. This interest was practically absent in the work of the author of "The Philosophy of Economy", who was fixated on the place of labor in the divine eternal plan of creation and salvation.

As for concrete questions, it is worth beginning with a point that Berdyaev shares with Bulgakov and, perhaps, with the majority of Christian thinkers who reflect on work. He considers work as a spiritual phenomenon, and not a mere "expenditure of nervous and muscular energy" as Marx thought. According to Berdyaev, neither capitalism nor socialism can correctly pose the question of work, because both remain within the error of "economism", which reduces man to economic values, whereas, in reality, the ultimate values are spiritual: the person, his inner life, and his destiny. They alone constitute an appropriate starting point for understanding the essence of work.[64] Marxists consider work under the merely quantitative aspect and praise it as if it were an end in itself, because they have lost the true end and meaning of human life.[65] They treat economics as a key that unlocks all mysteries, but it says nothing about the ends, only about the means.[66] The paradise promised to man as the fruit of the revolution is actually a bourgeois ideal: maximum consumption and minimum effort. However, Berdyaev argues, this is equivalent to leaving the spirit enslaved to matter. Socialism and capitalism are but two different forms of such slavery.[67]

68   *Andrzej Persidok*

In the face of such reductionism, the thinker calls for a return to addressing the issue of work as a spiritual issue.[68] According to him, work is determined externally (external conditions, social relations, etc.) and internally, the second dimension being the decisive one.[69] Solving the spiritual problem of work means finding its sacred dimension and its true motivation. What the philosopher proposes as the spiritual enlightenment of work is to live it either as a redemptive effort or as creativity. The tragic dimension of work in the postlapsarian world consists in the fact that only a few can carry out creative work *sensu stricto*, while the rest are condemned to drudgery and repetitive work.[70] According to Berdiayev, a general goal would be to free as many as possible from the need to do non-creative work. Corresponding to this general objective on the personal level is the imperative to work as creatively as possible, even at the lower levels of the "hierarchy of creativity".[71]

As it is clearly seen, in Berdyaev's philosophy, creativity is a supreme value. Situating it on the universal plane of salvation history, the Russian thinker proposes a kind of "Joachimism". According to his vision, there are three epochs in history: the epoch of the Law, under the Old Testament; the epoch of redemption, under the New; and the epoch of creativity, which has no Testament, since its presence would transform creativity back into obedience.[72] The essence of the third epoch, in which humanity will finally reach its fullness as "divine humanity" is the awakening of man's creative power.[73] If man is the "image of God", it is thanks to his capacity to introduce something new into being, to create things that have never existed before.[74] If for Sergey Bulgakov, the desire to create something absolutely new is a demonic ambition, for Berdyaev, it is at the heart of man's vocation in the present epoch. The author of "The New Middle Ages" argues that the fall of the world under the regime of determinism was the fruit of original sin. But in this fallen world, there is also the negative of determinism: human freedom, which is an absolutely indeterminate potentiality.[75] The path of the salvation of the world goes through human freedom and has two aspects. The first, in a negative sense, is redemption, which is equivalent to the healing of the wounds caused by sin. But there is also a positive side – creative activity, by which man rises to a level where he had never been before.[76] "Man – the philosopher argues – justifies himself before the Creator not only by the redemption, but by creativeness as well".[77]

From this comes Berdyaev's criticism of Bulgakov's sophiology and, conversly, his praise of Fyodorov's "Philosophy of the Common Task". Regarding the former, Berdyaev claims that in Bulgakov's system, there is no room for real creativity, but only for a "management" of what was granted to man.[78] Since everything that existed, exists, and will exist has its archetype in God, creativity in the strict sense is impossible.[79] This is an underestimation of human dignity. On the other hand, when the thinker deals with Fyodorov's system, he calls it "brilliant and audacious".[80] In "The Philosophy of Inequality", he is directly inspired by him, taking the idea of "cosmic economy" as his own. If the aim of economy consists in "overcoming the heaviness of the material world" and "mastering the chaotic elements of nature", this does not refer only to the natural processes on earth, but to the entire universe.[81] The transfiguration of the universe was an idea also present in Bulgakov, but, unlike him, Berdyaev considers it on a less theological plane, but more material and empirical. Moreover, he seems to grant a more relevant role to the ingenuity of mankind: while he does not exclude the principle of grace, he instead sees it as acting through human efforts and not as collaborating with them from outside. For this reason, without falling into atheism, he can maintain that it is man who must conquer the cosmic forces on which he has hitherto depended.[82] This conquest is a necessary condition for the fulfillment of the most important victory: the victory over death, which is, following Fyodorov, the root of all evil.[83]

In work and economy, Bedriayev sees a subject of utmost importance: the way in which the fulfillment of the world and human history is realized. In this context, however, it is worth emphasizing an idea that returns every time the philosopher deals with these issues. Today – he says – work, instead of perfecting man, generates "fictitious needs" and tries to satisfy them.[84] This type of misrepresentation of labor activity is generated above all by the capitalist system. Machines, technological progress, and human power all contribute to the growth of insatiable desire, wherein the concept of "bad infinity" manifests itself, an endless series of quantitatively different moments lacking true qualitative growth. This is only possible in the realm of the spirit, which in capitalism is totally suffocated by material dominance.[85] Thus, work, instead of bringing eschatological perfection closer, confines man in his own finitude and mortality. Nevertheless, even work that generates fictitious desires and objects and is not creative in its own sense has its dignity. Although it does not play its most noble role, it is still a redemptive, ascetic activity, which can have spiritual benefit for the working subject.[86]

The issue of economic growth, which no longer satiates but rather generates desires and false needs, is directly linked to that of mechanization. Berdyaev's reflections on this are among the most interesting and, in a certain sense, prophetic. "The issue of the machine belongs to the profound metaphysical problems" – says the philosopher.[87] According to him, the emergence of the machine profoundly changed man and his relationship to the natural world. From that moment man "ceased to live connected to the earth, surrounded by animals and plants". He now "lives in a new metallic reality, breathing polluted air".[88] The paradox consists in the fact that man, having freed himself from the power of nature, did not become his own master. Separated from the "carnal rhythms of nature", he now lives in a world formed by machines.[89] He is now the slave of his own invention.[90]

At first glance, all this seems to be one of many expressions of romantic nostalgia for the past. In reality, however, Berdyaev's position is more tragic than romantic. The thinker observes that a romantic who dreams in the twentieth century of returning to the pre-technical era has a false consciousness, since at every step he takes advantage of technique and depends on it.[91]

70 *Andrzej Persidok*

Moreover, he maintains that the machine does not kill the spirit, but matter, the "body of the world".[92] In fact, "the machine must lead to the destruction of one of the most perfect phenomena of nature: the human body; it must replace the body".[93] Despite this, the most valuable element in man remains intact. Instead of looking back, man must now find a new vital balance and seek a new beauty in the world transformed by technology. The advent of the machine is not a negative phenomenon, but an ambiguous one:

> The machine not only oppresses the human spirit, but also liberates it, as if with iron claws tearing it away from the organic matter in which it initially slumbered and from which it then began to awaken.[94]

The mechanization of life is the crucifixion of matter, but man must follow the paschal journey: through the cross to the resurrection.[95] The world must "experience the victory of the machine and the human spirit must survive this process, must free itself, and attain its highest dignity".[96]

Following Berdyaev's meditations on "the machine", we have apparently moved away from the subject of work. However, the technical revolution entails such a significant change in the conditions of labor that we cannot do without addressing it. How does work change as a result of the triumphant march of the machine? The Russian philosopher does not give a comprehensive answer. Rather, it seems fragmentary and even contradictory. On the one hand, as we have seen, in the introduction of technology he sees a kind of "paschal journey" that humanity has to travel in order to arrive through the cross of mechanization to the new life less dependent on matter and more spiritualized. This accords with his proposition to free humanity from the types of work that are less creative and more laborious, enabling them to concentrate their forces on creative activity.[97] But Berdyaev is aware that not everyone can perform creative work.[98] That is why the development of technology not only generates artists and creators, but also generates unemployment.[99] How can this problem be solved? Berdyaev's answer is enigmatic and not very concrete: if the nations want to experience a spiritual rebirth – he says – they have to follow the path of asceticism, the suppression of the desire for life and the spiritualization of economic activity.[100] But how to reconcile this perspective with the imperative to master – through technology – the cosmic processes in order to solve the problem of death? The philosopher seems to suggest two opposing paths, which, perhaps, correspond to two contradictory feelings that he carried within himself: horror at the triumphant machine and fascination for the possibilities it opens up.

Conclusion

Sergey Bulgakov and Nikolai Berdyaev were two great figures of the Russian "religious-philosophical renaissance" at the beginning of the twentieth century. Marxists in their youth, the two later came under the influence of

Human–divine synergy   71

Nikolai Fyodorov and Vladimir Solovyov. The inspiration that Bulgakov and Berdyaev found in the writings of these authors encouraged them to introduce the great topic of the twentieth century – labor and economy – into the heart of religious reflection. The former did so on a more theological plane. He developed his vision of the fulfillment of the divine plan through man's collaboration: as man works, the world is humanized and thus also approaches "sophinization", its ultimate destiny. By placing his reflection within the framework of "sophiology", Bulgakov has to emphasize that human labor is not absolutely creative, but develops the archetypes contained already from eternity in the "Sophia". The awareness that work, instead of being profitable for man, can also be destructive, makes him doubt that it has an eschatological role.

Berdyaev shares Bulgakov's sources of inspiration, but his perspective in looking at the problem of labor is narrower: he is not interested in the cosmic drama, but rather in the drama of the individual human spirit. He is even less optimistic than the author of the "Philosophy of Economics". According to Berdyaev, the role of man as a working being is tragic: his vocation is creative work, but only a few can work in this way. The rest have to do repetitive work, which does not contribute to the development of the spirit. One of the hopes for freeing man from this kind of work is technological progress – the appearance of the "machine". This phenomenon has, however, an ambiguous character. On the one hand, it frees man from the most arduous tasks, but, on the other hand, it enslaves him and tears him away from the motherly bosom of nature. According to Berdyaev, it is a paschal process: mechanization is a crucifixion of the human body, but it is also an opportunity to liberate his spirit and make it more creative, that is, more in accordance with its original vocation.

Despite the time that has passed since the publication of the main works of the two authors analyzed in this study, certain aspects of their reflections are surprisingly current. First, it is necessary to mention here the insistence of both of them on the spiritual, and not only physical and psychic, character of the phenomenon of work. Today, many debates on the subject of labor focus on such questions as the dignity of the worker or the influence of economic development on nature. Bulgakov and Berdyaev show that there is an even more important question: the meaning of labor, both in the subjective dimension (feeling that one's work is meaningful) and in the objective dimension (understanding that the common effort of the economy leads to some worthwhile end). The answers to this question can only be given at the level of the spirit that neither pure capitalism nor socialism can reach. Second, it is worth emphasizing that both authors make an attempt to combine a Christian perspective with a positive valuation of human creativity. Although neither of them forgets their possible deviation, they try to incorporate it into the divine plan of the fulfillment of the cosmos (Bulgakov) and of the full development of the human person as the image of God (Berdyaev). In this way, they show that the attitude of theology toward such values as progress or creativity

72 Andrzej Persidok

need not necessarily be critical, as is often thought. Finally, each of the two, building a theological–philosophical vision of their own, brings original ideas worthy of consideration. As for Sergey Bulgakov, his insistence on the paradoxical character of the relationship between the man-subject who works and the world-object transformed by work stands out. The Russian philosopher describes it as unity of subject and object. This idea of his may be of interest at a time when we are looking for ways to incorporate man back into the whole of the natural world, with a view to forging a vision of the economy that is more respectful of the environment. As for Nikolai Berdyaev, his description of the process of mechanization of the human world as a paschal process of death and resurrection stands out. This idea can be useful for framing technical progress without falling into nostalgic romanticism or excessive enthusiasm that forgets the price we pay for development.

In conclusion, it should be said that, on the subjects of labor and the economy, Bulgakov and Berdyaev are neither pessimists nor optimists. Economic progress, the mechanization of labor, the transforming power that man exerts on the cosmos, constitute a fact from which it is no longer possible to turn back. Nevertheless, they insist that they can and must be given a form that is beneficial to human beings. For this to be the case, economic issues must not be dealt with within the narrow framework of economics. This applies especially to work, which must be seen not only as an economic fact, but as a dimension of *human* life: bodily, psychic, spiritual, and social. In order not to lose sight of the true meaning of work, it is necessary to ask first of all, who is man and what does he live for? The fact of framing the labor problem in such a broad context seems necessary, so that the prodigious fruits of human progress do not end with humanity itself. Both Bulgakov and Berdyaev are clear that decent work cannot result in the alienation of the human being, with the latter functioning as a cog in the machine. Nor do they see a solution in individualism. Heirs to the ideas of Fyodorov and Solovyov, they understand that labor is, in reality, a true "common task" – participation in the great process of the transformation of the cosmos, in which both human freedom and divine grace have their irreplaceable role.

Notes

1 Cf. *Beyond Modernity: Russian Religious Philosophy and Post-Secularism*, eds. Artur Mrówczynski-Van Allen, Teresa Obolevitch, Paweł Rojek (Eugene, OR: Pickwick, 2016), 3.

2 Teresa Obolevitch, *Filozofia rosyjskiego renesansu patrystycznego* (Kraków: Copernicus Center Press, 2014), 41.

3 On the two currents and discussions between their representatives, cf. Obolevitch, *Filozofia rosyjskiego renesansu Patrystycznego* (Kraków: Copernicus Center Press, 2014), 40–62.

4 Serge Boulgakov, *La philosophie de l'economie* (Lausanne: Age d'homme, 1987).

5 Sergiusz Bułgakow, *Światło wieczności* (Kęty: Wydawnictwo Marek Derewiecki, 2010). According to Robert F. Slesinski, the two works form a "diptych",

Human–divine synergy   73

cf. Robert F. Slesinski, *The Theology of Sergius Bulgakov* (Yonkers, New York: St. Vladimir's Seminary Press, 2017), 40.

6 Thus is titled the first volume of his writings, edited by his disciples and friends in 1906, three years after his death, cf. Leonid Stołowicz, *Historia filozofii rosyjskiej* (Gdańsk: Słowo/obrazterytoria, 2008), 207.

7 Leonid Stołowicz, *Historia filozofii rosyjskiej* (Gdańsk: Słowo/obrazterytoria, 2008), 207.

8 Grzegorz Przebinda, "Wizje apokaliptyczne Mikołaja Fiodorowa i Włodzimierza Sołowjowa," in: ed. W. Szczukin, *Pamięć serca. Liber amicorum. Tom jubileuszowy dedykowany Danucie Piwowarskiej* (Kraków: Wydawnictwo Uniwersytetu Jagiellońskiego, 2008), 153

9 Cited in: Leonid Stołowicz, *Historia filozofii rosyjskiej* (Gdańsk: Słowo/obrazterytoria, 2008), 209.

10 Leonid Stołowicz, *Historia filozofii rosyjskiej* (Gdańsk: Słowo/obrazterytoria, 2008), 207.

11 Below we will explain what this current in Russian thought consists of.

12 Janusz Dobieszewski, *Włodzimierz Sołowiow. Studium osobowości filozoficznej* (Warszawa: Scholar, 2002), 80.

13 Janusz Dobieszewski, *Włodzimierz Sołowiow. Studium osobowości filozoficznej* (Warszawa: Scholar, 2002), 148.

14 Janusz Dobieszewski, *Włodzimierz Sołowiow. Studium osobowości filozoficznej* (Warszawa: Scholar, 2002), 160.

15 Janusz Dobieszewski, *Włodzimierz Sołowiow. Studium osobowości filozoficznej* (Warszawa: Scholar, 2002), 264.

16 Janusz Dobieszewski, *Włodzimierz Sołowiow. Studium osobowości filozoficznej* (Warszawa: Scholar, 2002), 270–272.

17 Janusz Dobieszewski, *Włodzimierz Sołowiow. Studium osobowości filozoficznej* (Warszawa: Scholar, 2002), 268; cf. Rev 21:1.

18 Cf. Sergiusz Bułgakow, *Światło Wieczności* (Kęty: Wydawnictwo Marek Derewiecki, 2010), 25–27.

19 For a summary of the early years of Bulgakov's life according to his notes; cf. Slesinski, *The Theology of Sergius Bulgakov* (Yonkers, New York: St. Vladimir's Seminary Press, 2017), 7–11.

20 Cf. Leonid Stołowicz, *Historia filozofii rosyjskiej* (Gdańsk: Słowo/obrazterytoria, 2008), 219–222.

21 Cf. Serge Boulgakov, *La philosophie de l'economie* (Lausanne: Age d'homme, 1987), 38.

22 Cf. Serge Boulgakov, *La philosophie de l'economie* (Lausanne: Age d'homme, 1987), 39.

23 Cf. Serge Boulgakov, *La philosophie de l'economie* (Lausanne: Age d'homme, 1987), 39.

24 Cf. Serge Boulgakov, *La philosophie de l'economie* (Lausanne: Age d'homme, 1987), 40.

25 Cf. Serge Boulgakov, *La philosophie de l'economie* (Lausanne: Age d'homme, 1987), 41.

26 Cf. Serge Boulgakov, *La philosophie de l'economie* (Lausanne: Age d'homme, 1987), 41.

27 Cf. Serge Boulgakov, *La philosophie de l'economie* (Lausanne: Age d'homme, 1987), 73.

28 Cf. Serge Boulgakov, *La philosophie de l'economie* (Lausanne: Age d'homme, 1987), 73.

29 Serge Boulgakov, *La philosophie de l'economie* (Lausanne: Age d'homme, 1987), 74.

74 *Andrzej Persidok*

30 Serge Boulgakov, *La philosophie de l'economie* (Lausanne: Age d'homme, 1987), 79–80.
31 For this reason, in a polemical tone against the postulates of Marxism, he maintains that it is not necessary to socialize production, since the economy is social by its very nature; cf. Serge Boulgakov, *La philosophie de l'economie* (Lausanne: Age d'homme, 1987), 84.
32 Serge Boulgakov, *La philosophie de l'economie* (Lausanne: Age d'homme, 1987), 87.
33 Cf. Serge Boulgakov, *La philosophie de l'economie* (Lausanne: Age d'homme, 1987), 88.
34 Cf. Antoine Arjakovsky, "The Sophiology of Father Sergius Bulgakov and Contemporary Western Theology," *St Vladimir's Theological Quarterly* 49, no. 1–2 (2005): 222.
35 Cf. Tomáš Špidlík, *Myśl rosyjska. Inna wizja człowieka* (Warszawa: MIC, 2000), 396.
36 Cf. Arjakovsky, "The Sophiology of Father Sergius Bulgakov," 223; the doctrine of the two Sophias was made explicit in Bulgakov's later works, for example in: Serge Bulgakov, *L'Épouse de l'Agneau: la création, L'homme, l'Église et la fin* (Lausanne: Age d'homme, 1984).
37 Cf. Serge Boulgakov, *La philosophie de l'economie* (Lausanne: Age d'homme, 1987), 100.
38 Establishing a single subject of history allows Bulgakov to see the unity of the historical process. However, contrary to Hegel, the Russian thinker does not identify him with God himself. Thus, he can speak of the unique meaning of history, without compromising the transcendence of God.
39 Cf. Serge Boulgakov, *La philosophie de l'economie* (Lausanne: Age d'homme, 1987), 101.
40 Cf. Serge Boulgakov, *La philosophie de l'economie* (Lausanne: Age d'homme, 1987), 110.
41 Cf. Serge Boulgakov, *La philosophie de l'economie* (Lausanne: Age d'homme, 1987), 111.
42 Serge Boulgakov, *La philosophie de l'economie* (Lausanne: Age d'homme, 1987), 111.
43 Serge Boulgakov, *La philosophie de l'economie* (Lausanne: Age d'homme, 1987), note 99.
44 Serge Boulgakov, *La philosophie de l'economie* (Lausanne: Age d'homme, 1987), 90.
45 Cf. Serge Boulgakov, *La philosophie de l'economie* (Lausanne: Age d'homme, 1987), 102.
46 Cf. Serge Boulgakov, *La philosophie de l'economie* (Lausanne: Age d'homme, 1987), 101.
47 Cf. Serge Boulgakov, *La philosophie de l'economie* (Lausanne: Age d'homme, 1987), 101.
48 Cf. Serge Boulgakov, *La philosophie de l'economie* (Lausanne: Age d'homme, 1987), 102.
49 Serge Bulgakov, *L'Épouse de l'Agneau: la création, l'homme, l'Église et la fin* (Lausanne: Age d'homme, 1984), 252.
50 It is worth emphasizing that the eschatological destiny of the economy and the fruits of human labor was a theme that occupied also Christian thinkers in the West, from Teilhard de Chardin to John Paul II. It might be interesting to trace the possible influences of Russian authors on Western work theology, cf. Paweł Rojek, *Liturgia dziejów. Jan Paweł II I polski mesjanizm* (Kraków: Wydawnictwo, 2016), 251–261.

Human–divine synergy 75

51 Cf. Serge Boulgakov, *La philosophie de l'economie* (Lausanne: Age d'homme, 1987), 102, note 83.
52 Cf. Sergiusz Bułgakow, *Światło wieczności* (Kęty: Wydawnictwo Marek Derewiecki, 2010), 490.
53 Cf. Sergiusz Bułgakow, *Światło wieczności* (Kęty: Wydawnictwo Marek Derewiecki, 2010), 496.
54 Cf. Sergiusz Bułgakow, *Światło wieczności* (Kęty: Wydawnictwo Marek Derewiecki, 2010), 503.
55 Cf. Sergiusz Bułgakow, *Światło wieczności* (Kęty: Wydawnictwo Marek Derewiecki, 2010), 509.
56 Cf. Sergiusz Bułgakow, *Światło wieczności* (Kęty: Wydawnictwo Marek Derewiecki, 2010), 490.
57 Cf. Sergiusz Bułgakow, *Światło wieczności* (Kęty: Wydawnictwo Marek Derewiecki, 2010), 513.
58 Cf. Sergiusz Bułgakow, *Światło wieczności* (Kęty: Wydawnictwo Marek Derewiecki, 2010), 514.
59 Cf. Leonid Stołowicz, *Historia filozofii rosyjskiej* (Gdańsk: Słowo/obrazterytoria, 2008), 265–269.
60 Mikołaj Bierdiajew, *Sens twórczości* (Kęty: Antyk, 2001).
61 Mikołaj Bierdiajew, *Filozofia nierówności* (Kęty: Antyk, 2006).
62 Mikołaj Bierdiajew, *Nowe Średniowiecze; Los człowieka we współczesnym świecie* (Warszawa: Fundacja Aletheia, 2003).
63 Mikołaj Bierdiajew, *O przeznaczeniu człowieka* (Kęty: Antyk, 2006).
64 Cf. Mikołaj Bierdiajew, *O przeznaczeniu człowieka* (Kęty: Antyk, 2006), 216.
65 Cf. Mikołaj Bierdiajew, *Nowe Średniowiecze; Los człowieka we współczesnym świecie* (Warszawa: Fundacja Aletheia, 2003), 88; 141.
66 Cf. Mikołaj Bierdiajew, *Filozofia nierówności* (Kęty: Antyk, 2006), 132.
67 Cf. Mikołaj Bierdiajew, *Filozofia nierówności* (Kęty: Antyk, 2006), 137.
68 Cf. Mikołaj Bierdiajew, *Nowe Średniowiecze; Los człowieka we współczesnym świecie* (Warszawa: Fundacja Aletheia, 2003), 73.
69 Cf. Mikołaj Bierdiajew, *O przeznaczeniu człowieka* (Kęty: Antyk, 2006), 218.
70 Cf. Mikołaj Bierdiajew, *O przeznaczeniu człowieka* (Kęty: Antyk, 2006), 218.
71 Cf. Mikołaj Bierdiajew, *O przeznaczeniu człowieka* (Kęty: Antyk, 2006), 220.
72 Cf. Mikołaj Bierdiajew, *Sens twórczości* (Kęty: Antyk, 2001), 86.
73 Cf. Mikołaj Bierdiajew, *Sens twórczości* (Kęty: Antyk, 2001), 87.
74 Cf. Mikołaj Bierdiajew, *Sens twórczości* (Kęty: Antyk, 2001), 88.
75 Cf. Mikołaj Bierdiajew, *Sens twórczości* (Kęty: Antyk, 2001), 89.
76 Cf. Mikołaj Bierdiajew, *Sens twórczości* (Kęty: Antyk, 2001), 85.
77 Cf. Mikołaj Bierdiajew, *Sens twórczości* (Kęty: Antyk, 2001), 92.
78 Cf. Mikołaj Bierdiajew, *Sens twórczości* (Kęty: Antyk, 2001), 85.
79 Cf. Mikołaj Bierdiajew, *Sens twórczości* (Kęty: Antyk, 2001), 117, note 8.
80 Cf. Mikołaj Bierdiajew, *Sens twórczości* (Kęty: Antyk, 2001), 92, note 6.
81 Cf. Mikołaj Bierdiajew, *Filozofia nierówności* (Kęty: Antyk, 2006), 189.
82 An interesting idea from the point of view of the current debate about artificial intelligence: for Berdyaev, human creativity has no limits in terms of self-improvement. However, the ambition to create beings does constitute such a limit; cf. Mikołaj Bierdiajew, *Sens twórczości* (Kęty: Antyk, 2001), 120.
83 Cf. Mikołaj Bierdiajew, *Filozofia nierówności* (Kęty: Antyk, 2006), 190.
84 Cf. Mikołaj Bierdiajew, *O przeznaczeniu człowieka* (Kęty: Antyk, 2006), 215–216; Mikołaj Bierdiajew, *Filozofia nierówności* (Kęty: Antyk, 2006), 190.
85 Cf. Mikołaj Bierdiajew, *Nowe Średniowiecze; Los człowieka we współczesnym świecie* (Warszawa: Fundacja Aletheia, 2003), 71.
86 Cf. Mikołaj Bierdiajew, *O przeznaczeniu człowieka* (Kęty: Antyk, 2006), 216.

76 *Andrzej Persidok*

87 Mikołaj Bierdiajew, *Filozofia nierówności* (Kęty: Antyk, 2006), 187.
88 Mikołaj Bierdiajew, *Nowe Średniowiecze; Los człowieka we współczesnym świecie* (Warszawa: Fundacja Aletheia, 2003), 204.
89 Cf. Mikołaj Bierdiajew, *O przeznaczeniu człowieka* (Kęty: Antyk, 2006), 229.
90 Mikołaj Bierdiajew, *Sens twórczości* (Kęty: Antyk, 2001), 241; cf. Mikołaj Bierdiajew, *Nowe Średniowiecze; Los człowieka we współczesnym świecie* (Warszawa: Fundacja Aletheia, 2003), 204.
91 Cf. Mikołaj Bierdiajew, *O przeznaczeniu człowieka* (Kęty: Antyk, 2006), 229.
92 Cf. Mikołaj Bierdiajew, *Filozofia nierówności* (Kęty: Antyk, 2006), 188.
93 Mikołaj Bierdiajew, *Filozofia nierówności* (Kęty: Antyk, 2006), 188.
94 Mikołaj Bierdiajew, *Filozofia nierówności* (Kęty: Antyk, 2006).
95 Cf. Mikołaj Bierdiajew, *Sens twórczości* (Kęty: Antyk, 2001), 242; cf. Mikołaj Bierdiajew, *Filozofia nierówności* (Kęty: Antyk, 2006), 187.
96 Mikołaj Bierdiajew, *Filozofia nierówności* (Kęty: Antyk, 2006), 188–189.
97 Cf. Mikołaj Bierdiajew, *O przeznaczeniu człowieka* (Kęty: Antyk, 2006), 219.
98 Cf. Mikołaj Bierdiajew, *O przeznaczeniu człowieka* (Kęty: Antyk, 2006), 216.
99 Mikołaj Bierdiajew, *Nowe Średniowiecze; Los człowieka we współczesnym świecie* (Warszawa: Fundacja Aletheia, 2003), 204.
100 Cf. Mikołaj Bierdiajew, *Filozofia nierówności* (Kęty: Antyk, 2006), 195.

5 Creative art and theology of work
Contributions from St. Bonaventure

Isabel M. León-Sanz

Introduction

This research seeks to explore new perspectives on work at the level of dogmatic theology.[1] Human work is situated at the heart of man's relationship with God, with each other and with the world; for this reason, it is necessary to contemplate it in a framework that includes who God is and who man is, with his unique dignity and the middle position that corresponds to him according to his corporeal–spiritual reality, as well as the meaning of the world and of history on the way to eschatological fullness.[2] The consideration of work from this approach cannot be reduced to a study of human action, or of its social context and its consequences, but must be based on a prior reflection on the being of man and the mission that is proper to him, and also on the characteristics of a universe available to work. We do not live in the midst of a chaos of bewildering arbitrariness but in an ordered cosmos: in the bosom of an intelligible nature that responds to rational laws and is susceptible to becoming a home for man through his work.

From the dawn of Genesis, Sacred Scripture offers the key to understanding these intertwined relationships: the knowledge of God as Creator, of creatures as true, good, and beautiful realities, and of man as the image of God, called to participate through his work in the lordship and development of nature.[3] The human being is called to collaborate with the very action of the Creator,[4] and this original vocation belongs to his essential definition.[5]

In order to enter into these questions, it is interesting to study St. Bonaventure, who thought with great depth about the creative action of God in analogy with art, and about the human artisan as the image of God, offering very suggestive elements for a theological reflection on work. Moreover, this author is characterized by an extraordinary capacity for synthesis,[6] and in this sense, the study of his work disposes us to consider human work not in isolation but in the network of relationships in which it exists and is configured.

So as to situate St. Bonaventure's contribution in its context, I will first present how the consideration and existential reality of work evolved in the European Middle Ages. Only certain coordinates will be traced, since it is a

DOI: 10.4324/9781003508212-6

78   Isabel M. León-Sanz

broad and complex topic.[7] Bonaventure also offers various reflections on the conditions and types of work – as a concrete dedication – in the vital context of thirteenth-century society, but this perspective affects less directly the question we are dealing with.

In the second part, I will focus on some elements of Bonaventurian thought that today can illuminate a theological reflection on work from a dogmatic point of view. I will present the understanding of man as the image of God, with the role of mediation and the lordship he exercises as such in the universe. Then, I will deal with the uniqueness of his action (the human person is the only being in the cosmos that acts artistically), to see how his work is illuminated in light of Trinitarian creative art.

Some features of the consideration of work in the western Middle Ages

During the long period usually referred to as the Middle Ages, new ways of understanding work were forged. In the assimilation of the multiple heritages that Europeans received from the past (Judeo-Christian, Greco-Roman, barbarian, and Indo-European peoples), a genuinely creative process is recognized through which the whole of these heritages was restructured and vivified in a way that allows us to speak of true novelty.[8]

In this period, the main source for understanding the meaning of work was the Bible. From the first chapters of Genesis and throughout the books that compose it, we find a double perspective. On the one hand, work is the fruit of God's creative call, linked to the precept of tilling and caring for the earth and bearing fruit (Gen 1:27 and 2:15); thus, from the beginning, work is part of man's reality, and is a sign of his dignity in the midst of the universe. In this sense, the people of Israel forged a culture of work, in which manual labor was also appreciated. On the other hand, as a consequence of sin, work is seen as a source of weariness and hardship. This ambivalence of dignity and cause of suffering runs through Sacred Scripture and is maintained also in the New Testament, where the positive vision is reinforced by the fact of the incarnation: Christ worked, performed a manual labor, preached and taught, and formed his disciples. At the same time, he took upon himself our fallen nature, in all things like us except sin; as a true man, he took upon himself the burden of the day and the heat, and the gospel testifies to the weariness that the exhausting days of preaching entailed for him. Thus Christ also took upon himself this penal dimension of work and turned it into a path of redemption and liberation.

This double consideration ultimately corresponds to the ordinary human experience. Work can be experienced as a more or less attractive task, a source of creativity and growth, of humanization of the natural and social environment. But at the same time, it also implies effort, the weariness of repetitive activities that follow one after another monotonously day after day, or the disappointment of not achieving the expected fruits. The Bible illuminates this common experience by making known the origin of both dimensions;

Creative art and theology of work 79

and with the understanding of work as a vocation, it makes it possible to counteract the prominence that the penal dimension often acquires on the existential level. In fact, this translated into a progressive appreciation of work in the varied complexity of its expressions, at the same time that a Christian-inspired civilization was taking shape.

Another element that stands out in the integration of the multiple inheritances that shaped the European Middle Ages is the valuation of manual labor: it ceased to be seen as an undervalued or slave task and was incorporated into the hierarchy of functions that sustain society and carry it forward. Undoubtedly, this valuation of manual labor was influenced by faith in the incarnation, as well as by the craftsmanship that Christ carried out during most of his life in history.

Along these lines, the influence of St. Benedict in the slow process of transformation of mentalities is often recognized.[9] Within monasticism, living by the work of one's own hands was considered an evangelical ideal rather than an obligation derived from necessity. And it was not only manual work that was appreciated, but work as such, which for St. Benedict had to be a serious task, not a mere occupation of time, and implied a true service to the community and the edification of the world.[10] At the same time, work was not seen as an end in itself, so that the obligation to work was adapted to the circumstances of age, health, and capacity of the monks. In keeping with this adaptation, the possible jobs were not limited to farm work or construction, but were extended to tasks such as copying manuscripts, teaching, or managing the monastery's properties. Thus, the consideration of work was broadened, not only covering the spectrum of agricultural and artisan activities, but also extending progressively to management and intellectual tasks. In addition, St. Benedict sought a balance between dedication to work, to the Divine Office, to study and to recreation; a balance that was difficult in practice, but which did not cease to be considered an ideal.[11] These approaches also influenced the progressive forging of medieval society.

Another issue of great relevance is the introduction of Sunday rest in the Carolingian calendar, which was a novelty compared to antiquity.[12] According to the account of the divine creation, it can be said that in some way, work is ordered to rest; this was translated into one of the ten commandments, which was protected and insistently demanded by the prophets in the Old Testament. The organization of time according to this rhythm, in which the days of labor are oriented toward the rest of Sunday, meant an authentic liberation of man, for it entails the idea that neither work nor social utility are ultimate ends, but are ordered to the person and, ultimately, to God. It was necessary to stop occupations not simply for psychological or health reasons, but above all to contemplate the reference of all things to God, and to celebrate and give thanks for his gifts. In this sense, characteristic of the medieval mentality is both an appreciation of work and a taste for feasting and celebration.[13] And although the need for rest was adapted to the requirements of the different trades (livestock breeding, harvest time, etc.), it can be

80   *Isabel M. León-Sanz*

said that this alternation of work and rest was proposed for everyone; leisure was not something reserved for a few elites of society.

On the other hand, as the spectrum of what was considered work broadened, there was actually little room left for those who "wandered". The tripartite scheme that distributed society into *oratores*, *bellatores*, and *laboratores* implied that there were different ways of being useful to society.[14] And among them, those who pray were considered to contribute in the first line to the common good. In the Middle Ages, the public prayer of the Divine Office was considered as indispensable to society as defending the country by arms or procuring the necessities of life.[15] Later on, this idea of contribution to the common good would justify linking wages to the work performed, not only in terms of the goods produced, and in this way, the demand for wages for tasks that are not directly manual or productive (study, teaching, commerce, etc.) would be introduced.[16]

From the dimension of service and usefulness to society in its different expressions, a double attitude was also derived. Those who did not work while being able to do so were frowned upon: there was a social rejection of the "lazy", of those who had no job and did not contribute to the good of the community. But at the same time, a whole series of charitable initiatives were developed to help the underprivileged.[17] This awareness of a common participation and responsibility through the trade performed influenced in some way the origin of the various forms of workers' associations in the last part of the Middle Ages.

In this contextual section, it is worth mentioning the absence in medieval Latin of a terminology equivalent to our word "work". In this period, several families of concepts and terms referred to this reality.[18] This plurality is already significant in itself, since it highlights the complexity of this dimension of human action, which is not easily delimitable or simplifiable; certainly, even today when we speak of work we are referring to very different realities that need to be analyzed, compared, and distinguished. This variety of Latin expressions can be summarized around three series of terms

a   *Labor, laborare, laboratores*
b   *Opus, operare, operatio*
c   *Ars, artifex, artificium, which are somehow related to industria, cura, ministerium.*

These words had a wide range of meanings, which is why they were often qualified with the help of adjectives: *ars mechanica* or *liberalis*, *labor corporalis*, *opus manuale*, etc. The use of *labor* and its derivatives frequently connotes the dimension of hardship and fatigue involved in work; in this sense, at the end of the Middle Ages, it can be seen that in medical books, this term came to be used as a synonym for ailment or illness.[19] The series related to *opus* and *operatio* has a more generic and neutral sense; it designates specifically human activity in general, without a pejorative character. *Ars* has

Creative art and theology of work   81

more to do with the performance of a trade, for which specific knowledge and skills are required; in this sense, it is also related to *industry* or to *cura* or *ministerium*, by reference to the execution of these tasks and the service provided through them.

This terminological approach projects the fundamental ambivalence to which we referred earlier. On the one hand, work implies effort, fatigue, repetition (it is *labor*). On the other hand, it is an expression of man's uniqueness in the universe as a whole, and of his capacity to transform and humanize nature (he is an artificer and artist, in the image of God). Many authors consider that the terminology related to *ars* and *artifex* would be the closest to the semantic scope of our current word labor.[20] In this sense, Hamesse indicates that the thinkers of the last stages of the Middle Ages did not elaborate their reflections from the terms *labor*, *opus*, or *industry*, but above all from *ars*, both the so-called *artes mechanicae* and, otherwise, the liberal arts.[21] In this way, the possibility of connecting art and work is raised, opening a space to think theologically about the relationship between the creative work of the divine artificer and that of the human artist through a two-way analogy.

At the end of this first part, it is interesting to note that the perspectives opened up by the Bible for the understanding of work (as highlighted in the chapters presenting the biblical approach to a theology of work) permeated the life and culture of European peoples in the gradual shaping of a Christian civilization.

Contributions of St. Bonaventure's thought for a theology of work

St. Bonaventure is a witness and testimony to how the consideration of work evolved in the Western Christian Middle Ages. The principal sources of his reflection are Sacred Scripture and the spirit of St. Francis, while he accepts the inheritance of tradition. For this topic, it is necessary to mention in a particular way St. Augustine, as well as the influence of the humanism of the twelfth century, with the reflections of Hugo of St. Victor or the contributions of Alain de Lille and other authors of the Chartres milieu.

In Bonaventure's writings, we can find very interesting indications about the existential and concrete reality of work along the lines presented in the previous section: as a trade, as service to the common good, in the appreciation of manual labor, in the consideration of intellectual work and the care of the faithful as true works, on the orientation of human activity to contemplative rest, on the *servus-liber* opposition posed on the level of the disposition of the subject who works and not on the type of work performed, in the criticism of "idleness" (those who do not work) together with the appreciation for recreation and good distractions, etc.[22] Here, however, I will focus on his thinking about art, as a way to open channels for a theological study of work. This path relates to the family of terms related to *ars* and *artifex*, which, as noted above, have the closest semantic proximity to the contemporary idea

82   Isabel M. León-Sanz

of work. This is a very broad topic cannot be presented in the space of this study.[23] For this reason, I will only propose some lines of reflection based on the understanding of man as the image of God, of his mediating function in the universe, and of the Bonaventurian idea of *ars* applied analogically to human work and divine creation.

Man, image of God

One of the distinctive features of Bonaventure's thought is the clear awareness of the dignity of man and his freedom,[24] which comes from the understanding of man as the image of God. These aspects have an immediate connection with a theological foundation of work.

St. Bonaventure considers that the being of the image consists in referring to the reality it represents, so that in itself it is only understood as being in reference. Therefore, the image as such essentially implies dependence and relationship.[25] This means that an image is not a first reality, but originated, and that it proceeds from the exemplar through an expressive emanation.[26] The original is expressed in its image, it is represented in it: the image makes it present in some way.[27]

In the universe, all creatures express in their own truth some likeness of the Creator, but only spiritual beings are images of him, because they alone represent him. This expressly representative likeness arises from the fact that they have the structure and operative order that God possesses in the intimacy of the divine life; St. Augustine explored this in such depth in his work *De Trinitate*: memory, understanding, will / *mens, notitia, amor*. St. Bonaventure makes the Augustinian affirmation that man is the image of God "quo eius capax est, eiusque esse particeps potest"[28] his own. That is to say, being an image entails the capacity of God, thanks to which man can become a sharer in the divine nature, enter into communion with Him. But he can live with the Trinity precisely because he possesses the faculties proper to a spiritual life, such as that of God.

St. Bonaventure indicates that the human creature "nata est ordinari in Deum immediate",[29] which implies that he is not subject to any other creature but depends and is directly oriented to Him. At the core of the divine image is freedom, by which man lives in immediate reference to God: he is not subjugated to natural forces or to other men or to angels. He is subject only to God and toward Him he freely directs himself as the object of his existence.[30] Moreover, he considers that *unibilitas* with God is one of the traits that characterize human nature.[31] And he is capable of this union because he naturally possesses the spiritual operative powers that give him a certain convenience of proportion and order with God, enabling and disposing him to enter into communion with Him through knowledge and love, which are also the vital divine operations.[32] Undoubtedly, attaining this union is a gift of grace, but God has made man capable by nature of being raised to communion with Him.

Creative art and theology of work   83

Thus, the essential dignity of every human being is rooted in the condition of the image of God. In the midst of the universe and among other men, each one makes God present, is the bearer of the light of his face.[33]

Man as the vertex, mediator, and rector of the universe

In accordance with this dignity and in connection with his nature, both corporeal and spiritual, St. Bonaventure contemplates man as a culmination of the sensible universe, and discovers in all corporeal beings an "appetite" or tendency toward perfection, which is attained in the human being.[34]

The human person occupies a middle place in the order of the universe, between purely spiritual beings and corporeal beings, and from the beginning is called to exercise a function of mediation between creatures inferior to him and God.[35] This approach is interesting because it indicates that man's preeminence in the world does not come only from his spiritual reality, but also includes his corporeality: he is a mediator precisely because he is body and spirit, he belongs to nature and transcends it.

Sentient creatures are not immediately ordered to God, but through man. By themselves they manifest a reflection of the glory of God, since in the light of truth which they possess and express a glimmer of the wisdom of their divine artificer is revealed. However, it is only thanks to human understanding that this luminosity becomes conscious and meaningful. Man's intellect is in a certain sense all things, as Aristotle affirmed, and the other beings of the universe have been constituted to be "written" in him, so that their likenesses may be "impressed" and "painted" in his mind. The whole universe represents God according to a certain sensible totality, but man represents him according to a certain spiritual totality, and because he is its image, he can understand the divine expressiveness embodied in the whole of the creatures, and give voice to the poem which, in the beauty of the universe, expresses the glory of its Creator.[36]

Related to these ideas is the Bonaventurian thesis that irrational creatures have been made for the service of man, who is in a certain sense the end of all other beings.[37] He is not an absolute end, but a true *finis sub fine*,[38] in conformity with the reference to God that defines him as an image. Moreover, St. Bonaventure considers that this service does not simply translate into the satisfaction of his material needs, but constitutes above all a path that leads him to his ultimate end: all of nature helps him to know and love God.[39] The divine artificer has made the universe as an expression of His infinite goodness and beauty, in order to offer man a way by which he can know Him, and to awaken in him the desire to correspond to His love.[40] St. Bonaventure synthesizes these ideas by affirming four reasons why God created animals and other corporeal beings: they allow man to exercise his rule over the universe; they decorate and beautify the world; they lead him to contemplate the wisdom of the Creator in so many different forms; and they move him to love Him.[41] St. Bonaventure adds a typically humanistic nuance, when he says

84   *Isabel M. León-Sanz*

that sentient creatures are ordered *ad solatium* of man, so that he may enjoy and take pleasure in them; and he discovers here the generous providence of God, who knows that we need beauty and delight in our life.[42]

There is thus a double direction of complementarity and reciprocal service between the universe and human beings. With intelligence and freedom, man receives lordship over other corporeal beings, as a collaborator of the Creator in the care and development of nature. He is God's interlocutor, the recipient of the beautiful message of the universe. And in turn, he represents the other creatures, giving them a voice to lead a song of praise to God in love.

For St. Bonaventure, free will is born of the conjunction between the two principal powers of the soul: intellect and affect, reason and will[43]; and it is thanks to them that it exercises dominion over the rest of creatures. This task does not only enter into the realm of knowledge or intentionality, but also extends to his work: the human being is called to become God's partner and collaborator in the development of creation.[44] Now, this authority is not arbitrary, but resides in his condition of divine image and, therefore, is exercised rightly to the extent that he lives in the direction of God and is assimilated to Him.[45] Therefore, St. Bonaventure brings together the terms *rector* and *rex* of the universe with the *conditio recta* of man, and explains that the lordship over the world implies a similarity and continuity with divine action. For this reason, it is necessary that in his work, he seek with his intelligence the measure of the supreme truth, and that with his will he conforms himself to the supreme goodness through love. Only then is his task an authentic prolongation of God's creative power.[46] After the original fall, this *conditio recta* was disturbed, causing man to easily consider himself as the ultimate end, and not *finis sub fine*. This curvature upon himself is what causes the passage from use to abuse in man's relationship with nature. However, through redemption, Christ opened up the possibility of restoring the order altered by sin, and man can once again fulfill his mediatorial mission according to God's original design.[47]

The human art in analogy with the divine art

It can be said that the artistic approach to creation constitutes one of the keys to Bonaventure's conception of the universe, in connection with exemplarism.[48] He developed it extensively on the basis of an interesting circularity between the analogical understanding of the divine operation and that of man:[49] human art helps to access the mystery of the creative act, and divine art helps to understand the work of man more deeply and its novelty with respect to the way nature acts.

St. Bonaventure distinguishes two noble modes of production, that which is proper to nature and that which proceeds from the will.[50] The first implies necessity, the second supposes freedom; art belongs to this second group. Since man is intelligent and free, he is the only agent in the world who can act artistically, in the image of God. And although from one point of view the natural operation is more perfect than man's finite art, from another perspective, the artistic capacity elevates him above all other beings, and makes him more like the divine artificer than any other creature.

St. Bonaventure understood art in a broad sense, encompassing both the fine arts and technique. And without violating his thought, it can be related in a more general way to work, in accordance with the lexicon common in the thirteenth century, to which we referred earlier. He conceives art as the production of an effect distinct from the agent in which the capacity, the knowledge, and the affective dimension of the artist[51] intervene in an articulated way. The artist freely produces his work according to the idea he has in his mind; that idea is the exemplar that directs his operation and configures the form of what is produced, giving that reality its being and its intelligibility as a work of art. What is produced is external to the agent first of all in the sense that it is an entity distinct from its author; that is why this notion of art can be applied to corporeal products as well as to products of the spirit (a poem, an investigation, etc.). Moreover, it is not a matter of the mere application of knowledge to production, nor of mere skill, but specifically includes interaction with the affective dimension. The artist is moved to act by love for the work he is going to make, and seeks to create a beautiful, useful, and lasting object.[52] In this way, with his art/work, man transforms reality by giving it a human measure, creates culture, and incorporates nature into history.

The use of artistic analogy to explain the origin of the universe has a foundation in Sacred Scripture, and for this reason was employed by Christian thinkers from the beginnings of theological reflection. As described in the first chapters of Genesis, in creation, we can discern a free and sovereign action (referring to the divine omnipotence), according to a preconceived plan (his wisdom), which effects a good and beautiful work (his goodness), as well as the joy of the divine artist, who loves his creatures. In creation, therefore, the power, wisdom, and benevolence of God are integrated, and the creatures are distinct effects of their divine artificer, possessing a consistency of their own. This structure is similar to that which articulates the artistic work of man according to the Bonaventurian understanding, which we have just presented. For this reason, the analogy with art was shown to be an adequate channel for reflecting on the origin of the universe, and provided the basis for explaining the reciprocally expressive and meaningful relationship established between the creative Artificer and his works.[53]

Moreover, this operative structure can be applied analogically to creative action in a Trinitarian perspective, where power and origin are attributed to the Father, wisdom, and exemplarity to the Son, and goodness and culminating love to the Holy Spirit.[54] In this perspective, St. Bonaventure points out that the Son is conceived as a completely similar Image and a perfectly communicative Word, in whom the Father expresses all his knowledge and power, and disposes whatever He wishes to do. Therefore, the Word proceeds from the Father as *ratio artificiandi*[55] and *ratio exemplandi*[56] of all things; and consequently, as expressive light of the truth of created beings, since

86   Isabel M. León-Sanz

it is proper to the exemplar to cause the form, and through it the veritative luminosity of the entity is shown. Because the Father has made all things by means of his Word, in it is the principle of the knowledge of beings,[57] since the truth of works of art is measured by the idea that directs their production and configures their reality.[58] In this way, the Word is the radical source of the intelligibility of all creation.

In projecting these reflections on human action, we must bear in mind that only God has the omnipotence necessary to create artistically the natural forms of beings.[59] Man only freely produces artificial forms, and by shaping them in reality with his work, he really endows the beings he produces with truth and meaning. But at the same time, he is not the ultimate source of the truth of things; he must always reckon with the proper measure they possess by themselves and with the laws that govern nature, whose origin is to be found in the creative Word. From the Word proceeds the phontal light that originates and sustains the truth of all that exists, in Him is the radical source of our light, of our capacity and of our life.[60] This approach is interesting because it disqualifies the excessive aspiration of a radical anthropocentrism, in the different versions that have been proposed in history. Human work is not the ultimate source of definition and meaning. But this approach is also liberating, because it exempts man from an enterprise that exceeds his finitude and disposes him to develop his enormous potential in respect and harmony with other beings.

As can be seen, these ideas open up extraordinary perspectives for the understanding of human labor. Here I will point out only two aspects.

The first, in relation to creativity, Bonaventure considers that man introduces true novelty in the repetitive sequences of nature. It is not a question of absolute originality, because human production is exercised from entities that possess a structure and certain laws. And on the other hand, the specimens that he invents in his mind have a root in reality, through the experiences that the agent keeps in his memory. However, with these ideas, he configures truly new objects that did not exist in the course of nature.[61] And this novelty does not only affect the external configuration of his works, for the form he gives to the materials he uses is the source of a new operativity, or expands the one they possessed by themselves. In this way, man can contribute effectively to the improvement and development of the natural energies of the universe.[62] In this sense, one could apply to human art the idea of obediential power:[63] with his work, he is capable of drawing from natural realities effects that they could not have achieved by themselves, bringing them to another order of perfection. By acting in this way, man unveils in his works unpublished aspects of the divine exemplar, the possibility of which was latent in nature, but which nature itself could not show. Thus the imprint of God is no longer only in natural beings but, in a new way, in culture, in the works produced by human labor. And it is significant that St. Bonaventure relates this feature to the intermediate position that corresponds to man, between God and the whole of the universe.[64]

The very work of man is thus, as such, a manifestation of the glory of God: both because of the dignity of the human artisan, who exercises and represents in a finite way the creativity and providence of the supreme artificer, and also because of the novelty of the objects produced, which reveal latent aspects of the beauty of the divine exemplar. These similarities were within the possibilities of nature, but could not be expressed without the intervention of human labor. Thus, it is not only that man can give voice to the glory of God manifested in the universe, but that he himself contributes with his work to make that glory shine with new nuances unknown to us until then.

The second aspect to which I would like to allude has to do with the Trinitarian dimension of divine creation. Following an idea of Pseudo-Dionysius, St. Bonaventure projects in the history of salvation the cycle of eternal love that describes the life of God. This idea underlines the conjunction between the beginning and the end in the divine action,[65] and shows that creation is a constant fruit of his love: everything proceeds from the supreme Good, is sustained by the supreme Good, and is led toward the supreme Good. Love is the source of the goodness that God communicates to all creatures as the root of their being.[66] With the triple appropriation of efficiency to the Father, the exemplarity to the Son and the completion or culmination to the Holy Spirit – mentioned above – it is possible to specifically transfer this eternal cycle to the creative work of the Triune God, contemplating creation as the effect of the same loving communion in which the three persons coexist eternally. Everything proceeds from the love of the Father, expresses the love of the Son, and is brought to fullness by the Holy Spirit, the mutual love of both, who brings creation to its perfection and enjoys contemplating the participation of beings in the infinite goodness and beauty of the Father and the Son.

This idea can be transferred analogically to human art, indicating the configuration that ultimately defines it. Beyond achieving or not achieving the desired fruit, a more or less brilliant genius, or a perfect realization, work is above all a task that has to be born of love, express love, and be ordered to love, according to an insight of St. Josemaría Escrivá in which we can see a translation of the Trinitarian perspective of creation.[67] It is in this way that the mediating function of man in the universe, in the image of God, is shown in the most profound way.

Some conclusions

These ideas, which would merit further development, offer elements of great interest for a theological deepening of work and the dignity of man's mission in the universe, valid for any era. They constitute a starting point rather than an end point.

We have observed how the light of revelation and subsequent theological reflection, initiated by the Fathers and developed throughout the Middle Ages, had a great potential for change and transformation in the life

88   *Isabel M. León-Sanz*

and organization of society. In the slow inculturation that took place during the first millennium of social freedom for Christians, there was a progressive recognition of the working person (overcoming the practice of slavery). The dignity of manual labor was understood, and at the same time the idea of work was extended to a wide spectrum of activities (management, commerce, study, teaching, etc.). The dimension of service and usefulness for the common good that characterizes all types of work was understood, and the awareness of participation and collaboration in a common responsibility was developed. The complementarity between work/rest/celebration was incorporated, and the festive dimension was extended to society as a whole, above all as an expression of gratitude and praise to God. In the implementation of the weekly work calendar, oriented to Sunday rest, the primacy of God and the preeminence of man were implicit: neither work nor social utility are ultimate goals.

The Bible also illuminated the ambivalent aspect of the daily experience of work, in its double dimension of lordship and penalty, and helped to overcome the immediacy of tiredness and pain by opening up the possibility of considering work as a vocation, and also as an evangelical ideal in light of Christ's work.

In this way, despite the limits attached to any human work, it is clear that theology drives history as a source of humanization and meaning that translates into concrete realities. Even today it is called to illuminate new forms of work and social organization based on the orientation provided by faith as to who God is, who man is, and what the meaning of the universe and of history is.

Some features of contemporary culture, such as the appreciation of human dignity, freedom and creativity, solidarity, the importance of work, and the value of nature, find a solid foundation in the theology of St. Bonaventure, based on the understanding of divine creation as a Trinitarian art and of man as the image of God. At the beginning, he stated that in the understanding of work, God, man, and the world are intertwined. If the human being isolates himself from this interconnection, the whole set of relationships that weave his life is disturbed; and this can be seen not only in personal experience but also in the dramatic consequences of the attempt to understand man without God, both in society and in relation to nature. In the thought of St. Bonaventure, the three terms of this relationship are solidly connected to each other precisely through the understanding of man as the image of God and from his mission as mediator. Man is not the image of an idol (symbol of a capricious power) but of a God who is the Trinity of persons who live in the free gift of self, in a full communion of wisdom and love from which their action proceeds. Man is a person, the image of God as a son, called to a communion in truth and love with other men – his brothers – and with the whole universe. He can understand himself only from his reference to God. He is not an ultimate end but a *finis sub fine*, however a true end in himself. This preeminence implies, among other things, that workers are the main capital of a company, and that profits are a necessary objective, but not the ultimate end of its existence as such a company. It also follows that work – whatever it may be – is configured as a service, the purpose of which is oriented to the good of individuals, families, and society.

Moreover, these ideas lay the foundations for a correct relationship between man and nature. The primacy of man is rightly exercised in respect for beings in their proper truth and good: nature is not the realm of the merely factual, the object of arbitrary use, but in itself is the bearer of definition and meaning, the expression of the creative Word. As such, it is the place where man encounters God, the occasion for joy and loving contemplation in and through work. Thus, contemplation and action aren't only not opposed, but interpenetrate each other in the work he performs. Moreover, it follows from this that nature is not ultimately something alien to human freedom, but can become a kind and beautiful place through the common work of men at a given time and through the generations.

Finally, I would like to highlight a consequence that emerges when considering the inseparable connection between omnipotence, wisdom, and love in divine art. Nor should capacity, intelligence, and love be dissociated in human work/art. Scientific and technical training – that which is specific to each task – is required to be able to work well. Likewise, intelligence knows the laws that govern a given process, directs its realization, and discerns the relationships of justice in the web of links that are generated throughout the phases of the work. However, it can be noted that capacity and intelligence are not enough. Creatural finitude so often causes a greater or lesser failure in carefully organized and performed activities. Moreover, once sufficient expertise is acquired in any given craft, the weariness of monotony and repetition can set in; although there is always room for initiative and study, the margins of creativity are limited in their formal dimension. On the other hand, in the sphere of love, novelty is always possible, freedom is renewed and the way is open to inventiveness despite the limits of capacity and circumstances. Any honest work can and must be an occasion to love the realities that receive the configuration of that work, to love the people with whom one works and to whom one directs the fruit of that work, to love oneself. And above all, to love God and to give him glory, sharing with him in the care and development of people and nature.

Notes

1 It is part of the project "The meaning of work in recent theology" at the School of Theology of the University of Navarra (2021–2025). For the dogmatic approach, cf. Gregorio Guitián, Ana Marta González, "Theology of Work: New Perspectives," *Scripta Theologica* 54, no. 3 (2022): 757–787, 767–771.

2 Chenu makes a list of questions that a theology of work should study today; they cover the whole of salvation history (creation, redemptive incarnation, eschatology): see Marie-Dominique Chenu, *Pour une théologie du travail* (Paris: Éditions du Seuil, 1955), 28–30.

90 *Isabel M. León-Sanz*

3 Cf. Second Vatican Council, Const. *Gaudium et spes*, 34 (*AAS* 58 (1966): 1052).
4 Cf. John Paul II, Enc. *Laborem exercens*, 4 and 24–25 (*AAS* 73 (1981): 584–585 and 637–641).
5 Mounier points out that man is essentially an *artifex*, creator of forms, maker of artifacts: cf. Emmanuel Mounier, *La petite peur du XXe siècle*, Les Cahiers du Rhône 76 (Neuchâtel: Éd. de la Baconnière – Paris: Éd. du Seuil, 1959), 29–30. Chenu comments on this idea by indicating that the human being is *homo sapiens*, but cannot be so, at least collectively, except by the fulfillment of *homo artifex*, which would be his first definition (cf. Marie-Dominique Chenu, *Pour une théologie du travail* (Paris: Éditions du Seuil, 1955), 17), as it includes and develops the previous one.
6 Jacques G. Bougerol, *San Bonaventura. Un maestro di sapienza* (Vicenza: L.I.E.F. Edizioni, 1972), 53: "non si può studiare nella sua opera l'uno o l'altro aspetto del suo pensiero, senza scoprire subito un movimento incessante tra la visione sintetica, in nome della quale ciascun elemento trova il suo posto esatto, e la luce che dà alla sua sintesi la precisione di ciascun elemento".
7 For an introduction to the understanding of work in medieval Europe, see for example: Robert Fossier, *Le travail au Moyen Âge* (Paris: Hachette Littératures, 2000); Jacqueline Hamesse, Colette Muraille-Samaran (éds.), *Le travail au Moyen Âge. Une approche interdisciplinaire*. Actes du Colloque international de Louvain-la-Neuve, 21–23 mai 1987 (Louvain-la-Neuve: Institut d'Études médiévales de l'Université catholique de Louvain, 1990); Geneviève Hasenohr, Jean Longère (éds.), *Culture et travail intellectuel dans l'Occident Médiéval. Bilan des Colloques d'Humanisme médiéval (1960–1980)* (Paris: Centre National de la Recherche Scientifique, 1981); Jacques Le Goff, *Pour un autre Moyen Âge: temps, travail et culture en Occident* (Paris: Gallimard, 1977); Patricia Ranft, "Franciscan Work Theology in Historical Perspective," *Franciscan Studies* 67 (2009): 41–70.
8 Cf. Jacques Le Goff, "Le travail dans les systèmes de valeur de l'Occident médiéval", *Le travail au Moyen Âge. Une approche interdisciplinaire*, éds. Jacqueline Hamesse, Colette Muraille-Samaran (Louvain-la-Neuve: Institut d'Études médiévales de l'Université catholique de Louvain, 1990), 7–21: 8–9. In this line, Verbeque considers that the medievalists were more critical and creative than the Renaissance in the assumption of antiquity (cf. Gérard Verbeke, "L'homme et son univers: de l'antiquité classique au moyen âge", *L'homme et son univers au Moyen Âge*, éd. Christian Wenin (Louvain-la-Neuve: Éditions de l'Institut Supérieure de Philosophie, 1986), 16–41).
9 Oexle points out in this regard: "... il convient de souligner qu'avec le début du XIe siècle une étape importante est franchie dans l'évolution de l'estime pour le travail manuel. Cette estime a été provoquée par le christianisme et sépare profondément les sociétés du Moyen Âge et celles des époques moderne et contemporaine de l'Antiquité. Je voudrais accentuer l'importance de (...) la naissance du Moyen Âge occidental avec le développement du cénobitisme, pour qui le vrai moine est celui que travaille (*tunc vere monachi sunt, si labore manuum suarum vivunt* [Regula Benedicti, 48, 8]" (Otto G. Oexle, "Le travail au XIe siècle: réalités et mentalités", *Le travail au Moyen Âge. Une approche interdisciplinaire*, éds. Jacqueline Hamesse, Colette Muraille-Samaran, 49–60: 58–59.
10 Jacques Dubois, "Le travail des moines au Moyen Âge", *Le travail au Moyen Âge. Une approche interdisciplinaire*, éds. Jacqueline Hamesse, Colette Muraille-Samaran, 61–100: 97.
11 Jacques Dubois, "Le travail des moines au Moyen Âge", *Le travail au Moyen Âge. Une approche interdisciplinaire*, éds. Jacqueline Hamesse, Colette Muraille-Samaran, 97–100.

12 Jacques Le Goff, "Le travail dans les systèmes de valeur de l'Occident médiéval," *Le travail au Moyen Âge. Une approche interdisciplinaire*, éds. Jacqueline Hamesse, Colette Muraille-Samaran, 10–11, 15–16.

13 Robert Fossier, *Le travail au Moyen Âge* (Paris: Hachette Littératures, 2000), 23–24.

14 Cf. Giles Constable, "The Orders of Society," ed. Giles Constable, *Three Studies in Medieval Religious and Social Thought* (Cambridge: Cambridge University Press, 1995), 251–360. Le Goff attributes a Hindo-European origin to this division, prior to the Greek scheme.

15 Robert Fossier, *Le travail au Moyen Âge* (Paris: Hachette Littératures, 2000), 20–21. Jacques Le Goff, "Le travail dans les systèmes de valeur de l'Occident médiéval," *Le travail au Moyen Âge. Une approche interdisciplinaire*, éds. Jacqueline Hamesse, Colette Muraille-Samaran, 16–17. Jacques Dubois, "Le travail des moines au Moyen Âge", *Le travail au Moyen Âge. Une approche interdisciplinaire*, éds. Jacqueline Hamesse, Colette Muraille-Samaran, 100.

16 Jacques Le Goff, "Le travail dans les systèmes de valeur de l'Occident médiéval," *Le travail au Moyen Âge. Une approche interdisciplinaire*, éds. Jacqueline Hamesse, Colette Muraille-Samaran, 19.

17 Robert Fossier, *Le travail au Moyen Âge* (Paris: Hachette Littératures, 2000), 23–24.

18 Cf. Jacqueline Hamesse, "Le travail chez les auteurs philosophiques du 12ᵉ et du 13ᵉ siècle. Approche lexicographique," *Le travail au Moyen Âge. Une approche interdisciplinaire*, éds. Jacqueline Hamesse, Colette Muraille-Samaran, 115–127; Robert Fossier, *Le travail au Moyen Âge* (Paris: Hachette Littératures, 2000), 13–15; Jacques Le Goff, "Pour une étude du travail dans les idéologies et les mentalités du Moyen Âge," *Lavorare nel Medio Evo. Rappresentazioni ed esempi dall'Italia dei secc. X–XVI*, Atti del XXI Convegno storico internazionale, Todi 12–15 ottobre 1980, Centro di studi sulla spiritualità medievale (Todi: Accademia Tudertina, 1983), 9–34, 14. It may be useful to consult Charles du Fresne, sieur Du Cange, *Glossarium mediae et infimae latinitatis*, 5 v. (Graz: Akademische Druck-u.Verlagsanstalt, 1954); Albert Blaise, *Lexicon latinitatis Medii Aevi* (Turnholti: Typographi Brepols Editores Pontificii, 1975).

19 Jacqueline Hamesse, "Le travail chez les auteurs philosophiques du 12ᵉ et du 13ᵉ siècle. Approche lexicographique," *Le travail au Moyen Âge. Une approche interdisciplinaire*, éds. Jacqueline Hamesse, Colette Muraille-Samaran, 118–122.

20 Fossier highlights the tendency toward an honorable valuation of work in its dimension of creativity and humanization of nature, from the consideration of *Deus artifex* as a model of the worker (cf. Robert Fossier, *Le travail au Moyen Âge* (Paris: Hachette Littératures, 2000), 22–23). Bultot also recognizes this evolution, which leads to the recognition in the thirteenth century of technical capacity as an expression of the dignity of man (cf. Robert Bultot, "Les sources philosophiques païennes de l'opposition entre «naturel» et «artificiel» en milieu chrétien," *Le travail au Moyen Âge. Une approche interdisciplinaire*, éds. Jacqueline Hamesse, Colette Muraille-Samaran, 101–113).

21 Jacqueline Hamesse, "Le travail chez les auteurs philosophiques du 12ᵉ et du 13ᵉ siècle. Approche lexicographique," *Le travail au Moyen Âge. Une approche interdisciplinaire*, éds. Jacqueline Hamesse, Colette Muraille-Samaran, 123–127.

22 Some of these reflections are placed in the context of the polemic that arose between the secular masters and the mendicants, or in various writings and dispositions related to the Rule and the Franciscan charism: *Quaestiones de perfectione evangelica*, q. 2, *Apologia pauperum*, *Determinationes quaestionum circa regulam fratrum minorum*, q. 12, *Epistola de tribus quaestionibus ad magistrum innominatum*. Cf. volume VIII of the critical edition of the writings of

92   *Isabel M. León-Sanz*

St. Bonaventure: *Doctoris Seraphici S. Bonaventurae S. R. E. episcopi cardinalis opera omnia*, studio et cura PP. Collegii a S. Bonaventura, 10 v. (Ad aquas claras (Quaracchi): ex typ. Collegii S. Bonaventurae, 1882–1902). Unless expressly indicated otherwise, the texts of St. Bonaventure will be cited according to this critical edition, indicating volume and page. On these subjects: Christian Wenin, "Saint Bonaventure et le travail manuel," *Le travail au Moyen Âge. Une approche interdisciplinaire*, éds. Jacqueline Hamesse, Colette Muraille-Samaran, 141–155; Cecylian T. Niezgoda, "Théologie du travail ou le travail des pauvres volontaires selon saint Bonaventure," *S. Bonaventura 1274–1974*, cura et studio Commissionis Internationalis Bonaventurianae, 5 v. (Grottaferrata (Roma): Collegio S. Bonaventura, 1974), IV, 685–717; Gabriel Banyangira Rusagara, "De la Fraternité à l'Ordre Mendiant. La place du travail manuel chez François d'Asisse et dans la vie des premiers frères mineurs," *Études Franciscaines* n. s., 5 (2012): 69–83.

23 I have developed these questions in Isabel M. León Sanz, *El arte creador en san Buenaventura. Fundamentos para una teología de la belleza* (Pamplona: EUNSA, 2016). Also of interest: Isabel M. León Sanz, "La creación como arte de la Trinidad en san Buenaventura," *Scripta Theologica* 47, no. 3 (2015): 579–605; Isabel M. León Sanz, "Algunas claves del pensamiento de S. Buenaventura que iluminan la posición del hombre en el universo según Laudato si'", *'Deus Summe Cognoscibilis'. The Current Theological Relevance of Saint Bonaventure*, éds. Amaury Begasse de Dhaem et al., Bibliotheca Ephemeridum Theologicarum Lovaniensum, 298 (Leuven-Paris-Bristol CT: Peeters, 2018), 239–250.

24 Jacques G. Bougerol, *Saint Bonaventure et la sagesse chrétienne* (Paris: Éd. du Seuil, 1963), 171–174; Giulio Bonafede, "Sulla dignità dell'uomo," *S. Bonaventura 1274–1974* (Grottaferrata (Roma): Collegio S. Bonaventura, 1974), III, 317–335. Francesco Corvino, "La dignità dell'uomo come motivo fondamentale del pensiero bonaventuriano," ed. Francesco Corvino, *Bonaventura da Bagnoregio francescano e pensatore* (Roma: Città Nuova, 2006), 512–530.

25 St. Bonaventure, *In Hexaemeron*, coll. 10, 7 (V, 378).

26 St. Bonaventure, *In I Sent.*, d. 27, p. II, a. un., q. 4, f. 1 (I, 489).

27 St. Bonaventure, *In I Sent.*, d. 3, p. 1, a. un., q. 3, ad 4 (I, 73).

28 St. Augustine, *De Trinitate*, XIV, 8, 11 (cf. *Opere di Sant'Agostino*, Nuova Biblioteca Agostiniana, a cura della Cattedra Agostiniana presso l'Augustinianum di Roma, 44 v., testo latino dall'edizione Maurina confrontato con l'edizione del Corpus Christianorum (Roma: Città Nuova Editrice, 1965–2011), IV, 582).

29 St. Bonaventure, *In II Sent.*, d. 16, a. 1, q. 1, concl. (II, 394b).

30 St. Bonaventure, *Quaestiones de perfectione evangelica*, q. 4, a. 1, s. c. 4 (V, 180): "ius naturae dictat, dignitatem imaginis esse servandam; sed imago est immediate a Deo et soli Deo subiecta". Cf. *In II Sent.*, d. 25, p. 2, a. u., q. 1, concl. (II, 611).

31 St. Bonaventure, *In Nativitati Domini*, sermo II, in the context of the incarnation: "Est etiam aliquo modo intelligere perfectionem in naturali dispositione. Ut nobilissima omnium potentiarum receptivarum, quae erat in humana natura plantata, scilicet unibilitas cum divina in unitate personae, non esset otiosa, est in actu reducta; per hoc autem, dum in actum reducitur omnis creatura, perfectio ultimatur, et in illo uno tota unitas consummatur". In this text I follow the version of the edition of Quaracchi: IX, 110a.

32 St. Bonaventure, *In II Sent.*, d. 16, a. 1, q. 1, concl. (II, 394–395).

33 St. Bonaventure, *In II Sent.*, d. 16, a. 1, q. 1, concl. (II, 395a): "quia enim ei inmediate ordinatur, ideo capax eius est, vel e converso; et quia capax est, nata est ei configurari; et propter hoc fert in se a sua origine lumen vultus divini".

34 St. Bonaventure, *Breviloquium*, II, c. 2 (V, 220a) and 4 (V, 221b). With this idea is connected the conception of man as a microcosm or *minor mundus*, which had been so dear to the theologians of the twelfth century. Cf. *In II Sent.*, d. 30, a. 1, q. 1, ad opp. 4 (II, 715).

35 St. Bonaventure, *Breviloquium*, II, 4 (V, 221–222). Cf. James McEvoy, "Microcosm and Macrocosm in the Writings of St. Bonaventure", in *S. Bonaventure 1274–1974*, II, 309–343: 323–330; Alexander Schaefer, "The Position and Function of Man in the Created World According to Saint Bonaventure," *Franciscan Studies* 21 (1961): 233–382: 314ff.

36 St. Bonaventure, *In II Sent.*, d. 16, a. 1, q. 1, ad 5 (II, 395–396). Cf. Aristóteles, *On the Soul*, III, 8 (431b). Cf. Isabel M. León Sanz, "El universo como poema divino: la expresividad de la naturaleza en San Buenaventura," *De Natura. La naturaleza en la Edad Media*, 2 v., eds. José L. Fuertes Herreros, Ángel Poncela González (Ribeirão: Ediçoes Humus, 2015), II, 567–575.

37 St. Bonaventure *In II Sent.*, d. 2, p. II, a. 1, q. 2, f. 2 (194a): "omnia corpora propter humanum obsequium sunt facta, unde «sumus nos finis quodam modo omnium eorum quae sunt»"; this last observation is inspired by Aristóteles, *Physics*, II, c. 2.

38 St. Bonaventure, *In II Sent.*, d. 15, a. 2, q. 1, concl. (II, 382b).

39 St. Bonaventure, *In Hexaemeron*, coll. 13, n. 12 (V, 389–390): "Notandum autem, quod mundus, etsi servit homini quantum ad corpus, potissime tamen quantum ad animam; et si servit quantum ad vitam, potissime quantum ad sapientiam. Certum est, quod homo stans habebat cognitionem rerum creatarum et per illarum repraesentationem ferebatur in Deum ad ipsum laudandum, venerandum, amandum; et ad hoc sunt creaturae et sic reducuntur in Deum". This thesis had been proposed by Hugo of St. Victor in *De tribus diebus*, XIV (cf. CCCM, no. 177, 30–31).

40 St. Bonaventure, *Breviloquium*, II, c. 11 (V, 229): "quia primum principium fecit mundum istum sensibilem ad declarandum se ipsum, videlicet ad hoc, quod per illum tanquam per speculum et vestigium reduceretur homo in Deum artificem, amandum et laudandum".

41 St. Bonaventure, *In II Sent.*, d. 15, a. 2, q. 1, concl. (II, 383a).

42 St. Bonaventure, *De plantatione paradisi*, n. 9 (V, 577a). He comments that God offers us the multiform beauty of creatures to prevent us from finding annoyance and weariness in knowing him and, instead, to make the path of piety pleasant for us.

43 St. Bonaventure, *In II Sent.*, d. 25 (V, 591–626).

44 Efrem Bettoni, *S. Bonaventura da Bagnoregio. Gli aspetti filosofici del suo pensiero* (Milano: Biblioteca Francescana Provinciale, 1973), 154.

45 St. Bonaventure, *In II Sent.*, Prooem. (II, 5): "Fecit igitur Deus hominem rectum, dum ad se convertendo sibi eum assimilavit, et per hoc omnibus praeposuit; et sic patet recta hominis conditio".

46 St. Bonaventure, *In II Sent.*, Prooem. (II, 4).

47 Laure Solignac, "«Ouvre les yeux, prête l'oreille». Le salut ou le monde retrouvé selon saint Bonaventure," '*Deus Summe Cognoscibilis'. The Current Theological Relevance of Saint Bonaventure*, eds. Amaury Begasse de Dhaem et al. (Leuven-Paris-Bristol CT: Peeters, 2018), 217–230. Stephania Parisi, "La caduta di Adamo e la redenzione nel pensiero di San Bonaventura," *Doctor Seraphicus* 62 (2014): 25–42.

48 St. Bonaventure, *In Hexaemeron*, 12, 2–12 (V, 385). Cf. Isabel León, "Hacia una comprensión artística de la creación. Fecundidad de esta analogía en el pensamiento de S. Buenaventura," *Pensar la Edad Media Cristiana: San Buenaventura de Bagnoregio (1217–1274)*, eds. Manuel Lázaro Pulido, Francisco León Florido, Francisco-Javier Rubio Hípola (Madrid: Servicio de Publicaciones de la UNED and Editorial Sindéres, 2019), 167–181.

49 Olegario González, *Misterio trinitario y existencia humana. Estudio histórico teológico en torno a S. Buenaventura* (Madrid – México – Buenos Aires – Pamplona: Rialp, 1965), 587.

94   Isabel M. León-Sanz

50 For example, *In I Sent.* d. 2, q. 4, f. 2 (I, 56): "non reperitur nisi duplex modus producendi nobilis; «omnis enim agens aut agit per modum naturae, aut per modum voluntatis», sicut vult Philosophus". This idea of Aristotle (cf. *Physics*, II, c. 3–ff: 194b–ff) was taken up by other masters of the thirteenth century.

51 St. Bonaventure, *In Hexaemeron*, 5, 13 (V, 356): "notitia igitur transiens in effectum extrinsecum est ars, quae est «habitus cum ratione factivus», et hic iungitur notitia cum faciente, praevia tamen affectione".

52 St. Bonaventure, *Ibidem*; cf. also *De reductionem artium ad theologiam*, 11 and 14 (V, 322–323).

53 Cf. Isabel M. León Sanz, *El arte creador en san Buenaventura. Fundamentos para una teología de la belleza* (Pamplona: EUNSA, 2016), chapter VII.

54 St. Bonaventure, *Quaestiones de mysterio Trinitatis*, q. 8, f. 6 (V, 113): "primum principium, hoc ipso quod primum, est simplicissimum et spiritualissimum: ergo necesse est quod intellectus; sed omnis intellectus principians principiat per verbum et donum amoris intrinsecum; omne autem principians per verbum et amorem prius concipit verbum et spirat amorem quam producat effectum exteriorem". In ad 7 of the same question, he reflects the Trinitarian scope of this idea: "quia enim Pater producit Filium et per Filium et cum Filio producit Spiritum sanctum; ideo Deus Pater per Filium cum Spiritu sancto est principium omnium creatorum; nisi enim eos produceret ab aeterno, non per illos producere posset ex tempore" (V, 115). Cf. Isabel M. León Sanz, "La creación como arte de la Trinidad en san Buenaventura," *Scripta Theologica* 47, no. 3 (2015): 579–605.

55 St. Bonaventure, *In I Sent.*, d. 10, a. 1., q. 1, ad 3 (I, 196).

56 St. Bonaventure, *In I Sent.*, d. 6, q. 3 (I, 129–130).

57 St. Bonaventure, *In Ioann.*, c. 1, nn. 9 and 12 (VI, 248 and 249).

58 St. Bonaventure, *In Hexaemeron*, 1, 10 (V, 331): "ad notitiam creaturae pervenire non potest nisi per id, per quod facta est".

59 St. Bonaventure, *In II Sent.*, d. 7, p. II, a. 2, q. 2, concl. (II, 202).

60 St. Bonaventure, *Sermo de ascensione Domini*, 4–ff (cf. Saint Bonaventure, *Sermons de diversis*, nouv. éd. crit. par Jacques G. Bougerol (Paris: Les éditions franciscaines, 1993), v. I, 345–ff).

61 St. Bonaventure, *In III Sent.*, d. 37, dub. 1 (III, 830): "anima enim facit novas compositiones, licet non faciat novas res".

62 St. Bonaventure, *In II Sent.*, d. 7, p. II, a. 2, q. 2, concl. (II, 202): seconding an idea of Richard of St. Victor, he points out that although "rem naturae non potest producere", man "operando in agricultura operatur ut artifex, et ideo naturam potest expedire et adiuvare".

63 St. Bonaventure, *In II Sent.*, d. 18, a. 1, q. 2, concl. (II, 436–437). Here he studies it in relation to the action of God, but his reasoning is analogically applicable to the action of human artisans.

64 St. Bonaventure, *Itinerarium mentis in Deum*, c. 2, 10 (V, 302). For a more detailed analysis, cf. Isabel M. León Sanz, *El arte creador en San Buenaventura*, 152–154 and 160–163.

65 St. Bonaventure, *In I Sent.*, d. 45, a. 2, q. 1 concl (I, 804–805): "«Unde divino amor est quidam cyclus aeternus, ex optimo, per optimum et in optimum». Ex quo colligitur, quod dicit coniunctionem principii cum fine, et ideo causam actu, quando vult facere". Cf. Dionysii Areopagitae, *De div. nom.*, c. 4.

66 St. Bonaventure, *In III Sent.*, d. 32, a. 1, q. 2, f. 3 and 4 (III, 699–700).

67 St. Josemaría Escrivá, *Christ Is Passing By*, 48 (cf. https://escriva.org/en/es-cristo-que-pasa/48/): "It is well to remember that the dignity of work is based on Love. Man's great privilege is to be able to love and to transcend what is fleeting and ephemeral. (...) This is why man ought not to limit himself to material production. *Work is born of love; it is a manifestation of love and is directed toward love.* We see the hand of God, not only in the wonders of nature, but also in our experience of work and effort" (emphasis added).

6 Daily life and work in the light of the mystery of Christ

Antonio Aranda†

Theological reflection on work admits and demands to be carried out taking into account the various perspectives that intersect in the event of the human creature (theology of creation, of the *imago Dei*, of sin, of the incarnation of God, of the redemptive work, etc.). All of them, in turn, direct our thought toward the consideration of the immense reality that unifies them and fills them with splendor: the mystery of Christ, true God, and true man. In this essay, these diverse perspectives and, especially, although very faintly, this splendor are pulsating.

Everyday life as an object of thought

The experience of everyday life arises, like all other human experiences, from the interpretation of reality as the domain of one's own existence unfolding over time; a time that is certainly limited, yet filled with events, relationships with others, consequences, and expectations. The experience of everyday life logically has a spatial dimension, but above all, since reality is made up of events, everyday life manifests an essential temporal structure. Therefore, everyday life primarily refers to temporality at various levels: either as a reflection of man's inner time, whose passing we are each aware of; or as a manifestation of time external to us, common to all, measured by the clock and socially established by the calendar. It is also a temporality with singular characteristics, because in everyday phenomena, the past is always somehow present ("things have always been like this"), and the future happens, in a certain sense, in advance ("things will continue to be like this"). For this reason, if there were no other expectations, everyday life could become monotonous, predictable: a routine flow of existence within a finite and standardized time.

But, fortunately, not everything is like that. In the experience of daily life, there are other elements that bring variety and vivacity. For example, the newness that is born of the encounter with others, of the capacity to love, to play, to act in conscience, to refuse, to allow oneself to be led freely by the needs of others.... Moreover, novelty always exists, particularly in the religious sphere, which brings transcendent meanings of faith, love, hope, but also of recognition, salvation, guilt, forgiveness, consolation, both in relation to others and above all in relation to God, to everyday life.

DOI: 10.4324/9781003508212-7

96 *Antonio Aranda*

In our era, it is common to contemplate ordinary life, which presents itself with the simplicity and normality of "every day", as the place and time of that which has little value, of that which lacks transcendent meaning. Religion itself, the relationship with God, has been seen as a way out of everyday life, as a way of performing "extraordinary" actions, far from concrete existence. God is often excluded from ordinary life, which ends up being identified with the profane. Even today, broad sectors of the dominant culture consider daily life as something opposed to what makes great men and women emerge: they identify it as an obstacle to personal freedom and to self-realization.[1]

The Christian conception, founded on the revelation of God in Christ, views daily life in a much more favorable light. Jesus Christ, Son of the Eternal Father, has revealed to the world through his incarnation a radically new reality: his own holy and sanctifying human existence, his filial fullness, from which we receive grace upon grace (Jn 1:16). In the light of Christ, daily life must be understood as the genuine place and time of a greatness not made up of clamorous actions and gestures, but interwoven with actions linked to the most normal vicissitudes and ordinary circumstances, experienced as a continuous discovery of supernatural values.

This is, then, in synthesis, the content of this chapter. My aim is to highlight the greatness and appeal of everyday life, especially in the work we routinely undertake, when its ultimate source of value and meaning is found, through the gift of faith, beyond ourselves. That is, in our identification with the Son of God made man. For this reason, the theological core of these pages is centered on the light shed by the true humanity of Jesus Christ in his daily work activity, during his 30 years of hidden life, as one among others.

Everyday life and work: some theological stances

I will confine my considerations solely to the realm of theology and spirituality. I have previously had the occasion to point out certain aspects of other areas, in particular philosophy and sociology.[2]

Formal or systematic developments on the topic of daily life in the field of theology and spirituality are not abundant, although one can find references to daily practice as a sphere and pathway for the experience of faith. Karl Rahner, for example, in one of his booklets on spirituality,[3] provides various considerations on ordinary things in the light of faith. Rahner tries to outline a "theology of everyday life",[4] in the sense of asking theology for the meaning of the ordinary realities of existence, such as working, walking, sitting, looking, laughing, eating, and sleeping. In this context, he mentions the "experience of grace in everyday life",[5] which should ultimately consist in the experience of being loved by God, and of wanting to love Him, as is seen in truly spiritual men and in the saints.

Bernhard Casper has also developed an interesting reflection on the experience of transcendence in everyday life under the title "*Everyday experience*

Daily life and work in the light of the mystery of Christ 97

and spirituality",[6] in which he tries to demonstrate how the experience of everyday life should be understood as the seat of the spiritual life. The terms he focuses on are varied; for example, the acceptance of one's own finitude, the awareness of sin and forgiveness, the experience of the other as the image of God, etc. The spirituality of the everyday in the light of faith is seen by Casper as founded on the experience of gratitude; on the understanding of work as effort, but also as cooperation in the work of creation and redemption; on the overcoming of the tension established between the difficulties of the present and the desire for salvation. Above all, it must be based on hope, the true driving force of Christian life "in the face of and in the midst of daily experience",[7] and it must be placed under the salvific sign of the cross.

On another note, and specifically reasoning within the field of the theology of the divine image in man, Leo Scheffczyk has developed a relevant thought on our topic.[8] Just as man's individual and social dimensions cannot be separated, Christian spirituality so emphasizes the connection between the relationship of each person with other human beings and his relationship with the rest of creation. Interpersonal relationships and relationships with the impersonal world constitute primary elements of the person's relationship with God, and are therefore theological determinations present in his being in the image of God. The progression of the image takes place within this dynamic circle of personal relationships with God and with others, in which the daily relationship with the world is also situated. In this second area, the relationship is one of mastery on the part of man, but also of responsibility toward creatures, which are *vestigia Dei* and have something to say to man. They come to meet him with their capacity to manifest the divine glory and demand a response from him: that of recognizing their creatural significance. When man releases the word that lies hidden in things, he also unveils their own meaning and relates it to God. By engaging with things, he himself moves within the sphere of God, in the mystery of the Creator, and is propelled by creation to the encounter with God. By unveiling the creatural meaning of things, man can find his own meaning in relation to creative Love, and with it, his own condition as an image.

For the Christian man, the relationship with the world is not reduced exclusively and primarily to a simple technical activity, which limits the understanding of the purposes of things to pure utility and the needs of men. Rather, this relationship must be an attitude of contemplation of the authentic value of creation as a divine imprint. Things then become a daily meeting place with God, and human work, as a *personal creative relationship with the truth of things, and as an activity that perfects the world*, acquires a new and profound meaning. An authentic theology of work is born, where the image of God and human activities tend toward the unity of their mutual fullness in Christ, with the help of grace. In my opinion, this is the theological terrain in which we must try to advance.

Man's work, work as such, is not part of the negativity introduced into the history of the world by the *mysterium iniquitatis*, but of the salvific reality

98 *Antonio Aranda*

of God's gift to the human creature. Work belongs by its own right to the *mysterium charitatis* in which we have been loved, created, and redeemed. Work is a holy and sanctifiable reality whose meaning shines forth in Christ. Christian holiness as the perfection of charity, as the fullness of identification with Christ, can therefore be expressed, as St. Josemaría Escrivá pointed out, as "sanctifying work, sanctifying oneself in work, and sanctifying others through one's work".[9]

The daily existence of Christ

Romano Guardini, in one of his Christological writings, offers this suggestive affirmation:

> Let us look at the features of his figure as outlined by Paul, at those highlighted by John and also at those found in the narratives of the Synoptics. All these traits belong to him, but beyond all of them rises an immeasurable reality, whose origin goes back to God, capable of breaking every limit that human reason could have conceived. Each one of these features leads to it, but it encloses them all in its ineffability. So it is, and that is Christ.[10]

This immense reality also stands before us, before our intention to reflect as Christians on the work of man, as the true starting point and at the same time the goal of our study.

In one of the most theologically dense paragraphs of *Gaudium et Spes*, the Second Vatican Council formulated the core of the issue we now wish to study, namely, the new meaning of fulfillment attained by ordinary human existence when it has been personally embraced by the incarnate Son of God as his own. The conciliar text states,

> Since human nature as He assumed it was not annulled, by that very fact it has been raised up to a divine dignity in our respect too. For by His incarnation the Son of God has united Himself in some fashion with every man. He worked with human hands, He thought with a human mind, acted by human choice and loved with a human heart. Born of the Virgin Mary, He has truly been made one of us, like us in all things except sin.[11]

In Christ, God has assumed not only the temporality of man, but, more profoundly, the common human existence with all its characteristics. In doing so, these characteristics have been elevated in Him and, by extension, in us, to the mysterious fullness of which they are capable. Christ has lived man's daily life as His own. He has illumined human daily life with His mystery: He has filled it with His personal reality, He has filled it with a new and definitive meaning.

Daily life and work in the light of the mystery of Christ 99

Since Christ, ordinary life must be understood as what it truly was in Him: the channel in which and through which His existence as God incarnate unfolded, the channel of the filial everyday life of the Word made flesh. A really interesting question, in my opinion, for a theology of daily life and work must therefore be this: what are the normative profiles, so to speak, the essentially defining features of the filial everyday life of Jesus Christ? This is not a question that can be answered simply, since the ineffable mystery of paternity and filiation is always implicit in the mutual love that is Trinitarian life. However, it is by no means a question about which we should remain silent, because upon it the lights of the revelation in Christ of the mystery of the Father and of His love, that is, the lights of the economy of salvation have been shown. These lights tell us something particularly central to our topic: the Word of God who was with the Father, the Only-Begotten who is in the bosom of the Father (cf. Jn 1:1,18), in assuming human reality, has filled it with His personal *proprium*, with the *personalitas Filii*, that is, with His filiation, without changing the human reality assumed.

In the incarnate Word, the human condition, everything that belongs to man, receives the determining imprint of divine filiation. The humanity of Christ, assumed in the person of the Word, is marked by a radically filial relationship with the Father. Therefore, in the incarnate Word, not only is human time a dimension of God, but more profoundly, all aspects of humanity, have entered into the sphere of divine filiation, where the key to the profound meanings is: "Father, hallowed be thy name". And the password, if we accept this image, simply says that: "Thy will be done on earth as it is in heaven". Only from these flashes of light can theological thought approach the mystery of Christ's daily existence on earth: an entirely filial daily life, lived under the sign of the mission that He had to carry out.

Christ's everyday life has the same common features of our existence: the materiality of passing days, the passage of time, the work to be done, and of the other duties toward family, friends, etc. However, His life is imbued (in the strongest sense of the word) and lived with the intimate awareness of personal filiation and the mission received on earth. This awareness means: to have the will to glorify the Father; to make His Name known – His paternity; to fulfill His works to the end; to manifest His mercy – His love for the world; to carry out the work of salvation for the Father's sake. The Church confesses in the Christological cycle of the Nicene–Constantinopolitan Symbol that the divine Word "came down from heaven for us and for our salvation, became incarnate by the Holy Spirit and became man". With this confession of faith as a backdrop, theology must also consider that the Son of God became man above all out of love of the Father and for His glory, to which, by the will of the Father, our salvation is intimately linked. The Son came to save man because He came to glorify His Father, fulfilling the mission He received. The Son wants only to love and glorify the Father in the Holy Spirit. Here, once again, lies the essential meaning of Christ's daily life, where the Christian must try to discover the meaning of his own.

100 *Antonio Aranda*

The work of Christ at Nazareth in theological reflection

Let us now reflect on a point – the work of Jesus in Nazareth – about which we lack precise historical references. Exegetes only pause to interpret what they find in the sacred text, and in this sense, although in commenting on the Gospels of the infancy they allude – briefly – to the life of Christ and the Holy Family in Nazareth, they are not particularly interested in the question we are studying here: His daily work. This also explains, for example, why Benedict XVI, in the aforementioned work, does not devote a single line to our topic.

We have, however, the certainty – certainly not small – provided by the testimonies of St. Matthew, St. Mark, and St. Luke. They tell us that Jesus lived in the small town in Lower Galilee (cf. Mt 2:23; 21:11; Mk 1:9; Lk 2:39,51), where He remained for about 30 years (cf. Lk 3:23). He was known by his fellow citizens as someone who practiced the trade of a craftsman – *tekton* – (cfr. Mk 6:3), the same that Joseph, who was considered His father (cfr. Mt 13:55), had also practiced (cfr. Mt 13:55) and would have passed on to Him the appropriate training, as was customary.[12] Although the information is so concise and there is no further specific documentation on the matter, it is worthwhile to reflect, not historically but theologically, on the issue we wish to study, in order to unveil some of its elements. Indeed, theology, in dialogue with the rather meager exegetical and historical studies on the subject, and with the support of the likewise infrequent contributions of the spiritual and doctrinal tradition on the work of Jesus, can bring to light certain aspects implicit in the Gospel accounts. That is what we aim to reason here.[13]

Of the various arguments to be studied within a Christian vision of man and man's work (historical, philosophical, magisterial, theological), we limit ourselves here to presenting some considerations – clearly fragmentary – pertaining to the theological sphere.

Data disclosed

The New Testament, after relating in some detail, in the first chapters of Matthew and Luke, various events of Jesus'childhood, is completely silent about the years of His life in Nazareth, prior to the beginning of His preaching and public ministry. The only information we have about those hidden years is the one already mentioned: in that small town where He spent his whole childhood, adolescence, and youth, or as Luke soberly says: "where he had grown up" (Lk 4:16), all His fellow citizens knew Jesus and His family,[14] and were therefore aware of the work that both He and Joseph carried out.[15] This is the information that has been transmitted to us. Its content and meaning are analyzed by the experts according to the laws governing their professional field and their specific interests.

Biblical studies, for example, delve into descriptions of Nazareth in the first century, its history, geography, etc.[16] With the support of historical and archaeological knowledge, etc., they present the characteristic traits of the

Daily life and work in the light of the mystery of Christ   101

family, religious, social, working life, etc., of a community like that one,[17] but nothing more.[18] On the subject that concerns us here – the work of Jesus – only generic considerations are made, or perhaps more specific but always not very concrete.[19] Thus, for example, Joachim Gnilka writes:

> "In everyday life he practiced a trade. For his trade and for Joseph's trade the same word is used: *tékton*, which we usually translate as carpenter (...) We can suppose that both exercised the trade of *tékton* and that Jesus learned the trade from Joseph, according to what we can see in late rabbinic Judaism".[20]

Other authors express themselves in a similar way.[21]

From a reading of the biblical texts from such a perspective, nothing of interest can emerge to advance the question we have posed. If we want to make further progress, a more theological and inquisitive approach is necessary, one that strives to bring to light other aspects of the reality of Christ the man, even if it has not been literally manifested.

Ideas in dialogue with Joseph Ratzinger-Benedict XVI

What we have just pointed out is what, for example, Joseph Ratzinger-Benedict XVI does in his magnificent study on Jesus of Nazareth,[22] although this work does not deal at any time with the work of Jesus either. The only references to Nazareth that may have some interest for what we are studying here are those that refer to the appellation of Jesus as "Nazarene". Starting from Mt 2:23, where it is said that Joseph "dwelt in a town called Nazareth, so that what had been spoken through the prophets might be fulfilled, 'He shall be called a Nazarene'", the author alludes to the two denominations of Jesus with that appellation in the NT: *nazōraîos* (Mt, Jn, Acts) or *nazarēnos* (Mk); Lk uses both.[23] Going back to the OT traditions, Nazarene can be interpreted in two ways:[24] (a) as a derivation of *nazir* (Judg 13:5–7), with the meaning of "man totally consecrated to God from the womb" (Samson), which has an extraordinarily dense meaning in Jesus; or, (b) as a derivation of *nezer* (Is 11:1), "offshoot" of the stem of Jesse, which can also be applied perfectly to Jesus: in him is fulfilled the promise of the branch that God was going to give to the stump of Jesse, on which the Spirit of God would rest. In being called Jesus Christ on the cross as the Nazarene (*ho Nazoraîos*) (cf. Jn 19:19), the title "takes on its full sonority": it indicates not only his origin but also, at the same time, his essence: "he is the 'offshoot', he is the one entirely consecrated to God from the womb to death".[25]

Joseph Ratzinger, in the work we are commenting on, says nothing more about it, and therefore we cannot deduce from it what he thinks about the hidden life of Christ and his work in Nazareth. Perhaps, however, the idea mentioned above can be of use to us: Jesus being par excellence the "offshoot", the one "entirely consecrated to God from the womb to death", the

102 *Antonio Aranda*

whole meaning of his existence and of his human work must be thought (imagined) from his full personal reference to the Father as Son. As the author points out in another of his works, "the whole testimony of the Gospels is unanimous in affirming that the words and actions of Jesus stemmed from the most intimate union with the Father".[26] Jesus is in person the Son, and in this denomination the historical figure of Jesus resonates most directly. In the same work just cited, we also read:

> All the evangelists agree that the last words of Jesus constituted an expression of his disposition towards the Father and a cry addressed not to someone or something but to Him [the Father]: to be in dialogue with Him constituted his most intimate essence.[27]

In my opinion, this is also applicable to his life's work in Nazareth, although nothing specific can be said about it that is historically or biblically documented. We are therefore arguing – and we consider it opportune to repeat this – that, when a theological reading is made of the Gospel texts about Jesus, it is possible that realities come to light that are not explicitly manifested in them, although they are present in an implicit way in his mystery as Man-God.

Going deeper into this idea, we can ask ourselves this question: what intentions filled the entire existence and, therefore, also the daily work activity of Jesus in Nazareth, before the beginning of his public life? Although we cannot shed a properly historical light on this question, we are in a position to shed some theological light on it, or on other similar questions, if we take into consideration, as is usual in Christian thought, the Christology implicit in the Gospel texts. Let us give an example. If at the dawn of his public ministry, after the imprisonment of John, Jesus calls for conversion and announces that the Kingdom is at hand (cf. Mk 1:15), is it speculative to suppose that the imminence of this proclamation and call were not already present in him in the time immediately before, when He was still living as an ordinary man in Nazareth?

What importance can be attached, as another example, to the mysterious words that the Child Jesus addressed to his parents in the temple of Jerusalem: "Why were you looking for me? Did you not know that I must be in my Father's house?" If this is what occupies the soul of the Child at the age of 12, when he lives daily with them and is being formed by Joseph in the doctrine of Israel and in his trade, how can we not think that this was also the attitude that occupied his soul in the following years of permanence and work in Nazareth? The Gospel summarizes in a few words that time:

> He went down with them, came to Nazareth and was subject to them. And his mother kept all these things in her heart. And Jesus *grew* in wisdom, and in age, and *in favor with God and man.*
>
> (Lk 2:51–52)

Daily life and work in the light of the mystery of Christ   103

What Our Lady kept in her heart, we can think, was not only what she saw in the Child when she found Him in the Temple, but also what she saw in Him (and heard from Him) at the time of Nazareth.

In this regard, what Benedict XVI points out in his *Jesus of Nazareth*, when meditating on the response of Jesus to his parents is very interesting.

> Jesus tells his parents: I am in the very place where I belong—with the Father, in his house (...)I *am* with my father. My father is not Joseph, but another—God himself. It is to him that I belong, and here I am with him. Could Jesus' divine sonship be presented any more clearly? A second element is directly linked with this. Jesus uses the word '*must*', and he acts in accordance with what *must* be. The Son, the child *must* be with his Father (...) He is already bound by the "must" at this early hour.[28]

And immediately, our author, going even further in his exposition, unveils the Christology implicit in the passage:

> The answer of the twelve-year-old made it clear that he knew the Father—God—intimately. Only he *knows* God, not merely through the testimony of men, but he recognizes him in himself. Jesus stands before the Father as Son, on familiar terms. He lives in his presence. He sees him. (...) He is with the Father, he sees everything and everyone in the light of the Father. And yet it is also true that his wisdom *grows*. As a human being, he does not live in some abstract omniscience, but he is rooted in a concrete history, a place and a time, in the different phases of human life, and this is what gives concrete shape to his knowledge.[29]

All of this is also perfectly applicable, in my opinion, to the long years of Jesus'work. To contemplate them realistically and grasp what they mysteriously mean, it is not enough to consider what type of work he did. However, such considerations are necessary, as He performed a specific job, with certain characteristics, and not another. Nor is it enough to discuss the Old Testament meaning of work, although it also must be to taken into account, since Jesus – as a good Israelite, well-versed in the Law of Moses – knew it and embraced it. Without forgetting these aspects, it is also necessary to consider what He who was the Son of the Father, identified with his will of salvation, kept in his heart, and reflected in his works. "This story opens a door to the figure of Jesus as a whole, which is what the Gospels go on to recount".[30] From these Gospel narratives we must infer those other dimensions of his work, which, because they were always present in the soul of Jesus the man, had to be present and operative in his daily life and work.[31]

One cannot logically meditate on the daily life of Christ on the basis of something we can only know approximately. The materiality of the ordinary

104   *Antonio Aranda*

life of Jesus in Nazareth is unknown terrain to us. We can only imagine it, on the basis of the various historical investigations carried out on the ordinary life of a Hebrew of his time, more specifically of a craftsman (*tékton, faber,* says the sacred text about Joseph and Jesus; cf. Mt 13:55; Mk 6:3). But, in reality, what interests us is not so much the exact or approximate content of that existence, but rather its hidden meaning. And this is illuminated by the light of his person and his mission, a light that shines with special intensity in these stories. For those familiar with the Gospel's essential aspects of Christ's public life – the glory of the Father, the fulfillment of his will, the coming of the Kingdom, the salvation of mankind through his own self-giving – the meaning of the hidden life in Nazareth, the everyday existence of the incarnate Son, does not raise any special questions. On the contrary, it holds a certain luminosity.

Some contemporary theological proposals

In contemporary theology, we find similar underlying positions, even if the topic addressed in them may not explicitly focus on Christ's work. As pointed out, for example, by the International Theological Commission in its 1985 document on "Jesus' awareness of himself and his mission", it must be maintained that:

> The life of Jesus testifies to the awareness of his filial relationship to the Father (…). He was aware of being the only Son of God, and in that sense, of being, himself, God.[32]

Likewise, it must be maintained that:

> Jesus knew the purpose of his mission: to announce the Kingdom of God and to make it present in his person, his actions and his words, so that the world might be reconciled with God and renewed.[33]

And finally, it must also be affirmed that:

> Christ's awareness of being sent by the Father for the salvation of the world and for the gathering of all men into the people of God implies, mysteriously, love for all men, so that we can say that 'the Son of God who has loved me and given himself up for me' (Gal 2:20).[34]

As we have been saying, it is opportune and legitimate to consider that this filial and soteriological awareness of Jesus, always alive and operative in his person, also filled his daily work with meaning. If this quality were not emphasized, the reality and meaning of that work would be poorly expressed.

A contemporary Spanish theologian, referring to the human existence of Jesus, has written that: "This existence serves as the medium through which

Daily life and work in the light of the mystery of Christ 105

God reveals Himself to us, and we grasp this divine revelation by knowing and appropriating this human existence".[35] He also points out that, in the analysis of the event of Jesus of Nazareth (Jesus himself and what he has meant in the history of humanity), three levels of knowledge must be distinguished. These levels are found simultaneously in the New Testament and include: (a) the facts, which require historical-scientific knowledge; (b) the meaning of those facts, that is, the deep intentionality behind them, and their exemplarity for us, which call for historical–sapiential knowledge; and (c) the divine revelation inherent in those facts, going beyond what Christ did to what God did in him and what He gave us through him, which demands a religious–believer knowledge.[36] The idea seems interesting and also applicable to our topic, because although the work of Christ in Nazareth is not known to us in detail, we do know three levels of his reality: (a) that he worked as an artisan (facts); (b) that the intentionality of that work was the same that governed his entire filial and redemptive existence (exemplarity); and (c) that God is revealing in Christ the worker the profound meaning of work, as a task proper to man in the order of creation.

Later on, González de Cardedal adds the following:

> By proclaiming the diversity of planes and cognitive accesses, and by hierarchizing them starting from the third, Christianity proclaims that the events of Jesus' life are truly understood when they are interpreted as the expression of a novel understanding of existence in the world and its relationships with the cosmos, society, and God. This perspective acknowledges that such a mode of existence is firmly grounded and nurtured in Jesus' self-awareness as the revealer, the sent one, the Christ, the Son.[37]

The humanity of a man has indeed been the humanity of God, and in that sense, the human self-consciousness of Jesus is the natural home of a supernatural revelation.[38]

And we, from our concrete interest, insist on the same thing: although the fact "the work of Jesus in Nazareth" is unknown to us in its empirical realization, it is known to us in its substantial reality: it is an event that really happened and was carried out by the Son of God made man. We can, therefore, apply these ideas to it, and meditate on what it reveals to us and on the exemplarity it entails.

Concluding summary

That concludes what we aimed to convey in this chapter. The essential content of what we have discussed can be summarized as follows:

a For those who, through the Gospel, know the essential aspects of the public life of Jesus Christ – the glory of the Father, the fulfilment of his

106   *Antonio Aranda*

will, the coming of the Kingdom, the salvation of all men through his self-giving, the redirection of all creation to God – the meaning of his hidden life and his daily work in Nazareth does not pose special questions. On the contrary, it somehow shines in the unity of his being and his mission.

b In the work of Jesus, it is necessary to consider above all what is an inescapable requirement of the perfection of his humanity (true humanity of the incarnate Word). But not only that, because considered from other theological perspectives, particularly as the work of the Son of God made man, it also signifies a work in full conformity with his filial condition and with his assent to the mission received from the Father.

c In Jesus' daily work during the 30 years of his life in Nazareth, the ultimate meaning of work is tacitly revealed as the channel of the creational relationship between man as a person and God – of whom he is an image – and with the impersonal world, which has been placed under his care.

* * *

Although we have not considered it directly here, in view of future research, it is also necessary to take into account that:

d Jesus, both in the years of his public life and in those of his hidden existence in Nazareth, wanted to show the meaning and content of an ordinary life, certainly marked by charity, humility, detachment, spirit of service, etc., but also marked by work humanly well done, with the desire to give glory to the Father, to serve men and to care for creation: a life, then, of sanctified work.

e If the Son of God assumed human work in Nazareth with naturalness and daily dedication, this work – because of the one who performed it and the purpose for which it was performed – was also sanctified.

f It can therefore be affirmed that the sanctification of work and through work is a sign of the Christological fullness of the divine image in man: something, therefore, that in Christ as a man, and as a working man, has been made known to us.

We have reached the end of our reflection, and the conclusion, the thesis that we defend, can be formulated very briefly. Ordinary life sanctified by the Son of God made man enables us to understand that the Christian's daily life is also, in Christ and in the Holy Spirit, sanctifiable. However, it will be so only if, and always if, it is informed by the reality of the Cross taken up each day – the unavoidable path of Christian holiness – and by the profound meaning of the Christ's Cross, which is also the true meaning of his daily life: a meaning of filiation and mission, a meaning of glorification of the Father, a meaning of love through deeds for all men, especially those who are most in need. From the Cross of Calvary, or rather from the Crucifix, a source

Daily life and work in the light of the mystery of Christ   107

of life and new meanings is born; a source that allows the renewal, without changing its nature, of men and all human realities. Ultimately, it allows for the renewal of the meaning of human daily life itself, understood as filial Christian daily life, which must become – in the repetition of the ordinary – a daily life also characterized by heroism.

Notes

1 Cf. Pierpaolo Donati, "Senso e valore della vita quotidiana," *La grandezza della vita quotidiana. vocazione e missione del cristiano in mezzo al mondo*, AA. VV, ed. Mariano Fazio (Roma: Edusc, 2002), 221–263.
2 Cf. Antonio Aranda, "Dimensioni della quotidianità, dimensioni della santità", *Tempo e spiritualità*, Pontificia Università Gregoriana (Istituto di spiritualità), (Napoli:Chirico, 2001), 73–106; also in "Studi Cattolici" 487 (2001): 596–603.
3 Karl Rahner, *Cose d'ogni giorno* (Brescia: Morcelliana, 1966). Cf. L. J. Card Suenens, *Vita quotidiana, vita cristiana* (Modena: Edizioni paoline, 1964).
4 Karl Rahner, *Cose d'ogni giorno* (Brescia: Morcelliana, 1966), 7–9.
5 Karl Rahner, *Cose d'ogni giorno* (Brescia: Morcelliana, 1966), 30–36.
6 Bernhard Casper, "Experiencia cotidiana y espiritualidad", eds. Thomas Luckmann et al. *Fe cristiana y sociedad moderna*, Vol. 25, (Madrid: Ediciones SM, 1990), 54–88.
7 Bernhard Casper, "Experiencia cotidiana y espiritualidad", eds. Thomas Luckmann et al. *Fe cristiana y sociedad moderna*, Vol. 25, (Madrid: Ediciones SM, 1990), 83.
8 Cf. Leo Scheffczyk, "Stand und Aufgaben der Imago-Dei-Theologie" *Münchener Theologische Zeitschrift* 20 (1969): 1–28; Leo Scheffczyk, "Image et ressemblance dans la théologie et la spiritualité d'aujourd'hui," *Dictionnaire de spiritualitè*, eds. Ferdinand Cavallera, Joseph de Guibert et al. Vol. VII.2 (Paris: Beauchesne, 1971), 1464–1472.
9 "I have repeated it constantly, since the day that our Lord chose for the foundation of Opus Dei! We have to sanctify our ordinary work, we have to sanctify others through the exercise of the particular profession that is proper to each of us, in our own particular state in life", Josemaría Escrivá, *Christ Is Passing By: Homilies* (Dublin: Four Courts, 1982), 122b.
10 Romano Guardini, *La figura di Gesù Cristo nel Nuovo Testamento* (Brescia: Morcelliana, 2000), 106.
11 Vatican Council II, Pastoral Constitution *"Gaudium et Spes" (on the Church in the Modern World)*, December 7, 1965, #22, https://www.vatican.va/archive/hist_councils/ii_vatican_council/documents/vat-ii_const_19651207_gaudium-et-spes_en.html.
12 The Jewish author Joseph Klausner, in his work *Jesús de Nazaret* (Barcelona: Paidós, 1989), after noting that in texts of Jewish literature from around the time of Jesus there are references to no fewer than 40 different types of craftsmen, including tailors, shoemakers, builders, masons, carpenters, millers, bakers, tanners, and many others, points out: "The trades passed from father to son, as explained by the expression of the Talmud: 'carpenter and carpenter's son'. The Judeo-Christian tradition says that Jesus and his father were carpenters" (171).
13 This question is not new to us, as we have previously touched upon it indirectly in our earlier research on the theological and spiritual insights of St. Josemaría. As is well-documented, our focus has been on the sanctification of the Christian through their everyday work, drawing inspiration from the life of Jesus Christ, who spent much of his earthly existence laboring in the workshop of Nazareth.

108 *Antonio Aranda*

Drawing from those investigations and long meditation, we delve deeper into these concepts in the following pages. Here, we reference some of those previous studies: (a) *Identidad cristiana y configuración del mundo. La fuerza configuradora de la secularidad y del trabajo santificado* (Roma, 2002), *La grandezza della vita quotidiana. Vocazione e missione del cristiano in mezzo al mondo*, AA. VV, ed. Mariano Fazio (Roma: Edusc, 2002), 175–198. (b) "Trabajo diario santificado y santificador. Sobre la contribución de san Josemaría Escrivá a la espiritualidad y a la teología", eds. Jon Borobia et al. *Trabajo y espíritu. Sobre el sentido de las enseñanzas de san Josemaría Escrivá en el contexto del pensamiento contemporáneo* (Pamplona: Eunsa, 2004), 19–44. (c) *Es Cristo que pasa*. Edición crítico-histórica (Madrid: Rialp, 2013), especially the study of the homily "En el taller de José", 321–372. (d) *Amigos de Dios*. Edición crítico-histórica (Madrid: Rialp, 2019), especially the study of the homily "Trabajo de Dios". (e) *El Hecho teológico y pastoral del Opus Dei. Una indagación en las fuentes fundacionales*, 2nd ed. (Pamplona: Eunsa, 2021).

14 "Isn't this the son of Joseph?" (Lk 4:22). "Is this not Jesus, the son of Joseph? Do we not know his father and mother?" (Jn 6:42). "Is not his mother named Mary and his brothers James, Joseph, Simon, and Judas?" (Mt 13:55; cf. Mk 6:3). "We have found the one about whom Moses wrote in the law, and also the prophets, Jesus, son of Joseph, from Nazareth" (Jn 1:45).

15 "Is he not the carpenter's son?" (Mt 13:55). "Is he not the carpenter?" (Mk 6:3).

16 Thus, for example, in Adolphe Legendre, "Nazareth", *Dictionnaire de la Bible. Suplément* (Paris: Letouzey et Ané, 1928ff), 1521–1542. Serafín de Ausejo, "Nazaret", *Diccionario de la Biblia* (Barcelona: Herder, 1981), 1326. Evaristo Martín Nieto, "Nazaret", F. Fernández Ramos (dir.), *Diccionario de Jesús de Nazaret* (Burgos: Monte Carmelo, 2001), 863.

17 For example, M-J. Lagrange, *Vida de Jesucristo según el Evangelio* (Madrid: Edibesa, 1999), while pointing out that to seek something about the hidden life of Jesus outside the Gospels is to lose oneself in vain conjectures, also says: "If it were permitted to refine the analysis of his human development, one would say that there was in him, as in others, something of the influence of his Mother; her grace, her exquisite refinement, her indulgent gentleness, belong to him (...). If Joseph taught his adopted son the art of planing boards, did he not offer himself to Jesus as the finished model of an honest worker worthy of the most pious Israelite" (54).

18 Günther Bornkamm, *Jesús de Nazaret* (Salamanca: Sígueme, 1977), for example, writes: "From the point of view of history, the childhood and youth of Jesus remain obscure to us (...) His family belonged to the Jewish fraction of the population that, since the time of the Maccabees, had become strongly linked to the cult of the temple of Jerusalem and to the legal practice of Judaism (...) His father was a carpenter and perhaps he himself was one" (55–56). Indeed, we can reflect that those years of Jesus remain obscure to us, but we can surmise something about them based on our knowledge of who Jesus was and what he was like. It is enough to consider what we do know that happens immediately after those 30 unknown years. Right from the outset of his preaching about the Kingdom of the Father, the evangelists portray a defining aspect of his historical persona: the immediate and widespread recognition of his authority. Where does this doctrinal authority, of which everyone was amazed, come from (Mk 1:22; Mt 7:29)? "This term 'authority' undoubtedly covers the whole mystery of the person and influence of Jesus as they are perceived in faith; thus he surpasses everything that is purely 'historical'. In the most varied encounters Jesus always displays an immediate 'authority' stemming from within himself" (Günther Bornkamm, *Jesús de Nazaret* (Salamanca: Sígueme, 1977), 63). From the very outset of his

Daily life and work in the light of the mystery of Christ 109

public ministry, which followed his years of quiet labor in Nazareth, Jesus' teachings resonate with profound depth. His doctrine about the Father, the imminent arrival of the Kingdom, the hour of salvation; his preaching on the beatitudes, and his call to repentance all reveal much about his character and, in a sense, the ideals that fill his soul. While these teachings may not directly recount his earlier life or the specifics of his work, they offer rich insights into his essence and the ideals that animate him. It is crucial to recognize that these aspects of his ministry did not emerge in isolation or suddenly; they must have been ingrained in his daily existence and his labor, for they stem from the core of his being. Jesus never explicitly refers to his 'vocation', yet he does speak of the arrival of the "hour" – the moment of his divine mission.

19 For example, in the voice *Travail* of the *Dictionnaire encyclopédique de la Bible* (Turnhout-Paris: Brepols, 1960), col. 1871, we read: "Jesus did not contribute new ideas in relation to human work [with respect to those of the Old Testament]. But, since he spent almost all his life working with his hands, he sanctified the work of men and thus ratified the high conception that the OT had in this respect". Joachim Gnilka, *Jesús de Nazaret. Mensaje e historia* (Barcelona: Herder, 1993), will say: "We know nothing concrete about the long time Jesus spent in Nazareth. The Gospels are completely silent. While he was a young child, Mary was in charge of his education. Then Joseph did it, who had to instruct him in the Torah. In the synagogue, Jesus heard the reading of Scripture, and the interpretation of Scripture in preaching" (97). It is not uncommon to find views such as this about the family life of Jesus, characteristic of Christian piety: "Obscure life, of Much and Humble Labor; of Poverty, Though not of Deprivation and Necessity; of Sacrifice and Prayer, but also of the Gentlest Union". Louis–Claude Fillion, *Nuestro Señor Jesucristo según los Evangelios* (Madrid: Edibesa, 2000), 89.

20 Joachim Gnilka, *Jesús de Nazaret. Mensaje e historia* (Barcelona: Herder, 1993).

21 For example, Armand Puig, *Jesús, una biografía* (Barcelona: Destino, 2005), who writes: "Under this denomination [*tekton*] can be included works made not only with wood, but also with stone and even iron (…) Jesus is, then, a craftsman of wood and iron, a man who knows how to work both materials and who earns his living in a workshop, inherited from his father (…) A workshop of these characteristics must be prepared to do work related to the agricultural world (…) or to domestic needs" (181).

22 Joseph Ratzinger, *Obras completas*, 6, 1: *Jesús de Nazaret. Estudios de Cristología* (Madrid: BAC, 2015). We will cite by this edition.

23 Joseph Ratzinger, *Obras completas*, 6, 1: *Jesús de Nazaret. Estudios de Cristología* (Madrid: BAC, 2015), 83; [Joseph Ratzinger–Benedict XVI, *Jesus of Nazareth. The Infancy Narratives* (London: Bloomsbury, 2012), 115].

24 Cf. Joseph Ratzinger, *Obras completas*, 6, 1: *Jesus de Nazaret. Estudios de Cristologia* (Madrid: BAC, 2015), 84–85 [Bloomsbury, 2012, 116–117].

25 Joseph Ratzinger, *Obras completas*, 6, 1: *Jesus de Nazaret. Estudios de Cristologia* (Madrid: BAC, 2015), 85. [Bloomsbury, 2012, 118].

26 Joseph Ratzinger, *Guardare il crocifisso* (Milano: Jaca Book, 2005), 17; cf. Pablo Blanco, *La teología de Joseph Ratzinger* (Madrid: Palabra, 2001), 388.

27 Ratzinger, *Guardare il crocifisso* (Milano: Jaca Book, 2005), 23. To what has already been mentioned we could further add the meaning of Christ's *pro nobis*, and his *pro-existence*, as emphasized by Ratzinger. This concept can only find its complete intelligibility precisely in *his being of the Father* (cf. Gabriel Richi Alberti, *Dios y hombre en un bocado*, in AA.VV., *Jesucristo en el pensamiento de Joseph Ratzinger* (Madrid: Publicaciones San Dámaso, 2011), 15. In this regard Richi quotes Ratzinger: "This 'I' is not at all something exclusive and independent but Being completely derived from the 'Thou' of the Father and lived for the 'You'

110   Antonio Aranda

of men" (Joseph Ratzinger, *Introducción al cristianismo* (Salamanca: Sígueme, 1969), 177 [*Introduction to Chrisitianity* (New York: Herder and Herder, 1970), 154]. Although the hidden life of Jesus is not mentioned in these texts, and therefore neither is his work in Nazareth, I think that it can also be seen from the perspective indicated by Th. Söding in his work: *Jesucristo según el Nuevo Testamento*, who, interpreting Ratzinger, points out that: "Jesus can only be understood historically if he is understood theologically: from God" (in the abovementioned AA.VV., *Jesucristo en el pensamiento de Joseph Ratzinger* (Madrid: Publicaciones San Dámaso, 2011), 80). That is, from the unity between the Father and the Son. And he adds: "The unity between Jesus and the Father, which Joseph Ratzinger develops in an intuitive and reflective way as the central perspective of his image of Jesus, is not only something given and experienced, but also something proven and suffered" (95). In a similar vein, Pierangelo Sequeri (*Jesucristo, el Testigo fiel*, in AA.VV., *Jesucristo en el pensamiento de Joseph Ratzinger* (Madrid: Publicaciones San Dámaso, 2011), 97–114) also quotes Ratzinger's *Introducción al Cristianismo*, where he says: "For what faith really states is precisely that with jesus it is not possible to distinguish office and person; with him, this differentiation simply becomes inapplicable. The person *is* the office, the office *is* the person (…) In other words, faith's decisive statement about Jesus lies in the indivisible unity of the two words 'Jesus Christ'" (Joseph Ratzinger, *Introducción al cristianismo* (Salamanca: Sígueme, 1969), 173–174 [Herder and Herder, 1970, 149–150]. Sequeri adds: "The exercise of the mission is a constitutive moment of the identity of Jesus with the Son, while the bond with the father is the very beginning of the fulfillment of the mission. The being-for-us and the being-of-the-Father form a circle that cannot be interrupted" (107). G. Uribarri also concurs (cf. *Jesucristo, el Hijo: la clave del "yo" de Jesús*, in the aforementioned *Jesucristo en el pensamiento de Joseph Ratzinger* (Madrid: Publicaciones San Dámaso, 2011), 115–156.

28 Ratzinger, *Obras completas, 6, 1: Jesús de Nazaret. Estudios de Cristología*, 89 [*Jesus of Nazareth. The Infancy Narratives* (London: Bloomsbury, 2012), 124].

29 Ratzinger, *Obras completas, 6, 1: Jesús de Nazaret. Estudios de Cristología* (Madrid: BAC, 2015), 91[Bloomsbury, 2012, 127].

30 Ratzinger, *Obras completas, 6, 1: Jesús de Nazaret. Estudios de Cristología* (Madrid: BAC, 2015), 91 [Bloomsbury, 2012, 127].

31 Angelo Amato (in his article: "Cristología católica", *Temes D'avui: Revista de teologia i qüestions actuals* 28 [2008] 38–62), following Ratzinger's *Jesús de Nazaret* and referring to the "implicit or pre-paschal Christology" patent in some passages of the Gospel – and specifically in the Sermon on the Mount – points out that: "The Beatitudes" have a great value for the disciple, since they have been previously lived and realized by Christ himself, as in their prototype. They are a sort of hidden biography of Jesus; his faithful portrait (Joseph Ratzinger-Benedetto XVI, *Gesù di Nazareth*, I, [Milano: Rizzoli, 2007] 98). They also contain concrete elements of an implicit or pre-paschal Christology, which the Pope, in this context, calls "hidden Christology" (Joseph Ratzinger-Benedetto XVI, *Gesù di Nazareth*, I, [Milano: Rizzoli, 2007], 124). Behind the Sermon on the Mount lies the figure of Christ, of that man who is god and who teaches his disciples the paths of true life. One might ask in this regard: should we not also speak, in broad terms, of the "implicit Christology" in the years of Jesus' hidden life and, more specifically, in the working life of Nazareth?

32 Comisión Teológica Internacional, "La conciencia que Jesús tenía de sí mismo y de su misión, proposición primera" eds. Comisión Teológica Internacional, *Documentos 1969–2014* (Madrid: BAC, 2017), 379–392.

Daily life and work in the light of the mystery of Christ   111

33 Proposición segunda (Comisión Teológica Internacional, "La conciencia que Jesús tenía de sí mismo y de su misión, preposición primera" eds. Comisión Teológica Internacional, *Documentos 1969–2014* [Madrid: BAC, 2017]).

34 Proposición cuarta (Comisión Teológica Internacional, "La conciencia que Jesús tenía de sí mismo y de su misión, proposición primera" eds. Comisión Teológica Internacional, *Documentos 1969–2014* [Madrid: BAC, 2017]).

35 Olegario González de Cardedal, *Jesús de Nazaret. Aproximación a la Cristología* (Madrid: BAC, 1975), 374. Our translation.

36 Cf. Olegario González de Cardedal, *Jesús de Nazaret. Aproximación a la Cristología* (Madrid: BAC, 1975), 361–365.

37 Olegario González de Cardedal, *Jesús de Nazaret. Aproximación a la Cristología* (Madrid: BAC, 1975), 368.

38 Cf. Olegario González de Cardedal, *Jesús de Nazaret. Aproximación a la Cristología* (Madrid: BAC, 1975), 371. In other work (cf. *Cristología* [Madrid: BAC, 2001], 436) González de Cardedal writes: "Jesus must be understood as every Jewish child is understood, growing up in a family marked by prayer, the synagogue, the temple, the learning of the law, the rites of initiation both religious and social, (…). Jesus owes the forging of his human soul to his parents, to his village, to the Torah and to the synagogue. To know that soul, one must know the soul of Mary and Joseph, the liturgical ordination of the synagogue of Nazareth, the currents of spirituality, the homiletic orientation and the social legislation, the political and religious situation of the moment in which Jesus was born". Indeed, Christ the man – I would say – had the deep sense of work proper to the Old Testament as God's law for man, as a task entrusted by the Creator, with a sacred value as a means of God's presence. A Rabbi friend of mine, Angel Kreimann Brill † once shared with me his admiration for St. Josemaría's teachings on the sanctification of work. He emphasized that work is also a pathway for a devout Jew to encounter God. However, beyond this, which helps us in contemplating and contextualizing the humanity of Jesus, only the New Testament provides a comprehensive response to the question, "Who Is Jesus?" The New Testament declares that Jesus Christ is the Son of God, who assumed human form and, through His birth from Mary, became fully human. From this perspective, it must be acknowledged that "the man Jesus is not an anomaly of the human to be explained, but, conversely, the goal and norm from which our humanity must be explained as a proficient form" (González de Cardedal, *Cristología* (Madrid: BAC, 2001), 456). The same applies to the meaning of our work.

7 Work, οἰκοδομή and πνεῦμα. A view from the Pauline categories

Juan Luis Caballero

In the New Testament, the reality of work appears in various forms: there is talk of professions and of those who exercise them; there are parables whose context is work; Jesus says that both Him and the Father work; Paul speaks of the need to avoid idle life and to work in order to eat; Luke tells us what profession the Apostle dedicated himself to, etc.[1] There is, however, a reflection on work that is not so explicit, carried out at the level of the theological and anthropological foundations of the gospel. In Paul, in a particularly clear manner, work is closely related to the mystery of Christ and the Church, a mystery that is inseparable from the doctrine of creation, the eternal plans of God and eschatology.

With this approach, we will arrive at a definition of work that we can already present here: all human activity whose purpose is to make the other members of the Body – the whole Body, therefore – participate in the material and spiritual goods that one has, thus contributing to the growth and development of the whole and, therefore, of each of its members. This definition is in line with that which constitutes the starting point of the project in which our study is integrated:

> A type of human activity oriented to the support of one's own life (or also of others' life), which responds to God's call to the perfecting of the person and to collaborate in the development of creation, and which is carried out in a social context, that is, in service to the needs of the human community to which one belongs.[2]

General approach

The reflections that follow intend, in their overarching framework, to contextualize the reality of the work in the context of ecclesiology, specifically Pauline ecclesiology.[3] In Paul's writings, there is an evolution in thought, always stemming from a core foundation. Paul's vision is, at the beginning, more partial, more centered on the concerns of the Judaism of his time. Little by little it will expand, as the mystery of Christ and the Church unfolds

DOI: 10.4324/9781003508212-8

Work, οἰκοδομή and πνεῦμα. A view from the Pauline categories   113

before his eyes.[4] For this reason, the most logical way to approach Paul's theological framework is to begin with his most programmatic writings, in which he expounds his gospel more fully: the Letter to the Romans and, as a harmonious deepening from there, the Letter to the Ephesians, whose reflections are, at the same time, "the starting point of the adventure of faith".[5]

If we read the discursive part of the Letter to the Romans (chapters 1–8) in reverse, a clear thread emerges:[6] God created man to share in the divine life and to procure life through the Spirit (Rom 8:6,13).[7] This life, which is a gift that exceeds mere condition of a creaturely existence, is the life of a son (Rom 8:15), and we have access to it precisely through the Son, who is the one who pours the Spirit into our hearts (Rom 5:5). The Book of Genesis speaks of it in terms of its mission: to govern and care for creation. What God has created is already done, but, at the same time, it is the seed of a newness, which God has placed in the hands of man so that he can make it manifest with his own creativity (Gen 1:26–30; 2:15,19–29). In Christ, it will be revealed to us that this "man" called to govern and care for creation is the Church, the Body of the Son. Furthermore, the Church embodies a mission in herself. The Church herself is gospel; she herself forms part of the gospel; she herself is at the heart of God's eternal plans. She is not simply the one who receives, guards, and proclaims the gospel. She herself is called by God to build herself up and to eternal life.

The normal development of this life, however, has been cut short by the irruption of sin and death into the world (Rom 5:12).[8] The plight of man in the grip of sin consists in the fact that, although he understands that this life is his deepest aspiration, he is unable to follow its paths. His heart, untransformed by grace, is governed by another law from which he is unable to free himself (Rom 7:19,21,22,25). In this context, Paul strives to illustrate what the work of Christ entails and how redemption and grace have lifted him from a self-centred mentality – something that radically affects the reality of work – opening him to conceive his own existence as worship, as service to God in the brethren (Rom 12:1).

Thus, we can say that in man, there is a "total tension" towards life, just as there is in all creation. But, in the case of man, it is a tension towards a life of which he alone is capable, albeit as something that is beyond his power to procure. This life is already begun through baptism (Rom 6:4), but at the same time, it is something that is still to be fully attained. This life is, moreover, intrinsically linked to the life of the Church, of its members in union with its head, Christ, who recapitulates and unites with the Father (1 Cor 15:20–28). This life has its own dynamic, in the image of the divine life. Paul speaks of it, based on the divine plan of creation described in Genesis, in terms of the building up of the Church, the Body of Christ, the family of God (Eph 2:19–22). It is here that the reality of work is situated, precisely as the building up of the Church, called to govern and care for the whole of creation, hence its cosmic dimension (Eph 4:12).

114 *Juan Luis Caballero*

Pauline images

In his writings, Paul frequently uses various images to describe the Church. We will focus on three images that are especially relevant to his ecclesiology. We could also mention others that are, in a certain way, closer to the world of work, specifically those that refer to professions: agriculture, sports, or the military. But we cannot delve into all of them, and for our intended illustration, the central ones are those related to the family, the house, and the body. In any case, there is contiguity between them. Suffice it to think, for example, that when Paul uses agricultural images – with great emphasis on the "fruits"[9] – there is a clear evocation of the vineyard and the vinedressers, a very ecclesiological image. God's vineyard is His people. We are His plantation, a plantation called to grow and bear fruit. Those who must work in it are men. To be able to work on it and care for it, we must look upon it with love, which is sometimes not easy – the vineyards are usually not particularly beautiful, but rather arid and desolate – and without possessiveness or mere profit. Thus, the vinedressers must work knowing that the vineyard is not theirs, but has been entrusted to them. They must work with the mindset of the owner, since they are not the owners. They should know that what is expected of them is to see to it that the vineyard bears fruit without exploiting it for their own benefit.[10]

But let's move on to the images we want to focus on, and then propose a working definition based on them.

The image of the family

Paul speaks of the Church as the mystery hidden from the ages and now revealed in Christ (Eph 3:3–9). We have already seen that Paul resorts to various images to speak of the Church. Although the image of the family of God is not the most common,[11] we can begin with it, because it best reflects an aspect of the core of the Church,[12] which is directly connected with what was prefigured in the Old Testament.[13] Once the essential aspect of his identity, namely, looking to God as Father,[14] was obscured after the first sin, having been removed from the tree of life (Gen 3:22–24), man must rediscover and learn, through his journey, his status as a son of God. From this realization stems his understanding of himself as a brother to other sons and daughters. The divine pedagogy thus begins with the formation of a people. To this people God makes promises and offers very particular aid to live the law that leads to life. He accompanies this people as a good pedagogue in their preparation to welcome the full revelation of what He offers them. Man is essentially defined by his relational nature,[15] as the image of God (Gen 1:27), specifically of the Son, and this relational being is lived in a very particular way by living as the people of God. This is precisely what was broken as the culmination of the rejection of God when we left Eden, when we built the Tower of Babel (Gen 11:1–9). And this is what must be rebuilt if man really wants the divine plans to be realized.

Work, οἰκοδομή and πνεῦμα. A view from the Pauline categories   115

Living as a son and as a people is expressed in an admirable way in the Decalogue, the essential law of life (Ex 20:1–17). In it, the sovereignty of God and his creative plan, realities of which the precept of the Sabbath speaks, are placed as the foundation. And after these, the laws that reach their full meaning when the people are conceived as a family, and that refer to their relational character, beginning with the veneration for the parents.[16] But the people do not know or do not want to live according to this plan, and they cyclically conform to the closed mentality of the surrounding peoples. This mentality emulates the self-sufficiency of sinful Adam, and identifies life with conquest and a certain type of domination, by force if necessary, and with separation from the rest of the peoples. In reality, in Israel's journey, there is a continuous mixture of motivations, a consequence of the darkness that clouds their hearts due to their unfaithfulness to the Covenant sealed with God. This erratic journey is what causes the people to end up dwindled and dispersed among the neighbouring peoples, except for a faithful remnant, from which the Church will be born.

Although Paul speaks of the Church – in one way or another – in all his writings, it is in the First Letter to the Corinthians and, above all, in the Letter to the Ephesians that he tries to expound this mystery with greater breadth and depth. God wants humanity to be one and at the same time diverse (cf. Jn 17:21–23). The Letter to the Ephesians speaks of this: the Church is a mystery to be believed in and lived, a mystery of unity in diversity, a mystery of communion in love, where we learn to love by being loved, where we learn to work by seeing the work of others. In Christ, all the walls of separation between peoples, between pagans and Jews, have been broken down. Now, in him, all have access to the same inheritance. Now, in him, the Church can grow as a harmoniously united Body (Eph 4:11–16).

In speaking of the family, Paul does not overlook that there is something that impedes its growth and development towards maturity: sin. From its origin, in Eden, it is a movement of possessiveness, pride, and greed. This desire has shaped man's heart to some extent – with wounds consistent with the nature of sin – directly impacting the reality of work, which is now self-centred, focused on one's own (misunderstood) fulfilment. on one's own benefit.[17] To refer to this sad reality, the Apostle uses these terms: emptiness, frustration, vanity, darkness, ignorance, hardness, insensitivity, licentiousness, impurity, old man, seductive appetites, sin, bad words, etc. All these expressions refer to ignorance and wickedness, to deceit and seduction, to worldly and self-absorbed mentality. The tragedy of the darkness of the heart is that it neither desires nor can it shape its life as service to others, to neighbors, to brothers, to the Body. And this causes him to languish, since he belongs to that same Body which he ignores. Hence the Apostle's insistence: "And to be renewed in the spirit of your minds, and to clothe yourselves with the new self, created according to the likeness of God in true righteousness and holiness" (Eph 4:23–24). It is this renewal that will enable man to truly become a family.[18]

116   *Juan Luis Caballero*

The image of the house

Also, in the Pauline writings, we find the image of the house applied to the Church, closely related to the terminology of building.[19] This image is completely intertwined with that of the family. On the one hand, the house itself is conceived as a home for the family. But it is not only that. The image, taken to the extreme, overlaps with that of the family when both realities are identified: the house, ultimately, is the family. However, this does not detract from the fact that the image of the house also has great force in relation to what we instinctively conceive of as house, and in its various elements. Thus, the Pauline writings speak of "the household of God, which is the Church of the living God, the pillar and bulwark of the truth" (1 Tim 3:15), a building constructed on the foundation of the apostles and prophets (Eph 2:20).

This image of the house evokes the solidity of the foundations, a common home in which to feel safe and loved, in which to rest, to feed, to relate, to learn and teach, to welcome with hospitality, to value, to share.[20] This living together is based on something that does not change, a spirit that enlivens everything. The house, moreover, is a structure that, on the one hand, lacks walls of separation, but, on the other hand, has rooms which enable the intimacy necessary for relationships. At the centre of the house is the place where food is shared, the source of life. This goes beyond the material aspect of eating. What builds the family is not so much each person being fed, but the sharing of food as a sacred encounter, insofar as it is directly related to life. This includes the giving of oneself to one another, with welcoming and listening. Ultimately, what is lived and shared is a spirit. Paul is no stranger to this, and in his writings, he speaks of the importance of nourishing oneself by giving thanks to God for all his gifts (1 Tim 4:4). Thus, as a whole, the image of the house, of the home, referring in itself to something perishable, that crumbles with time – a building made of stones – being intertwined with that of the family, also speaks of something permanent, which is precisely the family relationship that, when lived in the Church, builds it up as something called to last forever.

The image of the body

Paul finds in the image of the body an extremely useful instrument for speaking about the mystery of the Church.[21] Aletti says that there is a need for a renewed, in-depth study of the potential of this image: the Church is the body of the risen Christ![22] The approach that follows will seek to draw especially from the reality of the human body, of whose vital dynamics we all have an immediate experience and therefore find so familiar. Moreover, as science deepens our knowledge of the body in various dimensions, we gain more insight into the mystery for which the body has been used as an image. But without forgetting that the Body which is the Church participates in the life of the Risen One, it is vivified by His Spirit. The Church is not just any body. Its fullness is not just any fullness.

Work, οἰκοδομή and πνεῦμα. A view from the Pauline categories 117

Each image used by Paul seeks to illuminate an aspect of the mystery of God, of Christ, and of the Church. In fact, in each argument, it is only certain aspects that seek to be illuminated. No single image could encompass them all by itself. Thus Paul speaks of the body and its members, of their greater or lesser nobility, of weakness and strength, of cooperation or solidarity among them, of health and sickness and, finally, of capitality (cf. 1 Cor 12:12–27). Everything in the body works for the life of the whole and of each of its members. Its life is not the sum of the life of each member, but it is the life of the whole, to which all contribute, knowing that they are all subordinate to one another. Studies on the corporate personality have made it possible to deepen this vision of the body as applied to the Church.[23]

We could say, looking at the image of the body, that its life comes from everyone, moved by the head – which, acting through its spirit, is what gives unity and coherence to the whole, and therefore it is which provides growth (1 Cor 3:6–9) – putting what is unique to them, their potentiality, and their goods, in relation to others. Doing this allows everyone, after being given what they do not have, to develop their potentialities in turn. This is an open and dynamic system, in which each member does not think only of themselves, but are continually open to balance the imbalances that are produced by the relationship among themselves and with the external environment. This image is directly applicable to humanity understood as a body. It is not only that the life of each person is governed by what has just been described, but also that humanity as a whole has life and grows and develops to the extent that it follows this same dynamic, knowing that they are all members of the same body and knowing that they are all members of one another (Rom 12:5).

A definition of work

The three Pauline images mentioned in the preceding sections coincide in their essential elements: God's plans for man revolve around life, manifested in the dynamic of growth and development of the Body toward maturity;[24] relationships and mutual subordination; finally, life through the Spirit "in the Body of Christ". These elements can already be both explicitly and implicitly found in the divine command given to man:

> God blessed them, saying to them, 'Be fruitful and multiply and fill the earth and subdue it and have dominion over the fish of the sea and over the birds of the air and over every living thing that moves upon the earth',
>
> (Gen 1:28)[25]

but they only acquire their full significance in light of the revelation in Christ. Man, from the very moment of his creation, enjoys a natural grace that allows him to be open to God and to his plans.[26] It is sin that produces darkness and

118   *Juan Luis Caballero*

insubordination within man himself: distrust and disobedience to God result in a disruption in the dominion that man has over his own faculties and in the dominion – government and care – that man is called to exercise over creation with his own work, thus causing it to be subjected to frustration (Rom 8:19–23).

From this point, we can address these questions: What is it that must be governed and cared for, that is, what is it that must grow and be built? What is the dynamic of this building? What are the laws that govern it? What is to be said about those who build and about the mind with which they do it?

Work and building

We have previously spoken of three Pauline images: the family, the house, and the body. To these, we could add that of the temple. In his study of Pauline ecclesiology, Lucien Cerfaux says that the Apostle combines his images as he progresses in his understanding of the mystery of the Church.[27] Thus, man is called to collaborate in the construction of the heavenly Jerusalem, a city in which he will dwell with God, participating in his vital force. This heavenly city, whose foundation is the apostles and prophets and whose cornerstone is Christ –the one who provides consistency and cohesion – has the saints as its citizens, the "household of God". In it, those previously considered Gentiles will no longer be strangers without the right of citizenship, but will form with the others a single people, "fellow citizens with the saints and also members of the household of God" (Eph 2:19). But then, this city is seen as a holy temple of the Lord, "in whom you also are built together spiritually into a dwelling place for God" (Eph 2:22). This dwelling is the abiding in one another; it is relationship-communion.

Several essential elements are interwoven in this image. On the one hand, all of us are called to participate in a building with a heavenly vocation, which will be God's dwelling place through the Spirit. This construction is already beginning to be built here and is none other than the Body of Christ, "from whom the whole body, joined and knit together by every ligament with which it is equipped, as each part is working properly, promotes the body's growth in building itself up in love" (Eph 4:16). The Church, the Body of Christ, is therefore the heavenly temple that God builds, a new and spiritual temple that replaces the old one.[28] In this heavenly Jerusalem, there is no longer a temple, but the whole community constitutes the temple, all of it consecrated to spiritual worship (Rev 21:22). In Paul, the whole city is a temple, and the temple is mystically identified with the Body of Christ.[29]

Therefore, who builds and what is being built? God builds through men. What He builds is the Church, which is His dwelling place.[30] The one who guides this building is the head, Christ, and the one who makes it possible is the Spirit. What defines the Church is the communion among her members and of all of them with her head and, through her, the communion with God the Father. Therein lies her life, her vitality. The journey of building is the

Work, οἰκοδομή and πνεῦμα. A view from the Pauline categories 119

relationship governed by love,[31] with the firm awareness of being children of God in Christ and brothers and sisters among ourselves. For this reason, when Paul speaks to Christians – his letters are addressed to them – he expresses himself in the plural: he uses "we"; he uses "brethren", he uses expressions that refer to "one another".[32] The same concept of "charism", coined by him, refers to divine gifts received for the benefit or advantage of the whole Body (1 Cor 12:7).[33]

Thus, we could begin by defining work as every human activity whose purpose is to share with the other members of the Body – the entire Body, therefore – the material and spiritual goods that one possesses, thus contributing to the growth and development of the whole and, therefore, of each of its members. In other words, work would be every human action that seeks to provide nourishment to the rest of the Body, directly or indirectly. This nourishment is both material and spiritual, reflecting the nature of the Body.[34] Man is thus called to participate in the act of providing each individual with their nourishment in due time as designated by God.[35] It is the Body, therefore, in which each member lives and through and for which each member lives.

The dynamics of building

Paul tells the Corinthians that we are collaborators with God and that it is He who provides growth. Moreover, we are God's building, God's field (1 Cor 3:9). It is in this context that man's work is situated. The Johannine image of the vine and the branches is very illustrative in this regard: it is the vine that makes the fruit possible, but that fruit arises from the branch that is attached to the vine (Jn 15:1–11). Within the body, fruit represents strengthening, development, and growth. This idea of fruit is very present in the preaching of Jesus,[36] and resonates in all Pauline and Johannine theology.

Since man is created in the image and likeness of the Son and is therefore called to live as a son in the Son, the work of Christ illuminates the dynamics of human work in an extraordinary way. Christ lovingly takes on the whole of creation – in fact, at its origin is the wisdom and power of the Word – and frees it from the bonds that have led it to vanity, that impede or hinder the development of its life (Col 1:15–20). Christ invites us to assume the mandate given in Paradise with a renewed mind. Human work, therefore, possesses both an aspect of liberation and an aspect of construction, with inherent creativity empowered by the action of the Spirit.

We rely here, once again, on the image of the human body. Life arises through the act of giving within relationships. Thus, work can be conceived as a "gift" or "transfusion" of life. And also as "liberation" of a life that was hidden and was as "possible". All life has its origin in God, but man contributes, with his loving work, to bring it forth and extend it to where it was not before. This process also includes removing the obstacles that prevent it from flowing, fostering the conditions for it to emerge, and with his own ingenuity and creativity, discovering new synergies – relationships that provide

120   *Juan Luis Caballero*

life, that "liberate" it. Thus, the human organism possesses mechanisms of effusion of life and self-regulation in response to the imbalances produced by relationships, both within the organism and with the external environment, which can be sometimes intrusive and hinder life. Only when the organism is properly prepared can its life grow and develop. This is an expression, at this level, of the mandate given to man: life must be nurtured and governed in its growth and development, safeguarding what enables it.

This dynamic we are discussing is governed, in turn, by the law of the old and the new. That is to say, the liberation of life does not occur if the new is not given upon something that remains. What remains (the *logos*) is the condition of possibility for the new (the *agape*) to be true and truly fruit-ful, that is, something that remains in time. If this is not so, development and growth will be something fictitious, a mere façade. In fact, both Paul's theological model and the Johannine model emphasize the destructiveness of appearances and lies. One can work hard and creatively, but if it is done without regard to the nature of what one seeks to build, that is, the Church and, therefore, the divine plan for the world, one is not truly building. A lot of work can be done, but if it is done for a murky motive, it will not be edi-fied. And, in the end, it is the fruit – its presence or absence – that will show how it has been built up (1 Cor 3:10–15).

We can bring what has been said up to this point down to the realm of the ordinary, including the more socio-economic sphere. To work is to build. To build is to establish relationships – so that it can be shared – with the aim of giving life to the body, contributing the novelty that each one is and has, one's own genius. In order to be able to do this, it is necessary to cultivate each one's own capabilities and, at the same time, to internalize the ultimate meaning behind our occupations. Work does not depend only on having the possibility to work and to do it creatively, although this is fundamental. The uniqueness that is each of us, the novelty of our thoughts and works, will be enhanced to the extent that we open ourselves to God's plans and do not put ourselves in His place. It is striking how, in some aspects of science, we have advanced so little, although there is an appearance of significant progress – along with, at times, a setback. This is because something within the human spirit acts as a brake, a darkening of reason and weakening of the will and, not infrequently, a patent foolishness when it comes to proposing and developing projects. The path of life will always involve working on cre-ating unions through which life can flow – like a shared road, or a new link between blood circulatory pathways, for example – rather than separating and uniting the reality before us "on a whim", without considering whether what we do will directly or indirectly serve to unite people.

The laws of building

The recent document of the Pontifical Biblical Commission on Biblical Anthro-pology devotes a few pages to speak of the "laws of work".[37] This document

Work, οἰκοδομή and πνεῦμα. A view from the Pauline categories   121

states that human work must be carried out in accordance with certain laws in order to respond to the plan of the Creator and Lord:

> What is important is not so much the concrete work that is done, but the way it is done and the intentions with which it is carried out. Work cannot become a place of arrogant self-affirmation, tyranny or slavery to others, but must be true service: a gift for the benefit of others. God himself, by creating and being providentially present in human history, has placed himself at our service; from him we learn the true nature of work.[38]

At the heart of these laws is the "Sabbath", assuming the role of a limit, becoming a "sign" of the consecration of time ("to sanctify it") and a sign of the relationship with God ("for the Lord"). The Sabbath, moreover, in the perspective unique to Deuteronomy, serves to "remember" (Dt 5:15) Egyptian slavery, from which the Lord has rescued Israel.[39]

> The document also mentions the directives that refer to Sunday, the Lord's day, a memorial of salvation, a time of gratuitous prayer and solidarity, which has a prophetic dimension[40] and which is a symbolic anticipation of the new heavens and the new earth (Rev 1:10).[41]

Based on these considerations, we can place at the centre of the laws of work precisely the day of the week that reminds us that we are not creators, that we are not self-sufficient, that life depends on accepting limits, that we work to rest – it is the six days of work that give meaning to the day of rest – that the key to life lies in opening up to others and relating to them outside the realm of utility, without succumbing to the dictatorship of the "conquest of space",[42] that is, the dictatorship of technique, profit, efficiency, and possession. In fact, this law of the Sabbath is about recognizing oneself as a trustee of a power and an authority that come from God.[43] They must be used to govern and care according to the divine mind, not to prolong one's own self in the appropriation of others and of what is beyond oneself, placing the key to the desired life in the despotic dominion of what is beyond me.[44]

The essential law of truly human work is that of love. In practice, Paul articulates in a very radical way: it is a matter of living for the other (2 Cor 5:15), of living in the other, of remaining in the other, in Johannine terminology (Jn 17:11, 21–23). Love leads us to see ourselves in the other, not as a possessive act, but rather as an oblation act, with the awareness that working by giving oneself to others – thinking of the Body, being open to the Body – leads to an enhancement of the life of the Body to which one belongs. This, in turn, results in a life from which one benefits, but multiplied and enriched by belonging to a Body with many members.

This leads us to the fact that, *de facto*, the two laws that must govern our work are love of God and love of neighbor (Gal 5:14), in keeping with the

122   Juan Luis Caballero

nature of the Body that is being built. In reality, it is a question of a single law – that of charity – which encompasses these two statements, ultimately implying each other. But this love, again with a disconcerting expression of Paul, implies a breaking down of something so that something may be built up (2 Cor 4:16-5:10). What crumbles is the material; what is built up is the spiritual. What crumbles little by little is that which is outdated; what rises is that which endures. Thus, to bring the reasoning down to a more concrete level, in work, the most determining factor is not so much what is done – building a bridge, for example – as what that work achieves: that people can communicate and relate to each other. The bridge will eventually fall down, but the communion created between people will remain forever.

Building and the Spirit

Up to this point we have proposed a definition of work in the context of ecclesiology, starting from the Pauline images of family, house, and body. We have also mentioned that the Church is the Body of the Risen One, and therefore participates in its meaning – the communion produced by love – and potentiality – the power of the Spirit (Eph 1:15–19). This means that the communion to which the human family is called as Church cannot be reduced to a merely sociological conception, but is called to something that only grace can produce. Therefore, the concepts of union, collaboration, agreement, etc., are not enough. The communion in which we intend to situate the reality of human work goes beyond that. The building we have discussed cannot be identified with the construction of a material building, nor is it along the lines of an association of persons who share interests.

We start from the conviction that what ultimately defines human work is not so much the materiality of what is done, but the intention and the mind with which man carries out his activities. Therefore, beyond a question of organization, techniques, etc., there is something more fundamental: what is conceived as work, and therefore, the mindset of the worker. In Pauline terminology, this can be discussed by referring to the expressions "old man" and "new man". The Johannine images of "darkness" and "light" are along the same lines.

Old man and new man

One of the nuclear points of Pauline anthropology is found in his notion of the "new man". This man is presented in contrast to the old man, characterized by his way of "thinking," understood as the way of thinking about one's own existence, focused solely on oneself. The new man, on the other hand, is the one who has risen with Christ, who has been incorporated into the Church, who has received the Spirit, who has a renewed mind, who has opened himself completely to others, who is already capable of aspiring to the goods from above, and who has entered into the realm of divine wisdom guided by the Spirit.[45] Also in his great letters, Paul speaks of this reality (1Co 2:14; 2Co 5:16–17; Ga 5:16–17; Rom 12:2).

Work, οἰκοδομή and πνεῦμα. A view from the Pauline categories   123

This vision finds continuity in the captivity letters, where there is a further elaboration on the image of the kingdom of darkness and the kingdom of light, especially in Colossians and Ephesians, where he uses terms of realized eschatology (Phil 2:4–5.21; Col 3:1–3; Eph 2:5–6; 4:1).

Paul insists – particularly in these last letters – that the baptized individual has been liberated from the power of the law of sin and the dominion of darkness, which led him to have a futile mindset, to desire deeds of death, to live selfishly, and to lead a vain existence.[46] The presence of the Spirit has brought about a radical transformation for man, a regeneration which has opened him to another way of seeing the world and of conceiving his own existence. This is what characterizes the new man: the possibility of having the mind of a resurrected person, since he is part of the Body of the Risen One. With this mind, man can no longer conceive his life detached from the Body to which he belongs, he can no longer conceive his work detached from the life of the "organism" to which he belongs. This is what will enable him to manifest himself as a son of God and thus make it possible for creation to cease to be subject to vanity (Rom 8:19–22).

The action of the Holy Spirit

Throughout the exposition we have frequently mentioned the Holy Spirit. We have defined work in relation to the building of a spiritual edifice called to remain and which has an eschatological vocation. This spiritual edifice is built by God with the help of man, but specifically the "spiritual man," to use Pauline terminology. The one who makes the spiritual man is the Holy Spirit. All the Pauline letters devote considerable space to discussing the action of the Spirit in the baptized person, insofar as he or she is receptive to its interior influence. For this reason, in these reflections on work in the context of ecclesiology, a reference to the action of the Spirit in the new man cannot be missing.[47]

Paul himself, as Luke reminds us in his Acts of the Apostles, says that at the heart of his gospel is the fulfilment in Christ of the promises of God made to the people of Israel. These promises include the outpouring of the Holy Spirit, the transformation of the heart and the formation of a "new people". And all of this is an expression of the new creation, a reality that, in a certain way, Paul identifies with salvation.[48] In fact, the redeemed and baptized man is already a new creation, he is clothed, he is a new man – he is the Church (Eph 4:20–24). It is not that he has received a new light, but that he is a new light. To renew the mind is not to give it light from time to time, but to "make it luminous". We can then trace in the Pauline writings what the action of the Spirit in the baptized person is and what enables him to cooperate with God in nothing less than the new creation:

a In the first place, the Spirit *frees* us from the power of sin, opens our eyes so that we can return from darkness to light and from Satan's dominion to God. It is, therefore, the opposite movement to the "opening of the eyes" that sin produces (Gen 3:7), which leads to confusion and despair.

124 *Juan Luis Caballero*

Sin has "hindered" that "natural grace" that was in Adam and Eve, which allowed them to be open to God and his plans, and has introduced them into the world of selfishness and greed, which appear with the pretension of life.[49] The Spirit frees us from the clutches of this seduction and lie.[50] He helps us to have good self-control (Gal 5:1). He helps us to overcome pride and greed. He frees us from the desire for possessiveness. The Spirit brings peace and hope (Rom 5:1–2). The Spirit brings rest.

b The Spirit *enables* us to see things with greater breadth and depth, both in space and in time, introducing us into the breadth and depth of God (1 Cor 2:14) and making us participants in the treasures of His wisdom.[51] In fact, the Spirit renews the human heart, making it "intimate with the law of God" (Eph 4:23), which is the source of the highest wisdom.[52] In the Spirit (Rom 5:5) we can call God the Father (Rom 8:15) and open ourselves to his plans and accept and understand them, as far as a creature can. Without the Spirit, desires, aspirations, and endeavors easily become trapped in the present moment, focusing only on the here and now, disregarding the surrounding context and the implications in space and time. The Spirit places our desires, our decisions, and our work in a broader and deeper context. He makes us participants in Christ and his wisdom (Heb 3:14). In both the Pauline and Johannine writings, knowledge and wisdom, seen from this perspective, have a significant relevance (1 Cor 2:6–16).[53]

c The Spirit *inspires* in us the desire to support the divine plans and *gives* us *the strength* to do so (Phil 2:13), no longer as servants but as "friends" (Jn 15:15). Concretely, it enables us to have the same sentiments as Christ,[54] who loved the Church and gave himself up for her, to consecrate her and make her glorious (Eph 5:25–27). This is the spiritual edifice to which man, moved by the Spirit, devotes all his efforts (1 Cor 3:4–17). The Spirit opens us to the solidarity unique to communion and leads us out of the slavery of individualism. In this sense, the Spirit enables us to participate in the permanent newness of the Risen One through love, which is "the ever new," making us true collaborators with God in the transformation of the world and the establishment of his kingdom. The Spirit enables us to manifest ourselves as children of God (Rom 8:16,19).

d The Spirit *makes the Church*, making us all members of one another (Eph 4:25), allowing us to remain in one another, to feel with the same Spirit, and thus to live communion, unity in diversity, without anyone ceasing to be himself (Jn 17:21). The Spirit opens us to conceive human relationships not in terms of usefulness or efficiency, but in terms of gratuitousness, acceptance, and self-giving,[55] for the sake of mutual edification (Rom 14:1–15:13). This is the mystery of the communion of the baptized. Thus it is the Spirit who, with His gifts, empowers our good desires, helping us to live mutual charity and the Decalogue in its fullness, avoiding anything that separates, and yielding fruit to our works (Gal 5:22–23).

Work, οἰκοδομή and πνεῦμα. A view from the Pauline categories 125

Conclusions

The theology of work, in dialogue with the other sciences, must confront a wide variety of issues. In this study we have tried to focus, ultimately, on a specific aspect: the mind of the worker. The conviction with which these reflections have been made is that, although the job, salary, recognition, and job training are central issues, there is something of radical importance beforehand: how the worker conceives his work, something that is closely related to the conception of man–humanity that one has. Work is, in short, something that the Body of Christ does for and on behalf of the Body of Christ, remembering that all men are called by God to have fullness of life within this Body.

In the building of this Body and in the government and care of the creation entrusted to this Body, all can and must contribute. But for them to do so and bear true fruit, they must allow themselves to be guided by the Spirit of God, who liberates, enlightens, opens, inspires, strengthens, unites, and builds. This implies the continuous renewal of the "thinking" of each of the members of the Body, which implies a "cultivation" both materially and spiritually, so that, upon what is common and permanent, the singular, the creative, what is unique to each one can emerge and develop for the benefit of the whole. Life emerges from those new relationships that each one, moved by the mind of Christ, makes between created realities, liberating and providing ever new life. That is: bringing to light that possibility of newness that God has placed in everything created and that only becomes a reality in the personal relationship that each one has with others and with the rest of created beings. This work will be as diversified as its object: to care, to govern, to educate, etc.

But, emphasizing the question of novelty, intrinsically related to the renewal of the mind by the Spirit, we would like to conclude by bringing it down to a very practical aspect: something that characterizes truly human work is the awareness that everyone can contribute something new with his or her work. Renouncing this novelty, perhaps by only aspiring for a mechanical occupation and turning oneself into a "process" – that is, putting oneself at the service of a process, which is understandable if it is for the need of a salary – slows down the growth dynamic of the Body, called by God to continuously live from the novelty of Christ. Only this will allow it, little by little, to lovingly govern and care for this immense creation of which we still know so little.

Notes

1 Cf., for example, Mt 9:9; 21 33–46; Jn 5:17; Acts 18:2; 2 Thess 3:10.
2 Gregorio Guitián and Ana Marta González, "Theology of Work: New Perspectives," *Scripta Theologica* 54 (2022): 761.
3 Cf. Jean-Noël Aletti, *Essai sur l'ecclésiologie des Lettres de Saint Paul* (Paris: Gabalda et Cie, 2009); Jordi Sánchez Bosch, *Maestro de los pueblos. Una teología de Pablo, el Apóstol* (Estella: Verbo Divino, 2007), 393–690.

126 *Juan Luis Caballero*

4 Thesis of Lucien Cerfaux, *The Spiritual Journey of Saint Paul* (New York: Sheed and Ward, 1968).
5 Jean-Noël Aletti, *Saint Paul. Épître aux Éphésiens* (Paris: Gabalda, 2001), 325–326.
6 Jean-Noël Aletti, "Romans," *The International Bible Commentary,* ed. William R. Farmer (Collegeville, MI: The Liturgical Press, 1998), 1553–1600 (here, 1557–1588); Giuseppe Barbaglio, *Il pensare dell'apostolo Paolo* (Bologna: EDB, 2004), 185–209.
7 The "Vitality of this Life", its fruitfulness, whose source is the tree of life – God, in short, is marvelously expressed in passages such as Ezek 47:1–12 and Rev 22:1–3.
8 James D.G. Dunn, *The Theology of Paul the Apostle* (Grand Rapids, MI: Eerdmans, 1998), 102–127.
9 Cf. 1 Cor 3:6–9; 9:7,10; 15:20,23,36–38; 2 Cor 9:6–10; Gal 5:22–23; Rom 1:13; 6:21–22; 8:23; 11:16–24; 15:28; 16:5; Phil 1:11,22; 4:17.
10 Cf. Ps 80:9–19; Is 5:1–2; 27:2–5; Jer 2:21; 5:10; 6:9; 12:10; Ezek 15:1–8; 17:3–10; 19:10–14; Mt 21:33–46; Jn 15:1–11.
11 Raymond F. Collins, *The Power of Images in Paul* (Collegeville, MI: The Liturgical Press, 2008), 225–227.
12 Cfr. Rafael Alvira, *El lugar al que se vuelve. Reflexiones sobre la familia* (Pamplona: Eunsa, 2000); Eloy Tejero, *El evangelio de la casa y de la familia* (Pamplona: Eunsa, 2014).
13 Cf. Ramiro Pellitero, ed., *La Iglesia como familia de Dios* (Madrid: Rialp, 2010).
14 Thesis of Dominique Barthélemy, *God and His Image. An Outline of Biblical Theology* (San Francisco: Ignatius Press, 2007). After sin, man does the exact opposite of what the Son does: to stand before the Father, to look Him face to face (Jn 1:1–2).
15 José Manuel Fidalgo, *Antropología. Para entender al ser humano* (Pamplona: Eunsa, 2023), 103–127; Juan Luis Caballero, "Freedom and Dependence in the Pauline Writings. A Theological Approach according to Colossians and Ephesians," *Θεολογια* 93, no. 3 (2022): 7–33.
16 Cf. Carlos Granados, *El Decálogo. Diez palabras de vida* (Madrid: Didaskalos, 2023).
17 Paradoxical is what goes through Cain's heart when he offers God gifts for the fruits of his labor, which God does not consider as a true gift (Gen 4:5).
18 See in this line the household codes of Col 3:18–4:1 and Eph 5:21–6:9, in which the key is always found in the "in Christ".
19 Raymond F. Collins, *The Power of Images in Paul* (Collegeville MI: The Liturgical Press, 2008), 243–245.
20 Cf. Rafael Alvira and Rafael Hurtado, *Oikía y polis. La familia, raíz y alma de toda la sociedad* (Pamplona: Eunsa, 2023), 59–72.
21 Raymond F. Collins, *The Power of Images in Paul* (Collegeville MI: The Liturgical Press, 2008), 228–229; Pierre Benoit, "Corps, tête et plérôme dans les Épîtres de la Captivité," *Revue Biblique* 63 (1956): 5–44.
22 Jean-Noël Aletti, *Saint Paul. Épître aux Éphésiens* (Paris: Gabalda, 2001), 324–325.
23 Cf. Luis Sánchez Navarro, *Un cuerpo pleno. Cristo y la personalidad corporativa en la Escritura* (Madrid: Universidad San Dámaso, 2021).
24 This law of life is the law of charity. In charity one can always grow, so that maturity is not a closed point of arrival, but a permanent point of departure, expressed by Paul with the idea of permanent progress (cf. 1 Thess 4:1,10; Col 3:14).
25 Juan Luis Caballero, "Elementos para una teología paulina del trabajo. En torno al documento '¿Qué es el hombre?'," *Scripta Theologica* 53 (2021): 172–174.
26 Cf. Santiago Sanz, *Alfa e omega. Breve manuale di protologia ed escatologia* (Verona: Fede & Cultura, 2021), 176–203.

Work, οἰκοδομή and πνεῦμα. A view from the Pauline categories   127

27 Lucien Cerfaux, *The Church in the Theology of St. Paul* (Freiburg: Herder, 1959), 345–347.
28 Cf. Jn 2:19–21; Gal 4:26. In the background, is 28:16.
29 In John's gospel, the Temple is the resurrected body of Christ (cf. Jn 2:19). In the Apocalypse, the Temple is replaced by God and the Lamb (cf. Rev 21:22).
30 The idea of dwelling refers to that of rest, to which we will refer briefly below. This rest refers directly to God's plans for man, an invitation to accept God's sovereignty, thus accepting the limits of the creaturely condition, and consideration of that to which God calls with work: precisely to "rest" (in Him). See Abraham J. Heschel, *The Sabbath. Its Meaning for Modern Man* (New York: The Noonday Press, 1994), and the theology of the Letter to the Hebrews on rest. Cf. Iswadi Prayidno, "The New and Greater Exodus: an Implication of Unaccomplished Exodus in Hebrews 4:8," *Cuadernos Doctorales de la Facultad de Teología* 71 (2022): 7–83.
31 Cf. John Taylor, "Labour of Love: The Theology of Work in First and Second Thessalonians," *Work: Theological Foundations and Practical Implications*, eds. R. Keith Loftin and Trey Dimsdale (London: SCM Press, 2018), 49–68.
32 Rom 15:7; Col 3:13; Gal 5:13–14; 6:2; etc.
33 Cf. Enrique Nardoni, "The Concept of Charism in Paul," *Catholic Biblical Quarterly* 55 (1993): 68–80; Ugo Vanni, *L'ebbrezza nello Spirito. Una proposta di spiritualità paolina* (Roma: AdP, 2000); Albert Vanhoye, *I Carismi nel Nuovo Testamento* (Roma: Pontificio Istituto Biblico, 2011).
34 Cf. Jn 4:34; 6:27. The fullness of life is in the spiritual order, and we see this continually in daily life when people so often prefer a good personal relationship to an optimal material condition.
35 Cf. Lev 26:3–5; Ps 145:15–16; Mt 24:45.
36 Cf. Mt 21:18–22,33–46; 23:13–36; 25:14–30.
37 The Pontifical Biblical Commission (PBC), *What Is Man?: A Journey Through Biblical Anthropology*, (London: Darton Longman & Todd Ltd, 2021), 113–120.
38 Caballero, "Elementos para una teología paulina del trabajo. En torno al documento '¿Qué es el hombre?'", *Scripta Theologica* 53 (2021): 174.
39 PBC, *What Is Man? A Journey Through Biblical Anthropology*, (London: Darton Longman and Todd Ltd, 2021), nn. 114–115. Cf. Ex 20:8–11; 31:13–15,17; Num 15:32–36; Deut 5:12–15; Ezek 20:12.
40 Since it not only affirms the absolute primacy of God, but also the dignity of man that must prevail over any economic or organisational consideration (cf. PBC, *What Is Man? A Journey Through Biblical Anthropology* (London: Darton Longman and Todd Ltd, 2021) 117).
41 Caballero, "Elementos para una teología paulina del trabajo. En torno al documento '¿Qué es el hombre?'", *Scripta Theologica* 53 (2021): 175.
42 This is the terminology used by Heschel in the aforementioned book.
43 Jean-Noël Aletti, "Paul et les autorités politiques. À propos de Rm 13,1–7," in (dir.) Didier Luciani and André Wénin, *Le pouvoir. Enquêtes dans l'un et l'autre Testament* (Paris: Cerf, 2012), 263–288.
44 About power, cf. Heinrich Schlier, *Principalities and Powers in the New Testament* (New York: Herder and Herder, 1962); Romano Guardini, *Power and Responsibility: A Course of Action for the New Age* (Chicago: Henry Regnery, 1961); Byung-Chul Han, *What Is Power?* (Cambridge: Polity Press, 2018).
45 Heinrich Schlier, *Fundamentos de una teología paulina* (Madrid: BAC, 2016), 163–202; Giuseppe Barbaglio, *Il pensare dell'apostolo Paolo* (Bologna: EDB, 2004), 277–297; Karl Hermann Schelkle, *Theology of the New Testament, II: Salvation History – Revelation* (Collegeville, MI: The Liturgical Press, 1976), 221–235.

128 *Juan Luis Caballero*

46 Cf. Phil 2:3–4,21; Col 1:13,21; 2:13,20; 3:5–9; Eph 2:1–3,11–12; 4:14,17–19, 25–31; 5:3–8.
47 James D.G. Dunn, *Jesus and the Spirit* (Grand Rapids, MI: Eerdmans, 1975), 199–361, and *The Theology of Paul the Apostle* (Grand Rapids, MI: Eerdmans, 1998), 413–441; George T. Montague, *The Holy Spirit: Growth of a Biblical Tradition* (New York: Paulist Press, 1976), 127–236; Anthony Thiselton, *The First Epistle to the Corinthians* (Grand Rapids, MI: Eerdmans, 2000), 956–1146.
48 Acts 26:6–7. Cf. Jer 31:31–34; Ezek 36:24–32; 37:1–28, Joel 3:1–2.
49 The book of Revelation (cf. Rev 11:1–14) poses, as a backdrop, the confrontation between two ways of conceiving existence, two worlds with their own value systems, the immanent and the transcendent. Cf. Ugo Vanni, *Apocalisse di Giovanni, II: introduzione generale. Commento* (Assisi: Cittadella, 2018), 391–408.
50 Cf. Jn 8:41–47; 1 Thess 3:5; 2 Cor 10:4–5; 11:14; Col 2:8; Eph 4:14; 5:8; Heb 3:13.
51 Cf. Wis 9:1–18; 1 Cor 1:24; Eph 3:14–19.
52 Here, the Spirit connects with the rich sapiential and pedagogical tradition present in the Old Testament, which, embracing human wisdom fruit of observation, reflection, and experience, places the divine law (in Ecclesiasticus, the Mosaic Law) as its ultimate source.
53 Cf, for example, in the letters of the captivity: Phil 1:10; 3:8; Col 1:9;28; 2:2,18,23; 3:10,16; Eph 1:17; 3:4,10,18; 4:14,17,18,22,25; 5,4,10,11,15,27; 6,11.
54 Cf. Gal 2:20; 4:19; Phil 2:5.
55 Cf. 1 Cor 12:25–26; 2 Cor 5:15.

Part II
Integration

8 The value of work in the Book of Ecclesiastes (*Qoheleth*). Is an optimistic view possible given the onerous experience of many jobs?

Diego Pérez Gondar

Introduction

In a previous work, which is part of the research project of the University of Navarra Strategic Line: "The meaning of work in recent theology", the task of re-describing the original divine project for the human being was addressed. This work analyzed Gen 2:4b–25 in detail, with the aim of offering researchers a technical reading of the passage that would attend to all the nuances present in this biblical text.[1] This initial step was an attempt to describe the divine offer to humanity, full of hope and trust. In this analysis, the God who revealed himself was markedly different from the mythological stories of other cultures, and His plan for humanity was characterized by respect and love. The article emphasized that the vocation of the human being to family and work is synonymous. The spousal covenant, as a sign of the biblical covenant in salvation history, is the environment imbued with "joy" and "rest" in which God intends for human beings to work and develop their capacities, being His image in the world.

In any case, this initial project, full of optimism, differs greatly from the present experience throughout history, motivating our reflection on the meaning of human activity. While we can describe Gen 2:4b–25 as a marvelous ideal, our historical experience falls short of fully embodying it. This could lead to criticism of that article; however, this initial contribution was necessary as a prologue to what I intend to present here. Therefore, the analysis continues to follow the biblical passage, from an intertextual and holistic perspective. Only such a reading can understand the evolution of thought throughout the history of revelation, of which the biblical texts are witnesses and instruments of transmission.

In the biblical account, Adam's situation after sin is the situation we often experience in many burdensome and heavy labors (Gen 3:17–19). But if the origin of this toil is the separation from the divine plan, what solutions are offered? How is this universal problem to be solved, or in what way is it to be oriented? Is there any mention of this in the Bible?

Therefore, the objective now is to delve deeper into the original problem— the rejection of that first Covenant and its consequences. In short, the goal is

DOI: 10.4324/9781003508212-10

132 *Diego Pérez Gondar*

to better understand the primordial fracture that we continue to experience, and which is part of the present state of our existence. It is clear that the original divine design encountered an obstacle: human freedom acting apart from and against the divine plan. And the question is, is it possible to reverse the situation? How?

From a biblical studies perspective, the most effective approach to addressing this matter is to concentrate on the Book of Ecclesiastes, as its entire content revolves around this theme. A notable indicator of this focus is the frequent use of the root עמל, which denotes "to labor", "to weary" and "to strive", vividly conveying the burdensome dimension of human activity. Of the 76 occurrences of this root in the entire Hebrew Bible, 35 are found in the Book of Ecclesiastes (46%). This is a remarkable frequency considering the brevity of this book.

We will take the following steps: (a) interpreting the book throughout history in the classical Christian sphere, (b) re-reading of the book from an intertextual perspective centered on Gen 1–3, and (c) synthesizing the book's proposal based on recent contributions from biblical exegesis. As a result of this study, the final conclusions will offer some keys to suggest ways of dealing with the difficulties encountered in our day-to-day work.

The history of the interpretation of *Qoheleth*

I present a concise reflection on the historical interpretation of *Qoheleth*. In preliminary observations, it is evident that three noteworthy figures—Origen, St. Bonaventure, and Martin Luther—have played pivotal roles in shaping distinct perspectives on *Qoheleth*'s discourse.

The contemplative approach of Origen (second–third centuries AD)

It is crucial to contextualize Origen within the Christian milieu preceding the Edict of Milan, a period marked by persecution. Christian life during this era was exceptionally rigorous and, at times, heroic. To be a genuine Christian meant being willing to sacrifice everything. Simultaneously, it was an epoch of theological consolidation.

Origen played a substantial role in harmonizing the finest elements of classical philosophy with the Judeo-Christian phenomenon in this challenging environment. In this regard, Origen stands as a notable representative of the early tradition of interpreting *Qoheleth*, closely tied to a contemplative ascent through the wisdom literature attributed to Solomon.

> Origen's schema has the student ascend from Proverbs to Ecclesiastes to Song of Songs as three stages of the spiritual life. These stages correspond to the three schools of philosophy. Proverbs teaches ethical living, while the climax of the ascent, Song of Songs, teaches logic, which in the imagination of medieval interpreters is equated with theology,

The value of work from the Book of Ecclesiastes (Qoheleth) 133

"the science of divine contemplation". Between ethics and logic is physics, which in Origen's account is the topic of Ecclesiastes. Herein lies the contradiction. How can Ecclesiastes teach one simultaneously to flee the world and to study rigorously its physical features?[2]

Therefore, *Proverbs* would help situate the Christian in the world during his process of sanctification, providing a foundation for proper "ethics". *Qoheleth*, on the other hand, would teach an understanding of the "physical" characteristics of the world, including its limitations and dangers. Finally, *Song of Songs* would lead to a "logical/theological" contemplation of divine matters. It's important to note, however, that the concept of *contemptus mundi* has not appeared at any point.

The process of estrangement from everyday life was a phenomenon associated with the widespread adoption of the Christian social phenomenon during the time of Constantine. The anchoretic, cenobitic, and monastic movements surged in the fourth century, and were connected to the pursuit of an authentic experience of the evangelical faith. As Christianity spread extensively, the practice of many Christians fell short of the expectation set by the early Christians who had initially influenced the movement. St Jerome, in particular, began to view *Qoheleth* as an invitation to reject temporal realities.[3]

The penitential approach of St Bonaventure (twelfth century AD)

In medieval times, St Bonaventure inherited and enriched this tradition by offering a new interpretation of the triad of Solomonic books. Bonaventure associates the Solomon of *Qoheleth* with Adam, transforming the perspective into a penitential one. Similar to Adam, Solomon transitioned from a state of holiness and righteousness to one of brokenness and separation, which necessarily must be followed by a journey of penance. The concept of Covenant resurfaces here. The "Eucharistic" feast must come after a "penitential" journey (as depicted in Ecclesiastes). It seems clear that the journey is no longer that of contemplation of the divine through meditation on Scripture (as in Origen's approach) but rather on the ecclesial path of Christian initiation. *Proverbs* serves as preparation for Baptism, Ecclesiastes as a guide to Penance, and *Song of Songs* as the consummation of union in the Eucharist.

What characterizes St Bonaventure's interpretation is his conception of the meaning of *Qoheleth* as a call to detachment from the world. While Origen encouraged a metaphysical vision of God through created things, aligning with the biblical invitation and acknowledging the limitations of creation, St Bonaventure understood the book as Solomon's personal confession. According to him, Solomon's sin would have been an inappropriate *curiositas* toward the created, leading him to neglect the Creator.[4] Therefore, the proposed solution involves rejecting the created[5] and a turning away from worldly realities as the only option to ensure a truly contemplative way of

134   *Diego Pérez Gondar*

life. In this vision, the so-called *carpe diem* passages are interpreted as the autobiographical voice of Solomon during his phase as a sinner, indulging in *vanitas* understood as a *curiositas* that hinders true contemplation.

Despite the aforementioned perspectives, St Bonaventure regards creation as a manifestation of the inner world of the Trinity. He maintains an optimistic and positive view of creation by staying aligned with a biblical interpretation rooted in the best aspects of patristic thought. This is how Atkinson summarizes it:

> Every creature is a vestige, containing traces of the Trinitarian imprint. Humans bear more of the Trinity's imprint as image-bearers of God, because they are rational beings who reflect the rationality of the divine Word. They reflect the Trinity in their faculties of memory, intelligence, and will, corresponding to the Father, the Son, and the Spirit, respectively. Similitude is the highest tier of the created hierarchy in that it represents beatific union with God.[6]

We can hypothesize that St Bonaventure's interpretation of *Qoheleth* is conditioned by the way Christianity culturally crystallized in the West. This remained true for over a millennium, although its principles might have seemed unfamiliar in the early days of Christianity. St Bonaventure, and the entire school of thought he represents, can be considered correct in nearly every aspect except for the assessment of the historical construction of the "earthly city". In this perspective, the only way to interpret creation as a path of union and return to God would be a life of detachment from temporal realities, fraught with dangers. This is why St Bonaventure interprets *Qoheleth* as a "confession" of Solomon. In it, Solomon acknowledges his guilt and the state he was left in by following in the footsteps of Adam and Eve (Gen 3). Thus, the danger being warned against is the potential failure to perceive the "eternal vestige" of creation and turning it into a "false idol". Consequently, St Bonaventure advocates for a healthy "contemplation" as opposed to an unhealthy "curiosity". He does this by proposing the monastic ideal.

The Lutheran rejection of greed for the things of the world (sixteenth century AD)

The next phase in the process of interpreting *Qoheleth* is marked by Luther.[7] In his commentary on the book, he unequivocally expresses his opposition to the monastic phenomenon. According to Luther, *Qoheleth* extends an invitation to live amidst worldly matters without succumbing to their afflictions. It involves "conquering" their "malice", exercising control over the world perceived as inherently evil. The Christian is "called" to dwell in the world with a peaceful and tranquil heart, avoiding all disordered desires (*avaritia*). In this context, the approach involves establishing a proper *usus* which stands in opposition to a misguided *fruitio*.

The value of work from the Book of Ecclesiastes (Qoheleth) 135

The fundamental difference between the two visions described (Bonaventure *versus* Luther) lies in Luther's rejection of all metaphysics. According to him, there is no "exemplarity" in the created world as an emanation of the Word. The world is something in opposition to the divine due to all-pervading sin. However, for Luther, in the everyday realities of life—in the "use" of creatures—, calmly, human beings can discover God's call to enjoy His hidden Presence. Luther can be said to affirm that it is not necessary to renounce the mundane in order to attain the union depicted in the *Song of Songs*.

Luther interprets *Qoheleth* as God's definitive word and understands it as a call to "rest" that avoids all "restlessness". In short, Luther views *Qoheleth* as a kind of "Sermon on the Mount" by Solomon, inviting an "ethic" oriented toward enjoying the present without being burdened by the future.

From what has been said so far, it is clear that Luther rejects any vision that implies a process or progress in the Christian life. On the contrary, he advocates for a life where contact with the divine is drawn from the present. However, he does so by affirming both the evil of the world and its capacity to be a "language" for understanding the divine reality.

It is at this point that Luther initiates a new tradition that historically leads today's society to its more than obvious tensions. If the world is entirely corrupt and redemption is not effectively present (metaphysically), only an individual spiritual dimension (Jesus and the Gospels) and an earthly justice (Solomon and *Qoheleth*) remain. There would be two spheres: the ecclesiastical and familial on one hand, and on the other, the world of politics—a necessity arising after sin. This dichotomy establishes a dual framework with different laws and dynamics. It is this dichotomy that forms the basis of the current political, social, and economic systems in tension in the contemporary world.

On a personal level, Luther denounces *greed* as the main obstacle to living in "peace" and "calm". However, his vision remains individualistic, which is one of the limitations of his approach. In fact, the joy mentioned in *Qoheleth* is not individualistic. On the contrary, it is an ideal that can be achieved and shared by all within a properly constructed society.

Qoheleth in light of Gen 1–3: the human condition after the rupture of the Covenant

A close reading of Gen 2:4b–25 reveals that the divine command encompassed a broad invitation to eat of all the trees (except one), to grow, multiply, and fill the earth (Gen 2:16–17).[8] The smallness of the limit imposed compared with the grandeur of the invitation/command to enhance everything that God had made, which He bestowed upon human beings, is certainly striking. The constructive possibilities of human creativity are enormous, according to the narrative, but they have limits because not all options hold the same value, and some go against the order established by the Creator. Human beings possess autonomy, but it is not boundless. They must discern paths

136 *Diego Pérez Gondar*

that contradict the Covenant[9] in order to avoid them: they must not presume to be the creators of reality. Reality is something given that must be managed, not to control at will, lest they suffer the consequences and punishment.

If we create a conceptual map, the term "Covenant" is connected to others such as "gift", "gratuitousness", "freedom", "responsibility", "dignity", "consequences", "punishment", etc. All these terms are associated with "desire" and "dominion". It also seems logical to consider terms like "calculation", "thought", or "decision". In examining the texts concerning these terms, we find significant occurrences of the word תשוקה[10] and the root חשב.[11]

In the first case, the word that we translate as "desire" is a noun derived from the root שוק. As a verb, it means "to be abundant", "to overflow", or "to bestow abundantly". As a basic noun (שוק), it means "street" or "market". From the semantic point of view, its usage is abundant and clear, referring to the place where an abundance of goods is available and offered in a public way. Although the root is frequently used in biblical texts, the noun תשוקה is unusual and rare. However, due to the contexts in which it appears (Song 7:11; Gen 3:16; 4:7) and their strong thematic connection, they evoke particular interest.

It is useful to bear in mind that a necessary background for understanding the *Song of Songs* is Gen 1:1–2:25, and that a context for a proper reading of *Qoheleth* is provided by Gen 3:1–4:16.[12] The *Song of Songs* speaks of a joyful and fruitful covenant. *Qoheleth*, however, delves into an onerous and often meaningless existence, full of toil and despair. The former conveys "harmony", "joy", and "peace", while the latter explores "tension", "weariness", and "conflict". Since spousal language is prevalent throughout the Bible, "desire", "possession", and the danger of "unfaithfulness" are all-encompassing. And, as in all passionate conflict, a "love triangle" emerges.

The first text is Song 7:11: "I (am) for my beloved, and upon me (is) his desire" (אני לדודי ועלי תשוקתו). This statement is made by the beloved about his beloved. The entire Song is a play of desire-filled quests and encounters. Through this verse, the surrender to God and the exclusivity of the creature according to the original Covenant, along with God's desire over her, is expressed.

As pointed out in the previous work and following Beauchamp's aphorism, "all things of man signify the things of God",[13] we understand that the reality that best manifests the God of the Judeo-Christian Revelation is spousal love. This theme operates in biblical texts on both positive and negative levels. Indeed, to explain the rupture between the human being and the Creator, the same language is employed with some appropriate changes. Thus, as a consequence of disobedience, God says to Eve (Gen 3:16b): "And towards your husband (shall be) your desire and he shall rule in you" (ואל אישך תשוקתך והוא ימשל בך). Before sin, the desire was that of the beloved [God] toward the beloved [Israel/Church], and the beloved was to dominate over the created. Now, the order has been disrupted. And that cannot happen

The value of work from the Book of Ecclesiastes (Qoheleth)   137

without the intervention of a new agent: the third vertex of the "triangle", that is, sin.

Gen 4:7 is one of the most challenging verses in the entire Torah to translate and understand. In this passage, we hear the voice of God offering the decisive advice to Cain before his sin. God encourages Cain in his anger over the non-acceptance of his offering, the fruit of his labor. God tells him that if he does what is right, he will be happy, but if not, sin (עון) is portrayed as a crouching varmint ready to pounce on its prey. Although God informs him about sin, stating: "towards you (Cain) (is) his desire, yet you shall rule in it" (ואליך תשוקתו ואתה תמשל בו), unfortunately, this divine prediction is not fulfilled and Cain succumbs, leading to the killing of his brother Abel. This occurs despite God's assurance that, even though the desire of sin toward him is strong, he has the ability to overcome it if he so wills.

The enigmatic wording of Gen 4:7 alludes to another "principle" that desires mankind and introduces disharmony into the world by breaking the original covenant. Adam and Eve, along with Cain and his descendants, choose to relate to this new "principle", personified in the serpent of Gen 3, which sows distrust in the original plan. Everything was designed to proceed in a straight line, with an abundance of gifts, but from the beginning, this did not come to pass as the original covenant was broken. From then on, the escalation of the collapse accelerated, and the destructive frenzy was only halted when God recommenced the world with a new covenant with Noah after the Flood. Before this punishment, in Gen 6:5, the writer of Genesis had already recorded that "God saw how great (was) the wickedness of mankind on the earth, and that every imagination of the thoughts of his heart (was) only evil all the days of his life" (וירא יהוה כי רבה רעת האדם בארץ וכל יצר מחשבת לבו רק רע כל היום). The root חשב now appears, the second term referred to above, which helps to connect the presented texts.

In the wisdom reflection of *Qoheleth*, we encounter an important text in which this word appears: "God made man upright, but they sought many complications" (Qo 7:29) (עשה האלהים את האדם ישר והמה בקשו חשבנות רבים). There is a thematic connection between this verse and Gen 1:27: "[God] created [Adam], male and female God created them" (ברא אתו זכר ונקבה ברא אתם אלהים). The plural אתם of Gen 1:27 corresponds to the plural המה of Qo 7:29. God made the human being ישר ("upright", "righteous"), but their thoughts were entangled in manifold חשבנות ("musings", "inventions", "complications", "calculations", and "machines" or "contrivances"). The term חשבנות, expressed in the plural, means "plans", "designs", even "wits of war", and has a strong negative connotation. The same term expressed in the singular belongs to the semantic field of חכמה ("wisdom") and can be translated as "calculation" or "adjustment". The full reasoning of *Qoheleth* is as follows (in a proper and literal translation from the Hebrew):

[25]I turned I and my heart [went within me] to know, and to investigate, and to seek wisdom and "settling of accounts" (חשבון); and to know the

138   *Diego Pérez Gondar*

greatest error and the greatest stupidity;[26] and I found (that) more bitter than death (is) the woman; that she (is as) snares, her heart (as) nets, her hands (as) bonds. (Who is) good before God shall escape from her, but he who sins will be punished by her.[27] Note (in) this: I found that Qoheleth said when he sought a "fit" (חשבון) for everything:[28] what still my soul seeks and I found, one man among a thousand I found, but one woman among them all I did not find.[29] Only this only I found: that God made man upright (ישר), but they sought for themselves many complications (חשבנות).

(Qo 7:25–29)

One can observe a strong opposition in Qo 7:29 between ישר ("upright", "righteous") and חשבנות ("complications", "calculations", or "wits"). It clearly refers to human beings as a whole, given the use of plurals. To explain the origin of these "complications" outside the divine plan, a forceful allusion to the passage in Gen 3 arises, where Eve directs her "desire" toward the forbidden tree—a tree associated with the acquisition of "wisdom", but a wisdom in clear opposition to God's plan.

In the LXX, the term חשבן is translated as λογισμός. This word appears in Pauline texts with a strong negative connotation (Rom 2:15 and 2 Co 10:4) and points to internal deliberation, a judgment through a strategy in which an approach based on sophism or theory opposed to the divine design prevails.

The origin of evil in the world is, according to this biblical understanding, the result of human creative deliberation that does not respect divine boundaries, breaking both vertical and horizontal communion (with God and with others). This lack of unity and cohesion explains the conflict, as each human being pursues their own course in an "explosion" of decisions full of "complication", "calculation", or "interest", sidelining the common project. The world is thus transformed by human action, and reality becomes as we know it today, with all its contradictions, difficulties, and weariness. This is the experience of life depicted by the main character in Ecclesiastes (called "Qoheleth"), who expresses it with particular skill throughout the book.

However, *Qoheleth* does not contain only one voice. Occasionally, another, more positive voice appears, showing that within the mystery of the historical circumstances human beings live in, it is worth trusting in God's plan, and that what we have available in our lives should be used in moderation, living with gratitude.

God had "made man to rest" in the Garden of Eden (Gen 2,15). However, everyday experience reveals the lack of "rest" and "harmony/peace" in the performance of ordinary activities. The breaking of the Covenant implies consequences, a return to the situation before creation: a return to the chaotic waters (תהו ובהו). The "void" and "chaos" are the opposite of the "fullness" and "order" of the original divine design. The flood as a punishment or

The value of work from the Book of Ecclesiastes (Qoheleth)   139

consequence of the rejection of the divine plan implies a situation without rest. In the account in Gen 6–9, the narrator states:

> And the dove (היונה) [14] found no rest (מנוח)[15] for the sole of her feet and returned to him (Noah, נח), to the Ark (תבה)[16], for (there was) water upon the face of the earth, and he sent his hand and took it and brought it in towards him, towards le Ark.
>
> (Gen 8:9)

The entire history of salvation contained in the biblical texts speaks of a journey to a place of rest, a promised land. The Exodus itself is the story of an attempt to return to the initial situation willed by God and of resistance to entering that rest due to an unwillingness to accept God's offer. Psalm 95 summarizes the entire lengthy narrative by poetically capturing how the lack of rest is due to human rejection of the divine plan: "For forty years (I) abhorred this generation, and said, 'They (are) a wandering people at heart'. And they did not know My ways, so I swore in indignation: 'They shall not enter My rest' (אם יבאון אל מנוחתי)" (Ps 95:10–11).

With all this in mind, the statement of the author of the *Letter to the Hebrews* is better understood: "Therefore, we enter into rest who have believed (Εἰσερχόμεθα γὰρ εἰς [τὴν] κατάπαυσιν οἱ πιστεύσαντες), as it was said: 'Therefore, I swore in my wrath. They shall not enter into my rest, although the [divine] works were done from the creation of the world'" (Heb 4:3). In other words, the whole salvific message from the biblical perspective implies a new access to the original "rest/joy". For this reason, the question of how to inform the concrete reality of the human being's historical existence is at the center of all true humanistic reflection. For the author of *Hebrews*, access to this "new creation" is through faith in Jesus Christ.

Qoheleth witnesses a wisdom debate

With what has been said so far, we can better understand the interventions of the author of *Qoheleth* correcting the hopeless complaint of the main protagonist of the diatribe.[17] With this broader vision, we can comprehend the play of the internal dialogue of the book and overcome the temptation to see the so-called *carpe diem* passages (Qo 2:24–26; 3:12–13,22; 5:17–19; 8:15; 9:7–9; and 11:9) as an invitation to hedonism.[18] Thus, the book argues that what we should expect from this life is to enjoy it in moderation, following a healthy "reverential awe" of the Creator. Indeed, Qo 3:12–13.22 says:

> [12]I discovered that there is nothing good for them (human beings) but to enjoy and do good in their lives.[13]And also that for every human being to eat and drink and see the good in everything he strives for is a gift from God.[22]I see that there is nothing better than for a human being to

140   *Diego Pérez Gondar*

enjoy his task, because that is his "lot/portion", because who will take him to see what will be after him?

As early as 1913, Mitchell[19] quoted Genung as paraphrasing these optimistic passages from Ecclesiastes, when he described a worker as

> a man who can draw up to table with a good healthy appetite, sleep sweetly whether he eat little or much, because he has found his work, the expression of his plans and his skill and his individuality, and takes it as what God meant him to have, and makes it his own by rejoicing in it.[20]

Regarding the understanding of the design of *Qoheleth*, exegetes have not always agreed. It is clear that the book presents a set of competing assessments of human existence after the fracture of the original covenant. And the logical question for the reader is about the intentionality of the work, that is, about which voice is dominant and has the last word. In this sense, we can distinguish three main voices: (a) the voice of the author of the book, which mainly appears in the epilogue, (b) the pessimistic voice, disillusioned with existence, and (c) the voice of the *carpe diem* passages.

Leaving aside the first proposed voice, which goes unnoticed by many researchers, there are three possible interpretations about the voice that wins in Ecclesiastes: (a) the "pessimistic" one, with the *carpe diem* passages rejected for their "hedonistic" sense, (b) the "optimistic" and "hopeful" vision in which God calls human beings to enjoy the gift of life according to His plan, overcoming the "pessimistic" one; and (c) the invitation to unrestrained hedonism as the only way out of accepting the "pessimistic" situation. As we shall see, position (b) seems the most reasonable and makes sense of the whole.

For some exegetes of the first school of thought, such as Gerhard von Rad, the dominating voice in the book "has come to terms with his situation, even if it is with a resignation that can leave no reader unmoved...".[21] So too thought R.B.Y. Scott, R. Murphy, W. Zimmerli, J. Crenshaw, and R. Gordis initially.[22] However, since the work of R. Gordis, E. Good, and N. Lohfink, the view has shifted to the second interpretation. According to Gordis' perspective, closely followed by Good's,

> [f]or Koheleth, joy is God's categorical imperative for man, not in any anemic or spiritualized sense, but rather as a full-blooded and tangible experience, expressing itself in the play of the body and the activity of the mind, the contemplation of nature, and the pleasures of love.[23]

With all this in mind, it must be acknowledged that the two forces present in the book have their place. What is striking to our contemporary mind is that

The value of work from the Book of Ecclesiastes (Qoheleth) 141

two antagonistic positions coexist, resulting in a "tense" equilibrium. Simultaneously, it is true that the situation of the human being in concrete existence is fueled with הבל, i.e. "frustration" and "transience". At the same time, within the heart of the human being, there resides a desire for שמחה, i.e. "joy", "gladness", and "happiness". The former is a consequence of the breaking of the covenant, while the latter is regarded as an irrevocable gift from the outset.[24]

We can say that the book's proposal is oriented toward an "aesthetics of human action". In this sense, Ecclesiastes suggests "being", "dwelling" in a manner that allows us to derive enjoyment and find joy in every human action, regardless of its nature. It involves transforming each action into a contemplative and joyful cathartic experience. For this reason, I concur with Joubert when he encapsulates the meaning of Ecclesiastes by saying:

> None of the good things that God created lost any of their intrinsic or absolute goodness. It explains why things that are intrinsically good and good for us share essentially the same property: they underline, as opposed to, undermine the value of every person's life, well-being, or happiness. However, because of the reality of sin and other evils in our everyday lives, some things are now "good" and "bad" for us, and some "better than" or "worse than" others. To discern the difference requires prudence, which begins with the fear of God and obedience to his revealed moral will.[25]

Taking into account the background of Gen 2–3, it can be observed that, according to the biblical proposal, God is the "giver", and the human being is an intelligent and free recipient of divine gifts. As Ecclesiastes belongs to the wisdom literature, it aligns with a tradition of reflection on the best way to conduct oneself in life. Referring to Qo 2:26, we find that God "gives" the human being "good" "חכמה ודעת ושמחה" ("wisdom and knowledge and joy"), but to the חוטא, i.e., the human being who "errs in the way", God "gives" ענין, i.e., an "honourable commission", a "drudgery:" "to gather and collect for the good human being". Consequently, an important statement in Ecclesiastes is that "one cannot enjoy life unless God makes it possible. The consequence is that the way of wisdom is to enjoy the goodness of life as long as it is granted by God".[26]

In the wisdom context within which the book operates, it is evident that what is proposed is not centered on a selfish and individual enjoyment of life's pleasures, but rather on the recognition that everything depends on God and that His gifts remain accessible. The book makes it clear that, unlike the *do ut des* of "traditional wisdom" found in other ancient cultures and represented by the book of *Proverbs*, there is no automatic connection between right behavior and divine gifts. Many times, this dependency is contradicted by the experience expressed in the pages of Ecclesiastes. Therefore, the

142   *Diego Pérez Gondar*

meaning of existence should not primarily rest on human "mastery" over reality. Wisdom is not a knowledge or skill for achieving success in life, as it is not something contingent on a human decision; instead, it is a divine gift to be accepted with joy and simplicity.

The proposal of Ecclesiastes, therefore, comprises a receptive and optimistic attitude toward the world. Such an attitude could well be considered among the *prolegomena* of the Gospel, i.e., a preliminary step preceding the final revelation. As Johnston points out,

> [i]t is interesting to observe that the Septuagint translated this word (שׂמחה) into the Greek as εὐφρανοσύνη, and as such, it is used by the NT writers to speak of natural or common joy (e.g., the joy of a festive meal; cf. Lk 12:19), in contrast with one's joy in Christ (χαρά).[27]

From what has been discussed thus far, the alternative is to either attempt to control existence apart from dependence on God—recalling Gen 3—or to embrace the understanding that we are creatures blessed with divine gifts. In doing so, we must savor each moment in communion with our Creator, striving for that "rest" that arises from continually "choosing" to be what we are: "creatures". The thematic resonance with Gen 1–4 is evident here.[28]

Indeed, the study of *Qoheleth* has been influenced by a particular rhetorical analysis aimed at revealing the various perspectives presented and the main line of thought that provides a central solution. However, there is another, more dynamic perspective that aligns with the trajectory of returning to Eden, from which the human being was expelled. This perspective involves understanding the book as a proposal for spiritual transformation through joy "in the divine". In a recent and insightful work, Annalie E. Steenkamp-Nel demonstrates that

> Qohelet is not about paradox, but about a process. It is not about balance, but about movement, not being just observational, but transformational. Qohelet has not a heterodox character, but a transformational character. (...)
>
> Joy as an aspect of spiritual transformation is the faintly glistening thread that holds Qohelet together. It is of profound importance because it represents not only a spiritual shift but moreover a commitment to change the attitudes of believers. To come to God in faith is not an arithmetical, instant or result oriented affair. It takes time to grow into God(-likeness). Qohelet as a "bridge book" to the New Testament dispensation shows the (processual) way.[29]

The path that this author proposes includes: (a) "Experimentation: Joy in simple things",[30] (b) "Reinterpretation: Understanding God anew",[31] (c) "Realignment: Enjoying God",[32] and (d) "A new commitment: Enjoying others".[33]

The value of work from the Book of Ecclesiastes (Qohelet) 143

Conclusions and implications for contemporary work

With what we have seen so far, we can better understand the positions and limitations of Bonaventure and Luther. Is it possible to have an integrating vision that preserves the goodness of creation despite sin and does not divert human beings from the Genesis task of dominating, working, guarding, and caring for the "Garden"? I believe that if one reads *Qoheleth* in light of Gen 1–3, it is possible.

If we are searching for a point of connection between St Bonaventure and Luther, we could say that the term that points to it is the הבל of *Qoheleth*. For Bonaventure, "[o]nce the *curiosus* has acquired knowledge of an object, the object loses its novelty because the *curiosus* has quickly moved his glance from the newly old object to another one, in a vicious cycle".[34] In other words, if one is in the world and is carried away by its "mutability", one cannot grasp the "divine". Therefore, the best option is a simple life that can contemplate the divine projected into a future world (as Origen proposed). The question is whether this is inevitable or whether there is a way to connect involvement in the divine vocation to temporal work with the joy of the divine. Atkinson summarizes this thus:

> Both Bonaventure and Luther stress that in Ecclesiastes, the problem Solomon is confronting is not creation in itself, but the way in which humanity sees it and responds to it in word and deed. Both vices [*curiositas* for Bonaventure and *avaritia* for Luther] betray a discontentment with God's gifts and a failure to use (*uti*) them properly. The obsession with the acquisition of new things, be they objects of knowledge or material objects, on the one hand resists contemplation and on the other hand resists the intrinsic benefits of labor itself.[35]

If we connect this with the contemporary world, it can be asserted that the materialism and hedonism characterizing it would be well explained in the reflection made thus far. However, what solutions can be proposed? What is the appropriate biblical approach? I believe that the answer emerges from a re-reading of *Qoheleth* in light of Gen 1–3. God's gifts are irreversible and form the foundation of human dignity.

> Ecclesiastes invites the enjoyment of labor by stressing the time of the present as that which makes possible the experience of a new work of God. In so doing, it draws attention to the intrinsic value of the worker's labor. (...) [C]ontemplation through the Word and human activity that is done in anticipation of divine activity turns the worker away from self-referential and self-salvific pursuits and toward good speech and action for the sake of the neighbor.[36]

That is why I believe the most fitting interpretation of the biblical approach aligns with Origen's perspective. Human life is called to evolve, particularly

144 *Diego Pérez Gondar*

in its spiritual dimension. Furthermore, we have observed that this aligns well with the insights from the latest research on Ecclesiastes, which clearly exhibits optimism. Therefore, it becomes more evident that the biblical vision inherently adopts a wisdom approach to existence, and all this is elucidated by the points discussed so far.

If we revisit the beginning of this paper, we will recall the question of how to confront the challenges of today's work. Therefore, we conclude by presenting some ideas that may serve as inspiration for practical considerations.

One of the fundamental attributes of biblical wisdom texts is their timeless nature. Many of the teachings they encapsulate possess enduring value and remain relevant in various contexts, including the present day.

In contemporary times, work and joy are often not perceived as intimately connected. In the prevailing Western societal perspective, work is viewed as a means to attain the resources necessary for finding joy in a separate realm. These are considered two disconnected realities. However, this diverges from the biblical proposal, which is rooted in an anthropology that is absent in many cultural and economic approaches today. The biblical proposition lays out a path where being human is not an individualistic endeavor but a familial one. This perspective allows for self-understanding as openness to the spiritual freedom.

In the everyday enjoyment of life within the family, the human being becomes the image of God. The Creator desires for the human being to exercise stewardship over creation with care, following the divine plan that must be comprehended and creatively developed. Herein lies the greatness of the human being and the sacred call to work.

Some of the points discussed here may pave the way toward a social construct in which we limit certain "schemes" and "inventions", striving for increased "joy/peace" through a deeper understanding of one another and a more contemplative experience. This, in turn, results from a clearer vision of the divine inherent in creation: an authentic contemplative life. Perhaps this should be the most fervent of the "desires" that we seek to "master".

Notes

1 Cf. Diego Pérez-Gondar, "The Anthropology of Work from Biblical Theology. A New Consideration of Gen 2:4b–25," *Scripta Theologica* 55 (2023): 9–37. This work is a continuation of what has already been presented, and for this reason, it is useful to be familiar with this article in order to continue the thread of reflection. We will not conclude this exploration in this work because that could be achieved in a New Testament reading, which we leave to other members of the research project team. Other recent publications arising from this research project include: Gregorio Guitián and Alejo José G. Sison, "Offshore Outsourcing from a Catholic Social Teaching Perspective," *Journal of Business Ethics* 185 (2023): 595–609; Hélio Luciano, "La comprensión de la noción de trabajo en la teología brasileña del siglo XX," *Veritas* 54 (2023): 147–171; Pablo Blanco, "The Idea of Work: from Luther to Pentecostals in Recent Protestant Authors," *Teologia i Moralność* 17 (2022): 189–203; Juan Luis Caballero, "Freedom and Dependence

The value of work from the Book of Ecclesiastes (Qohelet) 145

in the Pauline Writings. A Theological Approach according to Colossians and Ephesians," ΘΕΟΛΟΓΙΑ 93 (2022): 7–33; Gregorio Guitián and Ana Marta González, "Theology of Work: New Perspectives," *Scripta Theologica* 54 (2022): 757–787; César Izquierdo, "El Trabajo en la filosofía de la acción de Maurice Blondel," *Libellus quasi speculum. Studi offerti a Bernard Ardura*, ed. Pierantonio Piatti (Cittá del Vaticano: Libreria Editrice Vaticana, 2022), 1003–1015; Juan Luis Caballero, "Elementos para una teología paulina del trabajo. En torno al documento «¿Qué es el Hombre?»," *Scripta Theologica* 53 (2021): 169–190 y Gregorio Guitián, "How Financial Institutions Can Serve the Common Good of Society. Insights from Catholic Social Teaching," *Business Ethics, the Environment & Responsibility* 32/S2 (2023) 84–95.

2 Tyler Atkinson, *Singing at the Winepress. Ecclesiastes and the Ethics of Work* (London: Bloomsbury T&T Clark 2015), 71–72. For an in-depth study of Origen's thought, cf. Diego Pérez-Gondar, "Una propuesta de enriquecimiento para la exégesis bíblica contemporánea. Claves del *De Principiis* de Orígenes," *Estudios Bíblicos* 77 (2019): 435–457.

3 It was Jerome who translated the Hebrew term הבל by the ambiguous Latin term *vanitas*. To a great extent, interpretation has always been closely tied to resolving this ambiguity. As we shall see, Bonaventure linked it with *curiositas* (as opposed to *studiositas*) and Luther identified it with *avaritia*.

4 Cf. Tyler Atkinson, *Singing at the Winepress. Ecclesiastes and the Ethics of Work* (London: Bloomsbury T and T Clark, 2015), 79.

5 The rejection or withdrawal from the world would refer primarily to the "Human Construction", rather than to the "natural".

6 Tyler Atkinson, *Singing at the Winepress. Ecclesiastes and the Ethics of Work* (London: Bloomsbury T and T Clark, 2015), 85.

7 Cf. Tyler Atkinson, *Singing at the Winepress. Ecclesiastes and the Ethics of Work* (London: Bloomsbury T and T Clark, 2015), 121–185.

8 For more on Gen 2:15–17, cf. Anto Popović, "Il compito, il permesso, il divieto e la punizione (Gen 2:15–17)," *Liber Annuus* 71 (2021): 9–45.

9 A covenant is a pact, "an agreement enacted between two parties in which one or both make promises under oath to perform or refrain from certain actions stipulated in advance. As indicated by the designation of the two sections of the Christian Bible—Old Testament (= covenant) and New Testament—, 'covenant' in the Bible is the major metaphor used to describe the relation between God and Israel (the people of God). As such, covenant is the instrument constituting the rule (or kingdom) of God, and therefore it is a valuable lens through which one can recognize and appreciate the biblical ideal of religious community" (cf. George E. Mendenhall and Gary A. Herion, "Covenant," *The Anchor Bible Dictionary*, dir. David N. Freedman [New York et al.: Doubleday, 1992], I,1179–1202, I,1179).

10 Cf. Franciscus Zorrel, *Lexicon hebraicum et aramaicum Veteris Testamentum* (Roma: Pontificium Institutum Biblicum, 1968), 830.

11 The noun comes from the root חשב, meaning "to think", but with the sense of "to knit", "to weave", or "to plot". Cf. Willy Schottroff, "חשב", *Theological Lexicon of the Old Testament*, eds. Ernst Jenni and Claus Westermann (Peabody, MA: Hendrickson Publishers, 1997), 631–635.

12 For an in-depth account of the close relationship between *Ecclesiastes and Genesis*, especially Gen 1–4, cf. Matthew Seufert, "The Presence of Genesis in Ecclesiastes," *Westminster Theological Journal* 78 (2016): 75–92.

13 Paul Beauchamp, *El Uno y el otro Testamento. Cumplir las Escrituras* (Estudios y Ensayos. Teología. 185; Madrid: BAC, 2015), 181.

14 It is striking that the noun "dove" coincides in Hebrew with the name Jonah. If we recall the narrative of the book of Jonah, the protagonist is thrown into

146 *Diego Pérez Gondar*

the raging sea by God because of his refusal to go along with God's plan for the salvation of Nineveh. In biblical symbolic language, the idea is repeated that the stormy waters that ravage the human being, leaving him exhausted, symbolise the consequences of opposing God's plan of salvation.

15 In Gen 2:15, it is striking that God, in commanding man to work in and care for the garden, "made him rest" (וינחהו בגן עדן לעבדה ולשמרה) in it. The activity that God wants human beings to engage in should be full of harmony, joy, and peace. At the time of the flood, while it or its consequences lasted, no one could find his rest (מנוח).

16 The word תבה is of Egyptian origin and is used 22 times in the story of the flood to designate the Ark that preserved the people and animals that survived the cataclysm and that would be the seed of a new beginning, of a new creation and covenant. It is the same term that is used twice at the beginning of Exodus to designate the "basket" in which Moses escapes from the slaughter of the Hebrew newborns, and the means of reaching Pharaoh's daughter floating on the waters of the Nile. The salvific meaning that links these texts is thus clear. This word is distinguished from the usual term for the Ark of the Covenant (ארון) that appears later in the biblical account and is no longer connected with the origin stories.

17 Since ancient times, commentators have interpreted several voices in the multiplicity of utterances in the Book of *Qoheleth*. However, there has been no consensus on their number and arrangement in the structure of the text. Despite this, the idea that the book presents a set of opposing points of view in the form of a diatribe has been peacefully received. By way of summary, we can accept that there are two main voices in the text. On the one hand, there is the "critical" and "hopeless" view that embodies a "pessimistic realism". On the other hand, an "optimistic" and "ambiguous" perspective that can be understood as a certain "ironic hedonism" or as a "hopeful" and "optimistic" proposal, despite the obvious difficulties of life. These two voices appear in the book "interpreted" by a fictitious character in the form of a polyphonic character called "Qohelet". What must not be overlooked is that there is a superior voice, that of the author of the book, which appears at decisive moments to make certain essential points clear in the wisdom reflection. One of the main moments of appearance of this authorial voice is the epilogue of the book: "9Qoheleth, besides being wise, transmitted knowledge to the people, listened, researched and composed many proverbs. 10Qoheleth tried to find a pleasant style and to write the truth correctly. 11The words of the wise are like goads; and the collections of the sayings of every author are like stakes well driven in. 12For the rest, my son, take heed: to compose many books is a never-ending thing, and to study much, it wearies the body. 13End of discourse. We have heard all: fear God and keep the commandments, for this applies to every man. 14God will judge whether all that is done is good or evil, even that which is hidden" (Qo 12:8–14). Also belonging to this "higher" voice of the book is the passage commented above from Qo 7:25–29.

18 Qo 2:24–26 says: "24 There is nothing better for a human being than to eat and drink and to show his soul good by his effort. This also I saw, that from the hand of God (is) this (the soul?). 25For, "Who shall eat and who shall enjoy besides me?" 26For to the human being who is good before Him He gave wisdom, knowledge, and joy, and to the one who sins He gave the charge to gather and assemble and give to the one who is good before God. This also is "emptiness/steam/futility" and fighting against the wind". The Hebrew version of v. 25 seems to bring some words in direct speech from God himself, "Who shall eat and who shall enjoy apart from me?" (מי יאכל ומי יחוש חוץ ממני). In a way, these words recall Ps 127:2: "Empty (is) for you who rise early to get up after lying down and eat the bread of toil for [God] will give it to his sleeping beloved (while he sleeps)". In

The value of work from the Book of Ecclesiastes (Qoheleth) 147

these words, there seems to be a reference to the "manna" of the wilderness. As the Hebrew expression in Qo 2:25 is somewhat ambiguous, the LXX wrote: "ὅτι τίς φάγεται καὶ τίς φείσεται πάρεξ αὐτοῦ;" ("For who shall eat or abstain (from eating) without the intervention of Him [God]?"). It is clear that the αὐτοῦ refers to God.

19 Cf. Hinckley G. Mitchell, "Work in Ecclesiastes," *JBL* 32 (1913): 123–138, 132.

20 John Franklin Genung, *Ecclesiastes, Words of Koheleth: Son of David, King in Jerusalem; Translated Anew, Divided According to their Logical Cleavage, and Accompanied with a Study of their Literary and Spiritual Values and a Running Commentary* (Boston: Houghton, Mifflin and Co., 1904), 83.

21 Gerhard von Rad, *Wisdom in Israel* (New York: Abigdon 1972), 223 (quoted in Robert K. Johnston, "'Confessions of a Workaholic': A Reappraisal of Qoheleth," *Catholic Biblical Quarterly* 38 (1976): 14–28, 16). Johnston himself synthesises the two ways in which the Book of *Qoheleth* is understood by leading scholars: "Returning to Ecclesiastes, it becomes apparent that if the goal of OT wisdom is seen to be that of mastering life, of wresting from its chaos some order, then Qoheleth must be viewed as carrying out a frontal assault upon the tradition as a whole, and his advice to enjoy the 'small' gifts (both work and play) that come man's way from God, as resigned or ironic conclusions that carry little consolation. If, however, the goal of Biblical wisdom is understood aesthetically as the 'art of steering', and its theological focus is seen as resting squarely in creation, then Ecclesiastes' "advice to enjoy life's work and play as given by God must be re-evaluated in this light. Rather than turning his back on the whole wisdom undertaking, as von Rad suggests, Qoheleth might better be understood as restating the central focus of the wisdom tradition itself. For Qoheleth, life in all of its dimensions is a question of common grace, not of hard work" (Robert K. Johnston, "'Confessions of a Workaholic': A Reappraisal of Qoheleth," *Catholic Biblical Quarterly* 38 (1976): 28).

22 Cf. Robert K. Johnston, "'Confessions of a Workaholic': A Reappraisal of Qoheleth," *Catholic Biblical Quarterly* 38 (1976): 16.

23 Robert Gordis, *Koheleth-the Man and His World* (New York: Shocken,³ 1968), 131. Text quoted in Edwin M. Good, *Irony in the Old Testament* (Philadelphia: Westminster, 1965), 192 and Robert K. Johnston, "'Confessions of a Workaholic': A Reappraisal of Qoheleth," *Catholic Biblical Quarterly* 38 (1976): 17.

24 Regarding the third means of interpretation, many commentators fail in their understanding of the book because they do not conceive that there can be several voices in the same composition. They also fail to read the text in light of the other books of the biblical corpus, especially Gen 1–4, and to look for definitive messages in every part of the *Bible*. They fail to realise that revelation is a progressive historical phenomenon that reached its fullness several centuries after Ecclesiastes. Indeed, the book sets out a reflection that will have its closure in the NT (cf. Callie Joubert, "The Axiology of Qoheleth and Life "Under the Sun": What is Good for Us to Do," *Conspectus* 27 [2019]: 173–191). However, for many recent scholars, the meaning of Ecclesiastes is plainly and simply an incitement to hedonism (cf. Callie Joubert, "The Axiology of Qoheleth and Life "Under the Sun": What Is Good for Us to Do," *Conspectus* 27 (2019): 175, citing the works of Michael V. Fox [1989], Gordon D. Fee and Douglas Suart [1993] and Philip G. Ryken [2010]). There is a parallel between the attitude or situation of the author of Ecclesiastes and that of the contemporary human being. It seems that we are currently in a period prior to the definitive manifestation of the divine. There seems to be a mixture of despondency and hope in a new way of inhabiting the world that we have not yet discovered. It can be said that our contemporary world, already post-Christian, is in a step prior to recognising the

148   *Diego Pérez Gondar*

definitive divine revelation and finds itself once again in the previous hesitations. Thus, every proposal will seem incomplete, but it will serve to open the way to new perspectives.

25 Joubert, "The Axiology of Qoheleth and Life 'Under the Sun': What is Good for Us to Do," *Conspectus* 27 (2019): 189.

26 Antoon Schoors, "Theodicy in Qoheleth," *Theodicy in the World of the Bible,* eds. Antii Laato and Johannes C. De Moor (Leiden, Boston: Brill 2003), 375–409, 384. Schoors reproduces a text from a work already cited here by Gordis (Robert Gordis, *Koheleth-the Man and His World* [New York: Shocken, 1968], 94): "Actually ḥōṭē' in these passages is used both in its non-moral sense of 'fool, one who misses the right path', and in its religious connotation of 'sinner', as Koheleth understands it, the man who violates God's will by failing to enjoy the blessings of God's world, as in the Talmudic parallels adduced above" (Antoon Schoors, "Theodicy in Qoheleth," *Theodicy in the World of the Bible*, eds. Antii Laato and Johannes C. De Moor [Leiden, Boston: Brill, 2003], 403–404). Gordis refers, for example, to b.Erub 54a (Talmud of Babylon), where it is stated that every human being who does not enjoy the gifts bestowed by God will be held accountable.

27 Robert K. Johnston, "'Confessions of a Workaholic': A Reappraisal of Qoheleth," *Catholic Biblical Quarterly* 38 (1976): 20.

28 This is the view present in recent works. This is how Kimmo Houvila and Dan Lioy summarise the biblical proposal when they state that: "Qohelet wants to teach about life, specifically about human limitations as a reason to give up an obstacle that hinders receiving joy as a gift from God. The obstacle is the attempt to find permanent profit in life. This attempt is bound to fail. This is relevant, as people who intellectually understand their mortality fail to live accordingly in their lives, trying to hoard wealth that they will lose anyway, and losing their joy in the process. They may attempt to gain security through wealth, but wealth is incapable of providing such security, as it is lost in earthly life or at death at the latest. If an opportunity to have joy is God's gift, it honours God to receive the gift. Overwork that takes away the joy God wants to give does not respect the divine gift-giver. Qohelet argues for his theology of joy on the basis of injustice and death as human limitations" (Kimmo Huovila and Dan Lioy, "Coherence in Ecclesiastes 3:16–22," *Conspectus* 33 (2022): 42–57, 56).

29 Annanlie Steenkamp-Nel, "Transformative joy in Qoheleth: A Thread that Faintly Glistens," *HTS Theological Studies* 75 (2019): 7. https://doi.org/10.4102/hts.v75i3.5126.

30 "During the spiritual journey towards authentic existence, the absurd creates a tension necessary to the maturation and authenticity of the religious person. tension has a function. It urges qohelet to move" (Annanlie Steenkamp-Nel, "Transformative joy in Qoheleth: A Thread that Faintly Glistens," *HTS Theological Studies* 75 (2019): 5).

31 "Qohelet's perception of God changed too. God is not just rules (Torah) and ritual or give just rite and ritual. God gives joy (Eccl 2:24, 25, 3:13, 9:7, 9:9). (…) To be joyful is Divine will. As a result, Qohelet places joy in the core of human life because God, who gives joy, is at the core of human life. He was no longer frozen in a literalist interpretation of the Torah. He became spiritually defrosted" (Annanlie Steenkamp-Nel, "Transformative Joy in Qoheleth: A Thread that Faintly Glistens," *HTS Theological Studies* 75 (2019):5).

32 "Joy matters, not just because life is short, death is near, and God is alive. Joy matters because it is an act that indeed produces internal transformation. The crest of joy is a "perpetual birth" that "creates and recreates those who give themselves to it" (Here, Steenkamp-Nel quotes: Johann Baptist Metz and Jean-Pierre Jossua, *Theology of Joy* [New York: Herder and Herder 1974, 89] (…). To enjoy

The value of work from the Book of Ecclesiastes (Qoheleth)   149

without God is only pleasure. To enjoy with God is joy. Pleasure is situational. Joy is transformational. Qohelet's joy gave readers a view of a future horizon" (Steenkamp-Nel, "Transformative joy in Qoheleth: A Thread that Faintly Glistens," *HTS Theological Studies* 75 (2019): 5–6).

33 "Happiness is thinking of myself; joy is thinking of others. Joy as an aspect of spiritual 'transformation is at the heart of societal transformation' (Here, it is quoted: Iain Provan, *Ecclesiastes, Songs of Songs, The New NIV Application Commentary* [GrandRapids, MI: Zondervan, 2011], 11). Joy moves us to service, because God incarnated in the sensorial becomes service. (…) So, joy is not an emotion. Joy in Qoheleth is 'joy in small things' in transit to 'joy is love for others'. In the previous phase, Qoheleth became aware that the agency was not with the individual. The initiative was/is with God. Where the dynamic between the parties begins and ends is a mystery. To manage (on) the earth became a mutual endeavour" (Iain Provan, *Ecclesiastes, Songs of Songs, the New NIV Application Commentary* [GrandRapids, MI: Zondervan, 2011]).

34 Tyler Atkinson, *Singing at the Winepress. Ecclesiastes and the Ethics of Work* (London: Bloomsbury T and T Clark, 2015), 96.

35 Tyler Atkinson, *Singing at the Winepress. Ecclesiastes and the Ethics of Work* (London: Bloomsbury T and T Clark, 2015), 191.

36 Tyler Atkinson, *Singing at the Winepress. Ecclesiastes and the Ethics of Work* (London: Bloomsbury T and T Clark, 2015), 192.

9 Rethinking work from the Book of Leviticus

Francisco Varo

At first glance, the Book of Leviticus might not appear to be the most obvious choice for establishing a theology of work. However, upon closer examination, this book reveals significant insights into labor, particularly when viewed through the lens of the pressing issues faced by today's workforce. Leviticus originated in a cultural and religious context vastly different from our contemporary world, yet it offers valuable keys that unlock unexplored perspectives for tackling the challenges of our time.

The limited literature addressing the topic of work in the Book of Leviticus is worth noting. There is only one specific publication on the subject, authored by Bob Stallman, as part of a comprehensive project on the theology of work that explores the concept of work in every book of the *Bible*. Stallman's contribution was initially published on the internet in 2013[1] and subsequently consolidated into a single volume alongside other contributions covering various biblical books.[2] The writing style adopted in this work resembles that of a "dictionary entry," offering considerations of notable pastoral interest based on a straightforward reading of the text, as informed by widely accepted commentaries on Leviticus. However, the author does not present groundbreaking original insights but instead offers sensible observations, which are undoubtedly indicative of a skilled preacher.

The lack of specific studies on this subject is not surprising, since the Pentateuch hardly speaks of work itself. The most common Hebrew words for work, *melā'kâ*, *'abōdah*, and their derivatives, appear only a few times in the text and often only marginally.

In Leviticus, the noun *melā'kâ* is used 15 times in various contexts, which do not significantly enhance the theological understanding of this activity. In one instance, the text refers to a "work tool (*melā'kâ*)" that requires purification when it comes into contact with a corpse (Lev 11:32). On another occasion, it is mentioned that God will eliminate anyone engaging in any "work (*melā'kâ*)" on the Day of Atonement (Lev 23:30). Finally, the term is used in the context of enforcing Sabbath rest: "You shall work (*melā'kâ*) for six days, but on the seventh, there shall be a day of complete rest, a sacred assembly, on which you shall not do any work (*melā'kâ*) at all" (Lev 23:3). In all other instances, the term appears in the expression "you shall do no

DOI: 10.4324/9781003508212-11

Rethinking work from the Book of Leviticus 151

manner of work (*melā'kâ*)" when referring to Sabbaths or other solemn rest periods (Lev 16:29; 23:3, 7, 8, 21, 25, 28, 30, 31, 35, 36).

References to work with terms from the root *'ābad* are even rarer. On one occasion, the people are instructed: "If your brother becomes impoverished while with you and sells himself to you, you shall not make him do the work (*'abōdah*) of a slave" (Lev 25:39). A little later, speaking of this impoverished brother, it is mentioned that "he shall work (*ya'abōd*) for you until the jubilee year" (Lev 25:40). And that's about it.

As mentioned earlier, we cannot extract much about work in the Book of Leviticus from a terminological study alone. However, from a different perspective, we believe that the Book of Leviticus has much to offer.

Our research will deviate from traditional biblical theology. This is why the title of this paper is not "Theology of Work in Leviticus," but rather "Rethinking Work from the Book of Leviticus." The rationale behind this choice is that we do not intend to investigate what the writers of Leviticus specifically thought about work, although some insights can be inferred from their writings. Instead, our focus is on uncovering theological clues within this book that can illuminate the contemporary reality of work.

Now, one might still question: Why look for theological clues about work in the Book of Leviticus rather than in another Hebrew *Bible* book where there might be more relevant elements for this purpose? Our decision is rooted in the fact that Leviticus is a paramount book within the Hebrew *Bible* concerning worship. In biblical texts, work and worship are intricately connected, as we will explore further below.[3]

Allow me to explain our methodology. In contemporary biblical exegesis, it's common to approach biblical texts from specific perspectives or contexts, aiming to explore particular dimensions of reality.[4] In the context of work, there has been a suggestion to delve deeper into the relational aspect of work by studying the early chapters of Genesis through the biblical concept of "covenant."[5]

From a methodological standpoint, we will be following this research framework. Specifically, we will approach the text of Leviticus through a particular lens, drawing from Mary Douglas' idea of the interrelationship between the sanctuary's worship and work as a fundamental aspect of the created world. This approach also considers the norms governing sacrifices in ritual contexts and the norms governing the conduct of the people of God in secular contexts, which are found in the "Holiness Code" or "Law of Holiness."[6] Our focus will particularly be on the anthropological and relational dimensions of work, encompassing personal fulfillment, well-being, and harmonious relationships with others, with God, and with nature.

The assertion we made earlier that work and worship are closely interconnected may not be immediately evident. Therefore, in the initial part of our study, we will dedicate our efforts to provide justification for this claim. Once this question has been addressed, the subsequent sections of this study will analyze the texts within the "Law of Holiness" that shed light

152 *Francisco Varo*

on the anthropological and relational dimensions of work, addressing their relevance to contemporary issues in today's world.

Work and worship of God in Genesis

For some years now, it has become almost commonplace in commentaries on the first chapters of Genesis to suggest that the first account has (Gen 1:1–2:4a) an "intent to depict creation as the fashioning of a cosmic temple, which like the later tabernacle and Temple would be a meeting place for God and the human person made in his image and likeness."[7] Indeed, the parallels that the biblical texts draw between the creation of the world and the construction of the sanctuary are evident: the separation of spaces, creation in seven phases, and humanity's role in bringing about, preserving, and maintaining God's work in accordance with the laws established by God or imprinted on nature. The entire universe is presented as a grand stage for worship.[8] The world is declared to be "very good" (Gen 1:31), and all ordinary human activity takes place in this vast temple known as the cosmos.[9]

Considering the parallel between the narratives of the Sanctuary's construction and the creation of the universe, it's worth noting that in Exodus, the Lord gives Moses very specific instructions: "Make me a sanctuary so that I can reside among them. You will make it all according to the design for the Dwelling and the design for its furnishings which I shall now show you" (Exodus 25:8–9). In other words, it's not merely a matter of erecting a sanctuary but, fundamentally, of ensuring it conforms to the pattern revealed by God. The craftsmen tasked with constructing the sanctuary must be in perfect harmony with the divine design. Just as in the creation and preservation of the universe, God intends for someone "in His image and likeness" to carry out His work in perfect accordance with His own design. This individual is tasked with exploring the laws God has established, so that everything may be in perfect order, and continuing the construction of the world in full fidelity to the intrinsic rules of nature that the Lord has bestowed upon each element.[10] This responsibility entrusted to humanity for the development and care of the created world is what we refer to as work.

It should be noted that the explicit statement in Genesis, where God created man and woman in His "image" and according to His "likeness" (Gen 1:26–27), directs the reader of the Hebrew Bible to the family sphere. It highlights what parents and children share and invokes the responsibilities they have toward one another.[11] The vocation of humans, both to work and to the family, represents the same underlying reality. Hence, "a renewal of the idea of what work is cannot take place without a profound reflection on human co-existence based on a healthy conception of what the family is."[12]

The biblical text goes on to say, "Let us make man in our image, after our likeness. They shall rule the fish of the sea, the birds of the sky, the cattle, the whole earth, and all the creeping things that creep on earth" (Gen 1:26). The verb "rule" (*rādāh*) belongs to the vocabulary associated with

Rethinking work from the Book of Leviticus 153

the responsibilities of a king (1 Kgs 5:1–5). In the context of the ancient Near East, the king is expected to care for his people in a manner similar to a shepherd tending to his flock (Ezek 34:1–4; Ps 72:8–14). It doesn't imply arbitrary enjoyment of possessions but rather entails taking responsibility for the well-being of that which is under one's dominion. The task of man, created in the "image" and "likeness" of God, is, as previously mentioned, to collaborate with Him in the preservation and maintenance of creation, in accordance with the laws God Himself has inscribed in nature.[13]

The subsequent account (Gen 2:4a–25) complements the first one. The Lord creates man and places him in the Garden of Eden, a description that literally includes features that immediately evoke thoughts of a sanctuary.[14] The mention of the rivers of paradise (Gen 2:10–14) serves to connect the geography of Eden with the geography of Earth, indicating a sense of continuity. Furthermore, the presence of four rivers flowing in different directions suggests that this garden is situated atop a mountain, akin to the Temple of Jerusalem.[15]

God placed man in the garden "to work it (*lĕ'ābdāh*) and keep it (*lĕšāmrāh*)" (Gen 2:15). The Lord provided man with a pleasant and agreeable environment for his life and assigned him a specific task. The verb *'ābad* means "to work, to serve," and also "to worship." These are not two distinct realities designated by the same word but rather two inseparable dimensions of the same reality[16]:

> It is significant that the Hebrew lexicon uses the same word, *'abodah*, to indicate the manual labor of the working day (Lev 23:7–8) and the cultic activity carried out in the temple (Num 4:4,19; 8:11; Josh 22:27). In reality, these are two aspects of the same reality: God dwells in the temple, while the world is the temple that narrates the presence of God; in both cases the realities are the presences of God to which the human being has been admitted in order to develop his own work of collaboration with the divinity.[17]

The verb *šāmar* means "to keep, to fulfill the commandments." In the biblical text, worship and work are intertwined, and work that brings glory to God is inherently connected to obedience of God's laws. It is only through respecting the laws inscribed by the Creator in the natural order that we carry out His work in the world, and our work itself becomes an act of worship.[18] In the world's sanctuary, God is worshipped through work,[19] whether by making the earth fruitful, understanding the laws of nature through observation, adhering to them, or collaborating with God in the ongoing process of creation. Humans are thus presented as the priests of this temple, offering worship to God through their work in tending the garden, while the family serves as the sphere where their lives flourish.[20]

These insights are not exclusive to contemporary exegesis. The rabbinic tradition has also emphasized the connection between the world, the

154 *Francisco Varo*

sanctuary, and human labor, which appears to be intertwined with the worship of God and the fulfillment of His commands:

> With love abounding did the Holy One, blessed be He, love the first man, inasmuch as He created him in a pure locality, in the place of the Temple, and He brought him into His palace, as it is said, "And the Lord God took the man, and put him into the garden of Eden to work it and to keep it" (Gn 2:15). From which place did He take him? From the place of the Temple, and He brought him into His palace, which is Eden, as it is said, "And he put him into the garden of Eden to work it" (*ibid.*). Perhaps thou wilt say: To plough (the fields) and cast out the stones from the ground. But did not all the trees grow up of their own accord?
>
> Perhaps thou wilt say: There was some other work (to be done) in the garden of Eden, (such as) to water the garden. But did not a river flow through and issue forth from Eden, and water the garden, as it is said, "And a river went out of Eden to water the garden" (Gen. 2:10)?
>
> What then is the meaning of this expression: "to work it and to keep it"? (The text) does not say "to work it and to keep it" except (in the sense) of being occupied with the words of the Torah and keeping all its commandments, as it is said, "to keep the way of the tree of life" (Gen. 3:24). But the "tree of life" signifies only the Torah, as it is said, "It is a tree of life to them that lay hold upon it" (Prv 3:18).
>
> (*Pirke Rabbi Eliezer* 12,1)[21]

Work and worship in Genesis and Leviticus

Just as Genesis is the main book on God's original designs for the world and humanity, Leviticus serves as the central book in the Pentateuch for worship.

The Book of Genesis, while addressing human work, hints at the idea that this human activity is also inherently meant to be an act of worship toward God. It provides a means of accessing Him and giving Him the glory He deserves. Through work, we can gain a deeper understanding of what worship truly entails.

However, in the Book of Leviticus, we approach the same reality from a different perspective. Here, we learn about legitimate worship and its requisites. Yet, it is crucial to recognize that what is established for worship within the framework of the sanctuary, which serves as a model for the world, is closely linked to the work of human beings in the broader universe. The standards established by the Lord for worship offer insights into the divine logic that should guide all work.

On this basis, let us now delve into the ritual norms found in Leviticus that provide answers to perennial questions about the nature, purpose, and reality of human work within God's divine plans.

Sacrifices and offerings at the Sanctuary

One significant observation regarding the relationship between worship of God and work in the Book of Leviticus pertains to the presentation of offerings and animals for various types of sacrifices. While in other books of the Bible it is mentioned that artifacts, vessels, and other cultic objects are offered to the Lord (e.g., Num 7:3), Leviticus predominantly emphasizes the presentation of animal or plant offerings. These offerings represent something that God provides in nature, yet they also require human labor, whether in the care of livestock (Lev 1 and 3) or in agriculture (Lev 2).[22]

Worship and livestock farming

Sacrifices are offered as a gift to the Lord, recognizing His sovereignty.[23] In the regulations for the burnt offering, it is stated that "when any of you presents an offering of cattle (*běhemāh*) to the Lord, he shall choose his offering from the herd or from the flock" (Lev 1:2). The term "cattle" (*běhemāh*) refers to "domestic quadrupeds."[24] Among these, cattle, such as oxen or cows, held the highest value among domesticated animals, not only in Israel but also throughout the Syro-Canaanite region. They provided essential resources like milk and its by-products and occasionally served as a plentiful source of meat. Consequently, they commanded a high price in trade. The act of sacrificing an ox, as required for the burnt offering, meant giving up something of significant value for one's own well-being, something acquired through hard work.[25]

However, not everyone had access to an ox. Therefore, the legislation on the burnt offering also allowed for offerings of small livestock, such as lambs or kids (Lev 1:10), and even for the poorest, two turtledoves or young pigeons (Lev 1:14). In every case, it demanded a high level of generosity from the offerer, as it meant giving up something valuable for sustenance. Additionally, the offering had to be of high quality, as it always required an "unblemished" animal (Lv 1:3, 10).

Wild animals could not be offered as sacrifices.[26] This was due, on the one hand, to the incompatibility of the ritual of sacrifice with hunting. However, it was primarily to convey recognition to God, as indicated by the inner sacrifice of giving up something whose possession had involved considerable effort, either in raising the livestock or in acquiring it from a livestock farmer.[27] Utilizing an animal caught in the wild without human involvement did not clearly express gratitude to God for the blessings received, as it did not represent something that resulted from human labor and, simultaneously, a gift from God.

All that has been discussed here applies similarly to peace offerings (Lev 3:1, 6), sin offerings (Lev 4:23, 28, 32), and guilt offerings (Lev 5:15, 18, 25).

156 *Francisco Varo*

Worship and the processing of agricultural products

The second chapter of Leviticus discusses the agricultural offerings presented to the Lord. The first one mentioned is as follows: "When anyone brings a grain offering as an offering to the Lord, his offering shall be of fine flour. He shall pour oil on it and put incense on it" (Lev 2:1). The use of "fine flour" implies meticulous grinding, resulting in a delicate and highly valued product.[28] It is also prescribed that the meal offering be either baked in a casserole or cooked in a frying pan, always mixed with oil (Lev 2:4–10). In other instances, offerings include roasted ears of corn and crumbled grain, to which oil and incense are added (Lev 2:14–15). Interestingly, the sanctuary facilities do not mention a designated area for roasting or cooking these products, thus requiring the Israelites to bring them already prepared from their homes.[29]

Furthermore, in Chapter 7, various types of agricultural offerings are mentioned again:

> If he offers it for a thanksgiving, then he shall offer with the thanksgiving sacrifice unleavened loaves mixed with oil, unleavened wafers smeared with oil, and loaves of fine flour well mixed with oil. With the sacrifice of his peace offerings for thanksgiving he shall bring his offering with loaves of leavened bread.
>
> (Lev 7:12–13)

It's worth noting that in all cases, the prescribed offerings involve processed products (wheat ground into flour, kneaded with oil, obtained from pressing olives; flour baked to make cakes, toasted ears of cereal). These offerings are both gifts of the earth that God has bestowed upon His people and, inseparably, the result of human labor. The various methods of preparing these offerings likely reflect common practices in preparing daily meals, as the people offer to God the sustenance they consume regularly. There is something inherently human in these offerings, and once presented to the Lord, they become "something very holy" (Lev 2:3).[30]

Worship and family celebration

Continuing with the topic of sacrifices, it's worth noting what is implied in the regulations regarding communion sacrifices. In this case, a portion of the victim was set aside as an offering to the Lord, which belonged to the priest who had performed the sacrifice. Apart from this reserved portion, the meat of the victim was given to the offerer to be consumed on the day of its offering, with nothing left over until the following morning (Lev 7:15).

Naturally, one person couldn't consume all the meat, making it a highly opportune moment to share it with others.[31] By sharing this meal, the participants invoked divine blessings that would enrich their daily work and

Rethinking work from the Book of Leviticus 157

safeguard their family members from harm.[32] These sacrifices served as not only moments of encounter between the offerer and God but also with other family members or members of the community, fostering a joyful and celebratory atmosphere. This was especially significant as, apart from the aristocrats, consuming meat in such quantities was a rare occurrence, happening only a few times a year.[33] These sacrifices presented an ideal opportunity to establish regular gatherings with extended family and strengthen the bonds of fraternity, all while including God in this intimate encounter.[34]

The shared joy among one's family, clan, neighbors, and friends further underscores this act of worship. If there is an intrinsic connection between worship and work, it encourages us to recognize that the pursuit of family and social well-being must also be closely linked to work.[35] In other words, work and communion, work and unity among people, are intertwined aspects of life.

The "holiness code"

The observations we have just made highlight the relationship between worship and work, which is evident in the sacrificial regulations where offerings to God always consist of the fruits of one's labor. However, in Leviticus, worship is not confined within the bounds of the sanctuary; it finds expression in the ordinary life of God's people. Let's now delve into these rules.

A substantial section of Leviticus (Lev 17:1–26:46)[36] is commonly referred to as the "Holiness Code" or "Law of Holiness." This section resembles an extensive legal code and encompasses a wide array of regulations pertaining to the worship of God in ordinary life. It includes various prescriptions. Mary Douglas, a renowned British anthropologist celebrated for her studies on biblical texts, particularly Leviticus,[37] explains that 'holiness' in this context signifies a moral order that grounds legal instructions in God and gives a unified meaning to these diverse regulations. Interestingly, this concept of "holiness" holds great potential for a reflection on work:

> Developing the idea of holiness as order, not confusion, upholds rectitude and straight-dealing as holy, and contradiction and double-dealing as against holiness. Theft, lying, false witness, cheating in weights and measures, all kinds of dissembling such as speaking ill of the deaf (and presumably smiling to their faces), hating your brother in your heart (while presumably speaking kindly to him), these are clearly contradictions between what seems and what is.[38]

The order implicit in the norms of the "Law of Holiness" reflects the order established by God in nature. Here, worship and work as human realities in the created universe are interconnected. As Mary Douglas also observes, there is a correspondence between the holiness required in ritual contexts and what members of God's people must do for each other in secular contexts.[39]

158   *Francisco Varo*

Within the comprehensive regulations of this legal code, the rules regarding justice in human relations, particularly in labor matters, and respect for nature (Lev 19:1–37) are highly relevant. These regulations are accompanied by instructions on sanctifying time through the celebration of feasts, the sabbatical year, and the jubilee year (Lev 23:1–25:55).

Holiness and social justice

In Chapter 19 of Leviticus, we encounter thought-provoking rules regarding reaping and harvesting. The text instructs:

> When you reap the harvest of your land, you shall not reap your field right up to its edge, neither shall you gather the gleanings after your harvest. And you shall not strip your vineyard bare, neither shall you gather the fallen grapes of your vineyard. You shall leave them for the poor and for the sojourner.
>
> (Lev 19:9–10)

These precepts are reiterated later:

> And when you reap the harvest of your land, you shall not reap your field right up to its edge, nor shall you gather the gleanings after your harvest. You shall leave them for the poor and for the sojourner.
>
> (Lev 23:22)

In contrast to other Near Eastern cultures where leaving produce in the field may have been seen as an offering to gods or spirits, here, it is specified that "you shall leave them for the poor and for the sojourner" (Lev 19:10).[40] This regulation aims to facilitate access to essential food for all and is rooted in the belief that "the land is mine, and you are strangers and sojourners with me" (Lev 25:23). God's sovereignty over Earth's resources is absolute, and He is the ultimate owner of all that the land produces. Yet, God does not neglect anyone, especially those in need. With this instruction, God establishes a system of social protection[41] that enables the poor and foreigners to sustain themselves with dignity through their labor.[42] Simultaneously, this rule restrains the Israelites' desire for excessive profit, a common tendency among landowners in any era.[43]

The subsequent rules cover various aspects of daily life and particularly address work-related matters. Among these, there is a rephrased version of a traditional precept: "You shall not steal, you shall not deal falsely, you shall not lie to one another" (Lev 19:11). The commandments of the Law of Holiness build upon those of the Decalogue, offering more comprehensive and nuanced guidance. While in Exodus and Deuteronomy, the command is expressed in the singular, it is now formulated in the plural and addressed to the entire community. Moreover, the regulations specify various forms of concealed theft, such as fraud or deception, leaving no room for exceptions.[44] God protects the property of every Israelite.[45]

Further along, the demands of justice are reiterated: "You shall not falsify measures of length, weight, or capacity" (Lev 19:35), providing detailed instructions for honest buying and selling transactions in the marketplace. God is vigilant about upholding honesty in commercial dealings.[46]

Justice in the realm of work relations carries significant implications, particularly when one party is vulnerable: "You will not exploit or rob your neighbour. You will not keep back the labourer's wage until next morning" (Lev 19:13). An important extension of "You shall not steal" is the prohibition of exploitation or mistreatment of one's neighbor, especially the weakest. The obligation to pay daily wages ensures that workers have access to the necessary sustenance for themselves and their families.[47]

In this context, the regulations extend to specific details regarding the treatment of disabled individuals: "You shall not curse the deaf or put a stumbling block before the blind" (Lev 19:14).[48] Jacob Milgrom notes that in the ancient Near East there is a glaring absence of laws protecting the disabled,[49] but in the "Law of Holiness" it is clear that the protection of people, especially the most disadvantaged, is close to God's heart. Harming or demeaning them contradicts the requirements of holiness that are essential for worship,[50] as it devalues the image of God in every human being.[51]

Finally, in a concise statement, this chapter reaches the pinnacle of all the rules presented for participating in divine holiness[52]: "You shall love your neighbor as yourself" (Lev 19:18).[53] The verb used (*'āhab*) for loving one's neighbor is the same as that used in Deuteronomy to describe love for God: "You shall love the Lord your God with all your heart and with all your soul and with all your strength" (Deut 6:5).[54] Indeed, love of God and love of neighbor are two facets of the same reality.

Holiness and respect for nature

One of the recurring themes that arise when seeking the foundations of the rules in the "Law of Holiness" is that of respecting nature. Natural goods belong to God, and humanity has no absolute authority over them. It is not our place to tamper with the inherent rules of their nature, which have been established by the Lord.

In this context, consider the following command: "You shall not let your cattle mate with a different kind; you shall not sow your field with two kinds of seed; you shall not put on cloth from a mixture of two kinds of material" (Lev 19:19). These customs have deep historical roots. Mary Douglas explains that they stem from the belief that purity is found in the unadulterated. Holiness is closely connected with order and is incompatible with chaos or disorder. There is an instinctual aversion, as the anthropologist notes, to the mixing of disparate entities that do not naturally go together.[55] This aversion arises as an instinctive reaction, reflecting a respect for the natural order

160 *Francisco Varo*

of things, emphasizing the need to avoid artificially altering natural processes. While these may appear to be ancient customs that have been surpassed, they perhaps suggest the importance of recognizing that there are limits to experimentation or creativity (consider, for instance, genetic manipulation) that should not be transgressed.[56]

Equally significant is the command regarding fruit trees:

> once you have entered the country and planted any kind of fruit tree, you will regard its fruit as uncircumcised. For three years you will count it as uncircumcised and it will not be eaten; in the fourth year, all its fruit will be consecrated to Yahweh in a feast of praise; and in the fifth year you may eat its fruit, so that it may yield you even more. I am the Lord your God.
>
> (Lev 19:23–25)

This means that during the first three years, the fruit should be removed before it fully matures, allowing the tree to allocate its energy toward strengthening its roots and branches.[57] In the fourth year, when the tree can produce an abundant yield for the first time, the entire harvest is dedicated to the Lord, and only from the fifth year onward may the fruits be consumed. This rule promotes respect for the natural laws and timing established by divine wisdom to facilitate the growth of trees. Simultaneously, it underscores God's sovereignty over the earth, which provides the sustenance we need, leading to the dedication of the tree's first fruits to Him.[58]

Closely tied to the belief in God's dominion over the earth is the practice of offering the first fruits of the harvest. At the beginning of the harvest season, a sheaf is brought to the priest as an offering to the Lord, representing the first fruits. This sheaf is presented before the Lord on the day after the Sabbath, accompanied by a lamb offered as a burnt offering along with its oblation (Lev 23:10–13). The first fruits of the harvest are reserved for the Lord, and nothing from the new harvest may be consumed until this ritual has taken place (Lev 23:14). This rule imposes a significant restriction on the laborers, who would naturally desire to satisfy their hunger as their energy wanes during their work.[59] Complying with this command serves as a continuous reminder that they are not ultimate owners of these resources; instead, the true owner of the land is the Lord. Although He provides the land for the people's sustenance, the offering of the first fruits from each harvest is a token of gratitude for the gift bestowed by God.

Holiness and rest

Chapter 19 of Leviticus begins with the characteristic formula of the "Law of Holiness": "Be holy, for I, the Lord your God, am holy" (Lev 19:1–2). Among the rules for observing this holiness, we find the command: "Keep my Sabbaths" (Lev 19:3). The Creator of the world instructs humanity in the

Rethinking work from the Book of Leviticus 161

proper functioning of all creation. In this context, periodic rest is of primary importance for the harmony of the whole. It allows people to pause and reflect on themselves, others, and on their relationship with God, and thus to detect promptly any dysfunctions that may arise in order to restore inner balance and interpersonal relationships, but above all to restore their own behavior before the Lord.

This rule also has a social dimension, as rest and participation in worship provide suitable occasions for bonding. It allows individuals to get to know others in a peaceful environment, separate from work. The Lord can prescribe the rule of Sabbath rest because, in addition to being the sole owner of the space where human life and work occur, He also owns time itself. Just as God establishes rules to ensure that all may benefit from Earth's produce, especially the most disadvantaged, He also sets prescriptions to govern time in the service of a person's integral fulfillment. Therefore, the "Law of Holiness" continues to emphasize what was already part of Israel's tradition: "You will work for six days, but the seventh will be a day of complete rest, a day for the sacred assembly on which you do no work at all" (Lev 23:3).

The Sabbath (*šabāt*) is etymologically related to the verb "to rest," as noted in the Genesis creation account, where God is said to have rested from all His work (Gen 2:2). In the Decalogue, the Sabbath day is commanded to be remembered to keep it holy. Both formulations of the Decalogue emphasize its character as a day of rest, though for different reasons: In Deuteronomy, it allows those who work to rest, recalling the slavery in Egypt (Deut 5:12–15), while in Exodus, the cessation of all work serves as a reminder of God's rest in creation (Ex 20:8–11).

However, the primary purpose of the Sabbath is not merely to refrain from work but to have time to dedicate to the Lord. This is why it is described as "a day of complete rest, a day for the sacred assembly" (Lev 23:3). It is also and inseparably a day of joy and delight, as the Book of Isaiah underscores:

> If you refrain from breaking the Sabbath, from taking your own pleasure on my holy day, if you call the Sabbath 'Delightful', and the day sacred to Yahweh 'Honourable', if you honour it by abstaining from travel, from seeking your own pleasure and from too much talk, then you will find true happiness in the Lord.
>
> (Is 58:13–14a)[60]

In a parallel manner, just as humans are to rest every seventh day to renew themselves, Earth must rest every seventh year to rejuvenate itself: "In the seventh year, the land will have a sabbatical rest, a Sabbath for the Lord" (Lev 25:4). This rest is "for the Lord," implying not just a cessation of work but a period of consecration to God, acknowledging His sovereignty over Earth and expressing gratitude for the gift of possessing it. These biblical texts from ancient times already contain implicit ecological sensitivity and concern for the care of the planet, issues that remain relevant today.[61]

162 *Francisco Varo*

Similarly, the conclusion of a series of seven jubilee years is marked by special solemnity:

> You will count seven weeks of years, seven times seven years, that is to say a period of seven weeks of years, forty-nine years. And on the tenth day of the seventh month you will sound the trumpet; on the Day of Expiation you will sound the trumpet throughout the land. You will declare this fiftieth year to be sacred and proclaim the liberation of all the country's inhabitants. You will keep this as a jubilee: each of you will return to his ancestral property, each to his own clan. This fiftieth year will be a jubilee year for you; in it you will not sow, you will not harvest the grain that has come up on its own or in it gather grapes from your untrimmed vine. The jubilee will be a holy thing for you; during it you will eat whatever the fields produce.
>
> (Lev 25:8–12)

Perhaps the most characteristic feature of the jubilee year is the return of property to its original owner: "You will keep this as a jubilee: each of you will return to his ancestral property, each to his own clan" (Lev 25:10; cf. 25:13). This rule is designed to address enduring issues: When a person falls into debt and circumstances turn against them, they may have to part with their property, and in extreme cases, they might become enslaved due to insurmountable debts. These were common situations in the ancient world and continue to occur during contemporary crises.[62] Economic upheavals can generate significant social disparities between a small group of prosperous individuals and a large mass of disadvantaged people struggling to make ends meet.

The jubilee year regulations provide periodic intervention in the economy to prevent dramatic cascades of bankruptcy and irreversible inequalities, which disrupt social harmony and individual well-being. These regulations stipulate that properties sold or disposed of in previous years, out of necessity or other reasons, should be returned to their original owners or their descendants. Additionally, those who had been reduced to slavery were to regain their freedom.[63]

The overarching principle of this legislation is that God, the Creator of all, is the sole owner of the earth. He places it at the disposal of His people by imposing on them the conditions that promote equity and the common good.[64] Thus, "land will not be sold absolutely, for the land belongs to me, and you are only strangers and guests of mine" (Lev 25:23). The owner is only the one who has the right to use it for his or her livelihood. Rather than buying or selling the land, what is sold are the remaining crops until the next jubilee year.[65] Ownership is conditional, and the concept of the "right of redemption" (*gĕ'ulāh*) is established (Lev 25:24) to rescue those who find themselves in compromised situations, unable to extricate themselves. In fact, the term *gĕ'ulāh* is related to the verb *gā'al*, which means "to redeem."

A look at contemporary work from Leviticus

We mentioned at the outset of our discussion that our aim was not to develop a comprehensive "theology of work" from the Book of Leviticus. Instead, we intended to identify and highlight the theological insights within this book that can offer perspective on the modern work landscape.

In contemporary discourse, there are numerous challenges related to work. Phrases such as "decent work," "inclusive labor protection," "evolving world of work," "just transition," and "environmentally sustainable economies and societies" frequently surface in public debates concerning the urgent issues arising from new and contemporary work environments.

When considering contemporary challenges faced by individuals, several issues come to the foreground. These include temporary employment, work conducted through platforms or telecommuting, the coordination of work hours and rest periods, effective time management in work planning, achieving a work-life balance, the development of contractual and wage policies, and their impact on time utilization, worker safety, and birth rates, as well as addressing the needs of migrants and workers with disabilities.[66] Similarly, when examining the transition toward a sustainable framework, questions arise regarding macroeconomic and industrial policies that can harness technological innovation, the necessity for requalification and the acquisition of new skills in rapidly evolving labor markets, and the consequences of these transformations on the job market, which may have adverse effects on certain workers.[67]

Can Leviticus offer any insights into addressing these questions? While most of its directives may not have direct applicability, and the conceptual framework that contrasts order versus chaos underpinning the norms of the Law of Holiness may not directly align with contemporary solutions, this book undeniably provides valuable sapiential insights that could be of interest.

When we contemplate the pressing challenges that contemporary professional life presents, such as the crucial need for coordination between work and rest or the proper balance between one's professional and family responsibilities, we can find guidance in the biblical texts we have examined. These texts reveal that the Creator of the world instructs man about the proper functioning of all creation. They establish important directives like observing the Sabbath rest and the feasts that govern the times at the service of the integral fulfillment of the person (Lv 23:1–44). Additionally, communion sacrifices, by their very nature, foster moments of encounter between the offerer and God, but also among people within a celebratory and joyous context. Thus, it becomes evident that rest and festivity are integral aspects of worship. The parallel between worship and work outlined in these texts encourages us to recognize that, within the divine design, the pursuit of family and social well-being is a fundamental reality that deserves full consideration in work planning. Any form of work that undermines family cohesion or obstructs social conciliation is ultimately meaningless.

164   *Francisco Varo*

Regarding the present challenge of "decent work," we can find valuable insights in the rules outlined in Leviticus, Chapter 19. These rules, while advocating for the strictest justice and the protection of individual property, prioritize the good of the community over the pursuit of maximum profits by property owners. The regulations pertaining to harvests and grape harvests, which we have previously discussed, are designed to ensure that everyone has access to the necessary food for their sustenance (Lev 19:9–10). It can be argued that God establishes a social protection system that enables the poor and foreigners to work with dignity for their livelihoods, while simultaneously curbing the Israelites' desire for excessive profits from their property. Additionally, the rules intended to safeguard personal property are highly relevant, as they delve into specific details of buying and selling transactions in the market, ensuring that these transactions are conducted fairly and honestly, without any form of theft, fraud, or deception (Lev 19:11–12).

Of utmost importance are the provisions aimed at shielding the weak or vulnerable from exploitation or oppression, as well as those that offer special protection for individuals with disabilities (Lev 19:13–18). These guidelines underscore that caring for migrants and people with disabilities is not an indulgence of affluent societies but a fundamental requirement for human dignity, a principle that the laws of Leviticus emphatically proclaim.

Attention to achieving an "environmentally sustainable" world, another undoubtedly topical issue, is also not foreign to this biblical book. As previously mentioned, the "Holiness Code" (Lev 17:1–26:46) conveys the order established by God in nature through various means. Within its rules, worship and work are interconnected realities. Importantly, the Code stipulates that just as humans are required to rest every seventh day to renew themselves, the earth itself is to have a period of rest every seventh year to rejuvenate, as mandated by the institution of the sabbatical year (Lev 25:1–7). Additionally, even the regulation regarding "uncircumcised" fruit (Lev 19:23–25), which mandates plucking fruit buds during the first three years after planting a tree, allowing the tree to channel its energies into root and branch growth, reflects a keen sensitivity toward efficient and sustainable agriculture.

Fundamentally, all the rules of the "Law of Holiness" are underpinned by a profound respect for nature and its inherent laws, established by the Creator. Consequently, humans cannot possess natural goods in an absolute manner, nor can they alter the rules that the Lord has assigned to them, as evidenced by the regulations related to the preservation of species and the prohibition of crossbreeding (Lev 19:19). While these customs may appear to us as ancient practices that have been surpassed, they nonetheless underscore the idea that there are limits to experimentation or creativity (consider, for instance, genetic manipulation) that should not be exceeded. Moreover, the cultic prescriptions, such as reserving the first fruits produced by trees or offering the initial harvest (Lev 19:23–25), emphasize God's sovereignty over the earth, which provides human beings with the means for their sustenance.

Rethinking work from the Book of Leviticus   165

One of the most significant challenges in today's world of work concerns the governance of labor transition toward a sustainable framework. This transition often brings adverse effects on some workers who may lack the capacity or opportunities to acquire the new skills demanded by a constantly changing labor market influenced by rapid technological innovation. Is it advisable to establish mechanisms to prevent, address, or resolve these crises that can push individuals or families into insurmountable ruin?

While operating in a vastly different cultural context, the regulations of the jubilee year (Lev 25:8–12) can be seen as an attempt to periodically intervene in the economy. This intervention aims to prevent the imbalances that arise within the social fabric due to various factors from triggering a devastating chain reaction of bankruptcies and irreversible inequalities. Such circumstances could ultimately disrupt social harmony and the well-being of the people. The central guiding principle underlying all jubilee year legislation is that God, the Creator of everything, is the sole owner of the earth. He places it at the disposal of His people while imposing conditions that promote fairness and the common good.

In conclusion, the Book of Leviticus does not present a fully developed theology of work, nor is it a comprehensive manual for addressing labor issues in any era. However, it does provide valuable theological and wisdom-based principles that can stimulate reflection and offer insights into contemporary work. In Leviticus, we come to understand that God's holiness embodies order as opposed to chaos, righteousness, fair dealings, and love for one's neighbor. In this vast temple, which is the world itself, the Lord has positioned human beings as intelligent interpreters of creation. The highest form of worship in this cosmic sanctuary is the act of interpreting the divine design through our labor.

Notes

1 Theology of Work Project and Bob Stallman, "Leviticus and Work". *Theology of Work Project* 19 (2013): (https://digitalcommons.spu.edu/tow_project/19).

2 Bob Stallman, "Leviticus and Work," *Theology of Work. Bible Commentary: Genesis through Revelation*, ed. Theology of Work Project (Peabody, MA: Hendrickson Publishers Marketing, 2016), 117–141.

3 The relationship between work and worship, as well-attested in biblical texts, is an integral part of the significant cultural and religious tradition of the ancient Near East. This subject has been thoroughly examined in a robust and well-structured monograph exploring Mesopotamian and biblical sources, including translations from Sumerian, Akkadian, and Hebrew. See: José Antonio Castro Lodeiro, *Venid y trabajad. ¡Es tiempo de alabar! La vocación del hombre en los relatos de creación mesopotámicos y bíblicos*, IBO 5 (Estella: Verbo Divino, 2020). The seventh chapter entitled "Worship: The Soul of Work" (pp. 269–302) is of particular interest.

4 For a more detailed explanation, with some concrete examples, see Santiago Guijarro, "La aportación del análisis contextual a la exégesis de los textos bíblicos," *Cuestiones Teológicas* 44 (2017): 283–300, http://dx.doi.org/10.18566/cueteo.v44n102.a04, especially 286–291.

166 Francisco Varo

5 Thus, for example, Gregorio Guitián and Ana Marta González, "Theology of Work: New Perspectives," *Scripta Theologica* 54 (2022): 757–787, 772, https://doi.org/10.15581/006.54.3.757-787. This proposal has been taken into consideration and developed in the study by Diego Pérez-Gondar, "The Anthropology of Work from Biblical Theology. A New Consideration of Gn 2:4b–25," *Scripta Theologica* 55 (2023): 9–37, https://doi.org/10.15581/006.55.1.9-37.

6 Mary Douglas, "Justice as the Cornerstone. An Interpretation of Leviticus 18–20," *Interpretation* 53, no. 4 (1999): 341–350, 348, https://doi.org/10.1177/002096439905300403.

7 Scott Hahn, "Canon, Cult and Covenant," *Canon and Biblical Interpretation*, eds. Craig G. Bartholomew et al. (Grand Rapids, MI: Zondervan, 2006), 209–235, 213.

8 For a more developed comparison between the early chapters of Genesis and the account of the building of the Sanctuary in Exodus see Joseph Blenkinsopp, *Prophecy and Canon* (Notre Dame, IN: University of Notre Dame Press, 1977), 59–69; Jon D. Levenson, "The Temple and the World," *The Journal of Religion* 64, no. 3 (1984): 275–298, https://doi.org/10.1086/487131; Jon D. Levenson, *Creation and the Persistence of Evil* (Princeton, NJ: Princeton University Press, 1994), 66–99; Richard E. Averbeck, "The Tabernacle and Creation" *Dictionary of the Old Testament: Pentateuch*, eds. T. Desmond Alexander and David W. Baker (Downers Grove, IL: InterVarsity Press, 2003), 816–818; Terje Stordalen, *Echoes of Eden: Genesis 2–3 and Symbolism of the Eden Garden in Biblical Hebrew Literature* (Leuven: Peeters, 2000).

9 Lifsa Schachter, "The Garden of Eden as God's First Sanctuary," *Jewish Bible Quarterly* 41, no. 2 (2013): 73–77; Jeffrey L. Morrow, *Liturgy and Sacrament, Mystagogy and Martyrdom: Essays in Theological Exegesis* (Eugene, OR: Pickwick, 2020); John Bergsma, "The Creation Narratives and the Original Unity of Work and Worship in the Human Vocation," *Work: Theological Foundations and Practical Implications*, eds. R. Keith Loftin and Trey Dimsdale (London: SCM Press, 2018), 11–29.

10 Cf. Jeremy H. Kidwell, *Drawn into Worship: A Biblical Ethics of Work* (Edinburgh: The University of Edinburgh – School of Divinity, 2013), 30.

11 Cf. Carly L. Crouch, "Genesis 1:26–7 as a Statement of Humanity's Divine Parentage," *The Journal of Theological Studies* 61, no. 1 (2010): 1–15, https://doi.org/10.1093/jts/flp185.

12 Cf. Pérez-Gondar, "The Anthropology of Work from Biblical Theology. A New Consideration of Gn 2:4b–25," *Scripta Theologica* 55 (2023): 33.

13 Cf. Félix García López, *La Torah. Escritos sobre el Pentateuco* (Estella: Verbo Divino, 2012), 99–101.

14 Cf. Gordon Wenham, "Sanctuary Symbolism in the Garden of Eden Story," *I Studied Inscriptions from Before the Flood*, ed. Richard Hess (Winona Lake, IN: Eisenbrauns, 1994), 399–405, 403.

15 Cf. Donald Parry, "Garden of Eden Prototype Sanctuary," *Temples of the Ancient World*, ed. Donald Parry (Salt Lake City, UT: Deseret Book, 2004), 126–151, 133.

16 On the relationship between the biblical creation narratives and man's vocation to work and worship, cf. Bergsma, "The Creation Narratives," 15–18.

17 Giuseppe Deiana, *Levitico* (Milano: Paoline, 2005), 36.

18 Cf. Francisco Varo, "Naturaleza, trabajo y dignidad del hombre. Gen 2, 4b–6 y su inserción en el canon judío," *Esperanza del hombre y revelación bíblica*, eds. José María Casciaro et al. (Pamplona: Eunsa, 1996), 333–350.

19 This is one of the numerous allusions in this second creation account to the world as the first great sanctuary. Cf. Schachter, "The Garden of Eden," 73–77.

20 Cf. Dexter E. Callender Jr., *Adam in Myth and History: Ancient Israelite Perspectives on the Primal Human*, Harvard Semitic Studies, 48 (Winona Lake, IN: Eisenbrauns, 2000), 29.

Rethinking work from the Book of Leviticus   167

21 *Pirke de Rabbi Eliezer*, trad. Gerald Friedlander (New York: Hermon Press, 1970), 84.
22 We do not intend to delve into the complex technical debate about sacrifices and offerings in Leviticus at this moment. Instead, we aim to highlight some observations about its norms and rituals that may be relevant for a theological reflection on work. For a comprehensive and up-to-date *status quaestionis* of scholarly studies on the subject, see Liane M. Feldman, *The Story of Sacrifice: Ritual and Narrative in the Priestly Source* (Tübingen: Mohr Siebeck, 2020), 7–26.
23 Cf. John E. Hartley, *Leviticus* (Dallas: Word Books, 1992), lxix–lxx.
24 Cf. Liane M. Feldman, *The Story of Sacrifice: Ritual and Narrative in the Priestly Source* (Tübingen: Mohr Siebeck, 2020), 53, n. 67.
25 Cf. Erhard S. Gerstenberger, *Leviticus: A Commentary* (Louisville, KY: Westminster John Knox Press, 1996), 27.
26 Cf. John E Hartley, *Leviticus* (Dallas: Word Books, 1992), 11.
27 Cf. Cornelis Van Dam, "The Burnt Offering in Its Biblical Context," *Mid-America Journal of Theology* 7, no. 2 (1991) 195–206, 201.
28 Cf. Erhard S. Gerstenberger, *Leviticus: A Commentary* (Louisville, KY Westminster John Knox Press, 1996), 39.
29 Cf. Feldman, *The Story of Sacrifice: Ritual and Narrative in the Priestly Source* (Tübingen: Mohr Siebeck, 2020), 55.
30 Cf. Ephraim Radner, *Leviticus* (Grand Rapids, MI: Brazos Press, 2020), 48.
31 Cf. Jeremy H. Kidwell, *Drawn into Worship: A Biblical Ethics of Work* (Edinburgh: The University of Edinburgh – School of Divinity, 2013), 216.
32 Cf. John E. Hartley, *Leviticus* (Dallas: Word Books, 1992), 42.
33 Cf. Jacob Milgrom, *Leviticus: A Book of Ritual and Ethics* (Minneapolis, MN: Fortress Press, 2004), 28–29.
34 Cf. Giuseppe Deiana, *Levitico* (Milano: Paoline, 2005), 64.
35 From another point of view, in the analysis of Gen 2:4b–25, Diego Pérez-Gondar reaches a similar conclusion about the intimate connection between work and family harmony. Cf. Pérez-Gondar, "The Anthropology of Work from Biblical Theology. A New Consideration of Gn 2:4b–25," *Scripta Theologica* 55 (2023): 33–34.
36 On the content and characteristics of the Law of Holiness, see: Félix García López, *El Pentateuco* (Estella: Verbo Divino, 2003), 233–238. On its composition process see Christophe Nihan, "The Holiness Code between D and P: Some Comments on the Function and Significance of Leviticus 17–26 in the Composition of the Torah," *Das Deuteronomium Zwischen Pentateuch und Deuteronomistischem Geschichtswerk*, eds. Eckart Otto and Reinhard Achenbach (Göttingen: Vandenhoeck & Ruprecht, 2004), 115.
37 Cf. Mary Douglas, *Leviticus as Literature* (Oxford: Oxford University Press, 2000).
38 Mary Douglas, *Purity and Danger An Analysis of the Concepts of Pollution and Taboo* (London: Routledge, 1966), 53–54.
39 Mary Douglas, "Justice as the Cornerstone An Interpretation of Leviticus 18–20," *Interpretation* 53, no. 4 (1999): 348.
40 Cf. Richard Hess, "Leviticus," *Genesis-Leviticus*, eds. Tremper Longman III and David E. Garland et al., Expositor's Bible Commentary, 1 (Grand Rapids, MI: Zondervan, 2008), 304.
41 Cf. John W. Kleinig, *Leviticus* (Saint Louis, MO: Concordia Publishing House, 2003), 409.
42 Cf. John E. Hartley, *Leviticus* (Dallas: Word Books, 1992), 314.
43 Cf. Sidney Greidanus, *Preaching Christ from Leviticus* (Grand Rapids, MI: William B. Eerdmans, 2021), 198
44 Cf. John E. Hartley, *Leviticus* (Dallas: Word Books, 1992), 315.
45 Cf. Sidney Greidanus, *Preaching Christ from Leviticus* (Grand Rapids, MI: William B. Eerdmans, 2021), 200.

168   *Francisco Varo*

46 Cf. Erhard S. Gerstenberger, *Leviticus: A Commentary* (Louisville, KY: Westminster John Knox Press, 1996), 280.
47 Cf. John E. Hartley, *Leviticus* (Dallas: Word Books, 1992), 315.
48 Cf. John E. Hartley, *Leviticus* (Dallas: Word Books, 1992).
49 Cf. Jacob Milgrom, *Leviticus 17–22* (New York: Doubleday, 2000), 1641.
50 Cf. Erhard S. Gerstenberger, *Leviticus: A Commentary* (Louisville, KY: Westminster John Knox Press, 1996), 269.
51 Gen 1:26–28. Cf. Richard Hess, "Leviticus," *Genesis-Leviticus*, eds. Tremper Longman III and David E. Garland et al., Expositor's Bible Commentary, 1 (Grand Rapids, MI: Zondervan, 2008), 751.
52 Cf. Mary Douglas, "Justice as the Cornerstone An Interpretation of Leviticus 18–20," *Interpretation* 53, no. 4 (1999): 349.
53 Cf. Jacob Milgrom, *Leviticus 17–22*, (New York: Doubleday, 2000), 1651; Sidney Greidanus, *Preaching Christ from Leviticus* (Grand Rapids, MI: William B. Eerdmans, 2021), 204–205.
54 Cf. James E. Robson, "Forgotten Dimensions of Holiness," *Horizons in Biblical Theology* 33 (2011): 121–146, 123, https://doi.org/10.1163/187122011X593000.
55 Cf. Mary Douglas, *Purity and Danger: An Analysis of the Concepts of Pollution and Taboo* (London: Routledge, 1966), 53.
56 Cf. Erhard S Gerstenberger, *Leviticus: A Commentary* (Louisville, KY: Westminster John Knox Press, 1996), 273–274.
57 Cf. Jacob Milgrom, *Leviticus 17–22* (New York: Doubleday, 2000), 1679.
58 Cf. John E. Hartley, *Leviticus* (Dallas: Word Books, 1992), 319.
59 Cf. Erhard S Gerstenberger, *Leviticus: A Commentary* (Louisville, KY: Westminster John Knox Press, 1996), 345.
60 Cf. Jacob Milgrom, *Leviticus 23–27* (New York: Doubleday, 2001), 1961.
61 Cf. Sidney Greidanus, *Preaching Christ from Leviticus* (Grand Rapids, MI: William B. Eerdmans, 2021), 230–231.
62 Cf. Gordon Wenham, *The Book of Leviticus* (Grand Rapids, MI: Eerdmans, 1979), 317.
63 It is fitting that such a year should begin precisely on the Day of Atonement. If on that date God's forgiveness for all sins was implored, it is only logical that the sincerity of that request should carry with it the intention that everyone should, in turn, forgive what his neighbor may owe him.
64 Cf. John W. Kleinig, *Leviticus* (Saint Louis, MO: Concordia Publishing House, 2003), 549.
65 The recovery of the ownership of family lands has, of course, economic implications for the setting of prices for the purchase and sale of land: "You shall buy according to the number of years since the year of jubilee, and your fellow countryman shall sell to you according to the number of years of harvest remaining. The more years that remain, the higher the price, the less years that remain, the lower the price: it is the number of harvests that is sold" (Lev 25:15–16).
66 All of these themes are elaborated upon in the report: International Labour Organization, *Leaving No One Behind: Building Inclusive Labour Protection in an Evolving World of Work* (Genève, 2023). For a comprehensive overview, see the table of contents on pp. 3–5.
67 These issues are discussed in the report: International Labour Organization, *Achieving a Just Transition Towards Environmentally Sustainable Economies and Societies for All* (Genève, 2023). A detailed list of these topics and more are found in the table of contents, on pp. 3–4.

10 From *homo faber* to *homo liturgicus*. Toward a theology of work in liturgical perspective

Félix María Arocena

Introduction

It is surprising that the close relationship between work and liturgy is hardly mentioned in the doctrinal statements of our time. Already in 2005, an editorial in *Rivista liturgica* pointed out this deficit in the "Compendium of the Social Doctrine of the Church" issued by the Pontifical Council *Justitia et pax*, where the results of liturgical theology were not taken into consideration, except for references to the sacrament of Baptism. Nor are there any liturgical theological studies of work in the bibliographies published by contemporary authors.[1] This situation is a particular reflection of a more general *status quaestionis*: the lack of attention to the interaction between current treatises on moral theology and those on liturgical theology.

We feel that such a circumstance invites us to understand more deeply what human realities – especially work – are and are meant to be, in accordance with the divine designs of creation and re-creation. Our aim is to propose a vision of work as a particular domain contained within the more general framework of the relationship between liturgy and life. To put it in existential terms: Where precisely lies the vital connection – or, conversely, the disconnection – between work and Christian life, particularly through worship? Indeed, worship mediates and sheds light on this integration.

This is one of the most fundamental questions a mature Christian can ask. On the one hand, a liturgical celebration that does not take up work in order to transform it from within is not a celebration of the Church, but pure ceremonial formalism; on the other hand, the efforts invested in the vicissitudes of work, detached from their insertion in the Paschal Mystery of Christ, would be purely human endeavor, an intra-worldly aspiration without hope.

The magisterium of the Second Vatican Council offers a balanced view of Christian existence when it teaches that "in the Church the human is ordered and subordinated to the divine, the visible to the invisible, action to contemplation, the present to the future city we seek".[2] For a believer, this principle governs the proper understanding of the relationship between worship and the world, or alternatively, between work and liturgy.

DOI: 10.4324/9781003508212-12

170   *Félix María Arocena*

The Constitution *Sacrosanctum Concilium* introduces us to a faith perspective according to which the Church celebrates Christ's Passover and actualizes in time the divine plan of salvation. There, the liturgy never appears as a disembodied reality because it is man, in his concrete life, who must be saved in the entirety of his destiny: the human which is realized here and the divine which is consummated there. The Church's prayer often speaks of heaven, but it does not affirm that heaven is everything and that earth is nothing. The *lex orandi*, faithful to biblical anthropology, adheres to a humanism open to man's transcendent destiny.

To say that man is ordered to the divine is to raise human values beyond their natural confines to the region of transcendence. And it is precisely here that the liturgical Mystery appears, because if our being and our acting encounter the divine, which is part of what defines the human, this is achieved by our insertion into the sacramentality of the liturgy, that is, into the symbolic matrix of the Christian rites. In this way, the human is not annulled, it is resized. In fact, "the expectation of the new earth should not dampen, but rather enliven, the concern to perfect this earth". [3]

Before continuing our discourse, it is worth pointing out the limits of our contribution, as well as the various contents that we are going to present. Faced with such a vast reality as the light with which the liturgical Mystery illuminates the complex reality of human work, it would be necessary to follow certain paths of research which would give a more complete overview. Among these questions are: the Word of God celebrated in the liturgy; the testimonies of the *lex orandi*, present – at least – in the ancient Roman Sacramentaries; the liturgy as *confessio fidei* in God the Creator; the liturgy as celebration of the work of "re-creation"; the biblical theology of the Hebrew *Shabbat* and the Christian celebration of Sunday.

Admitting these limits, it is illustrative to begin this reflection with a brief historical excursus on the subject of work and liturgy. Then, we will deal with that singular work, which, in the Christian sphere, we call "liturgy", and, from there, we will show the "bridge" necessary to unite the two shores: one, work, and the other, sacramental action and Christian existence as worship. Following these assumptions, we will then address a point of great significance for our case, which is the rite of the Preparation of the Gifts and its relation to work, justice, and solidarity. Finally, we will focus our attention on work and leisure in relation to the liturgy and the philosophical implications thereof in the light, above all, of the thought of Romano Guardini (†1968) and Josef Pieper (†1997).[4] The afterword offers a sapiential synthesis of some Christian realities, illuminated from the contents presented above.

Historical milestones

Remembering the past means purifying the present of unstable encrustations and striving for maximum authenticity in view of a better future.

From homo faber *to* homo liturgicus   171

It is therefore appropriate to approach the "liturgy-work" binomial from the lessons of history. Without wishing to be exhaustive, but simply trying to open some windows that can illustrate this question, we could summarize the historical periods to be revisited in five. We will do this by traversing the successive cultural epochs *per summa capita*, trying to identify some avenues of research that revolve around the relationship between "work and liturgy".[5]

Christian antiquity. The "work – liturgy" binomial was present and intensely lived in the ecclesial life of the third and fourth centuries with such close synergy that it is possible to speak of a mutual influence. Both the patristic literature and the early liturgical sources bear witness to the way in which Christian generations – far removed from us in space, time, and culture – perceived and lived the osmosis between the two realities. An in-depth study of Christian antiquity allows us to understand the close relationship between work and liturgy, as reflected in the ancient Sacramentaries (Veronese, Gelasian, Gregorian…).[6] This is a task that goes beyond the limits of the present contribution.

The Middle Ages. The memory of the best of the *Romanitas*, together with the barbarian cultures and civilizations, which, from a certain moment onward, merged with Christianity, gave rise to admirable conjugations of the binomial "work-liturgy". It was the testimony of the cultural heritage that had reached previous generations and was peacefully passed on from one to the other. In this period, some data emerges that sheds light on the symbiosis between work and liturgy:

a Western monasticism with the motto of the Rule of St. Benedict *ora et labora*,
b the birth of the guilds,
c the first Mass formularies especially linked to the agrarian world, for example, to ask for rain, for abundant harvests, for good weather…
d the abundant blessings of fields, of fruits….,
e the celebrations marking the beginning of the seasons – the Ember weeks – whose survival was cut short by the Tridentine reform.[7]

It is a rich heritage that reflects the commitment to sanctify all that Christians used in their activities and circumstances of life, and reveals a rural society involved in their respective works, impregnated by the spirit of the Gospel. It can be said that the Middle Ages, as a whole, further enlivened the "liturgy-work" binomial that came to it from Christian antiquity.

The Counter-Reformation, the Reformation, and the Renaissance. The inertia of the customs inherited from the Middle Ages, the effervescence, and activism that invaded Europe, heirs of new ideas about the way of conceiving work and the market, together with the respective ideas of sin and faith – united or disunited with works (Reformation or Counter-Reformation) – were elements that led to the rupture of work with respect

172   *Félix María Arocena*

to the view of it in the Middle Ages as a reality susceptible to sanctification and transformation into prayer and worship.

The recent past of ecclesial life. During the industrial revolution of the nineteenth century, the mentality that the liturgy had little influence within the experiences of those Christian generations intensified. This coincided with the period in which the liturgical movement emerged and developed. Its pioneers sought to lead the People of God to the liturgy and to lead the liturgy to the People of God; a people who, as far as work and liturgy were concerned, were living what the Catholic baroque had brought them to, i.e., an experience based more on popular religiosity than on liturgical consistency. Popular religiosity meant that each guild lived, in a certain way, the synthesis between liturgy and work in the feast of the Patron Saint, in the processions with the image of the Saint, in the novenas prior to his feast and in the subsequent octave.... Everything appeared to be governed by devotions, prayers, and indulgences. But the split between work and liturgy, accentuated in the praxis of this period, had already been foreshadowed in the roots of Renaissance humanism.

The present-day ecclesial life. Today, the first thing that stands out is a fact: We start from the current hiatus between work and liturgy, between Christian worship and social reality. Today, in a cultural world that is so distant from the discourse on God, the fracture that has existed for centuries – perhaps since the beginning of modernity – has become more acute, deeper, and more incisive. It is not Christian worship that is to blame for the existence of this hiatus, but rather the inability of the faithful, whose education on this point has had significant gaps, to synthesize. Christians capable of participating in the liturgy – if one can speak of "participation" – and then unable to bring to life what they have celebrated in the sacrament and to bring to the celebration what they live. We devoted a monograph some time ago to the existential implications of the "beyond" of the celebration.[8]

Liturgy "begins" as work and "is" work

We see, then, that work and liturgy are two realities that have much to say to each other. It is a question that has its roots in the biblical *humus*. If we go back to the origins of Christian worship, we can see that this pairing owes something to the profane sphere. Starting from the concept of work as action and work done for the benefit of a people, it is interesting to note how the very term "liturgy" carries within itself this same indelible reality. This is evidenced by the etymological roots of this term, which teach that *leitourgía* means "work of the people".[9]

From this etymological approach to the term *leiturgy*, we perceive that both "work" and "worship" share a common substratum.[10] Both, in fact, are revealed as an action aimed at favoring a community, with an eminently social purpose, and which always involves a community without exclusively private consequences.

From homo faber *to* homo liturgicus   173

This explains why the Christian liturgy celebrates the Mystery of Christ not in isolation, but by involving the whole cosmos and thus man and the human reality of work. In this regard, how can we fail to recall here the conclusion of the Roman Canon

> (...) through Christ, our Lord, through whom you continue to create all good things, sanctify them, fill them with life, bless them and distribute them among us.

referring to the blessing of the products of nature (oil, honey... as they appear in the ancient Sacramentaries)? It is a blessing which aims to bring earthly gifts as close as possible to the great blessing which Christ Himself instituted and in which He confers the highest consecration and fullness of grace.[11] Today we find valuable insights in three formularies in the Masses *ad diversa* of the Roman Missal: *"for the sanctification of human labour"*, *"in time of sowing"*, and *"after the harvest"*.[12] Something similar happens in the Lauds prayers of the Divine Office, where the first of the invocations that the Church makes in her morning prayer, as soon as the day begins, is usually an expression of the spiritual worship of Christians.[13] This is also true of the vast array of blessings relating to human work, as set out in the Book of Blessings.[14]

But, after this first illustration that has come to us from etymology, it is necessary to add that the liturgy – it itself – "is" work. The liturgy is a reality that does not belong primarily to the cognitive order, to the realm of "logic", but to the practical order, to that of *urgía*: It is an action (*ergon*), a "work", a total communication, made up of words and gestures, movements and symbols that come together in ritual action. The liturgy is an action, that is to say, an exercise, in spatio-temporal coordinates, of the priesthood of Christ, which, entrusted to the Church, is put into action for the sanctification of man and the glorification of God. From this point of view, it is worth highlighting a paragraph with a strong theological accent, such as number 7 of *Sacrosanctum Concilium*, which repeats three times the term *"opus – actio"*: "every liturgical celebration, being the 'work' of Christ the priest and of his Body, which is the Church, is a sacred 'action' par excellence, whose efficacy, with the same title and to the same degree, is unequalled by any other 'action' of the Church".[15]

The name that the Divine Office gives to the "intermediate hour" (Terce, Sext, and None) suggests that these are prayerful moments during the workday and are therefore structured as short prayers that facilitate listening to the Word of God and praise, so that also the time of work, and with it the worker himself, are sanctified.[16]

The liturgy is the "work of God" (*opus Dei*) which, following *Sacrosanctum Concilium*, we would call "the work of the sanctification of man", in synergy with the "work of man", that is, with "the work of the glorification of God". The joint work, then, of God and man, "theandric work".

174   *Félix María Arocena*

Hence the liturgy cannot fail to take the reality of work seriously and does so – we would say – inevitably. Benedict of Nursia (†547), in his Rule, never separates the two realities, but sees them profoundly united in the life of the monk, almost as an essential communion to the point of becoming the motto of Benedictine life: *ora et labora*. The monk, after listening to the Word of God and having sung His praises, prolongs them in his work.

Presuppositions for characterizing labor in liturgical categories

In view of a liturgical theology of work, it is necessary to clarify, first of all, two preliminary questions, two basic questions that act as presuppositions for the whole exposition and without whose understanding the liturgical theology of work would remain encrypted. These presuppositions are:

a first, to affirm that, within the Christian experience – which is constitutively liturgical – there is a celebratory moment and an existential moment;
b secondly, to articulate this life, which is existential worship (*logiké latreia*), with the liturgical celebration, which is ritual action. Let us consider both statements a little more closely.

a *Spiritual worship* (logiké latreia). The Christian experience is essentially cultic. It is so because the Christian, by Baptism, is always a priest of his own work. This is the question of the *logiké latreia* of Romans 12:

I exhort you therefore, brethren, by the mercies of God, to offer your bodies as a living sacrifice, holy, acceptable to God: this is your spiritual worship.[17]

Offering, living host, spiritual worship… are terms characteristic of liturgical language, whose content refers to the very life of the faithful. In Pauline anthropology, "offering your bodies" is equivalent to offering your persons, your real, concrete life, made up of work and rest (*otium et negotium*). We are faced with a vision of the Christian who lives his whole existence and work activity as a gift, transforming it into a sacrifice pleasing to God, giving an existential worship of which he himself is the priest and offerer. In this task, he has Christ as his paradigm, priest, and offerer of His own life, culminating in the supreme oblation of Himself on the Cross.[18]

It can therefore be affirmed that, on the basis of both New Testament revelation and the celebration of Christian initiation, the existence of the believer, which ordinarily takes place in an extra-sacramental sphere, is a cultic reality. The difficulty in understanding Christian life as a cultic reality, or the reluctance to speak of "the liturgy of life", lies in not distinguishing between liturgy and celebrations, or in thinking that liturgy consists only of "ceremonies", and that these exhaust the liturgy. It is true

From homo faber *to* homo liturgicus   175

that the whole liturgy is in every celebration, but it is false to say that the celebrations exhaust the liturgy.[19]

Christian initiation begins the transfiguration of the subject into an "existential memorial" of Christ.[20] This statement is important From the notion of liturgical memorial, by the expression "existential memorial of Christ", we mean that the life of the baptized person becomes a memory and presence of Christ's life. To be an existential memorial of Christ is more than being a mere propagandist of a cold external doctrine. It is to have been constituted as a living icon of the presence and action of the Risen One in the fabric of everyday life, here and now. Consequently, Christian identity is revealed as the iconic presence of Christ in the world, including, of course, the world of work. Thus, when we speak of the Christian worker, we cannot circumvent his theological–liturgical status, as described here: The baptized person is a priest of his own work.

A life of work, being a memorial of Christ's, manifests itself as praise, witness, and service, as a consequence of its participation in the *triplex Christi munus:* priestly, prophetic, and royal. As a result of the *perichoresis* between the *tria munera*, the baptized person celebrates the Mystery from his baptismal priesthood (*leitourgía*), without ceasing to proclaim Christ in the midst of his work as a witness (*martyría*), serving God and men at work by means of the charity (*diakonía*), which God Himself bestows on him.

b   *The ritual celebration.* The liturgical discourse on work would be incomplete if we do not establish the necessary dialogue between human work – *opus hominis* – and divine work – *opus Dei* – the latter being contemplated in its fontal and culminating instance, which is the Eucharistic celebration. We pass, therefore, to the confluence of spiritual worship, which is existential (*logiké latreia*), with ritual worship, which is sacred action, celebrated under the regime of signs and symbols. *Logiké latreia* and liturgical celebration are not identical realities, but neither are they separate. The adverbs of the Council of Chalcedon (451), concerning the relationship between the two natures of Christ, can also illuminate analogically the relationship between the two moments of Christian life: Worship and life are declined "without confusion or change, without division or separation".[21]

But why, for a liturgical theology of work, is the celebration of the Eucharist an unavoidable point of reference? Because the celebration of the liturgy, especially at its zenith, which is the Eucharist, gives spiritual worship its "sacramental expression", that is, it sacramentalizes the work that each Christian offers in exercising his baptismal priesthood on "the altar of his heart", to use an expression dear to the unanimous patristic tradition of the Christian East and West.[22] In the Eucharistic celebration, the spiritual sacrifices of the faithful, many of which are lived in the midst of work, are transfigured by the action of the Spirit, Who brings them into communion with the Sacrifice of Christ.[23]

176   *Félix María Arocena*

The celebrated Eucharist is the "place" where the Spiritual Sacrifice of the Bride enters into communion with the Paschal Sacrifice of the Bridegroom. All the acts of loving submission to God's will, of openness and charity toward others that the Christian performs when working – not an exclusive but important part of his daily spiritual sacrifice – fall under the transforming action of Christ's holy oblation. The toil and pain, the successes and failures of work are united to the Sacrifice of Christ, from which they are revalued by means of a transcendent plus. This is expressed in an anaphora from the Roman Missal: "We humbly ask you, holy Father, to accept us too, together with your Son (...)".[24] This opens up an unsuspected horizon for daily work, which is transformed into the divine by being inserted into the Eucharistic Mystery, since everything that participates in the Holy Mass is transformed into what it signifies.[25]

The rite of the preparation of the gifts

This truly essential question of human work inserted in the Sacrifice of Christ, which we have just mentioned, was taken into consideration precisely in 1968 when Annibale Bugnini (†1982) wrote to the relator of *cœtus* 10 of the *Consilium* asking him, in accordance with the wishes of Paul VI, to present for the presentation of the offerings "a single scheme of formulae expressing the concept of the offering of 'human work' included in the sacrifice of Christ".[26] This indication of the Pope is important, for it reveals how the participation of "human work" in the salvific economy is not limited to the mere provision of the bread and wine necessary for the Mass to be validly celebrated, but its offering becomes a way through which work – and the baptized through it – can be inserted into the Sacrifice of Christ. The very act of working brings man to conform himself in some way to Christ through the experience of weariness, pain, anguish, waiting, and apparent defeats, lived in the perspective of contributing to God's creative plan.[27] In this way, the liturgy teaches that work, by the power of the Holy Spirit, becomes "the image and effect of the work of the Father and of Christ" (*figura et effectus Christi Patrisque laboris*).

When the priest performs the rite of the presentation of the gifts, it is seen that the fruits of "man's labor" – bread and wine – which satisfy the body's hunger and thirst, will become food which will also satisfy its desire for eternity. There is a "revalorization" of human labor in the sense that the effort invested in it is somehow "rewarded" by making bread and wine the sacramental presence of Christ on earth, through the pneumatological epiclesis. Grinding the wheat and pressing the grapes entails the sweat of labor, which, in some way, cooperates with God's creative and redemptive – always salvific – plan. The Mass is therefore the "place" (*topos*) where man's two vocations meet: the vocation to work, received from God in Genesis, and the vocation to celebrate the Eucharist, received from Christ at the Last Supper: "Do this in remembrance of me". To both vocations responds the

From homo faber *to* homo liturgicus 177

close articulation of the two characteristic moments of the Christian liturgy: celebratory and existential.

In the procession of the offerings, the gesture of the hands of the faithful offering the priest the fruit of human labor is in some way related to the gesture of the presentation of the gifts which the priest will then make on the altar. And both gestures – that of the faithful and that of the priest – find their complete fulfillment in the epicletic gesture of the imposition of hands on the bread and wine, which the minister makes so that they become the Body and Blood of the Lord. This articulation of gestures is the liturgical way of showing the Christian worker cooperating in the redemption offered by Christ to the Father in the holy Pneuma through the liturgy.

The Eucharist and "going beyond" justice

The values of justice and legality, as essential values in the world of work, are also prerogatives with which the Eucharist educates the worker. Indeed, the Eucharistic table is the place where God feeds His people, offering to all who approach it the abundant food for eternal life. It is the place of divine justice and legality, that is, where the Risen One, recognizing the fruits of man's labor, remunerates far beyond an economic calculation, offering each one his "wage" not according to the "quantity" of his work, but according to his desire to collaborate with Him; a desire that each one keeps in his heart and that only the Lord can see and therefore reward to the utmost, by means of the denarius of eternal life.

Christ's offering to the Father is infinitely superior to man's offering of himself and his work to God. Therefore, the wages that man receives from God in the Mass are received as a gift and not as a grateful acknowledgment of what man has worked for. The wage that man receives from God is infinitely superior to the offering that man makes of himself to God; it surpasses any mathematical counting of minutes, hours, days, or years, because the wage of every worker is Christ Himself, His life given in Sacrifice for us.

The procession of the gifts: work and solidarity

It is worth returning once again to an element that was revived by the liturgical reform of the Second Vatican Council, namely, the procession of the gifts. This procession has a particular spiritual significance. Indeed, the offerings brought to the altar are the fruit of the work and sweat of the faithful: The bread, baked in the ovens of their own homes, and the wine, the fruit of the harvest of their own vineyards, made exclusively as a gift to the parish for the celebration of Mass, was a very lively way of expressing the immersion of their daily work in the Mystery of Christ, celebrated at the altar. In it, that work will be anointed by the dew of the Spirit to transform it into a sacrament of Christ.

But not only that, at the moment of communion, receiving the eucharisted bread and wine, which were originally the fruit of man's own labor, helps

178   Félix María Arocena

man to feel part of the Mystery which he himself celebrates with the whole Church. Here, in the midst of this *exitus* and *réditus*, is an eloquent expression of man's solidarity with God's plan, the profound understanding of the being of the liturgy, which is *actio Christi et Ecclesiæ*. Man responds to the love of his Creator and to His solidarity with man – especially with the incarnation of His Son – by cooperating with the Father in the unfolding of His saving plan in history.

A privileged expression of this solidarity is found precisely in the procession in which the faithful bring the gifts to the altar. The General Instruction of the Roman Missal foresees that not only bread and wine, which is the matter of the Eucharistic sacrifice, may be brought to the altar, but also other gifts:

> (...) money or other donations for the poor or for the church may also be brought, which the faithful themselves may present or which may be collected in the nave of the church, and thus be placed at the appropriate place outside the Eucharistic table.[28]

This means that the Eucharistic liturgy is celebrated at a table where everyone can find welcome and nourishment in the Bread of Life, even those without resources or work. There is one food – the Eucharistic food – that cannot be bought with money, for the Lord has already bought it at the price of His Blood shed on the Cross. That food cannot be bought with money because it is God's gift and because the Eucharist is the fruit of the solidarity with which man, united to the solidarity of Christ, shares the fruit of his work and his toil with those who have no work, or are not given the opportunity to work. This is the capacity of the Eucharistic celebration to build community around the table of the Lord.

In this way, the offertory procession reminds us that the fruits of our labor are not to be jealously guarded or, worse, squandered, but shared in charity and fraternity. The very collection of money during the Mass speaks of solidarity and proximity: He who has the most and to whom the most has been given, shares his abundance with those who do not have or are waiting to receive. It is the Eucharistic Memorial as a place and source of solidarity.

The procession of gifts, in short, is the ritual transposition of man's response to the vocation received in Genesis. Recalling Jesus' parable, we would say that the "servant" returns to present to his "master" not the same gifts he received before his departure, but the fruit of the elaboration and the investment that the servant makes with these gifts: the fruit of his work.[29] On the one hand, the Father gave the talents to the servant to make them bear fruit and he, returning with the fruit of his work in his hands, gives them back to Him – increased and multiplied – and places them on the altar so that the Father may put into act the *opus salutis*, making of these fruits of his labor the Body and Blood of His Son for the life of the world.

From homo faber *to* homo liturgicus   179

On the other hand, God Himself, in His turn, "works" these gifts, through the work of the sacred *Pneuma*, returning them to man "transubstantiated" into the food and drink of salvation, so that the fruits of the Eucharist may reach the whole world. God and man work together; man to the human and God to the divine. It is – we could say – the "co-liturgy" of heaven and earth.

"Otiari" and "negotiari"

Thus, the procession of gifts refers to the two values proper to those who are about to undertake work, the same values that the Lord points out in the parable of the talents: gratitude and gratuitousness. It refers to the ability to understand that what has been received has been received freely, and it also refers to the consequent awareness that it is necessary to be grateful, sharing with others. Here everything happens as if *homo faber* gave way to *homo liturgicus*, who, presenting to the Creator the fruit of his work, shows a kind of "visiting card" as he waits to receive from God the invitation to enter the eternal banquet as a reward for having corresponded to his vocation as a co-operator in the creative and redemptive design.

Hence the liturgy should be considered more as an *otiari*, that is, more as a time of leisure (*otium*) – according to Romano Guardini (†1968) – than as a time of work (*negotium*).[30] Aristotle, in his *Ethics*, famously posited that true leisure is unattainable for man unless something divine resides within him.[31] The liturgy is the time suspended and spent freely, that is, the time lost as opposed to the daily time of work and production, and yet a very active time in relation to God and the brethren, because of its power to give work and the whole of existence its full and total meaning.

In the biblical account of creation we read: "On the seventh day God finished his work which he had made, and he rested".[32] Here is work followed by rest. This mysterious divine rest, like the rest offered to the people of the Exodus with the entry into the Promised Land, is given a new light in the New Testament.[33] It is the *Shabbath*, the "Sabbath rest" into which Christ Himself entered with His resurrection and into which the whole People of God is called to enter as a prelude to eternal life. The Church, who is a *mystical* person, wishes for her departed sons and daughters that they may rest in peace, *requiescant in pace*. Both the expression *in pace* and the Latin verb *quiescere* – which, coming from the noun *quies* (stillness), means to rest – point to that rest which responds to the need to "make merry", so characteristic of human beings. Heaven is a celebration where everything is Communion and Feast.[34] If there were no space for rest, joy, and prayer on Sunday, we would be closed in such a restricted horizon that we would no longer be able to see heaven. Then, even if we were to dress up as for a feast, we would be inwardly incapable of "feasting". And without the festive dimension, hope would have no home to live in.

180 *Félix María Arocena*

Afterword

At the end of these considerations, we would like to conclude with some sapiential reflections, as a product of the decantation of the preceding contents. Perhaps one of the most serious effects of the current secularization consists in having relegated faith to the margins of work, and vice versa. As if faith were something useless for the development of society. The failure of this way of living as if God did not exist – *etsi Deus non daretur* – is today for all to see.[35] To overcome this situation, the Church offers the intense light that the Eucharist casts on work. If the Eucharist is a "mirror" of the values that surround the world of work, it is, at the same time, a warning to rediscover and revive those same values. Through the Eucharist, Christians are enabled to translate the Paschal Mystery of Jesus Christ into their ordinary tasks. Man's "doing" finds in the Eucharist the culmination of his own "offering", which is united with Christ's redemptive offering for humanity.

In singing the *Sanctus* at Mass, the assembly on earth joins with the assembly in heaven to exclaim: "Heaven and earth are full of your glory". To say that "the earth is filled with the glory of God" is one of the great affirmations of the Catholic faith. At the same time, the cosmos groans and suffers with birth pangs as it is subjected to the vanity of sin; that is, it has to hide what it should reveal, until it is freed from the slavery of corruption and becomes a definitive partaker of the glorious freedom of the children of God.[36] It is from this Pauline doctrine that the discourse of liturgical theology on work is based. Following in the footsteps of the Apostle, work is man's transforming activity aimed at making the earth "light up" the glory of God. It is the activity of *homo liturgicus*, of the man of *doxa*, of the priest of his own work.

Like a pregnant woman, the earth needs the help of a midwife to give birth to what she is pregnant with. The baptized – priests of their own work – are like that midwife who extracts from matter the glory enclosed within it. The architect Antoni Gaudí (†1926) experienced this reality so intensely that he placed the trisagion *Sanctus, Sanctus, Sanctus!* and the *hosanna!* on the walls of the Sagrada Família – sometimes openly, sometimes more discreetly – as if they were a doxology made of stone and faith. He, who knew how to unite the inspiration that came to him from his three great books – nature, the Bible, and the liturgy – also knew how to create a school for the children of the bricklayers who worked on the construction of the church and other poor children of Barcelona: from the table of the Eucharist to the table of charity.

But not only Antoni Gaudí, the 2,000-year history of the Church includes many Saints, whose existence is a precious sign of how, from the Eucharist, an intense assumption of social responsibilities is born, a development that has the person at its center, especially when he is poor, sick, or unfortunate.[37] The lives of some of the great Doctors speak before, more and better than their writings. Thus, for example, at the gates of the city of Caesarea, the great Basil (†379) founded a monastic citadel of charity which took his name – *the Basilica* – with orphanages, leper houses, schools of arts and

From homo faber *to* homo liturgicus   181

crafts... a great social work which foreshadowed the future hospitals and other reception centers which the Church would develop in later centuries. In Hippo, Augustine (†430) built a *domus caritatis* near his cathedral. At the end of the Sunday liturgy, he would go there to care for the needy of his local church.[38] Worship and social justice go hand in hand.

As he works, the Christian makes his work a praise of God (*leitourgía*), a service to his colleagues (*diaconía*), and a witness to Christ before the world (*martyría*). Matter, transformed by his work, shines with the glory it conceals. And so, by making his work a sacrifice of praise, *homo faber* becomes *homo liturgicus*. Our work, day by day, can restore a juncture, obfuscated by human sin, to its original noble brilliance, to the original will of its Creator for it. We turn what we touch into gold, renewing – in a way – the wonders of King Midas.

The circularity between the two characteristic moments of the Christian liturgy – celebrative and existential – generates a solid unity of life in the Christian immersed in his civil activity. This unity of life is the existential reflection of the mutual implication of the trilogy [Mystery – celebration – life]. Precisely by virtue of this unity of life, the activity of the baptized person is naturally integrated into the social teaching of the Church. The living witness of those who overcome apparent dichotomies between Christian faith and work and social behavior, with its demands for justice and loyalty toward superiors as well as toward equals or subordinates, is thus raised up.

It is not possible to summarize in a few lines the ethical and social achievements that can be attained when the baptized person goes about his work aware that the liturgy is at the basis of the worship that he gives to God with it. Here too, the celebrated Eucharist becomes a "working formula". A formula whose application informs professional activity from within. Work is not primarily sanctified from the outside, but from the inside, making it "Eucharist", allowing the energy of the celebrated sacrament to transfigure the Christian's fatigue into the fatigue of the Crucified One, into redemptive fatigue.

The capacity of believers to transform society arises from the matrix with which they themselves are transformed from within by the Eucharist. In other words, the baptized are constituted "leaven" for the world because the Eucharist makes them "leaven" with Christ. Ultimately, it is by participating in the Holy Mass that Christians rediscover the genuine value of the temporal realities which it is their right to manage.[39]

In this sense, a text taken from the liturgical memorial of St. Josemaría Escrivá is suggestive: "(make us) salt that preserves from corruption, light that enlightens the hearts of men, living leaven that brings the living Bread to every task".[40] These last words have a strong theological accent: Each of the baptized is constituted "a living leaven that brings the living Bread to all things". It is biblical language that speaks of the cultic fiber inherent in the Christian vocation. It is the Eucharistic, and therefore liturgical, way of "placing Christ at the summit of all human activities".[41]

182　*Félix María Arocena*

The expression "translating the Paschal Mystery into work" is meant to affirm that, for Christians, every work, every honest culture aimed at transforming creation, is called to express in a limited way the universal scope of Christ's oblation on the Cross and to unfold the inexhaustible salvific potential of His Passover. This reality would be unattainable without the Eucharist and is, for this very reason, a precious reality of the Church's faith, which is reflected in a text of the Book of Blessings:

(...) by faithfully carrying out his work and all that concerns temporal progress and humbly offering it to God, man purifies himself, develops with his intelligence and skill the work of creation, exercises charity, becomes capable of helping those who are poorer than himself and, associating himself with Christ the Redeemer, perfects himself in love for Him.[42]

Notes

1　With the exception of the compilation work by Marcio Couto, which covers the short period between the conclusion of the Second Vatican Council and 1980, and the contribution of Matteucci (cf. Marcio Alessandro Couto, "Bibliografia em torno da teologia do trabalho", *Trabalho e teologia* (São Paulo: Paulinas, 1979): 88–93; cf. Benvenuto Matteucci, "La Eucaristía y el trabajo humano", *Cuadernos Monásticos* 8/26 (1973): 507–516.w
2　Second Vatican Council, *Dogmatic Constitution "Sacrosanctum Concilium" (on the Sacred Liturgy)*, December 4, 1963, #2, https://www.vatican.va/archive/hist_councils/ii_vatican_council/documents/vat-ii_const_19631204_sacrosanctum-concilium_en.html
3　Vatican Council II, *Pastoral Constitution "Gaudium et Spes" (on the Church in the Modern World)*, December 7, 1965, #39, https://www.vatican.va/archive/hist_councils/ii_vatican_council/documents/vat-ii_const_19651207_gaudium-et-spes_en.html. Karl Barth (†1968) used to say that he held the Gospel in one hand and the newspaper in the other, and read events in the light of the Gospel.
4　Cf. Josef Pieper, *Antologia* (Barcelona: Herder, 1984) 147–154; Josef Pieper, *Una teoría de la fiesta* (Madrid: Rialp 2006); cf. Romano Guardini, *El espíritu de la liturgia* (Barcelona: Araluce, 1962).
5　For bibliographical references for each of the five Historical Periods that follow, cf. the extensive study by Achille Maria Triacca, "Diurno labore fatigati", nella liturgia il reverbero della mens biblica dei Padri. Una tensione catechetica bivalente", Sergio Felici (a cura di), *Spiritualità del lavoro nella catechesi dei Padri del III–IV secolo* (Roma: Libreria Ateneo Salesiano 1986) 225–262.
6　This task is feasible only with the help of the editions of the respective concordances, given that the analysis of the theology underlying a liturgical source requires this type of tool: cf. *Sacramentarium Gregorianum concordantia* (Roma: Pontificium Institutum Altioris Latinitatis – LAS, 2012); cf. Idem, *Sacramentarium Veronense concordantia* (Roma: Pontificium Institutum Altioris Latinitatis – LAS, 2013); cf. Idem, *Sacramentarium Gelasianum concordantia* (Roma: Pontificium Institutum Altioris Latinitatis – LAS, 2014); cf. *Missale Gothicum – Konkordanztabellen zu Den Lateinischen Sakramentarien* (RED Series Minor VI), 3 vols. (Rome: Herder, 1961); cf. Félix María Arocena, Adolfo Ivorra and Alessandro Toniolo, *Concordantia Missalis Hispano-Mozarabici* (Città del Vaticano-Toledo: Libreria Editrice Vaticana-Arzobispado de Toledo, 2009).

From homo faber *to* homo liturgicus   183

7   During the first millennium, both in some eucological productions and in various celebrations of the year, reference was made to man's work, although not always explicitly. Tertullian recalls the civil and profane origin of Terce, Sext, and None, representing three moments that correspond to the subdivision of the working day in the Greco-Roman world (cf. Tertullianus, *De ieiunio adversus psychicos* 10, 3, *Corpus Christianorum. Series Latina* (CCL) vol. 2, (Turnhout: Brepols, 1954) 267: Cur non intellegamus, salva plane indifferentia semper et ubique et omni tempore orandi, tamen tres istas horas, ut insigniores in rebus humani, quæ Diem distribuunt, quæ negotia distinguunt, quæ publice resonant, ita et sollemniores fuisse in orationibus divinis?.

8   Cf. Félix María Arocena, *Liturgia y vida. Lo cotidiano como lugar del culto espiritual* (Madrid: Palabra, 2011) (esp. the reference to work, 109–115).

9   Λαός [masculine archaic di λήῖτοσ (= "of the people")] = "public", "looking to the people"; and Έργον (verbally derived from ἐργάζομαι) = "work", "action", "deed". In the Helladic democracies the term *leitourgía* was used to define public services, for the common good or at least for the *polis*, usually provided by aristocratic or wealthy families who felt morally obliged to contribute to the community because of their social status, or perhaps because they were invited by the public administration itself. Over the centuries, the term will further expand its meanings with the acquisition of new contents, until it reaches the religious field and also enters Scripture. In fact, the Bible itself, in order to represent an action performed on behalf of someone, will use this term, which is more present in the Old Testament than in the New, in reference to the service of worship performed in the temple by the priestly classes and the Levites. It is therefore a technical word which reveals a public and official worship carried out by a certain category of people.

10 Cf. Manlio Sodi, "La latinitas tra culto e cultura – A servizio di un rinnovato umanesimo," *Salesianum* 72 (2010): 317–335.

11 Cf. Joseph Andreas Jungmann, *El sacrificio de la Misa* (Madrid: Herder, 1961) 942–943.

12 Cf. "Misas y oraciones por varias necesidades", *Misal Romano* (Madrid: Libros litúrgicos, 2016), Formularies 26, 27 and 28, 1036–1040.

13 Cf. *Liturgia de las Horas*, (Preces del viernes de la segunda semana de Pascua; del lunes y martes de la segunda semana del Tiempo ordinario) vol. 3 (1994), 670; vol. 4, 839.860: "Holy Father, you who, in raising your Son from the dead, showed that you had accepted his sacrifice, -accept also the offering of our day and lead us to the fullness of life". "Lord Jesus, eternal Priest, who willed that your people should share in your priesthood, -may we always offer spiritual sacrifices, pleasing to the Father". "We offer you, Lord, the desires and plans of our day, – deign to accept them and bless them as the first fruits of our day"...

14 We can see, for example, the current formulas for the blessing of work tools, of a laboratory, of a workshop or trade, of the work that prepares the structure of a new building... (cf. *Bendicional*, [Barcelona: Coeditores litúrgicos, 1986], chapters 21, 16, 9, 347–354; 300–308; 229–231).

15 The English version of *Sacrosanctum Concilium* uses the verb "to work" to refer to the liturgy. The term "worship" also has the same root as the verb "work". In the anaphora of the English Missal, the work of the Holy Spirit is designated as the "working" of the Holy Spirit: "the power and working of the Holy Spirit" (cf. *The Roman Missal Renewed by Decree of the Most Holy Second Ecumenical Council of the Vatican, Promulgated by Authority of Pope Paul VI and Revised at the Direction of Pope John Paul II, Third Typical Edition* [London: Catholic Truth Society, 2010] 684). This designation is in the tradition of the sacred Pneuma as "Artificer" (Artifex) of the wonders of God, which are the Sacraments (*Catechism of the Catholic Church*, 741: "the Holy Spirit, artificer of the works of

184   *Félix María Arocena*

God (...)" – "Artifex operum Dei"; cf. Jean Corbon, *Liturgia y oración* (Madrid: Cristiandad, 2006), 189.

16 Just by way of example, we can consult the prayer of Terce on Monday: "Most excellent Father, our God, you have willed that we men should work in such a way that, cooperating with one another, we may achieve ever greater success, so help us to live in the midst of our labors, always feeling that we are your children and brothers and sisters of all men"; and the prayer of Sext on Tuesday: "Our God, who revealed to Peter your plan to save all nations, give us your grace that all our labours may be pleasing in your sight and useful to your design of universal love and salvation."

17 Rom 12:1. This text is situated at the beginning of Chapter 12, which is the point that marks the beginning of the parenetic part of the epistle. Up to this chapter, the Apostle has shown the *Kerygma*; now he goes on to show the fruits that derive from it on the ethical-existential level. And at the beginning, as a primary value, Paul presents "spiritual worship" *(logiké latreia)* as the baptized person's response to the Paschal Mystery of Jesus Christ, who has justified, liberated, and saved him.

18 Cf. Paulinus of Nola, *Epistula* 11, CSEL 29, 67–68: "Christ is priest of the Victim, who is Himself, and is the Victim of His own priesthood" – *"Victima sacerdotii sui, et sacerdos suæ victimæ"*. This same Christological truth appears in the Gelasian Sacramentary (n. 476): *"qui (Christus) oblatione sui corporis remotis sacrificiis carnalium victimarum seipsum tibi pro salute nostra offerens idem sacerdos et sacer agnus exhibuit"*. The doctrine of Paulinus of Nola is the source of a preface found in the current Roman Missal, which presents Christ as "priest, victim and altar" (cf. *Misal Romano* (Madrid: Libros litúrgicos, 2016), *Misas y oraciones por varias necesidades*, Ordinario de la Misa, Prefacio pascual, 5, 470): "(...) and, offering Himself for our salvation, He manifested Himself as Priest, Altar and Victim at the same time".

19 Cf. Jean Corbon, *Liturgia fontal* (Madrid: Palabra, 20092), 260.

20 "Memorial" is a category and, at the same time, a biblical-liturgical reality through which a salvific event is made present in time and space repeatedly and simultaneously with its "load" of salvation, although not, obviously, with the historical coordinates related to the event, since the latter have happened once and for all. This presence is given through the salvific coordinates. These, described in the sacred text and circumscribed in time and space the first time they happened, have been inscribed forever in the continuity of a *Hodie* (cf. Heb 4,7) of salvation, which the liturgy acts in the celebratory *hic et nunc*. In our discourse, we apply this notion, *servatis servandis*, to the life of the baptized.

21 Cf. Heinrich Josepf Denzinger and Peter Hünermann, *El magisterio de la Iglesia. Enchiridion symbolorum definitionum et declarationum de rebus fidei et morum* (Barcelona: Herder, 1999), 302: "inconfuse, immutabiliter, indivise, inseparabiliter".

22 Among the Fathers of the Church and ancient writers who have dealt with the heart as an altar, we note the following: Ignatius of Antioch, *Ep. ad Romanos* 2, 2, ed. Franz Xaver von Funk, vol. 1, 254; Augustine of Hippo, *De civitate Dei*, lib. 20, 10, CCL, vol. 48 (Turnhout: Brepols, 1955), 720; Richard of Cremona, *Mitrale sive summa de officiis ecclesiasticis*, PL 219, 19; Peter Chrysologus, *Sermo 108*, CCL, vol. 24A (Turnhout: Brepols 1981), 668–671; Leo the Great, *Sermo 4, 1*, CCL, vol. 138 (Turnhout: Brepols, 1977), 16–17; Gregory the Great, *Homiliarum in Ezechielem prophetam libri duo* 2, 10, 19, SCh 360, 522–523; John Chrysostom, *In Epistulam Secundam ad Corinthios Homilia*, 20, 3, PG 61, 540; Methodius, *Convivium decem virginum* 6, PG 18, 108; N. Cabasilas, *La vida en Cristo* (Madrid: Rialp, 1994) 172. For a more detailed study of the altar of

From homo faber *to* homo liturgicus   185

the heart, cf. Félix María Arocena, *El altar cristiano* (Barcelona: CPL, 2006), 136–155. We have dealt with the "theology of the three altars" (the altar of the heart, the altar of the temple, and the eschatological altar) Félix María Arocena, *Teología litúrgica. Una introducción.* (Madrid: Palabra, 2017), 227–231.

23 Cf. Vatican Council II, *Dogmatic Constitution "Lumen Gentium" (on the Church)*, November 21, 1964, #34: "For this reason the laity, dedicated to Christ and anointed by the Holy Spirit, are marvelously called and wonderfully prepared so that ever more abundant fruits of the Spirit may be produced in them. For all their works, prayers and apostolic endeavors, their ordinary married and family life, their daily occupations, their physical and mental relaxation, if carried out in the Spirit, and even the hardships of life, if patiently borne—all these become "spiritual sacrifices acceptable to God through Jesus Christ" (1 Pt 2:5). Together with the offering of the Lord's body, they are most fittingly offered in the celebration of the Eucharist. Thus, as those everywhere who adore in holy activity, the laity consecrate the world itself to God" (https://www.vatican.va/archive/hist_councils/ii_vatican_council/documents/vat-ii_const_19641121_lumen-gentium_en.html).

24 *Misal Romano* (Madrid: Libros litúrgicos, 2016), Plegaria eucarística de la reconciliación II, 617.

25 Cf. Benedict XVI, *Post-Synodal Apostolic Exhortation "Sacramentum Caritatis"*, 22 February, 2007, #89, https://www.vatican.va/content/benedict-xvi/en/apost_exhortations/documents/hf_ben-xvi_exh_20070222_sacramentum-caritatis.html.

26 Annibale Bugnini, *La riforma liturgica (1948–1975). Nuova edizione riveduta e arricchita di note e di supplementi per una lettura analitica* (BELS 30) (Roma: CLV-Edizioni Liturgiche, 19972), 366 (quotation marks are ours).

27 In the following paragraphs we will draw inspiration, though not exclusively, from Pier Angelo Muroni, *"Frutto della terra e del lavoro dell'uomo…". – Eucaristia e lavoro l'opus hominis nell'opus Dei quale culmine della cooperazione al disegno della creazione*, Francesco Maceri (a cura di), *Il lavoro dell'uomo – Tra creazione e redenzione*. Saggi in occasione della 48 Settimana sociale dei cattolici in Italia (Cagliari: University Press, 2017) 52–72.

28 "Instrucción general del Misal Romano" 73, *Misal Romano* (Madrid: Libros litúrgicos, 2016), 46.

29 Cf. Mt 25:14–30.

30 In 1918, Romano Guardini, "The Spirit of the Liturgy", reacts against the religiosity of his time, understood as a mixture of morality and subjective devotion. He relates liturgy to playfulness, the essence of which is "in-utility". It does not seek utility, but it does make sense. It is "in-utility", but it is neither "in-sensate" nor "in-significant". It escapes instrumental reason. This intuition was later developed by Hugo Rahner, who also takes up the contributions of Johan Huizinga's "Homo ludens", but makes it clear that worship includes the ludic, but goes beyond it (cf. Romano Guardini, *El espíritu de la liturgia* [Barcelona: Araluce, 1962]).

31 In this sense – notes Josef Pieper (†1997) – secularization has less to do with de-Christianization than with the loss of fundamental concepts of natural wisdom. This is what Aristotle indicates in the Ethics: (cf. J. Pieper, *Antología* [Barcelona: Herder, 1984], 147–154).

32 Gen 22.

33 Cf. Ex 33:14; Heb 4:9.

34 Cf. *Catechism of the Catholic Church*, 1136.

35 Expression of the Dutch jurist and theologian Hugo Grotius (†1645) in the context of a secularism that would save Europe from the self-destruction to which the continuous wars of religion were leading it (cf. Hugo Grotius, *De iure belli ac pacis libri tres*).

186 *Félix María Arocena*

36 Cf. Rom 8:21–22.
37 Cf. Benedict XVI, *Homily at the Closing of the Eucharistic Congress*, Ancona, 11 September 2011. https://www.vatican.va/content/benedict-xvi/en/homilies/2011/documents/hf_ben-xvi_hom_20110911_ancona.html.
38 Cf. Sozomeno (†c.450), *Historia ecclesiastica* 6, 34, PG 67, 1397; cf. Adalbert-Gauthier Hamman, *Vie liturgique et vie sociale* (Paris: Desclée, 1968).
39 Cf. Cruz González-Ayesta, "El trabajo como una Misa," *Romana* 50 (2010): 200–221, 220.
40 Hymn *Ipse magister* from the office of reading in the liturgical memorial of Saint Josemaría Escrivá de Balaguer (26 June): "*Sal, quod præservet a corruptione, lumen, humana pectora collustrans, vivum fermentum, ferens panem vivum omni labori*".
41 Josemaría Escrivá, *Forja* (Madrid: Rialp, 20077), 678.
42 *Bendicional*, (Barcelona: Coeditores litúrgicos, 1986), 671.302.

11 The personal good of work. A comprehensive reading of the subjective dimension of work

Hélio Luciano

Introduction: the objective and subjective dimensions of work

The theological understanding of work has followed a long historical path since the Fathers of the Church. However, it is since the Industrial Revolution, and the problems that arose during this period, that theology has attempted to understand the meaning of work more systematically.

The encyclical letter *Rerum Novarum*[1] arose as a response to the problems of the proletariat, Marxist materialism, and liberalism. To a large extent, both theology and the magisterium of the Church took this as a starting point for understanding the notion of work today. Subsequently, *Quadragesimo Anno*,[2] *Mater et Magistra*,[3] *Laborem Exercens*,[4] *Centesimus Annus*,[5] as well as other magisterial documents continued the discussion initiated by the first social encyclical, contributing important elements for reflection.

Given the social problems related to work in the nineteenth and twentieth centuries, it was necessary to make the value of work in the moral life of the individual clear. Until before the Second Vatican Council, this value was presented in two ways: the first with a more eschatological charge, which presented work as a sacrifice that leads to a future encounter with God;[6] and the second, perhaps more profound, as a personal activity (in its physical and spiritual dimension), destined to the realization of a product (it needs to be a transitive activity), with a common utility and a service to others (it is directed toward a good useful to man and, through him, useful to all others).[7] Both perspectives are interesting, but they still lacked a more systematic exposition of the subjective and objective dimensions of work and, logically, they also lacked an explanation that would integrate these dimensions more deeply.

Since the Second Vatican Council, the theological understanding of work has become more evident in the understanding of the sanctification of work. Work came to be understood not as a punishment, not even as a necessity extrinsic to the subject, but as man's participation in creation.[8] The connection of work with the universal call to holiness became more evident, and broader visions of this understanding found echoes in the Universal Church, such as the message of Opus Dei since the late 1920s.[9]

DOI: 10.4324/9781003508212-13

188   *Hélio Luciano*

After the Council, the understanding of work relations and social injustices became more present in theological reflection. This issue was presented in two different ways: firstly, from a more horizontal understanding, in which the Kingdom of God would be achieved only through the restoration of just relations. Secondly, making it clear that the social problems derived from the injustice of work relations are important points of theological reflection on work. It is true, however, that work does not necessarily lose its value in relation to personal sanctification, even within these unjust relationships.[10]

In the pontificate of John Paul II, the encyclical *Laborem Exercens* insists on this dimension of personal sanctification, while also highlighting the problems related to injustice and the objective problems that are derived from certain work relations:

> Man has to subdue the earth and dominate it, because as the "image of God" he is a person, that is to say, a subjective being capable of acting in a planned and rational way, capable of deciding about himself, and with a tendency to self-realization. As a person, man is therefore the subject of work. As a person he works, he performs various actions belonging to the work process; independently of their objective content, these actions must all serve to realize his humanity, to fulfil the calling to be a person that is his by reason of his very humanity.[11]
>
> Besides wages, various social benefits intended to ensure the life and health of workers and their families play a part here. The expenses involved in health care, especially in the case of accidents at work, demand that medical assistance should be easily available for workers, and that as far as possible it should be cheap or even free of charge. Another sector regarding benefits is the sector associated with the right to rest. In the first place this involves a regular weekly rest comprising at least Sunday, and also a longer period of rest, namely the holiday or vacation taken once a year or possibly in several shorter periods during the year. A third sector concerns the right to a pension and to insurance for old age and in case of accidents at work.[12]

In this sense, both theology and the magisterium have recurrently presented two dimensions of work: the subjective and the objective dimension. In the subjective dimension, there would be this personal sanctification, in correspondence to the divine call to work – the dominion of the earth (Gen 1:28) – and by man's identification with Christ, who sanctified work during his life. In this dimension, we find the dignity of work and the personal relationship of the worker with God. On the other hand, in the objective dimension, there would be the elements directly related to the materiality of work and the social relations derived from it. They participate in work, but they would not be its deepest dimension of sanctification. In this dimension, one may find the material conditions of work. These include remuneration,

The personal good of work 189

employer–employee relations, and even broader social dimensions, such as man's participation in the construction of the common good and solidarity.

The importance of both dimensions in the understanding of work is undeniable and helps to understand this complex reality. It is essential that the moral life of a Christian subject unifies these two dimensions and that work life – also in its two dimensions – is oriented toward the *ordo amoris*.[13] However, it is the subjective dimension that is essential for understanding work and to convert it into a true identification of the moral subject with Christ. However, highlighting the subjective dimension cannot be an exclusion or a downplaying of the objective dimension, but rather of incorporating the objective elements into the life of the subject. In the words of Benedict XVI:

> Technology is the objective side of human action whose origin and raison *d'etre* is found in the subjective element: the worker himself. For this reason, technology is never merely technology. It reveals man and his aspirations towards development, it expresses the inner tension that impels him gradually to overcome material limitations.[14]

This understanding of the subjective dimension is necessary in order to achieve a deeper vision of work as opposed to a merely objective and horizontal understanding of work activity. It is also coherent with the theological circumstances of the time in which John Paul II expounded these two dimensions, in which he wanted to make clear the transcendence of the notion of work, that is, to understand work not only as an extrinsic activity, but as man's personal relationship with God, with others, and with the world. The distinction between the subjective and objective dimensions was primarily pedagogical, aimed at facilitating understanding of a unitary process.

However, the proposed division has unintentionally acquired certain dualistic overtones and, in practice, ends up affecting the understanding of the subjective–objective unity of the notion of work.[15] This excessive division gives rise to problems that are difficult to solve without the integration of the two dimensions. By way of example, we can ask ourselves to what extent work under extremely unfair conditions can be considered morally good, or even true.[16] In the context of excessive separation, it would be difficult to answer whether working and receiving a just reward is morally equivalent to working and not receiving a reward, because it would be difficult to integrate the reward understood only from an objective perspective. Even in the context of another very current discussion, with this excessive division, it would not be easy to answer whether it is the same thing to live on the resources acquired by personal work as to live on a universal basic income.[17]

These issues highlight the need to emphasize the integration of the subjective and objective dimensions of work. Although the deeper essence of the meaning of work lies in its subjective dimension, the objective dimension is not external to this deeper relationship, but rather acquires its true meaning in it. Consequently, the objective dimension cannot be something simply

190   *Hélio Luciano*

extrinsic or accidental, but, when integrated into the subjective dimension, it is part of the very moral valuation of work.

In this framework, the aim of this chapter is to understand the unity of the subjective and objective dimensions from the unitary understanding of the moral act. To this end, in the first section, we will explain our understanding of the origin of all human action in affective union, as well as the free human response that commands us to love. In this way, we will explain the moral unity of action and, consequently, the unity that exists between the objective and subjective aspects in the moral act. Then, in the second section, we will apply these dimensions of moral understanding to the human reality of work, understanding this moral action from the perspective of affective union, as well as from the perspective of the free response to the *ordo amoris*.

The affections and the *ordo amoris* as the foundation of the unity of the subjective and objective dimensions of human labor

Human work, like all human actions, is immersed in a dynamic of gift and response on the part of the individual, orienting his or her life toward meaning. Moreover, by considering human work as a dimension of human action, it is possible to understand that work is part of personal identity. It is not merely an activity, but, in a certain way and without exhausting its being, it represents something that the man or woman is. To explain this unity, it is necessary to enter into an understanding of the meaning of the affections and of affective union from the dynamics of gift (a) and in the orientation of the human moral response – and, consequently, of his or her whole life – toward the *ordo amoris* (b).

Affections and affective union as the starting point of moral action

As Pérez-Soba has explained, it can be affirmed that the beginning of any human action, even before it is properly free, is given from elements that affect us.[18] However, we do not refer to this affective dimension from the perspective of passions and desires, that is, from a deficiency that moves us to a perfection that we grasp as necessary,[19] but rather the affective dimension is understood here as something prior: human action needs to be moved beforehand by an affective union. This affective union occurs in the key of the presence of the beloved in the lover, and it is the tension of the lover toward the beloved that moves the free action.[20] With a simple example, the fact that a person does not offend his or her mother is moved first by the affective and loving union toward his or her mother and only afterward by the free and rational decision not to offend her.

What we defend here is that this loving and affective dimension that moves to action is known – by practical reason – from the intentional dimension of prudence,[21] which, to a certain extent, knows and moderates the whole

The personal good of work 191

affective dimension according to the virtuous life of the subject. In this sense, it is worth the redundancy, the affections will affect each person according to the reality of his loving relationships and oriented to the loving end, according to the depth of the virtuous life of each subject. Returning to the previous example, in the relationship of a daughter with her mother, the order with which she grasps the things that affect her will be proportional to the depth of the affective union she has with her mother. Developing the example, in the intentional dimension of prudence, the same severe punishment imposed by the mother can be perceived as something annoying, but ordered to her good, or as a violence that deserves an act of rebellion – the different way of perceiving that which affects her (the punishment) will be given by the objectivity of the fact and by the different degree of affective union she has with her mother.[22]

If it is the subjectivity of personal relationships where affective union takes place, we can say that an action is always moved by an initial gift, which has its origin in this union. In this sense, we can say that the things that affect us from outside – I repeat, not in the dynamic of desire/passion as a lack of something I need, but as the initial loving movement of every action – are an expression of this gift received. Consequently, the loving gift is prior to all our actions. It is important to emphasize that when we refer to this loving gift we do not affirm it within an emotivist or sentimental understanding: for example, in the face of a serious injustice with the workers of a company, we may be affected by a strike movement – this affection, considering the injustice, would be an expression of the loving gift.

In human relationships, this dynamic of the gift will always be limited, for human love is not perfect – the affective union of a son with his mother is true and is the origin of his free acts in his relationship with his mother, but it is not perfect. On the other hand, in man's relationship with God, the beginning of the action comprised in the gift will be perfect in its origin. Imperfection – to varying degrees – will occur in the human response to the gift.[23]

Based on affective union and, consequently, on the affections received as a gift, we can better understand the intentional dimension of prudence. Based on the depth of affective union, we grasp the affections in a more ordered way the more ordered our virtuous life is. For example, an unvirtuous person may see the money in the cash register of the store where he or she works as a possible object of theft, whereas a virtuous person does not even entertain the idea of stealing it. We are addressing this aspect before the free decision of the concrete action, which independent of this prior affective and prudential dimension (although affected by it), can still be virtuous.

The ultimate end as ordo amoris and man's free response

The ultimate end of the subject is always beatitude, even when he is not aware of it. There are not two distinct ends, one natural and the other supernatural, since every human being is called to a single end in God.[24] Thus,

192 Hélio Luciano

even in the natural virtuous life of man who is unaware of his relationship with God, this end manifests itself in the end of the virtues, that is, in a less profound but real dimension of the *ordo amoris*.[25] In this way, the things that affect us – within the dynamics of the gift and moderated by the intentional dimension of prudence to which we referred above – must be brought to the intellective and volitional dimension, that is, to the *ordo rationis*, where, in profound continuity with the above, the human response is configured in the freedom of acts. It is there that one decides whether or not to reciprocate the affection received, whether or not to align oneself or not with what is appropriate, and whether or not to order one's life in accordance to the gift.

In this sense and considering personal freedom, it is prudence, now in its elective dimension,[26] which balances and guides the other virtues and, consequently, the action itself toward the *ordo amoris*. If in the previous section we said that affective union occurs in the subjectivity of personal relationships, we can now affirm that the human response demands coherence with the objectivity of this real relationship. For this reason, however much the subjective dimension is emphasized – we are always dealing with subjective loving relationships – there is no room for a subjectivist understanding of the human moral response. The dynamic of the gift in the affective union is completed by the freedom that corresponds to the reciprocity demanded by the gift received. As in the dynamics of love and gift, the perfection of the gift received will be given in the relationship with God. The human response will always be limited, but it will be more perfect the better it responds objectively to the affection received as a gift.

To summarize, we can say that action has its origin in an affective and loving union. Practical reason, through the intentional dimension of prudence, grasps the things that affect me, understood and moderated from that affective union. Intelligence and will – through the elective dimension of prudence and the just measure of the other moral virtues – freely choose to align the action with the *ordo amoris* or away from this end. This movement is what explains every free action and the virtuous life.

Affections and the ordo amoris in the Christian subject

In addition to all the above, it is also necessary to consider the Christian subject. Grace does not destroy this natural dimension, but rather elevates it, transforming this dynamic.[27] In the first place, even in the affective dimension, the gifts of the Holy Spirit act by moderating the reception of the affections.[28] Reason, permeated by faith,[29] understands the meaning of action more deeply, which is driven by hope as the tension and real possibility of living love.[30] Nevertheless, it is the concreteness of charity that permeates these actions and becomes the form of all the virtues,[31] shaping human action into the action of Christ.[32]

The personal good of work   193

Application in the understanding of work

On this basis, work is also found within human actions and, therefore, participates in this whole process. The affective movement, that is, that which drives human beings to work, even before the exercise of their freedom, is a crucial point in the subjective understanding of work. The actions related to the specific work that a person performs will depend, to a great extent, on the affections that drive him and on the depth of one's own virtuous life, which orders those affections.

The free response of this person, in the concrete action of the work he/she carries out, will also be a decision to correspond or not to the affections received and a decision to orient or not his/her life toward the *ordo amoris*. In this way, his/her identity as a working person will be linked to the degree to which he/she decides to orient his/her life to the *ordo amoris*. Considering that work is a profound dimension of life, both as a free act that shapes one's own life, as well as the hours of the day dedicated to this activity, the understanding of the meaning of one's own life and one's own personal identity also passes through this work dimension.

It is in these relationships that the subjective dimension of work is understood, since it is in them that the person and the very meaning of his or her work-related actions are found. And it is in this subjective dimension that the objective elements acquire their true meaning, for the one who works is the subject. In short, human work, as an essential dimension of human action, is found in a dynamic of gift and response that gives meaning to the life of the person and shapes his or her identity.

The integration of the objective dimension in the subjective work relationship

Based on the above, one might think that, with the emphasis given to the subjective dimension, the objective dimension would be relegated to a secondary role, without influencing the meaning of work. In some perspectives prior to the Second Vatican Council, in which work was perceived more as a punishment for sin than as a form of participation in the life of Christ,[33] the objective aspects were to be considered and even resolved, but not necessarily incorporated into the subjective dimension. Even in the encyclical *Rerum Novarum*, which addresses the objective issues related to work, there is still no deep consideration of the subjective dimension in the meaning of work, and the objective elements are presented simply juxtaposed:

> Moreover, the earth, even though apportioned among private owners, ceases not thereby to minister to the needs of all, inasmuch as there is not one who does not sustain life from what the land produces. Those who do not possess the soil contribute their labor; hence, it may truly be said that all human subsistence is derived either from labor on one's

194   *Hélio Luciano*

own land, or from some toil, some calling, which is paid for either in the produce of the land itself, or in that which is exchanged for what the land brings forth.[34] (...) It is surely undeniable that, when a man engages in remunerative labor, the impelling reason and motive of his work is to obtain property, and thereafter to hold it as his very own. If one man hires out to another his strength or skill, he does so for the purpose of receiving in return what is necessary for the satisfaction of his needs; he therefore expressly intends to acquire a right full and real, not only to the remuneration, but also to the disposal of such remuneration, just as he pleases.[35]

Even before the Council, even in more nuanced theoretical perspectives, such as Romeu Dale's meticulous reflection on work,[36] it is evident that the issues and challenges related to work require careful analyses and the injustices identified must be resolved efficiently. However, the approach and resolution of these problems are not integrated within the fundamental conception of the notion of work itself.

As mentioned above, after the Council *Laborem Exercens*, it was pointed out that work, besides being a participation in the work of creation and a means of personal sanctification in identification with Christ, has two intrinsic dimensions: the objective and the subjective. The deepest meaning of work resides in the subjective dimension, addressing aspects such as personal fulfillment and the end for which one works.[37] However, in some later interpretations,[38] with the didactic distinction established between the objective and subjective dimensions of work, the unified conception of this activity was somewhat diluted. This has led to certain difficulties in the comprehensive understanding of the labor phenomenon. Thus, in many cases, the objective elements, which include aspects such as working conditions, remuneration, and job security, were perceived as components simply juxtaposed to the subjective dimension – the latter understood in a spiritual and disembodied way. This lack of integration between the two aspects has generated a fragmented and limited vision of work, making it difficult to construct a more unitary and harmonious approach that would make it possible to adequately address the various issues and challenges related to the work experience as a whole.[39]

It is understandable that, given the historical and ideological challenges associated with the intricate notion of work, the differentiation of the two dimensions is necessary to facilitate a better understanding of the reality of work, at least from a cognitive perspective. It must be recognized that the heart of understanding work lies in the connection between the subject and the action he/she performs, as well as in the meaning he/she attributes to that action and to his/her own life. However, for a more complete understanding, it is imperative not to dissociate the two dimensions, but rather to integrate them into the subjective dimension. The interrelation and complementarity of the objective and subjective aspects of work are essential to effectively navigate the many facets and challenges that arise in the workplace.

The personal good of work 195

Affective union and perfectibility in the understanding of work

In the first place, when approaching this integration, it is necessary to take into account the dimension of affective and loving union. The moral subject's experience in the work environment and the objective elements motivating him to work – prior to the voluntary exercise of the work activity – significantly influences the subjective interpretation of work life. This in turn, influences the meaning he attributes to such work and, consequently, his own personal identity. Thus, even considering their objective character, these elements must be analyzed within the subjectivity of the personal relationship, since they are part of the meaning the subject gives to his or her work. This interrelation between objectivity and subjectivity in the work environment allows for a deeper understanding of the work experience and its impact on the personal and emotional development of individuals, recognizing the importance of both aspects in the construction of an identity and a sense of purpose in working life.

Still in the realm of affective understanding, it is crucial to address the subject's moral experience. In this regard, we can argue that the conception of life, the meaning attributed to work, previous work relationships, the individual's socioeconomic context, working conditions, and perceived remuneration are objective elements that will directly impact the person. Thus, these factors are integrated into this unit of understanding not as juxtaposed or extrinsic elements, but as an intrinsic part of the meaning of their work. Although these elements are not the product of free decisions per se, they will greatly affect the free dimension, and thus the moral valuation of the work performed. By recognizing and analyzing the interaction between these objective factors and the subjective experience of the subject, the understanding of the work dimension and its influence on decision-making, personal identity, and the meaning given to work is enriched.

This is not about defining, with a manualistic approach, what would be the minimum criteria for a job to have as its starting point an affective union and to be guided within the context of the *ordo amoris*. Nor is it a question of penalizing or diminishing those job prospects that do not start from a loving radicality. It is simply a matter of understanding that there are different levels of perfection in understanding work activity: for example, we can say that work originating from a profound understanding of the meaning of work, as participation in the God's creative work and solidarity in the construction of the common good, will be more perfect than work that is born from a simple understanding of the material need for subsistence.

On the other hand, by contemplating the affections not only in their facet of affective union, but also in their assimilation as gifts in personal life, that is, in the realm of the intentional dimension of prudence (which will affect the free decisions of the individual), it can be asserted that these affections mold and structure the individual's perception of work. It is undeniable that in the *ordo amoris* – whether in its manifestation of natural virtues or in its deeper dimension linked to the *sequela Christi* – the subject is committed to

196   Hélio Luciano

that which gives meaning to his own action. Thus, the incorporation of the affections and the orientation of how he relates to them in the context of his life preclude a perspective in which one can distinguish, separately, the objective and subjective dimensions of his work.

Thus, an individual's moral interpretation of the meaning of work will influence his working life and, consequently, he will voluntarily choose to perform in accordance with the meaning he gives to work. This objective component – his moral experience – will determine whether or not he integrates the various dimensions of the meaning of work – such as means of subsistence, personal self-realization, service to society, transformation of the world, and identification with Christ – into his work performance.

If any of these dimensions that the individual subjectively perceives as an intrinsic part of the meaning of his work is not satisfied, his work activity will be affected in a moral sense. He will not understand that his work stems from an affective union, and what motivates him to work will not be understood as a gift. Similarly, if any of these dimensions that give meaning to his work is only partially fulfilled, it will also affect the perfective value of that work, since not all work activities possess the same depth and moral significance. For example, if a person's affective understanding of work (as presented in the previous section) does not include an immediate contribution to the promotion of the common good, that work will be less perfect for that person. Once more, the goal is not to extrinsically define the perfectibility of each type of work, but to understand it from the subjective comprehension and meaning. It is logical that, objectively – and grounded in truth, it is possible to assist in understanding the value of each job. However, until this assistance is not assumed from the subjective and personal dimensions, the work performed will continue with an imperfect personal understanding.

Therefore, it is important to understand that it is not only about the work activity performed, but also about the understanding of work as an integral element of life and personal identity. In this way, the emphasis is not only on the objective materiality of work, but also on its deeper relevance in that it gives meaning to this person's life.

As a result of the above, it is true that the meaning of work rooted in personal identity implies that the individual is able to subsist on the product of his own labor. In this aspect – and not in others – Marx's critique may be valid in considering the unjust alienation of the product of personal labor as violence. Certainly, the just remuneration of the worker is essential in this perspective. Instances of slave labor or severe injustices – whether in remuneration or in working conditions – can significantly affect the reality of labor itself. Therefore, although it may seem counterintuitive, income distribution policies that are not based on the labor activity of the individual – such as universal minimum income projects – will similarly become more instruments of alienation and dependence than real means for personal fulfillment.

From a very different epistemological perspective, this difference in depth in the understanding of work may have common ground in the explanations given by the concept of "meaningful work", a focal point of the

The personal good of work 197

social sciences.[40] In this context, Cilla's differentiation between the moral conditions of work – which exist in an area extrinsic to the person but should be guaranteed by governments and employers – and meaningful work are insightful. In our interpretation, meaningful work lies in the understanding of work from the affective union, in the subjective meaning that integrates what are commonly referred to as objective elements, given by each person.[41]

Work as a free response in the ordo amoris

Still in the integration of the objective and subjective dimensions of work, we move on to consider the dimension of responses, which depend on the freedom of the worker. We do so from the moral understanding laid out above, i.e., rooted in the affective union and as a response in the *ordo amoris*.

Analyzing the human response to the affections, there are objective elements that contribute to the moral consideration of human work. The dimension of inner freedom is one of these elements. We are not referring only to freedom from coercion, which affects an extrinsic level of freedom, but to the deeper aspect of subjectively wanting to convert our action into real work. In this context, we can maintain that even in circumstances of external violence or in situations of slave labor – without downplaying the grave moral wrongdoing, the sin of those who attack personal freedom, or the urgency to eradicate such unjust situations – despite coercion, there remains the possibility to view and experience the work undertaken as a true avenue for personal perfection and/or expression of love for God. Therefore, it primarily revolves around the free dimension of wanting to work and find meaning in one's work. Building on what was explained in the previous section, it is about a voluntary commitment, in concrete actions, to respond to what one lives in the affective union that gives meaning to ones work.

In this same regard – and without excluding the problems of the meaning of work mentioned in the previous section (especially regarding the necessity for the person to be able to sustain himself on the outcome of his work) – even if these conditions do not manifest and affect the meaning of work in its deepest dimension, in his affective response, the person may be able to give meaning to his work.

Simultaneously, we can argue that certain jobs driven solely by the need for survival without an internal sense of practical reason, despite sharing the condition of work like the others, may in reality be a greater imposition to the freedom of the worker than a true avenue personal perfection. Once again, it is not a question of defining whether it qualifies as work or not, but rather of understanding the degree of perfectibility that work can assume.

Within this unity of action – where the objective dimension is integrated into the subjective – the aim is not to advocate for a moral subjectivism where conscience would determine the truth and goodness of action. Rather, it seeks to understand that all human action – including work – belongs to the concrete subject in its real and historical embodiment in the world.

198   *Hélio Luciano*

In this framework, we can use the definition of work from which this book is based:

> (...) we propose a theological definition of work as a type of human activity oriented to the support of one's own life (or also of others' life), which responds to God's call to the perfecting of the person and to collaborate in the development of creation, and which is carried out in a social context, that is, in service to the needs of the human community to which one belongs.[42]

Certainly, it cannot be said that this is a definition in the strict sense, for if it were so, realities lacking these characteristics could not be qualified as work. However, they exhibit characteristics that align with a more understanding of labor activity, integrating the objective dimensions into the subjective ones, since it is the individual who works. Explicitly, that which lacks these characteristics - assessed through practical reason and without requiring a personal speculative understanding of the action performed – would be considered work in a more limited moral dimension. However, even within actions that fit this definition, the integration of the objective and subjective dimensions will provide insight into the moral quality of such work. In some cases, this perception could lead to the consideration that certain work activities, from a moral point of view, cannot be understood as work.

Even considering the process of integrating the objective and subjective dimensions of work, it is crucial to recognize that the social aspects, although objective, must also be incorporated into the subjective dimension of work. They acquire their deepest moral meaning in that realm. It is worth remembering that the human being is not an isolated entity, but an inherently social individual, intrinsically connected with others. Therefore, human participation in the construction of the common good and solidarity should not be considered as extrinsic or merely qualitative aspects of labor action. In reality, they are fundamental elements in the labor relationship and contribute to the overall meaning of work. The notion of work as merely personal perfection, disregarding and ignoring this horizontal dimension of action, would be insufficient and would not lead man toward the *ordo amoris*.

The importance of integrating rather than juxtaposing the social dimension in work lies in the fact that this enables a broader and deeper understanding of the purpose and nature of human work. This implies considering work as part of personal development in its contribution to collective well-being, promoting an integral approach that embraces interaction and cooperation between individuals and communities. Such a perspective helps to orient man toward his ultimate goal. In this way, a fuller and deeper understanding of work as a means of personal perfection will be achieved, not parallel, but realized through contribution to the common good.

Conclusion

Considering all of the above, it is possible to understand that while the Industrial Revolution brought unimaginable material progress for the world, it also gave rise to associated problems. From this new reality – in the very execution of work and in relation to the problems that arose – there arises a need to reflect on the meaning of work. This need is also present in the theological realm.

The first reflections in this context focus more on the objective aspects of the problem, as a need to respond to concrete social problems. However, throughout the twentieth century, a deeper understanding of the meaning of work developed, focusing on its subjective dimension, while the objective elements came to be considered in juxtaposition to this deeper subjective understanding.

Although a richer notion of work has been achieved in this subjective dimension, the mere juxtaposition of the subjective and objective dimensions results in the loss of the unity of action. This excessive separation between the two dimensions – subjective and objective – leads to oversimplifications in the understanding of work. It becomes necessary to recover this unity, integrating the objective elements within the subjective relationship. In this way, the objective elements acquire a profound moral value in the context of work activity.

The integration of both dimensions is achieved from the understanding of one's own moral life. We have seen how the objective elements influence the person who works – even before the actual free action, in the affections and in the affective union that moves them – and participate in their free response during the work activity they perform. It is therefore necessary to understand them within this dynamic of gift and response that gives meaning to personal life in the direction of the *ordo amoris*.

In this way, a unitary understanding of labor activity is achieved, in which elements previously valued, but considered secondary within the notion of work – such as fair remuneration, subsistence, personal identity, solidarity, the common good, coercion, and inner freedom – acquire relevance in the very meaning of the notion of work, affecting the essence of its moral understanding. Thus, a more complete and enriching approach to the concept of work and its importance in the life of the individual and of society as a whole is achieved.

As a result, we hope to have contributed to framing the tensions that exist between the subjective and objective dimensions of work and, above all, within a Christian conception, to understand them within the unity of human action with its origin and end in love. In a parallel way and without being the main objective of this chapter, this work also opens a wide path for research on the integration between the affective and cognitive human dimensions through the virtue of prudence.

200 Hélio Luciano

Notes

1 Leo XIII, *Rerum Novarum*, May 15, 1891, ASS 23 (1890–1891), 641–670.
2 Pius XI, *Quadragesimo Anno*, May 15, 1931, AAS 23 (1931), 177–228.
3 John XXIII, *Mater et Magistra*, May 15, 1961, AAS 53 (1961), 401–464.
4 John Paul II, *Laborem Exercens*, September 14, 1981, AAS 73 (1981), 577–647.
5 John Paul II, *Centesimus Annus*, May 1, 1991, AAS 83 (1991), 793–867.
6 Boaventura Kloppenburg, "O valor religioso da atividade humana na ordem temporal segundo o Vaticano II," *Revista Eclesiástica Brasileira* 27, no. 1 (1967): 22–42.
7 Romeu Dale, "Teologia do trabalho," *Revista Eclesiástica Brasileira* 15 (1955): 595–606, 596.
8 Second Vatican Council, *Gaudium et Spes*, 22; Second Vatican Council, *Lumen Gentium*, 34.
9 José Luis Illanes, *La santificación del trabajo. El trabajo en la historia de la espiritualidad*, 10th ed. (Madrid: Palabra, 2001), 31–80.
10 Hélio Luciano, "La comprensión de la noción de trabajo en la teología brasileña del siglo XX," *Veritas* 54 (2023): 147–171, 166–167.
11 John Paul II, *Laborem exercens*, September 6, 1981.
12 John Paul II, *Laborem exercens*, September 19, 1981.
13 With this concept we refer to the ordering of the whole moral life toward the love of God. We can assume here the understanding of the term from St. Augustine, without discarding the later development given to the concept: "But if the Creator is truly loved, that is, if he himself is loved and not another thing in his stead, He cannot be evilly loved; for love itself is to be ordinately loved, because we do well to love that which, when we love it, makes us live well and virtuously. So that it seems to me that it is a brief but true definition of virtue to say, it is the order of love; and on this account, in the canticles, the bride of christ, the city of God, sings, "order love within me". Augustine of Hippo, *The City of God*, XV, 22.
14 Benedict XVI, *Caritas in Veritate*, July 7, 2009, AAS 101 (2009), 641–709, 69.
15 Without diminishing the merit of the work, which brings together many elements on an understanding of work, this vision with certain dualistic nuances can be seen, for example, in Élio E. Gasda, *Fe cristiana y sentido del trabajo* (Madrid: San Pablo-Universidad Pontificia Comillas, 2011).
16 Certainly, these questions arise from sociology; however, they must also be answered through the subjectivity and objectivity of labor dimensions from a broader perspective. See Nicholas H. Smith, Jean-Philippe Deranty, and Emmanuel Renault, "Unemployment and Precarious Work" *The Return of Work in Critical Theory. Self, Society, Politics*, eds. Christophe Dejours, Jean-Philippe Deranty, Emmanuel Renault, and Nicholas H. Smith (New York: Columbia University Press, 2018), 23-41.
17 Without entering into the discussion on this strategy, see Raúl González, "La renta básica universal: fundamentos, debates y posibilidades" *Polis Revista Latinoamericana* 21, no. 62 (2022): 11–31.
18 Juan José Pérez-Soba, *Vivir en Cristo, la fe que actúa por el amor* (Madrid: Biblioteca de Autores Cristianos, 2018), 261–270.
19 Juan José Pérez-Soba, "El Papel de los afectos en la acción humana: una exégesis de «S. Th.», I-II, q. 28, a. 6," *Scripta Theologica* 53, no. 3 (2021): 625–663, 646.
20 Juan José Pérez-Soba, "El papel de los afectos en la acción humana: Una exégesis de «S. Th.», I-II, q. 28, a. 6," *Scripta Theologica* 53, no. 3 (2021): 647.
21 Enrique Colom and Ángel Rodríguez Luño, *Elegidos en Cristo para ser santos. Curso de teología moral fundamental* (Madrid: Palabra, 2001), 200–204. In these pages, the authors explain the intentional dimension of the virtuous life and

The personal good of work 201

the intentional dimension of prudence, but they do not combine them with the affective dimension as we explain it here.

22 Although it is not the main object of this essay, it is worth clarifying that we understand the intentional dimension of prudence in its two dimensions – as a moral and intellectual virtue – and within the Thomistic understanding of habit. In this way, what St. Thomas calls knowledge by connaturality is not understood as knowledge independent of reason, but as habitual affective knowledge through the virtue of prudence. On this specific point – of the intentional dimension of prudence – we speak of this knowledge in its dimension prior to freedom, which orders the affections and makes them truly cognitive. It is still necessary to consider also that this intentional dimension of prudence is previously formed by the free virtuous life, in the elective dimension of prudence. This understanding will be systematized in a later work. The elements of this development can be found in the works we cite below, although it should be noted that these authors do not present it unified in the way we do – Sebastián Buzeta, *Sobre el conocimiento por connaturalidad.* Cuadernos de Anuario Filosófico. Serie universitaria (Pamplona: Servicio de publicaciones de la Universidad de Navarra, 2013); Ángel Rodríguez Luño, *Ética general* (Pamplona: Eunsa, 2014); Colom and Rodríguez Luño, *Elegidos en Cristo para ser santos. Curso de teología moral fundamental* (Madrid: Palabra, 2001); Pérez-Soba, *Vivir en Cristo, la fe que actúa por el amor* (Madrid: Biblioteca de Autores Cristianos, 2018).

23 Pérez-Soba, *Vivir en Cristo, la fe que actúa por el amor* (Madrid: Biblioteca de Autores Cristianos, 2018), 65–87.

24 Henri de Lubac, *El Misterio de lo sobrenatural* (Madrid: Encuentro, 1990), 92.

25 Authors differ in the name and in the nuances used to refer to this virtuous end. Some refer to this end from the understanding of the rightness of reason, others understand it from the very purpose and ordering of virtue. Although there are different nuances, for the purpose of this chapter, the term *ordo amoris* shows more clearly the subjective dimension that we wish to emphasize. See Daniel Granada, *El alma de toda virtud. «Virtus sependet aliqualiter ab amore»: Una relectura de la relación amor y virtud en santo Tomás* (Siena: Cantagalli, 2016), 428.

26 Colom and Luño, *Elegidos en Cristo para ser santos*, 204–207.

27 Thomas Aquinas, *Summa Theologiae*, I, q.1, a.8, ad.2.

28 Pérez-Soba, *Vivir en Cristo, la fe que actúa por el amor* (Madrid: Biblioteca de Autores Cristianos, 2018), 271–277.

29 Thomas Aquinas, *Summa Theologiae*, II–IIae, q.4. a.2.

30 Thomas Aquinas, *Summa Theologiae*, II–IIae, q.18, a.1.

31 Thomas Aquinas, *Summa Theologiae*, II–IIae, q.23, a.8.

32 Thomas Aquinas, *Summa Theologiae*, II–IIae, q.24, a.7.

33 According to Boaventura Kloppenburg OFM, this vision did not have a sufficient notion of the salvific reality of the temporal order, considered only as a springboard to eternal life. See Boaventura Kloppenburg, "O valor religioso da atividade humana na ordem temporal segundo o Vaticano II," *Revista Eclesiástica Brasileira* 27, no. 1 (1967): 22–42.

34 Leo XIII, *Rerum novarum*, May 15, 1891, ASS 23 (1890–1891), 8.

35 Leo XIII, *Rerum novarum*, May 15, 1891, ASS 23 (1890–1891), 5.

36 Romeu Dale, "Teologia do trabalho", *Revista Eclesiástica Brasileira* 15 (1955): 596.

37 The main reference points are points 5 and 6 of *Laborem exercens*, entitled respectively "Work in the objective sense: technology" and "Work in the subjective sense: man as the subject of work."

202 Hélio Luciano

38 As mentioned above and without detracting from the merit of the work, we cite as an example: Élio E. Gasda, *Fe cristiana y sentido del trabajo* (Madrid: San Pablo-Universidad Pontificia Comillas, 2011).

39 Daniel Granada, "Consideración unitaria del trabajo como acción en la historia de la teología del trabajo," *Scripta Theologica* 56, no. 2 (2024): 377–406.

40 See Ruth Yeoman, Catherine Bailey, Adrian Madden, and Marc Thompson, eds. *The Oxford Handbook of Meaningful Work* (Oxford: Oxford University Press, 2019).

41 Joanne Ciulla, *The Search for Ethics in Leadership, Ethics and Beyond* (Newark: Springer, 2022), 197–210.

42 Gregorio Guitián and Ana Marta González, "Theology of Work: New Perspectives," *Scripta Theologica* 54, no. 3 (2022): 757–787, 761.

12 Contemplation at work. Social contemplation and mysticism for an integral ecology of work[1]

Martin Schlag

Introduction

The title of my chapter expresses that I place my reflections on human work into the framework of integral ecology, i.e., an ecology that takes all dimensions of the human person into consideration. I do so inspired by the teaching of Pope Francis, whose social magisterium is characterized by a strong emphasis on a "prophetic and contemplative lifestyle...capable of deep enjoyment free of the obsession with consumption,"[2] a lifestyle that hears "both the cry of the poor and the cry of the earth."[3] In Pope Francis' writings, contemplation has become a category also of Catholic Social Thought: Contemplation means overcoming reductionism by perceiving the beauty of creation and of the other person who "is beautiful above and beyond mere appearances."[4] The contemplative gaze discovers God's presence in our cities[5] and discloses the mystical meaning of creatures.[6] Fraternity in solidarity is based on grateful contemplation[7] that receives creation and other human beings with reverence[8]: "Authentic contemplation always has a place for others."[9] In his Wednesday catechesis on the Catholic social principles, Francis links contemplation to solidarity by attributing solidarity to the outpouring of the Holy Spirit at Pentecost, the great Christian "anti-Babel:" "With Pentecost, God makes himself present and inspires the *faith* of the community *united in diversity and in solidarity*."[10] God creates community by inspiring faith in a common Father who makes us discover each other and all creatures as brothers and sisters. The way to healing, when community is ruptured, is "a *mystical* fraternity, a contemplative fraternity."[11] Francis rejects egotistic anthropocentrism, exploitation, and reduction of creatures to their usefulness. He grounds our capacity to discover the intrinsic value of nonhuman beings in contemplative spirituality and singles out our "mystical capacity" as a protective antidote to the evil tendency to treat others as slaves. He stays in a theocentric framework that regards the world as a gift of the Creator.[12]

The question that I want to address is what it might mean to contemplate God in work. A first answer is: Contemplation at work means seeing God in work and looking at work in the world with the eyes of God.

DOI: 10.4324/9781003508212-14

204 *Martin Schlag*

However, the question is challenging in the case of secular work in the world, understood as a theological category in the sense of 1 Jn 2:15–17: a fallen world dominated by the threefold concupiscence (sensual lust, enticement for the eyes, and a pretentious life) and opposed to God. Human work in business, finance, politics, media, and all other professions seems to be inextricably tied up with a sinful world that follows rules different from the world to come. Moral theology has developed norms to justify material cooperation with evil. But is justifying the inevitable negative consequences of what we do as non-intended and proportional a satisfactory path to sanctification of work and contemplation of God therein?

I want to approach an answer via ecotheology. This branch of theology takes up a contemporary cultural sensitivity which reacts to one of the existing social sins or sinful structures of society: the exploitation of nature through human work. Nature frequently is left without the necessary resources for regeneration because of human work organized by business interests. Environmental concern is an important value that moves an increasing number of people and has been doing so for a long time. How should humans relate to nature in their work?

Christopher Stone attempted to tackle the question from a legal perspective. In 1972, he published a seminal article on the legal standing of trees.[13] In it, he argues for a change in US law that would allow environmental advocacy groups to speak in the name of nature and to claim nature's "right" to be made whole from pollution and other environmental harm. His arguments can be incorporated into existing legal categories, which rest upon an anthropocentric conception of law. Here, rights of nature would codify a duty of man—his duty to care for nature—rather than grant nature rights in the strict sense of the word. Likewise, traditional claims of rights of nature from a theological perspective remain in an anthropocentric framework. For instance, James Nash recognizes that he is

> in effect defining human responsibilities, since only humans are moral agents capable of respecting rights. These rights, then, are justifiable claims on humans for the basic conditions necessary for the well-being of otherkind. They are specifications of the content of human ecological responsibility.[14]

In contrast, in other publications, the "rights of nature" paradigm is interpreted as an expression of ecocentrism or of biocentrism. Paul Taylor, an early influential scholar of environmental ethics, bases his system on the conviction of human interconnectedness and relationality with all other beings, but also on the explicit rejection of the belief that humans are "inherently superior to other living things."[15]

The common matrix that undergirds Taylor's proposal and can be found, formulated in varying degrees of radicality, also in other authors who endorse ecocentrism, is the conviction that animals, plants, inanimate

Contemplation at work 205

objects, and the whole of nature are beings in their own right that deserve recognition and respect as something natural and outside the power of human manipulation. They possess intrinsic value independently of their instrumental value for humans. However, ecocentrism or biocentrism can turn into anti-humanist ideologies that are inconsistent with the Catholic tradition.[16] Human work, by definition, is anthropocentric as it shapes and affects nature and therefore uses it as an instrument—for better or for worse. Is there a Catholic alternative to ecocentrism that is based on revelation and allows human work to be part of the salvific dispensation of God, by living in harmony with creation?

For the sake of greater clarity, I repeat the four questions I ask in the preceding pages:

What might it mean to contemplate God in work?

Is justifying the inevitable negative consequences of what we do as non-intended and proportional a satisfactory path to sanctification of work and contemplation of God therein?

How should humans relate to nature in their work to please God?

Is there a Catholic alternative to ecocentrism that is based on revelation and allows human work to be part of the salvific dispensation of God, by living in harmony with creation?

Before attempting to answer these questions, some methodological remarks are in order.

Theological backdrop

General remarks

In my considerations, I follow three methodological orientations that set the course of my thoughts and that I formulate as three general remarks:

1 We should be wary of attempts to reinterpret the tradition in light of contemporary issues but rather strive to understand contemporary issues in light of the tradition. In its Pastoral Constitution *Gaudium et Spes*, the Second Vatican Council offers dialogue as a hermeneutical key to reading the signs of the times in the light of the faith. The Church learns from the world, but she also proclaims the faith as her specific contribution to help the world better understand itself as world, without alienation.[17]

2 Before and after the Second Vatican Council, the Church proclaimed a "new humanism" in what has been termed the "anthropological turn" focused on the question "who is man?"[18] It is my impression that our culture has shifted to a social perspective: From "who is man?" (which we have not been able to agree on) we have moved on to the question "how do we wish to live together?" (which we must agree on).

206 *Martin Schlag*

3 Finally, every wrong answer is an answer to a correct question that we cannot ignore. It is not sufficient to reject the wrong answer, while ignoring the question. We must at least try to propose a better answer.

In application of these general remarks, I now turn to human work in relation to the ecology as a theological topic.

The greening of Catholic Social Thought

Already in 1989, Roderick Nash spoke of the "greening of religion" and described the birth of ecotheology in the 1980s.[19] More recently, Stephen Ellingson has analyzed the emergence of religious environmental movements and categorized their different approaches.[20] What the movements have in common is that they are not religious duplicates of their secular counterparts. Their aim is not primarily to address only environmental issues but to renew faith by spreading a new awareness that care for creation is an integral part of faith.[21] What distinguishes the movements are the different theological frames of the ethics of care for creation they promote. All three are relevant for human work. Ellingson groups these frameworks into three categories: stewardship ethic,[22] ecojustice, and creation spirituality.[23] The stewardship model is more common among conservative or moderate groups. It emphasizes God's mandate to humans as God's image to care for the earth. Environmental problems are seen as rooted in sin or alienation from God:

> The stewardship ethic tends to locate the environmental problems and their solutions at the individual level and thus does not push religions to consider the systemic or structural causes of environmental degradation or identify how power relations are implicated in environmental degradation.[24]

In this frame, environmental responsibility concentrates on individual virtues at work. Environmental ethics based on ecological justice, the second group, calls attention to the Bible's prophetic tradition of denouncing social injustices committed against the poor, the marginalized, the weak and oppressed, and extends these notions to the environment. Ecological justice underscores the deleterious effects of unjust systems, inequities, and power structures, and motivates religious believers to ameliorate the situation. In this frame, the emphasis for environmental awareness at work considers our participation in unjust structures and strives to overcome them. The third frame, creation spirituality or ecospirituality, was developed by Catholic thinkers and "rejects religious anthropocentrism and argues that humans and nature are mutual partners in God's cosmic plan."[25] It calls on humans to discover their own embeddedness in God's creation, and their interconnectedness with all beings, in whom we can contemplate God in a pan-en-theistic way. Ecospirituality is "the way one relates to or with the sacred, or the way the sacred

Contemplation at work   207

informs one's way of being in the world."[26] It focuses on experiences more than theoretical conceptions and is exercised in practices of spiritual awareness that lead to gratitude, respect, and love for the natural world, the sacred, and God.[27] Contemplation at work seems to fit into this frame neatly. It is important to realize that these frames are not mutually exclusive but rely on each other. They form expanding circles as can be observed in the development of Catholic social teaching.

Building on Ellingson's work, Lukas Szrot analyzes the development of papal Catholic social teaching on the environment between 1959 and 2015.[28] His analysis offers evidence of a shift in Catholic social teaching toward a "greening" of the tradition without, however, endorsing eco- or biocentrism. Over the decades, the magisterium, in dialogue with cultural trends, has widened the framework of stewardship to ecological justice and to aspects of creation spirituality. The notion of stewardship remains a central theme in the magisterium both of Benedict XVI and of Francis. Benedict XVI was explicit:

> There exists a certain reciprocity: as we care for creation, we realize that God, through creation, cares for us. On the other hand, a correct understanding of the relationship between man and the environment will not end by absolutizing nature or by considering it more important than the human person. If the Church's magisterium expresses grave misgivings about notions of the environment inspired by ecocentrism and biocentrism, it is because such notions eliminate the difference of identity and worth between the human person and other living things. In the name of a supposedly egalitarian vision of the "dignity" of all living creatures, such notions end up abolishing the distinctiveness and superior role of human beings. They also open the way to a new pantheism tinged with neo-paganism, which would see the source of man's salvation in nature alone, understood in purely naturalistic terms. The Church, for her part, is concerned that the question be approached in a balanced way, with respect for the "grammar" which the Creator has inscribed in his handiwork by giving man *the role of a steward and administrator with responsibility over creation*, a role which man must certainly not abuse, but also one which he may not abdicate.[29]

Nevertheless, more and more theologians share the conviction, that the mere stewardship model is ambiguous and not enough.[30] Thomas Massaro, e.g., writes:

> With the publication of *Laudato si'*, Pope Francis has definitively confirmed Catholic social teaching's adoption of a creation-centered approach, after decades of gradual but fitful movement in this direction. With this strong and heartfelt statement of deep concern for all of creation, there is no turning back to a model of mere stewardship.[31]

208 *Martin Schlag*

The skeptical stance toward the stewardship model may have to do with the fact that the notion of stewardship avoids the question of whether the original acquisition of the good held by the steward was just. A steward who has acquired his position fraudulently or forced himself into it or has a disproportionate part is inequitable even though his administration might be technically perfect. The uniqueness of the word "steward" to the English language and its etymological roots in royal power, abused by Henry VIII to confiscate Church property, do not make it easier to accept the term.[32] In Laudato Si, Pope Francis does not reject the notion of stewardship. Quite to the contrary, he endorses it[33] but complements it with co-creationality, relationality, interconnectedness, embeddedness, and personification.[34] Francis refers to the earth as "mother" and "sister," implying a kind of kinship with creation and underscoring the shift toward creation spirituality. However, as Szrot observes, Francis remains in the ecojustice framework, stopping short of embracing the creation spirituality model fully and not personifying nature in the legal sense.[35] Francis himself explained his position in a carefully worded address to the United Nations after the publication of his social encyclical on the common home:

> First, it must be stated that a true 'right of the environment' does exist, for two reasons. First, because we human beings are part of the environment. We live in communion with it, since the environment itself entails ethical limits which human activity must acknowledge and respect. Man, for all his remarkable gifts, which 'are signs of a uniqueness which transcends the spheres of physics and biology' (Laudato Si', 81), is at the same time a part of these spheres. He possesses a body shaped by physical, chemical and biological elements, and can only survive and develop if the ecological environment is favorable. Any harm done to the environment, therefore, is harm done to humanity. Second, because every creature, particularly a living creature, has an intrinsic value, in its existence, its life, its beauty and its interdependence with other creatures. We Christians, together with the other monotheistic religions, believe that the universe is the fruit of a loving decision by the Creator, who permits man respectfully to use creation for the good of his fellow men and for the glory of the Creator; he is not authorized to abuse it, much less to destroy it. In all religions, the environment is a fundamental good (cf. ibid.).[36]

Pope Francis explains the right of the environment in an anthropocentric way: The right of nature is presented as a human right to a healthy environment. However, for Francis, the last foundation of such a right is God. The intrinsic worth and beauty of all creatures reside in God. The alternative to ecocentrism is not mere anthropocentrism but theocentric anthropocentrism.

The three theological phases that we have sketched (stewardship—ecojustice—creation spirituality) are not mutually exclusive but form concentric expanding circles, as stated above. Creation spirituality opens our ears

Contemplation at work   209

for the cries of the poor and of the environment and hears them in one voice without withdrawing into a state of contemplative detachment. Ecological justice corrects wrong interpretations of stewardship by questioning social structures, economic models, and styles of life (consumerism, throw-away culture, indifference, etc.). Stewardship appeals to personal responsibility for creation.

Identifying Francis with the secular ethical frame of ecospirituality would miss the point that Francis is using contemplative, mystical language. He even quotes St. Francis' canticle, which is a prayer to the Creator God, as the title of his encyclical. According to the Catholic tradition, living beings and elements of inanimate nature are morally considerable. There is a peremptory need to protect the environment, to reduce carbon emissions, to save endangered species, to treat animals well, to serve our common home with the gifts God has given us. It is not that ecocentrism says too much; it says too little. Christian theology has much more to offer.

I therefore now sketch what I think could be a Catholic alternative to ecocentrism that is based on revelation and allows human work to be part of the salvific dispensation of God, by living in harmony with creation and thus pleasing God. I thereby hope also to contribute to our initial question of what it might mean to contemplate God in work in a world stricken by sin, beyond the mere rules of material cooperation with evil. I am inspired by "Green Thomism" (as exemplified by Christopher Thompson, Steven Long, Daniel Scheid, and others)[37] and the notion of the sacramentality of creation, at home mostly in the Byzantine tradition.[38]

A Catholic alternative to ecocentrism

Green Thomism

In this section, I will only obliquely touch on the ability of Thomas' theology to ground direct moral concern for nonhuman beings, as my topic is how ecological awareness can serve as an example for what it means to be contemplative in work amid a sinful world. Green Thomism, that is, the study of the philosophy and theology of Aquinas with the lens of environmental ethics, will be a prompt to arrive at my conclusion that work can be liturgical. Aquinas' teachings contain numerous elements that can serve as a foundation for a theory of environmental concern and for the theme of contemplation at work. It shares the tradition of philosophical realism that affirms the goodness of all that exists and strives to cleanse it of sin.

Many in the ecological conversation see human reason as the destructive force behind the manipulation and commodification of nature. But from a Thomistic perspective, reason, when properly understood, can help us live more in harmony with what we know—including nature. For Thomas, reason is *intellectus*, which can "read inside," as the Latin words *intus* (inside) *legere* (to read, to gather) denote. Intellect gathers knowledge and wisdom about the meaning, purpose, and connections of persons and things. John

210 Martin Schlag

Paul II called this way of perceiving the world a "contemplative outlook."[39] Pope Francis refers to the world as a "joyful mystery to be contemplated with gladness and praise."[40] All this is deeply rooted in the Catholic tradition as expressed by the angelic teacher. Aquinas teaches that truth comes before goodness, because knowledge precedes inclination (*cognitio naturaliter praecedit appetitum*).[41] In other words, truth comes before usefulness. Intellect is not in the first instance calculation of what human industry can make out of something, but knowledge of what the creature is in itself. Knowledge is an attitude of receptivity of the intrinsic worth of being and its goodness.

With Thomas' view of reason, anthropocentrism and harmony with nature are actually mutually implicative. While Aquinas affirms the intrinsic goodness of all creatures because they are ordered toward God, he also leaves no doubt about the subordination of all corporeal beings to the human person. "Less noble creatures exist because of (*propter*) the more noble ones, as subhuman creatures are because of (*propter*) man."[42] Humans are the proximate aim of all nonhuman creatures, whereas God's goodness remains the last end of all.[43] On a basic level, and expressed as a general rule, we are allowed to use the animals and plants for our food, but always with moderation and temperance.[44] More importantly, we need nonhuman beings to recognize God through creation. This is because everything in our minds, even the highest spiritual knowledge, has initially passed through our senses.[45] Errors about nature, therefore, lead to errors about God and the faith.[46] Thus, while all nonhuman creation exists for our sake, a warped view of it will warp us—and ultimately our mind's access to God.

Based on Aquinas' arguments of natural teleology (all subhuman beings are created for the sake of intellectual nature) and eschatology (in the new heaven and the earth, animals and plants will cease to exist), Ryan Patrick McLaughlin affirms that Thomas Aquinas' philosophical and theological teachings can be used to "expand our indirect moral concern for the welfare of the nonhuman creation within the borders of an anthropocentric conservation."[47] Here, our moral concern would not be based on the intrinsic value of nonhuman creation. Whatever one might think of McLaughlin's thesis, I doubt that his arguments regarding Aquinas' teachings are altogether sound. And I reference his article mainly for one omission that is important for the question of contemplation at work: the choirs of angels and their hierarchy, into which we are inserted. First, however, let us turn to questions of eschatology, as they are important for contemplation. McLaughlin affirms that according to Aquinas' eschatology, there will only be humans and minerals in the new heaven and the new earth.[48] This is based on the *Supplementum* to the Third Part of the *Summa Theologiae*, a reconstruction by Thomas' secretary of the end of the *Summa Theologiae*: "Therefore plants and animals will altogether cease after the renewal of the world."[49] McLaughlin corroborates that the author of the Supplement authentically conserved the mind of Thomas by pointing to Aquinas' affirmations of a

Contemplation at work   211

purportedly similar content in *Summa Contra Gentiles* IV, 97 and IV, 83–86. In the new earth, humans will not need animals and plants as ladders to God through contemplation nor will they need to eat them.[50]

Certainly, Aquinas could not assume a continuing "personal" identity of animals and plants, as they are not endowed with an eternal spiritual soul and are therefore not persons. However, would Aquinas really have excluded the possibility that God might create animals and plants for the new earth? In *Summa Contra Gentiles* IV, 97, Aquinas affirms that all bodily creation will be transformed.[51] Does this not include all corporeal beings, thus also animals and plants? In *Supplementum*, q. 82 a. 3 and 4, Aquinas' posthumous editor strongly insists that humans will have bodily senses (vision, hearing, smell, touch, taste) after the bodily resurrection (with the possible exception of taste because we will not have to eat). What would bodily senses be good for without objects that we could behold and contemplate (outside of God)? In a passage that is relevant for contemplation, Aquinas explains that the risen saints will see God in all things:

> When of two things the first is the reason for the second, the attention of the soul to the second does not hinder or lessen its attention to the first…And since God is apprehended by the saints as the reason for all things that will be done or known by them, their efforts in perceiving sensible things or in contemplating or doing anything else will in no way hinder their contemplation of God, nor conversely.[52]

How can we see God in all things if there are only rocks? Aquinas is adamant that God's glory is made manifest by the diversity of creatures more than by the perfection of a single one of them.[53] In any case, it seems to me that this is a rather speculative question. Little has been revealed of how the new heaven and new earth will be, except that it goes beyond anything the human heart can desire. It might be that we will see everything in the Trinity itself with no need for mediation. However, this assumption just does not seem to fit with the idea of a new earth. For now, we need to focus on our present world and eon.

Importantly for our eon, for the world we are in here and now, McLaughlin omits any reference to the angels and the notion of hierarchy, despite the fact that they take up considerable space in Thomas' *Summa Theologiae*.[54] Thomas says that for the creatures to be able to imitate God perfectly, there must be diverse levels of being, a hierarchy among creatures.[55] He puts human order in parallel with angelic hierarchies, after which society is modeled.[56] By God's grace (not by our human nature), after the resurrection, humans will be inserted into the choirs of angels and so there will be one society before God.[57] Aquinas' theocentric anthropocentrism takes on a different quality when we realize that we are not the crown of creation immediately under God but under nine choirs of angels. Angels are higher, purely

212 *Martin Schlag*

spiritual intellectual beings in comparison with whom our own dignity pales. Aquinas' metaphysics and ethics are not anthropocentric but hierarchically cosmological, in the positive sense that Aquinas inherited from Ps.-Dionysius who probably invented the word "hierarchy."[58] In the conception of Ps.-Dionysius, hierarchy has a positive, elevating, and salvific meaning. His explanation is worth quoting in full:

> The goal of a hierarchy, then, is to enable beings to be as like as possible to God and to be at one with him. The hierarchy has God as its leader of all understanding and action. It is forever looking directly at the comeliness of God. A hierarchy bears in itself the mark of God. Hierarchy causes its members to be images of God in all respects, to be clear and spotless mirrors reflecting the glow of primordial light and indeed of God himself.[59]

In this description, there is no hint at domination and even less at exploitation of subordinate beings. Those who have been endowed with the divine image turn into transmitters of the same grace to those entrusted to them:

> It ensures that when its members have received this full and divine splendor they can then pass on this light generously and in accordance with God's will to beings further down the scale. ...If one talks then of hierarchy, what is meant is a certain perfect arrangement, an image of the beauty of God which sacredly works out the mysteries of its own enlightenment in the orders and levels of understanding of the hierarchy, and which is likened toward its own source as much as is permitted.[60]

The implications for human work shaping the world are not difficult to perceive. Working in conformity with our needs in a way that avoids harm and virtuously promotes social and ecological justice is cooperation with God.

> Indeed, for every member of the hierarchy, perfection consists in this, that it is uplifted to imitate God as far as possible and, more wonderful still, that it becomes what scripture calls a "fellow workman for God" and a reflection of the workings of God. Therefore, when the hierarchical order lays it on some to be purified and on others to do the purifying, on some to receive illumination and on others to cause illumination, on some to be perfected and on others to bring about perfection, each will actually imitate God in the way suitable to whatever role it has.[61]

According to Golitzin, in this passage Ps.-Dionysius presents hierarchy as revelation and saving presence, as an icon or image of God's own beauty.[62] Hierarchy is a path or means of union with God.[63] The vision of creation as

Contemplation at work   213

a universe ordered in a hierarchy as a ladder to union with God opens up a sacramental worldview that sees all things as signs of God's loving presence. For contemplation in work in a fallen world, especially in business, politics, and other socio-economic realities, such a vision is important. Work is contemplative in itself when it is connected to truth and goodness whose last source is God.[64] We receive illumination and strength from the choirs of angels above us and are appointed priests of creation below us to illuminate, heal, and elevate it through our virtuous work—like the angels do for us. Our work participates in the cosmic liturgy.

Sacramental worldview and work as part of cosmic liturgy

A sacramental view of the world sees God in all things. Environmentalism reveals, in my view, a secret human longing for the *Logos* who holds all creatures together and sums up all things in heaven and on earth.[65] The Psalmist sings: "I keep the LORD always before me,"[66] which we can also translate as "I see God in all things." "Therefore, my heart is glad, my soul rejoices; my body also dwells secure."[67]

> All creatures look to you to give them food in due time. ...Send forth your spirit, they are created, and you renew the face of the earth. May the glory of the LORD endure forever; may the LORD be glad in his works![68]

This is an invitation to understand nature as a liturgy, as a kind of sacrament. Christianity de-divinizes the world, rejects any form of pantheism and subordination of human beings to subhuman order. At the same time, it sacralizes the world. The demarcation lines between sacred and profane have been torn down by Christ.

If work is a liturgy, the role of the human person redeemed by Christ is to act as a priest for nature, offering up to God our completion of what he has started. In creation, Thomas Aquinas says, God made his invisible beauty visible through the beauty of the earth. In the incarnation of Jesus Christ he has made his beauty even more visible.[69] It is significant that the Word incarnate worked as a secular craftsman: Most of his life on earth, Jesus made God's beauty visible through human work. Through the incarnation, Christ has also united each one of us to himself. We are no longer man or woman, of one nation or the other, of one socio-economic status or the other; we are all one in Christ.[70] All that we are and have—including our work—has been incorporated into Christ and thus, through the incarnation, makes God's beauty more visible than the universe in its totality. As nature is a manifestation of God's glory through which we can know the Creator, so our work can be the manifestation of God the Redeemer. Through our work others can find God. Our work is a revelation of God, a path to the knowledge of the existence of God and his worship. This is because Jesus Christ has reestablished human

214   *Martin Schlag*

work as an exercise of his own priesthood. Through work, we are priests of creation who participate in the cosmic liturgy, as I will try to explain.[71]

The cosmos, in which humans work, was created as God's temple and thus his place of presence and worship. In a careful analysis of biblical and extrabiblical sources, Gregory K. Beale explains that "[t]he rationale for the worldwide encompassing nature of the paradisal temple in Revelation 21 lies in the ancient notion that the Old Testament temple was a microcosm of the entire heaven and earth."[72] The outer court symbolizes the visible earth (altar made of stones) and sea (washbasin). The holy place symbolizes the visible heaven (the lampstand with seven lamps symbolizing the lights on the heavenly vault). The holy of holies symbolizes the invisible heaven where God dwells with his Cherubim and Seraphim who guard the entrance to paradise (the Ark is God's footstool; the Cherubim are on the Ark).[73] However, it is important to note that Israel's earthly Tabernacle and temple reflect and recapitulate the first temple in the garden of Eden. Eden is the unique place of God's presence, and, at the same time, it is the place of the first priest, Adam. Adam was supposed to rule as a priest and king in God's image and to expand the garden sanctuary of God to the whole cosmos, as formulated in Gen 1:28. When Adam fails in this duty through his sin and negligence, the Cherubim must take over the priestly role of guarding the tree of life. Later, in the time of the Tabernacle and the temple, the Cherubim are assisted by the Levites who continue Adam's priestly role of serving and guarding the place of God's presence in the temple.[74]

From a different but complementary perspective, Michael LeFebvre shows that the creation week at the beginning of Genesis "was designed as a guide for faithful work and sabbath worship ...."[75] His thesis is that Gen 1:1–2:3 is not meant to be a chronological history or a scientific account but a normative liturgical guidance for the celebration of creation. The original intention of the first priestly narrative of creation is to inculcate the sabbath rest after six days of work.[76] The whole festive liturgical calendar of Israel centered around agriculture, growth, fruitfulness, and harvest. It is no surprise that also the week of creation is centered around these same themes of making the world fruitful and feasting on its fruits.[77] LeFebvre thus presents the creation week narrative as a liturgical calendar based on the history of God's ordering of the world. Israel's observance of the sabbath as well as of the monthly and annual festivals is a schedule for stewarding that order with labor and worship.[78]

More importantly for our theme of work, the creation narrative depicts God the Creator as a model laborer who works from sunrise to sunset to inspire humans to imitate him in their own work and worship.[79] God teaches us how we should work and rest, thus continuing His work as priests of creation. Men and women are created as stewards and vice regents of everything to continue the world's fruitfulness and nurture.[80] Our work is liturgy, as it conforms us with God and leads up to the communion with

Contemplation at work   215

him on the day of rest. Ex 20:8–11 explicitly commands us to imitate God's rhythm of work:

Remember the sabbath day—keep it holy. Six days you may labor and do all your work, but the seventh day is a sabbath of the LORD your God. You shall not do any work, either you, your son or your daughter, your male or female slave, your work animal, or the resident alien within your gates. For in six days the LORD made the heavens and the earth, the sea and all that is in them; but on the seventh day he rested. That is why the LORD has blessed the sabbath day and made it holy.

From the notion of the cosmos as God's temple which we must cultivate and protect against defilement through our work, it is apparent that liturgy cannot be reduced to ceremonies in Church. Liturgy is a wider concept that St. Paul even applies to tax collectors, arguably one of the most resented though necessary institutions of the Roman Empire.[81] The New Testament reinforces the liturgical vision of the cosmos. The incarnation, death, resurrection, and ascension of Jesus Christ, God's new temple, have profoundly renewed the Old Testament's conception of human work in the cosmos as liturgy. Reflecting on the fact that the body of Christ is the new temple, Eric Peterson draws the conclusion that Christ's ascension into heaven breaks open the cosmos and converts heaven and earth into temple and throne room of God's Kingdom. "The glory of God no longer dwells in the temple at Jerusalem, but in the temple of Christ's body, which has ascended into heaven."[82] The prophetic vision in Rev 4 develops those in Ez 1 and Is 6. In the Old Testament prophecies, the triple cry of "holy, holy, holy" by the Cherubim is uttered in the temple in Jerusalem. In the book of Revelation, the angels' cry fills all of heaven and is unceasing, day and night.[83] The 24 elders in Rev 4:4–11 enact the royal priesthood—they are in the throne room together with the angels in exercise of their royal office, but they are also there as priests offering adoration and praise to God, thus performing the celestial liturgy together with the angels.[84] The Church's liturgy on earth is a participation in the liturgy of the angels and saints in heaven.

Our work on earth, every humanly honest work, even if it is modest and humanly insignificant, participates in the redemptive work of Christ. It is part of the cosmic liturgy that we perform in union with the angels, as the higher orders of being. If we are united with Christ in the Church, our work is part of the angelic *Sanctus*, the noise of our machines is incorporated into the angelic song and the stench of our sweat into the fragrance of the incense offered to God by the saints.

This urge towards incorporation in the liturgy of the church does not originate in any human need for order, but for the sake of that divine

216   *Martin Schlag*

decree which appoints redeemed man to be the tenth ordo of the nine ordines angelorum.[85]

Along similar lines, Daniel Toma, sees the "cosmos as a ladder of liturgical perfection."[86] He claims that the whole universe is structured as a liturgy built around the progression from purgation to illumination and from illumination to final union with God. This liturgy comprises heaven and earth, the immaterial and material world. Each is structured in three hierarchies, each of which is correlated to one of the levels of vicinity to God. Toma references the three hierarchies into which the nine choirs of angels are divided. He then attributes the highest hierarchy of three angelic choirs to union, the next three to illumination, and the lowest hierarchy of Principalities, Archangels, and Angels to purgation (or means). These hierarchies constitute the liturgical structure in heaven.[87] More remotely, the material universe mirrors this liturgical pattern: Union is represented by human beings, illumination by animals, and purgation by plants:[88]

> The unitive function of human beings led early Christian thinkers to speak of the human being as a microcosm of reality and the Church, the heart of which is the liturgical structure of union, illumination, and purgation. The human being sees in the universe his own very structure. Ultimately, every human person is like a little liturgy, a being whose nature is built as a platform of praise and adoration of God. He belongs in a liturgical setting and society, in union with a community of persons. His home is ultimately in the Church, united to the Persons of the Trinity. His very structure allows him to know and understand the universe, which itself participates in the liturgical structure of the Church and is a means of ascent to God.[89]

Returning to Ps.-Dionysius' vision of the hierarchy of beings connected by cooperation and help, I imagine this hierarchy as a structure of overflowing water basins. The higher order of rational beings joyfully pours their wisdom and love into the one below, in a communication without envy or selfishness. When we humans participate in the cosmic liturgy through our work in union with Christ, we form the tenth choir of angels and unite all creation below us with the angels above us and finally God. In our work, we are "a platform of praise and adoration of God."[90] This vision of the cosmic liturgy is, I think, the essence of what we mean when we speak of contemplation in work. It leads us to the apex of Christian liturgy, the Eucharist. In it, Christ offers the Father His body and blood in holy obedience, the only acceptable sacrifice that overabundantly intercedes for humanity and heals our sins. Our contribution to the cosmic liturgy can only reach the heavenly throne through Jesus Christ, as we humbly pray, that "these gifts be borne by the hands of your holy Angel to your altar on high in the sight of your divine majesty."[91]

Contemplation at work 217

One caveat must be mentioned against sugarcoating the idea of contemplation in work. Being contemplative means living in union with Christ through the Cross. In the Eucharist, source and summit of all Christian life, we pray:

> Be pleased to look upon these offerings with a serene and kindly countenance, and to accept them, as once you were pleased to accept the gifts of your servant Abel the just, the sacrifice of Abraham, our father in faith, and the offering of your high priest Melchizedek, a holy sacrifice, a spotless victim.[92]

In these words, we ask that we, not the sacrifice of Christ, be accepted. Christ's sacrifice is unfailingly accepted by the Father. It is we who need to pray that our daily work, united to the divine sacrifice, be acceptable to God. A short reflection on what we are saying in the Roman Canon can make us realize what is demanded of us. Abel gave his life, and the blood of Christ, the true Abel, cries to God louder than that of Abel. Abraham left his home, family, and possessions for an uncertain destination, at one word of God. He obeyed, giving God even his only begotten son, all his hope and future. Melchizedek offered bread and wine because he was the just king of peace and priest of God the Highest. Life and blood, complete obedience, justice, and peace are demanded of us in the fulfillment of our duties at work. Contemplation at work starts with a passionate love for the world but it leads to a purification of the world from sin. This passes through the Cross of Christ and our sharing in it. Only on the Cross, can work contribute to reordering the world toward God as the universal common good and reestablish the natural teleology in creation.[93]

In this context, on a philosophical level, the distinction between the (neo-) Platonic-Augustinian tradition and the Aristotelean-Thomist might be helpful. The (neo-)Platonic-Augustinian conception of the political, legal, and economic order is that it is basically derived from original sin. This tradition sees the inner-worldly social order as post-lapsarian structures that are necessary to repress evil, but not in themselves perfective elements of God's original plan of creation and salvation. On the other hand, the Aristotelian-Thomist vision considers socio-political and economic realities, if correctly ordered toward God as the final cause of the universe, as in themselves perfective and constitutive elements of human virtuosity and holiness.[94] Thus, Aquinas explicitly recognizes the virtues of Pagans, if their actions in themselves are ordered to the ultimate end of human life (God), as real, albeit imperfect, virtues.[95] In such a context, it makes sense to say: "Understand this well: there is something holy, something divine hidden in the most ordinary situations, and it is up to each one of you to discover it."[96]

Conclusion

The Church's teaching on the environment is the result of a contemplative and mystical vision of the world, beheld with the eyes of God. With this

218 *Martin Schlag*

contemplative gaze, we comprehend both the beauty and connectedness but also the suffering and misery of our brothers and sisters. Anna Rowlands puts it this way: "Contemplation is not what happens when we run out of answers but rather the very ground that births and sustains a vision of knowing and of social action and transformation."[97] Contemplation pulls us out of ourselves and stretches us toward God in the cosmic liturgy of human work. Peterson notes that we always transcend ourselves: We move either toward the angels who are in constant movement or toward the demons who are alienated from their true self.[98] Work can become demonic idolatry and hell, but our original vocation is to live in this world according to the laws of heaven in joyful and peaceful prophetic testimony.

I hope now to be able to answer the four initial questions.

What might it mean to contemplate God in work?

Contemplation at work means seeing God in work and looking at work in the world with the eyes of God. This implies understanding work as "cosmic liturgy" which all men and women perform as priestly co-workers with God.

Is justifying the inevitable negative consequences of what we do as non-intended and proportional a satisfactory path to sanctification of work and contemplation of God therein?

Applying the rules of the morality of actions with double effect to work in a sinful world is necessary but not sufficient for contemplation in work. A positive ethical approach is also needed. Every effort of sanctification begins with love for what exists. In a second step, and as part of our original mission in work, we are called to cleanse the world of sin. We can only do this united with the Paschal Mystery of Christ made present in the Eucharist.

How should humans relate to nature in their work to please God?

We are cooperators of God as royal priests and prophets when we respect the teleology of creation as expressed in natural and moral laws. This implies avoiding all that harms and doing what is in our power to preserve and promote ecosystems through our work. This is not possible without sacrifice united to the Cross of Christ.

Is there a Catholic alternative to ecocentrism that is based on revelation and allows human work to be part of the salvific dispensation of God, by living in harmony with creation?

Yes, there is. It is a sacramental worldview that avoids divinizing subhuman creation but also realizes that Christ's incarnation has sacralized all elements of nature except sin.

Notes

1 I gratefully acknowledge Frank Scarchilli's edits and useful comments that have improved this chapter.
2 Francis, Encyclical *Laudato Si': On Care for our Common Home*, May 24, 2015, n. 222. https://www.vatican.va/content/francesco/en/encyclicals/documents/papa-francesco_20150524_enciclica-laudato-si.html.

Contemplation at work 219

3 Francis, Encyclical *Laudato Si': On Care for our Common Home*, May 24, 2015, n. 49.
4 Francis, Apostolic Exhortation *Evangelii Gaudium* (On the Proclamation of the Gospel in Today's World), November 24, 2013, n. 199. https://www.vatican.va/content/francesco/en/apost_exhortations/documents/papa-francesco_esortazione-ap_20131124_evangelii-gaudium.html.
5 See Francis, Apostolic Exhortation *Evangelii Gaudium* (On the Proclamation of the Gospel in Today's World), November 24, 2013, n. 71. https://www.vatican.va/content/francesco/en/apost_exhortations/documents/papa-francesco_esortazione-ap_20131124_evangelii-gaudium.html.
6 See Francis, Encyclical *Laudato Si': On Care for our Common Home*, May 24, 2015, n. 233. https://www.vatican.va/content/francesco/en/encyclicals/documents/papa-francesco_20150524_enciclica-laudato-si.html.
7 See Francis, Encyclical *Laudato Si': On Care for our Common Home*, May 24, 2015, n. 214. https://www.vatican.va/content/francesco/en/encyclicals/documents/papa-francesco_20150524_enciclica-laudato-si.html.
8 See Francis, Encyclical *Laudato Si': On Care for our Common Home*, May 24, 2015, n. 127. https://www.vatican.va/content/francesco/en/encyclicals/documents/papa-francesco_20150524_enciclica-laudato-si.html.
9 Francis, Apostolic Exhortation *Evangelii Gaudium* (On the Proclamation of the Gospel in Today's World), November 24, 2013, n. 281. https://www.vatican.va/content/francesco/en/apost_exhortations/documents/papa-francesco_esortazione-ap_20131124_evangelii-gaudium.html.
10 Francis, General Audience "Healing the World—5. Solidarity and the Virtue of Faith," September 2, 2020, https://www.vatican.va/content/francesco/en/audiences/2020/documents/papa-francesco_20200902_udienza-generale.html. Emphasis in original.
11 Francis, Apostolic Exhortation *Evangelii Gaudium* (On the Proclamation of the Gospel in Today's World), November 24, 2013, n. 92. https://www.vatican.va/content/francesco/en/apost_exhortations/documents/papa-francesco_esortazione-ap_20131124_evangelii-gaudium.html. Emphasis in original.
12 Francis, General Audience "Healing the world—7. Care of the common home and contemplative dimension," September 16, 2020, https://www.vatican.va/content/francesco/en/audiences/2020/documents/papa-francesco_20200916_udienza-generale.html.
13 Christopher Stone, "Should Trees Have Standing?- Toward Legal Rights for Natural Objects," *Journal of Human Rights and the Environment* vol. 3, Special Issue (2012), 4–55. Reprint from *Southern California Law Review* vol 45 (1972): 450–501. In US law, legal standing refers to the right to bring a case to court and to be heard in due procedure. Standing is linked to legal personhood and the possession of rights.
14 James A. Nash, *Loving Nature: Ecological Integrity and Christian Responsibility* (Washington, DC: Abingdon Press, 1991), 186.
15 Paul Taylor, *Respect for Nature: A Theory of Environmental Ethics – 25th Anniversary Edition* (Princeton: Princeton University Press, 2011), 100; see also See David R. Boyd, *The Rights of Nature: A Legal Revolution that Could Save the World* (Toronto: ECW Press, 2017), xxiii.
16 See Benedict XVI, "Message for the Celebration of the World Day of Peace: If You Want to Cultivate Peace, Protect Creation," January 1, 2010, n. 13; https://www.vatican.va/content/benedict-xvi/en/messages/peace/documents/hf_ben-xvi_mes_20091208_xliii-world-day-peace.html; Robert W. Lannan, "Catholic Tradition, and the New Catholic Theology and Social Teaching on the Environment," *Catholic Lawyer* 39, no. 4 (1999–2000): 353–388, at 369. For examples of

220   *Martin Schlag*

misguided Christian anti-natalist movements, see Matthew Levering, *Engaging the Doctrine of Creation: Cosmos, Creatures, and the Wise and Good Creator* (Grand Rapids: Baker, 2017), 193–226; and for an extreme example, see anti-natalist groups that advocate for voluntary human extinction, see the voluntary human extinction movement that has as its mission "Phasing out the human race by voluntarily ceasing to breed [to] allow the Earth's biosphere to return to good health": "The Voluntary Human Extinction Movement, Accessed April 3, 2023, https://www.vhemt.org/.

17 See Second Vatican Council, Pastoral Constitution on the Church in the Modern World *Gaudium et Spes*, no. 40–45.

18 See Dries Bosschaert, *The Anthropological Turn, Christian Humanism, and Vatican II: Louvain Theologians Preparing the Path for 'Gaudium et Spes' (1942–1965)* (Leuven–Paris–Bristol, CT: Peeters Publishers, 2019).

19 Roderick Frazier Nash, *The Rights of Nature: A History of Environmental Ethics* (Madison: The University of Wisconsin Press, 1989), 87–120.

20 Stephen Ellingson, *To Care for Creation: The Emergence of the Religious Environmental Movement* (Chicago and London: The University of Chicago Press, 2016).

21 Stephen Ellingson, *Care for Creation: The Emergence of the Religious Environmental Movement* (Chicago and London: The University of Chicago Press, 2016), 3.

22 Squarely in the stewardship ethical approach are: Lucia A. Silecchia, "The Call to Stewardship: A Catholic Perspective on Environmental Responsibility," *American Law from a Catholic Perspective: Through a Clearer Lens*, ed. Ronald J. Rychlak (Lanham: Rowman & Littlefield, 2015), 213–227; International Theological Commission, *Communion and Stewardship: Human Persons Created in the Image of God* (Vatican City: Libreria Editrice Vaticana, 2004), nos. 25 and 71–76. https://www.vatican.va/roman_curia/congregations/cfaith/cti_documents/rc_con_cfaith_doc_20040723_communion-stewardship_en.html.

23 Stephen Ellingson, *Care for Creation: The Emergence of the Religious Environmental Movement* (Chicago and London: The University of Chicago Press, 2016), 9.

24 Stephen Ellingson, *Care for Creation: The Emergence of the Religious Environmental Movement* (Chicago and London: The University of Chicago Press, 2016), 10.

25 Stephen Ellingson, *Care for Creation: The Emergence of the Religious Environmental Movement* (Chicago and London: The University of Chicago Press, 2016).

26 Rachel Wheeler, *Ecospirituality: An Introduction* (Minneapolis: Fortress Press, 2022), 1.

27 Rachel Wheeler, *Ecospirituality: An Introduction* (Minneapolis: Fortress Press, 2022), 2–5.

28 Lukas Szrot, "From Stewardship to Creation Spirituality: The Evolving Ecological Ethos of Catholic Doctrine," *Journal for the Study of Religion, Nature and Culture*, 14, no. 2 (2020): 226–249.

29 Benedict XVI, "Protect Creation," n. 13. See also Theological Commission, *Communion and Stewardship: Human Persons Created in the Image of God* (Vatican City: Libreria Editrice Vaticana, 2004), nos. 25 and 71–76; and Lucia A. Silecchia, "The Call to Stewardship: A Catholic Perspective on Environmental Responsibility," *American Law from a Catholic Perspective: Through a Clearer Lens*, ed. Ronald J. Rychlak (Lanham: Rowman and Littlefield, 2015).

30 See Richard Bauckham, "Being Human in the Community of Creation: A Biblical Perspective," *Ecotheology: A Christian Conversation*, ed. Kiara A. Jorgenson and Alan G. Padgett (Grand Rapids: Eerdmans, 2020), 19–20.

Contemplation at work 221

31 Thomas Massaro, *Living Justice: Catholic Social Teaching in Action* (Lanham–Boulder–New York–London: Rowman & Littlefield, 2016 [third classroom edition]), 183.
32 See Kelly S. Johnson, *The Fear of Beggars: Stewardship and Poverty in Christian Ethics* (Grand Rapids–Cambridge: Eerdmans, 2007), 73–84.
33 See Francis, Encyclical *Laudato Si': On Care for our Common Home*, May 24, 2015, nos. 116 and 236. https://www.vatican.va/content/francesco/en/encyclicals/documents/papa-francesco_20150524_enciclica-laudato-si.html.
34 See Francis, Encyclical *Laudato Si': On Care for our Common Home*, May 24, 2015, nos. 202–245. https://www.vatican.va/content/francesco/en/encyclicals/documents/papa-francesco_20150524_enciclica-laudato-si.html.
35 Lukas Szrot, "From Stewardship to Creation Spirituality: The Evolving Ecological Ethos of Catholic Doctrine," *Journal for the Study of Religion, Nature and Culture*, 14, no. 2 (2020): 242.
36 Francis, "Meeting with the Members of the General Assembly of the United Nations Organization: Address of the Holy Father," September 25, 2015, https://www.vatican.va/content/francesco/en/speeches/2015/september/documents/papa-francesco_20150925_onu-visita.html.
37 Christopher J. Thompson, *The Joyful Mystery: Field Notes Toward a Green Thomism* (Steubenville: Emmaus. 2017); Steven A. Long, "The Teleological Grammar of the Created Order in Catholic Moral Discourse," *On Earth as It Is in Heaven: Cultivating a Contemporary Theology of Creation* (St. Paul: St. Paul Seminary Press, 2021), 37–55; Daniel P. Scheid, "Saint Thomas Aquinas, the Thomistic Tradition, and the Cosmic Common Good," *Green Discipleship: Catholic Theological Ethics and the Environment*, ed. Tobias Winright (Winona: Anselm Academic, 2011), 129–147.
38 See, e.g., John Chryssavgis, *Creation as Sacrament: Reflections on Ecology and Spirituality* (London–New York: T&T Clark, 2019).
39 John Paul II, *Encyclical Evangelium Vitae* (Vatican City: Vatican Press, 1995), n. 83. Pope Francis returns to the same theme when he warns against the technocratic paradigm.
40 Francis, Encyclical *Laudato Si': On Care for our Common Home*, May 24, 2015, n. 12. https://www.vatican.va/content/francesco/en/encyclicals/documents/papa-francesco_20150524_enciclica-laudato-si.html.
41 Thomas Aquinas, *Summa Theologiae* I, q. 16 a. 4 c., edited and translated by Thomas Gornall, S.J. (London – New York: Blackfriars, 1964), 84-86.
42 Thomas Aquinas, *Summa Theologiae* I, q. 65 a. 2 c., edited and translated by William A. Wallace, O.P. (London – New York: Blackfriars, 1967), 10-13.
43 Thomas Aquinas, *Summa Theologiae* I, q. 65 a. 2 ad 2., edited and translated by William A. Wallace, O.P. (London – New York: Blackfriars, 1967), 12-13.
44 Thomas Aquinas, *Summa Theologiae* II–II, q. 141 a. 6 c., edited and translated by Thomas Gilby O.P. (London – New York: Blackfriars, 1968), 24-26.
45 Thomas Aquinas, *De Anima*, art. 15, q. unica, c: "Manifestum est etiam quod potentiae sensitivae sunt nobis necessariae ad intelligendum non solum in acquisitione scientiae, sed etiam in utendo scientia iam acquisita. Non enim possumus considerare etiam ea quorum scientiam habemus, nisi convertendo nos ad phantasmata; ... Manifestum est etiam quod in revelationibus quae nobis divinitus fiunt per influxum substantiarum superiorum, indigemus aliquibus phatasmatibus; ..." ("It is evident too that we need the senses for understanding, not only in the acquisition of knowledge but also in the utilization of knowledge already acquired. For we cannot even reflect upon the things we know without turning to phantasms [images in our fantasy stemming from the sensitive powers] ...It is evident also that we have need of certain phantasms in things divinely revealed to

222 *Martin Schlag*

us through the influence of superior substances." Translation modified by author taken from https://isidore.co/aquinas/english/QDdeAnima.htm#15)

46 Thomas von Aquin, *Summa Contra Gentiles: Gesamtausgabe in einem Band. Lateinisch und Deutsch*, ed. and transl. Karl Albert, Karl Allgaier, Leo Dümpelmann, Paul Engelhardt, Leo Gerken, and Markus H. Wörner (Darmstadt: WBG, 2009), II, 3.

47 Ryan Patrick McLaughlin, "Thomas Aquinas' Eco-Theological Ethics of Anthropocentric Conservation," *Horizons* 39, no. 1 (2012): 69–97, at 97.

48 Ryan Patrick McLaughlin, "Thomas Aquinas' Eco-Theological Ethics of Anthropocentric Conservation," *Horizons* 39, no. 1 (2012): 87.

49 *Supplementum*, q. 91 a. 5.

50 *Supplementum*, q. 91 a. 1.

51 "Quia vero omnia corporalia sunt quodammodo propter hominem...tunc etiam totius creaturae corporeae conveniens est ut status immutetur, ut congruat statui hominum qui tunc erunt. Et quia tunc homines incorruptibiles erunt, a tota creatura corporea tolletur generationis et corruptionis status. Et hoc est quod dicit Apostolus, Rom. VIII, quod 'ipsa creatura liberabitur a servitute corruptionis in libertatem gloriae filiorum Dei.'" ["Because all bodily beings are in a certain sense for the sake of humanity...then (after the Resurrection) it is fitting that the state of all bodily creation be changed in accordance with the state of the humans who will then be. And because then humans will be incorruptible, the state of generation and corruption will be removed from the whole of bodily creation. This is what the Apostle says in Rom 8: 'that creation itself would be set free from slavery to corruption and share in the glorious freedom of the children of God.'"] *Summa Contra Gentiles: Gesamtausgabe in Einem Band. Lateinisch und Deutsch*, ed. and trans. Karl Albert, Karl Allgaier, Leo Dümpelmann, Paul Engelhardt, Leo Gerken, and Markus H. Wörner (Darmstadt: World Bank Group, 2009), IV, 97.

52 Thomas Aquinas, *Summa Theologiae*, Suppl, q. 82, a 3 ad 4; the translation follows that in Ernst Burkhart and Javier Lopez, *Ordinary Life and Holiness in the Teaching of St. Josemaría: A Study in Spiritual Theology*, vol. 1 (New York: Scepter, 2017), 249.

53 Thomas Aquinas, *Scriptum Super Libros Sententiarum* I, dist. 44, q. 1, art. 2, ad 6.

54 See Thomas Aquinas, *Summa Theologiae* I, q. 50–64, which fills the whole volume 9 of the Blackfriars publication, edited and translated by Kenelm Foster OP, (London – New York: Blackfriars, 1968) and q. 106–114, spread out over volume 14, edited and translated by T.C. O'Brien (London – New York: Blackfriars, 1975), 88-167 and volume 15, edited and translated by M.J. Charlesworth (London – New York: Blackfriars, 1970), 2-87. (both sections analyze demonic activities in one question each among the many other questions on the good angels).

55 Thomas von Aquinas, *Summa Contra Gentiles: Gesamtausgabe in Einem Band. Lateinisch und Deutsch*, ed. and transl. Karl Albert, Karl Allgaier, Leo Dümpelmann, Paul Engelhardt, Leo Gerken, and Markus H. Wörner (Darmstadt: World Bank Group, 2009), II, 45.

56 See Thomas Aquinas, *Summa Theologiae* I, q. 108, a. 2., edited and translated by T.C. O'Brien (London – New York: Blackfriars, 1975), 124-128.

57 See Thomas Aquinas, *Summa Theologiae* I, q. 108, a. 8, edited and translated by T.C. O'Brien (London – New York: Blackfriars, 1975), 152–157. In this affirmation, Aquinas quotes (Pseudo-)Dionysius.

58 See Ephrem Reese OP, "Thomas Aquinas and Dionysian Ecclesiastical Hierarchy," *Journal of Medieval and Early Modern Studies* 52, no. 2 (2022): 191–217; for the influence of Ps.-Dionysius on Aquinas' metaphysics, see Fran O'Rourke, *Pseudo-Dionysius and the Metaphysics of Aquinas* (Notre Dame: University of Notre Dame Press, 2005 [reprinted 2010]).

Contemplation at work 223

59 Pseudo-Dionysius, "The Celestial Hierarchy," *The Complete Works*, trans. Colm Luibheid (New York–Mahwah: Paulist Press, 1987), 165A–C, 154.

60 Pseudo-Dionysius, "The Celestial Hierarchy," *The Complete Works*, trans. Colm Luibheid (New York–Mahwah: Paulist Press, 1987), 154.

61 Pseudo-Dionysius, "The Celestial Hierarchy," *The Complete Works*, trans. Colm Luibheid (New York–Mahwah: Paulist Press, 1987), 154.

62 Alexander Golitzin, *Mystagogy: A Monastic Reading of Dionysius Areopagita*, ed. Bogdan Bucur (Collegeville: Liturgical Press, 2013), 172–3.

63 See Bernhard Blankenhorn, OP, *The Mystery of Union with God: Dionysian Mysticism in Albert the Great and Thomas Aquinas* (Washington, DC: The Catholic University of America Press, 2015), 5: "Hierarchy is necessary for Union."

64 See David C. Schindler, "Work as Contemplation: On the Platonic Notion of Technê," *Communio* 42 (Winter 2015): 594–617.

65 See Col 1:15–17 and Eph 1:10.

66 Ps 16:8.

67 Ps 16:9.

68 Ps 104:27, 30–31.

69 See Thomas Aquinas, *Summa Theologiae* III, q. 1 a. 1., edited and translated by R.J. Hennessey O.P. (London – New York: Blackfriars, 1976), 88–167

70 See Col 3:28.

71 This beautiful idea of Maximus Confessor, taken up by Hans Urs von Balthasar, was dear also to John Paul II: "This varied scenario of celebrations of the Eucharist has given me a powerful experience of its universal and, so to speak, cosmic character. Yes, cosmic!" Hans Urs von Balthasar, *Cosmic Liturgy: The Universe According to Maximus the Confessor*, trans. Brian E. Daley, S.J. (San Francisco: Ignatius Press, 2003); John Paul II, Encyclical *Ecclesia de Eucharistia* (On the Eucharist in its Relationship to the Church), April 17, 2003, n. 8. https://www.vatican.va/content/john-paul-ii/en/encyclicals/documents/hf_jp-ii_enc_20030417_eccl-de-euch.html.

72 Gregory K. Beale, *The Temple and the Church's Mission: A Biblical Theology of the Dwelling Place of God* (Downers Grove: InterVarsity Press, 2004), 31.

73 Gregory K. Beale, *The Temple and the Church's Mission: A Biblical Theology of the Dwelling Place of God* (Downers Grove: InterVarsity Press, 2004), 31–36.

74 Gregory K. Beale, *The Temple and the Church's Mission: A Biblical Theology of the Dwelling Place of God* (Downers Grove: InterVarsity Press, 2004), 66–81. See also John Bergsma, *Jesus and the Old Testament Roots of the Priesthood* (Steubenville: Emmaus Road, 2021), 7–43.

75 Michael LeFebvre, *The Liturgy of Creation: Understanding Calendars in Old Testament Context* (Downers Grove: InterVarsity Press, 2019), 7.

76 Michael LeFebvre, *The Liturgy of Creation: Understanding Calendars in Old Testament Context* (Downers Grove: InterVarsity Press, 2019), 127–135.

77 Michael LeFebvre, *The Liturgy of Creation: Understanding Calendars in Old Testament Context* (Downers Grove: InterVarsity Press, 2019), 142.

78 Michael LeFebvre, *The Liturgy of Creation: Understanding Calendars in Old Testament Context* (Downers Grove: InterVarsity Press, 2019), 117.

79 Michael LeFebvre, *The Liturgy of Creation: Understanding Calendars in Old Testament Context* (Downers Grove: InterVarsity Press, 2019), 119.

80 Michael LeFebvre, *The Liturgy of Creation: Understanding Calendars in Old Testament Context* (Downers Grove: InterVarsity Press, 2019), 141.

81 Rom 13:6.

82 Eric Peterson, *The Angels and the Liturgy*, trans. Ronald Walls (New York: Herder and Herder, 1964), 18.

83 See Rev 4:8.

84 See Peterson, *The Angels and the Liturgy*, trans. Ronald Walls (New York: Herder and Herder, 1964), 1–13.

224 *Martin Schlag*

85 Peterson, *The Angels and the Liturgy*, trans. Ronald Walls (New York: Herder and Herder, 1964), 24, quoting Gregory the Great, Homily in Ev I.II.H 34, PL 76, 1249C; Augustine, Sermo 341, 9 PL 39 S 1500; Enarrationes in Ps. 36 S. III PL 36, 385.
86 Daniel Toma, *Vestige of Eden, Image of Eternity: Common Experience, the Hierarchy of Being, and Modern Science* (Steubenville: Franciscan University Press, 2019), 262.
87 Daniel Toma, *Vestige of Eden, Image of Eternity: Common Experience, the Hierarchy of Being, and Modern Science* (Steubenville: Franciscan University Press, 2019), 264–267.
88 See Daniel Toma, *Vestige of Eden, Image of Eternity: Common Experience, the Hierarchy of Being, and Modern Science* (Steubenville: Franciscan University Press, 2019), 268.
89 Daniel Toma, *Vestige of Eden, Image of Eternity: Common Experience, the Hierarchy of Being, and Modern Science* (Steubenville: Franciscan University Press, 2019), 269.
90 Daniel Toma, *Vestige of Eden, Image of Eternity: Common Experience, the Hierarchy of Being, and Modern Science* (Steubenville: Franciscan University Press, 2019), 269.
91 Roman Missal, Eucharistic Prayer I.
92 Roman Missal, Eucharistic Prayer I.
93 We can read Rom 8:19–23 as referring to the sanctified and sanctifying work of the children of God who have died in Christ to the devil, sin, and flesh. See also, International Theological Commission, *Communion and Stewardship: Human Persons Created in the Image of God* (Vatican City: Libreria Editrice Vaticana, 2004), n. 76. https://www.vatican.va/roman_curia/congregations/cfaith/cti_documents/rc_con_cfaith_doc_20040723_communion-stewardship_en.html.
94 See George Duke, "The Principle of the Common Good," *Christianity and Global Law*, eds. Rafael Domingo and John Witte, Jr. (London and New York: Routledge, 2020), 251–266, at 253; Paul J. Weithman, "Augustine and Aquinas on Original Sin and the Function of Political Authority," *Journal of the History of Philosophy* 30 (1992): 353–76, at 371–72.
95 See Thomas Aquinas, *Summa Theologiae*, II-II, q. 23 a 7., edited and translated by R.J. Batten O.P. (London – New York: Blackfriars, 1975), 26-31.
96 Josemaría Escrivá, *Conversations with Saint Josemaria Escrivá* (New York: Scepter, 2008), no. 114.
97 Anna Rowlands, *Towards a Politics of Communion: Catholic Social Teaching in Dark Times* (London, New York: T& T Clark, 2021), 5.
98 See Peterson, *The Angels and the Liturgy*, trans. Ronald Walls (New York: Herder and Herder, 1964), 47.

Part III
Challenge

13 Work in Protestant perspective
A not so unintended Reformation

D. Stephen Long

Introduction

The thesis of the following essay is that a theological perspective on work first requires attention to the vocation to be what God intended humans to be – fully alive. Such a vocation relativizes work as a job, as primarily or exclusively, a means to a paycheck. It first challenges what has become known as "the Protestant work ethic". This challenge is relatively easy because I will first argue no such ethic existed prior to Max Weber's invention of it in 1905. Drawing upon the criticisms of R. H. Tawney and others, the Protestant work ethic reflects changes in commercial society occurring since the fourteenth century. It is not the cause but the result of those changes. These changes marked shifts in desire. Ethics, economics, and theology cannot be attended to well without attention to the fundamental question, "What do you want?" If we have not rational means to adjudicate among our desires, then we have no resistance to what became known as the Protestant work ethic. The economy, like ethics, should be directed to ends that are fitting with desires worthy of human creatures. Such an economy is central to Tawney's work in Christian socialism. A second step situates Tawney within Christian socialism by discussing two Anglican theologians, F. D. Maurice and his student Stewart Headlam.

This discussion is more than antiquarian. If work is to fit within the divine vocation for a fully alive human, then attention to the social and political contexts that promote that vocation must be set forth. We have paradigms of such contexts in what Lenin disparaged as "municipal socialism". Headlam referred to it more positively as "Gas and Water socialism". The city of Milwaukee, Wisconsin had a version of it for nearly four decades known as "sewer socialism". Christian socialism resembles well these municipal forms because it emphasized that focusing on workers as workers was inadequate. Something more than work was necessary for workers to flourish. The third step in what follows discusses the return of Christian socialism. I find this return intriguing. It seems to be gaining traction among a variety of thinkers and movements, but I make no claim that it will become a dominant force in

DOI: 10.4324/9781003508212-16

228   D. Stephen Long

the future. Its ability to sustain itself may depend upon the alliances it makes with non-Christian versions such as sewer socialism. Christian and sewer socialism share a conviction that something more than economic reform is necessary for social reform. Unlike Marxism, the flourishing of workers will not be found by turning the world into a factory system where workers own the means of production without fundamentally shifting what work is. Owning the means to your own enslavement to work is not liberating; nor is a Protestant work ethic that prizes work and its remuneration above the vocation to live life well.

A Protestant perspective on a Protestant work ethic

Let's begin with how workers came to be in the modern economy. Without telling us where it came from or how the workers came to it, Adam Smith (1723–1790) begins his 1776 *Wealth of Nations* with a pin-making factory. Workers are already in place, the division of labor set, and each toils away at his single task. How did this come to be? Smith neglects any discussion of the political and social conditions that made this transformation of work possible. However, in his *Principles of Political Economy*, the earlier British economist Sir James Steuart (1712–1782) addresses what Smith neglects. He counsels politicians on what they need to do to move persons from their farms, off the commons where they fish and hunt, and into the newly developing factory system. He divided people into two classes. First are "those, who, without working live upon the spontaneous fruits of the earth, that is upon milk, cattle, hunting, etc". Second are "those who are obliged to labour the soil"[1] In order to "rationalize" the economy, which is Steuart's purpose in his treatise, politicians must find means to move persons from the first class into the second. Slavery is one means to this end, but Steuart argued that it is ineffective. Instead, shifts in desire and the conditions necessary to fulfill those desires are required. Steuart wrote,

> slavery in former times had the same effect in peopling the world that trade and industry have now. Men were forced to labour because they were slaves to others; men are now forced to labour because they are slaves to their own wants.[2]

He sees this shift positively as a means toward a rational economy.

What Steuart offers that Smith neglected is the importance of desire in political economy. Force, coercion, and enslavement are insufficient means to keep persons working. They incite resistance and rebellion. For people with desires that are primarily satisfied through their work, it becomes a means to satisfy those desires. Increase those desires and presumably work increases. What Steuart neglects is whether these desires are rational; that is to say, whether they are fitting for a well-lived life. He lacks any ethical analysis. This politics of a rational desire contributed to what often goes

Work in Protestant perspective 229

by the name "the Protestant work ethic". Kathryn Tanner explains it well as follows:

> That Protestant work ethic was composed of a set of values in which hard work was a moral virtue, rewarded with good pay, where the expectation was for a kind of linear, gradual advancement along a single career track often at a single company – all of which suggested the reasonableness of delayed gratification and long-term commitment.[3]

How this work ethic became associated with Protestantism and "reasonableness" is perplexing. A tradition, or traditions, since Protestantism is a confusing mélange of beliefs and practices, that began by critiquing "works righteousness" and emphasizing life lived according to the theological virtues of faith, hope, and love, becomes associated with something called a "work ethic". The person who developed this concept was Max Weber in his 1905 *The Protestant Ethic and the Spirit of Capitalism*. It poses a considerable obstacle for understanding "work" in a Protestant perspective. The Protestant work ethic was a late invention and it misunderstood "Protestantism", "work", and the capitalist spirit.

It misunderstood the capitalist spirit because work, working for wages, is seldom if ever the way for "linear, gradual, advancement" that the desires formed by the so-called Protestant work ethic promised. History would seem to demonstrate how irrational this desire is. It becomes an insatiable desire for more that cannot be fulfilled in a never-ending quest for growth. (It previously was understood as the vice of *pleonexia*). Rather than diminishing the demands of work, it intensifies them. John Maynard Keynes was convinced that the efficiency of the market would result in his grandchildren working 15 hours per work. (Keynes had no children or grandchildren.) That did not happen and seems to have disappeared as a goal among economists. Thomas Piketty's $r > g$ formula challenges the reasonableness of any so-called Protestant work ethic.[4] Advancement does not occur through labor but through ownership, and the increasing divide between them results in increased labor for many and increased ownership for others leading to the global inequality that we witness today. Whether Piketty's analysis is accepted, the promise of a "Protestant work ethic" has lost its formative role in much of western culture. It not only misunderstood the capitalist spirit, it misunderstood work.

The most interesting analyses of work acknowledge that the term is unintelligible without attending to the social conditions that make such work possible. No one just opens a pin-making factory and people show up instantaneously to throw off their old way of life and adopt a new one. Likewise, no one, or at least very few, take on work in today's gig economy or slaughterhouse or sign up to work for a maid-company because they expect advancement or fulfillment. Work, working, labor are terms with histories. Those histories comprise social, cultural, and political conditions that render how we work intelligible, conditions inevitably associated with desire that should

230   D. Stephen Long

ask the question, "What do we want out of life"? Of course, we cannot but want certain basic creaturely goods such as food, water, shelter, health, and security. Such goods must me produced and distributed, but if work is solely for basic goods, then it reflects the curse that mere labor is in Genesis 3:19, "By the sweat of your face you shall eat bread until you return to the ground, for out of it you were taken; you are dust, and to dust you shall return". Of course, in Christian theology, the curse of work has been lifted, the judgment overcome by the Judge who was judged (to quote Karl Barth). Arduous labor and the concomitant desires that keep us at it are not the source of advancement or human fulfillment. They are curses to be overcome.

For Protestantism (and I'm confident the same is true of Catholicism), human fulfillment occurs through faith in Christ. To cite the *Confession of Faith* of the United Methodist Church: "The offering Christ freely made on the cross is the perfect and sufficient sacrifice for the sins of the whole world, redeeming man from all sin, so that no other satisfaction is required" (Article VIII). Likewise, the Anglican Articles of Religion state, "The Offering of Christ once made is that perfect redemption, propitiation, and satisfaction for all the sins of the whole world, both original and actual; and there is none other satisfaction for sin, but that alone" (*Articles of Religion* XXXI). In fact, these articles not only reject works righteousness, but they also go so far as to claim, in a hyper-Augustinian form, that works done outside the gift of grace are faulty. Article XIII states:

> Works done before the grace of Christ, and the Inspiration of his Spirit, are not pleasant to God, forasmuch as they spring not of faith in Jesus Christ. (...) we doubt not but that they have the nature of sin.

The term "works" here, of course, is not univocal to "work" within political economy. Yet there is a family resemblance. Whether it be to earn salvation or advance in natural flourishing, people work for a reason. Work is human action that expects remuneration. A perplexing question is how a protesting tradition of reform that rejected the expectation of remuneration for work in the theological domain and went so far as to suggest works outside of grace were sinful, became associated with a meritocratic Protestant work ethic in the economy. Max Weber offers one analysis, R. H. Tawney a different one.

Max Weber argued that the sixteenth-century Puritans unintentionally caused the transition from a critique of "works righteousness" to a Protestant work ethic. His argument begins with the psychological consequences caused by Calvinism's "eternal decree".[5] The decree is found in Chapter 3 of the 1647 Westminster Confession: "By the decree of God, for the manifestation of his glory, some men and angels are predestinated unto everlasting life, and others fore-ordained to everlasting death". This controversial decree has since been challenged within and without Reformed Christianity. It not only questioned the redemptive character of good works, but also made it difficult to identify what *good* works might be. Faith was divided from

Work in Protestant perspective   231

works and became the primary, if not exclusive virtue, for what constitutes a good work. It led to the kind of judgment found in Article XIII above that works that did not arise from "faith in Jesus Christ" were sinful. Even if they appeared good, they could not be, because their source was faulty.

Weber argues that the decree had psychological consequences; it led to "a feeling of unprecedented inner loneliness of the single individual" that could not be helped by priest or sacraments or church.[6] In this lies the "absolutely decisive difference" between the so-called Protestant and Catholic ethics. Protestantism eliminated "salvation through the Church and the sacraments".[7] That is a woeful misunderstanding of Protestantism, especially Lutheranism, Anglicanism, and Methodism. Luther held to a high doctrine of baptism and Methodism recovered not only weekly but daily Eucharistic practice. Perhaps it fits pietism and Puritanism which are the only Protestant sects that fit Weber's sociological analysis.

For Weber, the transition from opposition to works righteousness to a Protestant work ethic occurs through a Puritan ascetic morality that turns against "the spontaneous enjoyment of life and all it had to offer". The Puritans rejected sport, religious art, theater, and anything that they thought smacked of superstition. Such a worldly asceticism was suspicious of wealth but only because it was "a temptation to idleness and sinful enjoyment of life".[8] The discipline of labor, however, was affirmed as a "performance of duty" to the "calling" within which God placed each person. A "calling" to work in everyday life marks the crucial transition to the Protestant work ethic. Weber writes,

> the religious valuation of restless, continuous, systematic work in a worldly calling, as the highest means to asceticism, and at the same time the surest and most evident proof of rebirth and genuine faith, must have been the most powerful conceivable lever for the expansion of that attitude toward life which we have here called the spirit of capitalism.[9]

Without directly intending the accumulation of capital, it unintentionally did so and had an ethics for its justification, a justification that included a providential ordering for an "unequal distribution of goods".[10] The spirit of worldly asceticism led unintentionally to the economic rationalization of capitalism. Weber's well-known statement toward the conclusion of his influential work captures this memorably:

> The Puritan wanted to work in a calling; we are forced to do so. For when asceticism was carried out of monastic cells into everyday life, and began to dominate worldly morality, it did its part in building the tremendous cosmos of the modern economic order.[11]

The Puritan Richard Baxter's claim that "external goods" should be worn like a "light cloak" was turned into an "iron cage".[12]

232 D. Stephen Long

Weber's analysis met immediate challenge. One of the earliest was Lujo Brentano's 1916 *Die Anfänge des modernen Kapitalismus* that traced capitalism's origins to the Renaissance in Catholic communities. Lisa Jardine takes up a similar argument.[13] Although he faults Protestantism along Weberian lines for unintentionally contributing to a secularized society and the market's dominance, Brad Gregory acknowledges Weber's narrative is flawed and sides with Jardine.[14] Gregory nonetheless argues that Weber is right but for the wrong reasons. He states,

> (...) correlative to the ways in which Lutheran and Reformed Protestantism departed from medieval Christian ethics, by separating salvation from morality these traditions indirectly influenced the long-term development of economic behavior in ways that the sixteenth-century leaders would have deplored. In this broad sense, Weber was right – although almost certainly not because of the alleged psychological effects on English Puritans of Calvinist predestination that was subsequently secularized.[15]

For Gregory, the unintended consequences of the Reformation arose from reducing justification to faith and ignoring "its traditional subordination to *caritas* among the three theological virtues". The loss of the virtues led to an ethics of rules.[16] This ethics, he argues, undergirds capitalism:

> Friedman, Hayek, and their respective followers are quite right: modern capitalism and consumerism cannot be understood apart from the formal ethics of rights and the individual freedom politically protected by modern liberal states. Modern liberalism, individualism, and capitalism are profoundly intertwined.[17]

Weber and Gregory differ on the details but agree that a Protestant work ethic arose because the Reformation unintentionally led to a disenchanted, secularized society in which an individual's "calling" became inextricably linked with their work or labor.[18] Both place ideas originating in Protestantism at the origin of a modern work ethic indissolubly linked with capitalism. Both are critical of this work ethic and so they are also, by implication, critical of the Protestant ideas that give rise to it. I will not disagree with them in what follows. In fact, I think Gregory is onto something important when he argues that the subordination, if not near elimination, of the virtues of hope and charity to faith in strands of Protestant thought lends itself to the liberal and neoliberal dominance of an anthropology known as *homo œconomicus*. I will, however, suggest that Weber and Gregory overlook a challenge that came out of an important Protestant tradition known as Christian socialism. It raises the question that Weber never did – what constitutes rational economic desire? Rejecting an anthropology of *homo economicus* with its calculating rationality, this tradition assumes a Christological rationality

Work in Protestant perspective 233

governing creation that requires cooperation rather than competition. I find this tradition returning among a younger generation of Protestant thinkers and activists that could be promising for developing an *intentional* Protestant approach to reforming work unlike the dominance of the unintended consequences in Weber, Gregory, and Adam Smith. We are never in an iron cage; history is not fate because intentional ethical action matters.

Christian socialism: R. H. Tawney, F. D. Maurice, and Stewart Headlam

The term "Christian Socialism" was coined in the mid-nineteenth century by the Anglican priest F. D. Maurice and his lawyer friend John Ludlow. It resulted in a rich tradition that is often neglected on the left because of its emphasis on religion and on the right because it affirms "socialism".[19] The young Marx ridiculed it, opting for a putative "scientific" socialism. Indeed, Christian socialism lacks the "scientific" approach to economics present in Marx or Hayek and Friedman for that matter. One consistent theme among its advocates is that economics should be understood within theology and ethics. One of the most interesting Christian socialists was Tawney (1880–1962) who professed that economics can only be reasonable when something more than economics renders it intelligible. Although he was no theologian, he inherited this claim from theologians such as Stewart Headlam (1847–1924) and F. D. Maurice (1805–1872).[20] Tawney's historical analysis in his 1922 Holland Memorial Lectures remains one of the best analyses of the relationship between *Religion and the Rise of Capitalism*, which is the title of his published lecture. Tawney argued that neither Catholicism nor Protestantism had an adequate ethics to challenge the rise of modern economic developments, especially that of wage labor, and that put him at odds with Weber.

Tawney wrote the foreword to the 1958 edition of Weber's famous book and was in part sympathetic. He agreed that examining "the influence of religious ideas on economic development" is an important task, but he also argued that the analysis should consider the reverse causation, "the effects of the economic arrangements" on "the province of religion".[21] Rather than assuming that religious ideas, even unintentionally, give rise to a capitalist spirit, Tawney asks how the capitalist spirit malforms religion. Following Brentano, he traced the rise of capitalism to historical developments that predate Protestantism. The "capitalist spirit" was present in the fourteenth century in Venice and Florence and the fifteenth in Antwerp.[22] He brought three criticisms to bear on Weber's "overstrained" argument in the published version of his lectures. First, Weber gives too much causal power to "moral and intellectual influences" in the rise of "capitalist enterprise" rather than examining the pre-Reformation historical developments in Venice, Florence, Flanders, and elsewhere. Changes in "the organization of commerce, finances, prices, and agriculture", especially the rise of enclosures, led to modern economics more so than religious ideas, but Tawney was not a materialist. Ideas

234   D. Stephen Long

mattered. Such changes could only occur because of changes in political ideas. Society became construed as naturalistic or mechanical rather than religious.[23] This naturalistic or mechanical understanding conceives of society as working outside the intentions of human agents, moral or otherwise. Second, Weber neglects or "touches too lightly on" non-moral and non-religious influences such as can be found in Machiavelli. Third, he "appears greatly to over-simplify Calvinism itself".[24] The "capitalist spirit", he wrote, "is as old as history and was not, as has often times been said, the offspring of Puritanism".[25] For Tawney, competition for the sake of profit signifies the capitalist spirit. The Medieval Catholic church as well as the Reformation churches opposed this spirit through similar ethical teachings, especially with their common suspicion against financial capitalism by the prohibition of usury. An economic ethics, then, is no dividing issue between Catholicism and Protestantism. Luther and Eck, who debated each other, equally opposed usury as did nearly every church except for the Calvinists who moderated the prohibition against it. But Eck defended the triple contract that was a round-about way of affirming usury. The differences, Tawney suggests, were not that stark.

Although Catholicism and Protestantism shared much in common in their economic ethics, neither were prepared to address wage labor and the shifts it brought to workers. Wage labor was not at the origin of early economic developments. It came after shifts in commerce, finance, and agriculture.[26] Rather than the Protestant work ethic giving rise to the capitalist spirit, Protestantism lacked an ethics of work that could do anything but reflect back changes that occurred on other grounds. In that sense, Weber got things backward. An ethics of work was not yet present in the sixteenth century because wage labor did not yet exist. Slavery and serfdom did, and for Tawney, the inability of the church adequately to address it was a sign of moral failure that contributed to a failure to develop an adequate ethics of work. Neither Catholicism nor Protestantism was prepared for the shifts in understanding labor from the industrial capitalism that followed on the previous financial capitalism. The church had a criticism of the latter but was ill equipped to address the former, to speak to the changes brought about in Smith's pin-making factory and Steuart's new economics of desire. The reason that they were ill equipped was because of the hierarchical ethic that looked at society in organic terms. Its antiquated teaching viewed society in terms of head, hands, and feet – "feet were born to labor, the hands to fight, and the head to rule".[27] This "static view" affirmed equality within classes but not between them. When an "outburst of commercial activity and of economic speculation" arose in the mid-fifteenth century, the teaching was incapable of addressing the shifts. Tawney stated,

"The gross facts of the social order are accepted in all their harshness and brutality. They are accepted with astonishing docility, and, except on rare occasions, there is no question of reconstruction".[28] Both Catholicism and Protestantism lacked the intention to reconstruct society on something other than the emerging commercial society.

Work in Protestant perspective 235

An implication of Tawney's teaching is that the capitalist spirit dominated not because of a Protestant work ethic, but because it lacked one. The "economic virtues" triumphed over the theological. He acknowledges that the Puritans played a decisive role in that triumph, but they were merely reflecting back an ethics of the new commercial society.[29] Tawney states, "The social teaching of the Church had ceased to count, because the Church itself had ceased to think".[30] The church was ill prepared to respond to the change brought about by "a wage-earning proletariat".

> [The Church] had insisted that all men were brethren. But it did not occur to it to point out that, as a result of the new economic imperialism which was beginning to develop in the seventeenth century, the brethren of the English merchant were the Africans whom he kidnapped for slavery in America, or the American Indians whom he stripped of their lands, or the Indian craftsmen from whom he bought muslins and silks at starvation prices.[31]

Tawney ends his analysis of religion and the rise of capitalism on a negative and a positive note. Negatively, no "compromise" can be had "between the Church of Christ and the idolatry of wealth, which is the practical religion of capitalist societies". Positively, "A reasonable estimate of economic organization must allow for the fact that, unless industry is to be paralyzed by recurrent revolts on the part of outraged human nature, it must satisfy criteria which are not purely economic".[32] Rational desire includes more than purely economic desire. If it only has the latter, desire cannot be rational.

Tawney was an economic historian more so than a theologian, but he stood in a tradition of Christian socialism that originated in the mid-nineteenth century with the Anglican theologian F. D. Maurice. Maurice reacted against philosophers of his age who sought to narrow ethics and economics to systems. Against William Whewell, he wrote, "He avowedly endeavoured to construct a system of Morality. I have declared that I have no such object, that I shall even strive diligently against the wish to pursue such an object".[33] Ethics could not be taught or learned well by looking to systems but to persons, for it was about life. The same was true for economics. Ethics concerns life and cannot be parceled out through a division of intellectual labor.[34] He and the Christian socialists who followed him argued strenuously that questions of economics and labor had to be placed within moral theology and the life of the church. Socialism answered those questions, but socialism without Christianity failed to challenge the dominance of economic rationality.

Maurice's friend Ludlow had traveled in France during the 1848 revolution and was impressed with the movement that he witnessed. He wrote to Maurice and stated,

> Socialism was a real and a very great power which had acquired an unmistakable hold, not merely on the fancies but on the consciences

236   D. Stephen Long

of the Parisian workmen, and that it must be Christianized or it would
shake Christianity to its foundation, precisely because it appealed to the
higher and not the lower instincts of the men.[35]

That distinction was important. Capitalism appealed to competition and
self-interest. Socialism aimed higher to cooperation and common goods, but
these needed to be grounded in something higher yet, the Wisdom by which
all things were created. Central to Christian socialism were the doctrines of
the Trinity and Incarnation. Maurice agreed with Ludlow and two years later
wrote to him stating that Christian socialism was "the only title which will
define our object, and will commit us at once to the conflict we must engage in
sooner or later with the unsocial Christians and the unchristian Socialists".[36]
Their Christian socialism was understood as a reflection of Divine Wisdom
through, by, and for whom all things were created. This Wisdom made possible the higher instincts in human creatures by which they could intend the
world as God intended and that required intending it with charity. Maurice
explicitly critiqued the Reformers for placing faith above charity. On this
point, he would have found himself in agreement with Gregory. Protestant
emphasis on justification by faith too often subordinated charity to faith.

Maurice's Protestant teaching on justification challenged any works righteousness. He wrote,

> Has he made himself God's child by some services which he has ren-
> dered to Him? No! these are the world's ethics; in these lies that self-
> righteousness which the Bible denounces, and which the conscience in
> us revolts against. Christian ethics proceed on the opposite principle.[37]

However, this did not result in a critique of works. Maurice continues, "We
do not attach ourselves to Christ by performing righteous acts. We are able
to perform righteous acts because we are attached to Him".[38] Christianity
requires an ecstatic agency in which we find ourselves by losing ourselves. It
is only when our agency is located in another that we become who we are
called to be. Although this makes Maurice thoroughly Protestant, he explicitly rejected beginning with faith rather than charity. As Paul teaches, only
charity remains, for it alone characterized God. Charity is "the key to unlock
the secrets of Divinity as well as of Humanity".[39] For Maurice, Charity is
Trinity; Trinity is Charity. "Writers" in the patristic and medieval era, "speak
continually of the Trinity as the 'Eternal Charity,' and as the foundation of
all human life".[40] Charity requires cooperation among God's creatures and
was the central reason Maurice called for Christian socialism. For Maurice,
Christian socialism begins in the church, its doctrines, and liturgy. It reflects
the Trinitarian love that is the basis for creation and is found in baptism, a
common creed, the Eucharist, the ministry, and Scripture.

Christian socialism lacks scientific precision. It violates disciplinary divisions, refusing to grant economics an independent domain for fear that such

Work in Protestant perspective 237

independence treats human workers as input or output units in a calculating rationality that forgets what it means to be human. Stewart Headlam, one of Maurice's students, stated that people "were made for nobler things (...) than mechanical works". If they fail to "train themselves intellectually and spiritually" then they become "a mere machine".[41]

Neither Maurice nor Headlam mentioned or defended a Protestant work ethic. Defending a Protestant work ethic could easily repeat the pattern of making work itself more central to the divine economy than it should be. Headlam controversially defended Music Halls and theaters for laborers so that they could lead "more joyful lives". He organized an "anti-Puritan league" that had G. K. Chesterton as a member for a short period of time.[42] People were made to dance, create art, enjoy food, wine, and life.[43] He spoke out against church leaders who "put a ban on Sunday games and recreation and healthy outdoor life and cheerful social intercourse". Such persons, Headlam suggested, oppose "Social Reform". It is not only about insuring that everyone has work whether that work has any meaning or not. It concerns an equitable distribution of labor and goods so people can get to the vocation that matters most, "to lead full, delightful human lives".[44]

Headlam's perspective on work subordinated socialism to the church because socialism needs religion or it becomes one.

> For, owing to the divorce of Socialism from the Church, there has grown up a tendency among some Socialists to exalt Socialism itself into a kind of religion, and to maintain that it contains in itself a reasoned theory and philosophy of life.[45]

Socialism's role was not to be an all-encompassing philosophy of life. If it were to fulfill its purpose, it needed to recognize its limits. To recognize its limits, it needed a philosophy of life. Headlam, like Maurice, found that in Christianity. Christianity offers a philosophy of life that limits socialism while pointing to it. Baptism "abolishes class distinctions". The Eucharist generates conditions for the bonds of solidarity. Here were two "essential sacraments" that could provide "wage-earners" with an "irresistible power as social reformers".[46] The Eucharist could unite Christendom "making for Internationalism" and relativizing nationalisms.[47] Within the life of the church, a new form of the expression "Workers of the World unite" could emerge that would create "a bloodless revolution" because Christ's blood-shedding "was sufficient for all", a "perfect sacrifice".[48]

Headlam saw an intervention taking place with Maurice in 1850 who "first gave utterance to that most pregnant phrase, Christian Socialism. And from that time onwards there have always been Churchmen who have insisted that the principles of Socialism are distinctly Christian principles".[49] I think Headlam is correct, and this makes the previous discussion of Christian socialism of more than historical interest. As the illusory nonsense of the Protestant work ethic comes more clearly into focus, both that there ever

238 D. Stephen Long

was one and that if there had been, it would have been salutary, I find more and more Protestant theologians mining this tradition for a theological ethics that can fill in the void that Tawney identified. The Protestant work ethic did not fail; it never existed. What existed were changes in commercial life that were reflected back in a theological ethic. The focus of that commercialized "theological" ethic was a providential ordering of society that made labor, arduous labor, not a curse to be overcome but a form of ethical discipline administered by God's invisible hand. Such an austere discipline conflated vocation with labor and constructed a society in which the pursuit of individual profit, even when little profit was to be had, would bring about societal harmony. It is an irrational society that cannot fulfill humanity's restless desire for something more.

A Christian theology of life (the role of work)

Dissatisfied with Christianity in the United States and how it merely reflects its market-state society and dissatisfied with the dominance of that society over our lives by expressions such as 24/7 and ROI, some theologians have begun to retrieve Christian socialism. In 2021, Phillip Turner published *Christian Socialism: The Promise of an Almost Forgotten Tradition*. Many persons might be surprised that one of the leading US Protestant theologians, Stanley Hauerwas, wrote the foreword to Turner's work. For some, Hauerwas's emphasis on an ecclesial ethics rejects engagement in politics and economics. He sought to revise Christian social ethics by insisting that the church does not have a social ethic but is a social ethic. He opposed Christendom, Constantinianism, and any hint of Christian nationalism. He recognized that Maurice was favorable toward a kind of nationalism and attempted to "return to Christendom", to view the church as the "soul of a nation". Hauerwas set his reform of social ethics against such positions. Nonetheless, he expressed his affirmation of Christian socialism. The legacy of Maurice, the originator of Christian socialism, was "to make the church an alternative to capitalism", and that he considers to be a pressing matter. "Nothing is more important because our imaginations are now held captive by the presumption there is no alternative to the market". Hauerwas then affirms the possible "social bonds" that Christian socialism generates that could "make possible a pluralism that can act as a check on nationalism".[50] I see a convergence occurring between an ecclesial ethics and Christian socialism that puts work into a salutary, theological perspective to address the problems.

In 1981, Hauerwas set forth "ten theses toward the reform of Christian social ethics". Several of those theses hold forth new promise, but they need revision to address what has occurred economically since he first set them forth. The sixth stated, "Christian social ethics can only be done from the perspective of those who do not seek to control national or world history, but who are content to live 'out of control'". Private ownership is control.

Work in Protestant perspective 239

To relinquish or share it is to live out of control. The fifth stated, "the primary social task of the church is to be itself", and it was this thesis that prompted many to accuse him of sectarianism, but he went on to suggest that the church being itself might accomplish two ends. First, it "might gain a critical perspective on those narratives that have captivated our vision and lives". And second, "By doing so, the church may well help provide a paradigm of social relations otherwise thought impossible". The eighth stated, "For the church to be, rather than to have, a social ethic means we must capture the social significance of common behavior, such as acts of kindness, friendship, and the formation of families".[51] I would add to that, "and the formation of corporations". This extension to the formation of corporations connects Hauerwas's ecclesial ethics to Maurice's worker cooperatives. Christian socialism is a logical outworking of Hauerwas's reform of social ethics (or vice versa). It offers a criticism as to how our imagination is captured by capitalist forms of exchange and offers an alternative paradigm, one present in the worship life of the church that can and should be extended as a paradigm for social relations, especially economic ones. In light of his 2021 affirmation of Christian socialism, perhaps it is appropriate to rewrite his earlier well-known eighth thesis: "For the church to be, rather than to have, a social*ist* ethic means we must capture the social significance of common, *economic* behavior".

Given the current state of the church, the culture, and politics, such a socialist vision seems impossible. We should not be optimistic. Yet, as Terry Eagleton reminds us, hope is not optimism. Theology has resources for hope, especially since it names one of its central virtues, unavailable to the political partisans who too often assume the lesser, competitive system that holds us captive. All the means at our disposal – preaching, writing, art, and so forth – should be used to set forth this hope that privileges faith in a cooperative, mutual love by which God moves the world. One way to do so is by returning to the task of strengthening workers' cooperatives begun by Maurice, taken up by others, and still present residually within Christian and non-Christian communities. Jonathan Tran's recent work *Asian Americans and the Spirit of Racialized Capitalism* shows how such a task is being pursued within an ecclesial setting that provides an alternative paradigm that could be emulated by those outside it. He offers a field study of "Dayspring Partners", a 3.1-million-dollar software company whose owners divested their primary interest in it and made it a "subsidiary of a church with an average annual budget of $500,000". They did this to make possible spiritual, educational, and economic possibilities otherwise unavailable to a poor, primarily African American community in which their largely Asian church had relocated.[52] Here is an example of what it means for the church to "capture the social significance of common behavior, such as acts of kindness, friendship, and the formation of *corporations*".

Charity refuses to allow a few to own and control the labor of many. The church fulfills its vocation when it humanizes work by challenging the relations between employer–employee, even if they appear benevolent. If this

240   D. Stephen Long

requires governmental regulations at the level of a village, city, state, or nation to insure that a few do not dominate the majority, then it is incumbent on the church to manifest to the faithful and all people of goodwill how such regulations are consistent with the cardinal virtue, the hinge, that renders creation intelligible and makes the infused virtues of faith, hope, and charity not only more basic than the acquired virtues of temperance, prudence, courage, and justice but exposes the vice of greed, economic competition, vast inequality, and the acquisitive disposition that comes with capitalism and its exaltation of work. These two ways of life want different ends.

A Christian socialism would not fit every version of socialism. It rejects any Stalinist or Maoist versions. Nor does it advocate violent rebellion. If socialism requires the destruction of life for the sake of life, it will represent the contradictions present in some previous socialist societies. Richard Wolff writes, "The role of the state is no longer the central issue in dispute". Instead, "21st-century socialism focuses on and prioritizes something else – namely, the transformation of workplaces from capitalism's hierarchical internal structures to fully democratic worker cooperatives".[53] Moreover, no specific class exists that one could eliminate thereby ridding the system of its oppressors and liberating the oppressed. As James Steuart noted, the disciplining of desire capitalism enacts is something we do to ourselves. In so doing, politics itself is dissolved into governance and management that undoes democratic possibilities. As Wendy Brown puts it, neoliberal "reason recasts political rights, citizenship, and the field of democracy itself in an economic register; in doing so, it disintegrates the very idea of the demos".[54] Christian socialism, gas and water socialism, and sewer socialism do not require violence to reintegrate ethics, politics, and economics. For instance, in a fascinating chapter on "sewer socialism" in Milwaukee, Wisconsin from 1910 to 1946, John Nichols explains how it was an attempt at "a legal and peaceable revolution" and opposed American militarism as much as it opposed the inequality that arose from the private control of vast amounts of capital.[55] Sewer socialism was denounced by Lenin just as Marx and his son-in-law denounced Christian socialism.[56] It refused to advocate revolutionary change through the destruction of the class structure and sought "incremental progress". Sewer socialists agreed but responded that what they did was more than a theory; it worked in practice.

The sewer socialists ran Milwaukee for more than three decades because they were honest and trustworthy. They were known for "a passion for orderly government; and by a contempt for graft and boodling". Emil Seidel, one of Milwaukee's socialist mayors, understood socialism similar to Headlam. Explaining how they proudly adopted the invective "sewer socialists", he unapologetically claimed that their goal was to put "sewers in workers' homes". He goes on to say how much more they wanted:

> We wanted our workers to have pure air; we wanted them to have sunshine; we wanted planned homes; we wanted living wages; we wanted

Work in Protestant perspective 241

recreation for young and old; we wanted vocational education; we wanted a chance for every human being to be strong and live a life of happiness. And we wanted everything that was necessary to give them that: playgrounds, parks, lakes, beaches, clean creeks and rivers, swimming pools, social centers, reading rooms, clean fun, music, dance, song and joy for all.[57]

They accomplished much of this for more than three decades. It was eventually defeated and many of the gains, such as parks, playgrounds, swimming pools, and more have fallen in disrepair, especially after the neoliberal turn in the 1970s. Nonetheless, the legacy of sewer socialism continues to give Milwaukee possibilities that cities without this vision lack.[58]

Although many of the leading sewer socialists were German Lutherans, they did not share the sacramental communism found in Maurice and Headlam. That would not worry either of them for they were convinced that Wisdom permeated creation so that every culture and nation could not help but, in some sense, reflect it. The church has a mission as Hauerwas put it, to "provide a paradigm of social relations otherwise thought impossible", and also to recognize and imitate such paradigms when they are found pursuing creaturely goods in cooperation with joy and delight wherever they are found.

So what would this mean for a Protestant perspective on work? First, cooperation and mutual love need to be named within the church as that which is most basic not only to Christian life, but to life per se. Any work that does not reflect it must be identified as opposing God's good creation. Work that cannot sustain workers; work that isolates and forbids basic social intercourse; work that consumes time as if it were a commodity; work that lacks any meaning or purpose; work that claims to give persons their only meaning or purpose; such work must be protested against. This could be a valuable Protestant work ethic. Second, the picture that holds us captive to a lesser vision should be identified so that we can be liberated from it. A vision of so-called entrepreneurial leaders who should be conceded ownership over the labor of others, and to whom the laborers should be grateful, must be broken. We generate myths around "leadership", "entrepreneurs", or "job-creators" that sanction dominating relationships by capturing our imagination that corporate relations cannot be otherwise and speak nonsense such as "if we redistribute wealth and lessen the gap between leaders and those they lead, we will take away the incentives for those with the requisite leadership skills to guide us into the unknown future". Someday soon, we must hope, this nonsensical language will make as much sense as arguments that refused to grant women the right to vote because they are too hysterical or Blacks civil rights because, as William Buckley once put it, equal rights will diminish the white race rather than lift up Blacks. Those arguments, once widely held, are now considered by reasonable people to be repugnant. So too, Christian socialism hopes, is the current economic relations

242 *D. Stephen Long*

between employers and employees, administrators and adminstratees and the nonsense that sustains them. Anyone who works in a corporation by their very labor makes that corporation possible and should share ownership in it. Third, the ethics of the current corporate structure must be rejected as a lie. The problem with capitalism is the hierarchical structure of the corporation, the business, the university, etc. that gives a few people maximum control over the labor of others with little accountability for their lives. CEOs, chief administrators, and members of the ownership class primarily have fiduciary duties to the trustees or shareholders, which is another way of saying that they primarily put faith in themselves and others like them, and not in the cooperative, mutual love that moves creation. Faith has a misplaced object and that has material consequences that enrich the few at the expense of the many; it feeds Mammon and forgets God. Yet God, not Mammon, creates us and our hearts are restless until they rest in God. That is the most rational of desires.

Notes

1 James Steuart, *Principles of Political Economy*, 21. See https://www.marxists.org/reference/subject/economics/steuart/book1.htm#ch01.
2 James Steuart, *An Inquirty Into the Principles of Political Economy: Being an Essay On The Science Of Domestic Policy In Free Nations* (London, A. Milland T. Cadell, 1767), 40. See https://archive.org/details/inquiryintoprinc01steu/page/40/mode/2up. Accessed Sept. 2, 2024.
3 Kathryn Tanner, *Capitalism and the New Spirit of Capitalism* (New Haven, CT: Yale University Press, 2019), 27.
4 For Piketty, *r* equals the "annual rate of return on capital, including profits, dividends, interest, rents, and other income from capital, expressed as a percentage of its total value" and *g* equals the "rate of growth of the economy" (25). His calculations, which examined the history of return on capital compared to growth rates of the economy over an extended period of time suggested a 6 to 1 ratio such that it would take six years of labor to equal the economic advance made by one year of the rate of return on capital. And this "inequality", he stated, "has nothing to do with market imperfections. Quite the contrary: the more perfect the capital market (in the economist's sense), the more likely *r* is to be greater than *g*" (27). His analysis is not without its detractors, especially among American economists. He responded, "To put it bluntly, the discipline of economics has yet to get over its childish passion for mathematics and for purely theoretical and often highly ideological speculation, at the expense of historical research and collaboration with the other social sciences" (32). Thomas Piketty, *Capital in the Twenty-First Century*, trans. Arthur Goldhammer (Cambridge, MA: Belknap/Harvard, 2014).
5 Max Weber, *The Protestant Ethic and the Spirit of Capitalism* (New York: Charles Scribner's Sons, 1958), 99–101.
6 Max Weber, *The Protestant Ethic and the Spirit of Capitalism* (New York: Charles Scribner's Sons, 1958), 104.
7 Max Weber, *The Protestant Ethic and the Spirit of Capitalism* (New York: Charles Scribner's Sons, 1958), 104–105.
8 Max Weber, *The Protestant Ethic and the Spirit of Capitalism* (New York: Charles Scribner's Sons, 1958), 163, 166–168.

Work in Protestant perspective 243

9 Max Weber, *The Protestant Ethic and the Spirit of Capitalism* (New York: Charles Scribner's Sons, 1958), 178.

10 Max Weber, *The Protestant Ethic and the Spirit of Capitalism* (New York: Charles Scribner's Sons, 1958), 178.

11 Max Weber, *The Protestant Ethic and the Spirit of Capitalism* (New York: Charles Scribner's Sons, 1958), 181.

12 Max Weber, *The Protestant Ethic and the Spirit of Capitalism* (New York: Charles Scribner's Sons, 1958), 181.

13 Lisa Jardine, *Worldly Goods: A New History of the Renaissance* (New Haven, CT: Yale University Press, 2005).

14 Brad S. Gregory, *The Unintended Reformation: How a Religious Revolution Secularized Society* (Cambridge, MA: The Belknap Press of Harvard University Press, 2012), 241.

15 Brad S. Gregory, *The Unintended Reformation: How a Religious Revolution Secularized Society* (Cambridge, MA: The Belknap Press of Harvard University Press, 2012), 262.

16 Brad S. Gregory, *The Unintended Reformation: How a Religious Revolution Secularized Society* (Cambridge, MA: The Belknap Press of Harvard University Press, 2012), 208–209.

17 Brad S. Gregory, *The Unintended Reformation: How a Religious Revolution Secularized Society* (Cambridge, MA: The Belknap Press of Harvard University Press, 2012), 242.

18 Eugene McCarraher Challenges the Disenchantment Narrative in his *The Enchantments of Mammon: How Capitalism Became the Religion of Modernity* (Cambridge, MA: Harvard University Press, 2019). For an illuminating discussion between McCarraher and Mary Hirschfeld, see "Is Capitalism Good for us?" here https://www.youtube.com/watch?v=tztujzv_fQ8.

19 Gary Dorrien's *Social Democracy in the Making: Political & Religious Roots of European Socialism* (New Haven: Yale University Press, 2019) is the most thorough account of the history of Christian Socialism. He notes that the movement was "ridiculed by young Marx for trying to co-opt a revolutionary upsurge". He finds it to be advantageous to Marxism because it affirms ethics, eschews economic determinism, and rejects the violence of a "catastrophic mentality" (4–5).

20 Maurice's Great Granddaughter was the Controversial Economist Joan Robinson.

21 Tawney, "Foreword", to Max Weber, *The Protestant Ethic and the Spirit of Capitalism* (New York: Charles Scribner's Sons, 1958), 11.

22 Tawney, "Foreword", to Max Weber, *The Protestant Ethic and the Spirit of Capitalism* (New York: Charles Scribner's Sons, 1958), 7. In his earlier *Religion and the Rise of Capitalism*, Tawney stated, "If capitalism means the direction of industry by the owners of capital for their own pecuniary gain, and the social relationships which establish themselves between them and the wage-earning proletariat whom they control, then capitalism had existed on a grand scale both in medieval Italy and in medieval Flanders. If by the capitalist spirit is meant the temper which is prepared to sacrifice all moral scruples to the pursuit of profit, it had been only too familiar to the saints and sages of the Middle Ages. It was the economic imperialism of Catholic, Portugal and Spain, not the less imposing if more solid achievements of the Protestant powers, which impressed contemporaries down to the Armada. It was predominantly Catholic cities which were the commercial centers of Europe, and Catholic bankers who were its leading financiers". R. H. Tawney, *Religion and the Rise of Capitalism* (New York: Harcourt, Brace & World, Inc., 1954), 76.

23 R. H. Tawney, *Religion and the Rise of Capitalism* (New York: Harcourt, Brace & World, Inc., 1954), 20. He also stated that the ethics emerging from

244 *D. Stephen Long*

these changes "was the natural counterpart of a social philosophy which repudiated teleology, and which substituted the analogy of a self-regulating mechanism, moved by weights and pulley of economic motives, for the theory which had regarded society as an organism composed of different classes united by their common subordination to a spiritual purpose" 161. For his fascinating discussion of the role that enclosures played in the "new medicine for poverty", see 211–216.

24 R. H. Tawney, *Religion and the Rise of Capitalism* (New York: Harcourt, Brace & World, Inc, Inc., 1954), 262.

25 R. H. Tawney, *Religion and the Rise of Capitalism* (New York: Harcourt, Brace & World, Inc, Inc., 1954), 188.

26 David Graeber offers a similar analysis in his *Bullshit Jobs: A Theory* (New York: Simon & Schuster, 2018). Like Tawney, he recognizes that wage labor is a "latecomer" in modern economic developments. It involved changes in the understanding of time as well as technological and moral changes such that a laborer's time now became something that could be rented. Wage labor existed in the Middle Ages in port cities by unfree persons. So Graeber asks this question, "So how did we get to the situation we see today, where it's considered perfectly natural for free citizens of democratic countries to rent themselves out in this way, or for a boss to become indignant if employees are not working every moment of 'his' time?" He answers, "It is usually laid at the feet of Puritanism, and Puritanism certainly had something to do with it; but one could argue equally compellingly that the more dramatic forms of Calvinist asceticism were just overblown versions of a new time sense that was, in one way or another, reshaping the sensibilities of the middle classes across the Christian world", 82–92.

27 R. H. Tawney, *Religion and the Rise of Capitalism* (New York: Harcourt, Brace & World, Inc., 1954), 55.

28 R. H. Tawney, *Religion and the Rise of Capitalism* (New York: Harcourt, Brace & World, Inc., 1954), 27.

29 Despite his criticisms of Puritanism, Tawney affirms their contribution to democracy. While he would be as critical of Hayek, Friedman, and individualism as Gregory, he would be more affirmative of modern democracy. The problem with liberalism and neoliberalism was not its affirmation of freedom, but its inability to recognize the inequalities built into it because of the unwillingness to address the new forms of economic divisions that it inherited from previous forms. It awaits a Protestant ethic of work. R. H.Tawney, *Religion and the Rise of Capitalism* (New York: Harcourt, Brace & World, Inc., 1954), 225.

30 R. H. Tawney, *Religion and the Rise of Capitalism* (New York: Harcourt, Brace & World, Inc., 1954), 157.

31 R. H. Tawney, *Religion and the Rise of Capitalism* (New York: Harcourt, Brace & World, Inc., 1954), 156–157.

32 R. H. Tawney, *Religion and the Rise of Capitalism* (New York: Harcourt, Brace & World, Inc., 1954), 233– 235.

33 F. D. Maurice, *The Conscience: Lectures on Casuistry* (London and Cambridge: MacMillan and Co. 1868), 26.

34 Maurice was the last significant theologian to hold the Knightbridge Chair. Established in 1683, it is one of the oldest and most prestigious chairs in Cambridge (the current holder is the philosopher Rae Helen Langton). Maurice held it from 1866 to 1872 when its full name was "Knightbridge Chair of Moral Theology, Casuistical Divinity, and Moral Philosophy". When Maurice's protégé Henry Sidgwick received the chair in 1883, he reduced the name to "Moral Philosophy". Sidgwick rejected Christian Theology. In a move directly contrary to

Work in Protestant perspective 245

Maurice, he endeavored to teach ethics with "scientific precision" as a discipline independent of theology, metaphysics, or politics. Sidgwick taught John Keynes (John Maynard Keynes's father) and as the chair of Moral Sciences, hired Alfred Marshall. Maurice had been put up for the Professorship of Political Economy at Oxford by leaders of the Oxford Movement until they realized that despite his strong sacramentalism, he was not of their movement. Frederick Maurice, *The Life of Frederick Denison Maurice: Chiefly told in his own Letters by his son Frederick Maurice*, Vols. I and II (London: MacMillan, 1885), 210–213.

35 Frederick Maurice, *The Life of Frederick Denison Maurice: Chiefly told in his Own Letters by his son Frederick Maurice*, Vols. I and II (London: MacMillan, 1885), Vol. I, 458.

36 Frederick Maurice, *The Life of Frederick Denison Maurice: Chiefly Told in his own Letters by his son Frederick Maurice*, Vols. I and II (London: MacMillan, 1885), Vol. II, 35.

37 F. D. Maurice, *The Epistles of St. John: A Series of Lectures on Christian Ethics* (London: MacMillan and Co., 1893), 174.

38 F. D. Maurice, *The Epistles of St. John: A Series of Lectures on Christian Ethics* (London: MacMillan and Co., 1893).

39 F. D. Maurice, *Theological Essays* (London: James Clarke & Co. Ltd., 1853/1957), 22–24.

40 Frederick Maurice, *The Life of Frederick Denison Maurice: Chiefly told in his Own Letters by his son Frederick Maurice*, Vols. I and II (London: MacMillan, 1885) II, 416.

41 John Richard, *Stewart Headlam's Radical Anglicanism: The Mass, the Masses, and the Music Hall* (Urbana and Chicago: University of Illinois Press, 2003), 27, cited in Orens. Orens notes that Headlam read Aristotle's *Ethics* with Maurice and brought together his sacramentalism and orthodoxy with a radical socialism.

42 Orens, John Richard, *Stewart Headlam's Radical Anglicanism: the Mass, the Masses, and the Music Hall* (Urbana and Chicago: University of Illinois Press, 2003), 29, 132.

43 Stewart Headlam, *The Socialist's Church* (London: George Allen, 1907), 13.

44 Stewart Headlam, *The Socialist's Church* (London: George Allen, 1907), 59–60.

45 Stewart Headlam, *The Socialist's Church* (London: George Allen, 1907), 49.

46 Stewart Headlam, *The Socialist's Church* (London: George Allen, 1907), 5–6.

47 Stewart Headlam looked to "The Mass" in order to united British Christians "with the rest of Christendom, destroying our English isolation, making for Internationalism". *The Socialist's Church* (London: George Allen, 1907), 21.

48 Stewart Headlam, *The Socialist's Church* (London: George Allen, 1907), 25.

49 Stewart Headlam, *The Socialist's Church* (London: George Allen, 1907), 1.

50 Stanley Hauerwas in Phillip Turner, *Christian Socialism: The Promise of an Almost Forgotten Tradition* (Eugene, OR: Cascade Books, 2021), xi–xii.

51 Stanley Hauerwas, *A Community of Character* (Notre Dame, IN: University of Notre Dame Press, 1981), 10–12.

52 Jonathan Tran, *Asian Americans and the Spirit of Racial Capitalism* (New York: Oxford University Press, 2021), 224.

53 Wolff, Richard D., *Understanding Socialism*, (New York: Democracy at Work, 2019), 51.

54 Wendy Brown, *Undoing the Demos: Neoliberalism's Stealth Revolution* (New York: Stealth Books. 2015), 151–152.

55 John Nichols, *The 'S' Word: A Short History of an American Tradition... Socialism* (London: Verso, 2015), 101–139.

246   D. Stephen Long

56 "Denouncing Headlam's efforts to woo the left, Marx's son-in-law Edward Aveling dismissed Christian socialism out of hand. Christianity and capitalism, he wrote, were the nation's twin curses". Orens, *Stewart Headlam's Radical Anglicanism*, 57. Aveling wrote *Christianity and Capitalism*. With Charles L Marson and Stewart D Headlam. (London: Modern Press, 1884).

57 John Nichols, *The 'S' Word: A Short History of an American Tradition... Socialism* (London: Verso, 2015), 111.

58 Milwaukee also suffered from racist housing and discrimination policies that emerged after the Socialist mayors that continue to plague the city.

14 Labor of love

The meaning of work in the household

Mary L. Hirschfeld

In the opening line to his best-selling textbook, *The Principles of Economics*, Greg Mankiw writes:

> The word economy comes from the Greek word oikonomos, which means "one who manages a household". At first, this origin might seem peculiar. But in fact, households and economies have much in common. A household faces many decisions … [about allocating] its scarce resources among its various members… Like a household, a society faces many decisions.[1]

Mankiw's instinct to link the two words by finding a commonality in the necessity of making decisions is instructive. For economists, the central feature of "decision-making" revolves around the question of how to allocate resources so as to most efficiently achieve whatever ends we desire. Because resources, most notably time and money, are scarce, this involves making trade-offs. Given that I have ten dollars, I can either have lunch or a new pair of socks, but not both.

For economists, the necessity of making decisions that take the form of allocating scarce resources permeates human life. It is thus meaningful to extend the economic way of thinking to areas we would not normally think of as belonging to economics. There is an economics of crime, for example, and an economics of religion. And there is an economics of the family, which covers questions like whom one should marry, whether one should stay married, how many children one should have, and how the spouses should divvy up the work necessary to maintain the household.[2]

Construing human life as essentially an exercise in allocating scarce resources elevates concerns about economic efficiency. If there is not enough to go around, surely it would be better to work to generate more of those scarce resources so that we can at least get more of whatever it is that we desire. This worldview is accompanied by a thin understanding of labor. For individuals, labor is understood to be the "disutility" one accepts in order to receive a wage, with individuals choosing the point which maximizes net

DOI: 10.4324/9781003508212-17

248 *Mary L. Hirschfeld*

utility (i.e. the difference between the utility one derives from being paid and the disutility involved in working). For firms, labor is understood to be a factor of production to be employed up to the point where the value of the laborer's work is no longer greater than the cost of the wage.

To the extent that our culture is formed by this worldview, it is difficult to arrive at a thicker conception of labor. There is a two-fold problem. First, as already suggested, work is viewed purely as a disutility that we bear in service of getting the goods we think we want. But as St. Pope John Paul II reminds us, the value of work is not limited to its "objective" dimension, i.e. the value of the goods it produces. Work also has a subjective dimension, one that allows us to participate in God's creative activity in the world, to fulfill our own talents, and to serve our communities.[3] Second, even if we did just want to focus on the "objective" dimension, the modern economy only values producing more and more goods and services, without reference to the ends that will be served by those commodities. It does not distinguish between goods that are genuinely valuable, and those which at best do not advance human flourishing and at worst actively hinder it. To see what is at stake, simply contrast the meaning and purpose of work for the laborer who is producing nourishing bread, with the meaning and purpose of work for the laborer who is producing junk food. Again, St. Pope John Paul II provides us with a useful distinction. True progress involves advancement in "being". In other words material progress is meant to serve spiritual development – the pursuit of the true, the good and the beautiful, the cultivation of community, and the development of personal excellence. But our culture thinks of progress as advancement in "having", i.e. expanding our command over goods and services, irrespective of whether they are well-ordered to our higher ends.[4] Work that is ordered to progress understood as advancement in "being" would necessarily be valued according to both its objective and subjective dimensions. And it would have a greater sense of meaning and purpose.

What is instructive about Mankiw's opening observation about the subject of economics is that he begins in precisely the same place that Aristotle begins, with the connection between the household, or *oikos*, and the economy. For Aristotle, however, the connection is pernicious – a threat to the integrity of the household, which plays a crucial role in the project of creating a polity capable of cultivating and sustaining the good life. Indeed, economists' inability to see that there is any alternative to the sort of decision-making they describe is a symptom of what happens when the misguided economic project of maximizing income colonizes the entire culture, starting in the household.

As we reflect on the theological significance of work, we need to think about the strong headwinds present in our culture reflected in the preeminent position occupied by economics. One way to do that is to return to Aristotle's own distinction between what he calls the natural art of acquisition that is proper for households pursuing virtue, and the artificial art of acquisition that threatens that project. Aristotle's question was about how households

Labor of love: the meaning of work in the household 249

secure the material resources they need to in order to pursue their higher ends. His basic story was that while specialization and exchange in the market could be ordered to the natural art of acquisition, it could easily be corrupted into the artificial art of acquisition wherein making money becomes an end and not a means. That story could be mapped onto the history of the west wherein the expanding reaches of market activity corresponded to a shift to understanding happiness as a matter of material prosperity rather than a life with a sense of meaning and purpose. This chapter will briefly sketch out that story, but primarily to push beyond it.

Household economic activity is not limited to the question of how to acquire the material necessities of life produced by others. There remains a type of production that necessarily takes place in the household. We might think in terms of cooking and cleaning, but there is more involved in household production than simply those sorts of activities. Part of the story of the development of the modern economy is the steady decline of household production alongside a loss of understanding of its importance. In the household, labor is done by and for the members of the family. The relational nature of labor is thus impossible to overlook. Moreover, household production represents the final stage of economic activity wherein material goods are made ready for their ultimate use. It is the stage of production in which the ultimate purpose of economic activity is realized. The story of the decline of household production, then, is intimately connected to the story of how our economic activities became detached from the higher purposes they are meant to serve.

The transition from *Oikos* to economy: first take

I begin with Aristotle. It is important to concede from the start that Aristotle fails to appreciate the human goods that are secured through labor. The "subjective" dimension of labor is invisible to him. Instead, he believes that we only divert our time toward work as a matter of necessity. Labor is only valuable insofar as it produces the material goods that allow us to survive and to pursue our higher ends. And because the need to work is a cruel necessity, it is better that some should shift the burden of work onto others, namely onto slaves, so that the masters might be free to cultivate virtue, participate in the *polis*, and pursue philosophy.[5] Aristotle likewise thought that free craftsmen were engaged in activities that made it more difficult for them to achieve full human flourishing.[6] Although Aristotle cannot help us think about the subjective meaning of work, he provides us with crucial distinctions that can help us think more clearly about work's objective dimension. In particular, Aristotle insists that economic activity should be limited to serving genuinely important ends. And he warns against the dangers involved in pursuing unlimited economic progress without reference to the real goods economic activity should serve.

Aristotle identifies the divergent understandings of economic life in Book I of *Politics*, in which he takes up the question of the role of the "art of

250 *Mary L. Hirschfeld*

acquisition" in the functioning of the household. As Aristotle puts it, there are two modes of the art of acquisition. The first he calls "natural", observing that it is finite. We need only so much food, clothing, and other material instruments to sustain life and cultivate virtue.[7] The second he calls "artificial", observing that it is infinite. This is economic activity ordered to accumulating money, and the desire for such wealth has no limit.[8] The latter form of acquisition is rooted in *pleonexia*, the vice that urges us to think of happiness in terms of extension; one more promotion or one more raise (and then another one and another one). Of the two modes of acquisition, only the natural form is ordered toward "living well" as Aristotle puts it. The art of artificial acquisition, by contrast, is simply ordered to "living", which quickly gives way to a desire to live enjoyably, something which one can only really do if one has "superfluity".[9] The economy that pursues the artificial art of acquisition orders work to goods that have no higher purpose, thereby degrading the objective value of labor.

Unfortunately, there is a tendency for the art of natural acquisition to be corrupted into the art of artificial acquisition. The reason for this is that the two arts involve the same act, namely producing some good or service for sale in the marketplace. Although Aristotle does not formally discuss the importance of the division of labor for economic life, his analysis presupposes that it exists. The idea, simply, is that a household that sought to supply all its material needs out of its own labor would be very poor. As Adam Smith suggests, the division of labor greatly improves economic productivity.[10] The simplest way to see the enormity of the value of the division of labor would be to imagine how much of the standard of living you presently enjoy you could reproduce if you had to do everything yourself – even if you were supplied with all the machines and technological knowledge that is available to modern manufacturers. Economists like to remind people that there is no such thing as a free lunch. But the social dividend that results from the division of labor is a very large free lunch that we enjoy simply by virtue of participating in the economic life of the community.

So, all households have very good reason to specialize, and then to trade whatever goods or services they produce on the market. What distinguishes the two forms of the art of acquisition, then, is not the act of specializing and selling goods or services in the market. What distinguishes them is the end served by that activity. Material goods are instrumental goods, valuable insofar as they are ordered to higher goods. Aristotle offers an analogy with medicine. Like material wealth, medicine is instrumental. If it takes two aspirin to cure a headache, then, that is what I want. Just so, the virtuous household thinks about the standard of living that is appropriate for them, and the various activities the members wish to undertake, and determines how much wealth is necessary to secure those ends. Thus, for the virtuous household, the art of acquisition is in service of an end that is limited. The household adjusts its productive activities to meet those needs. By contrast, the household engaged in the art of artificial acquisition seeks wealth as an

Labor of love: the meaning of work in the household 251

end in itself, perhaps ordered to some open-ended wish of ever-increasing degrees of convenience and comfort in the standard of living. For that household, the art of acquisition aims at maximizing income; the household then determines what standard of living it can afford.[11] In doing so, they undermine the meaning of purpose of work, which shifts from being in service of producing and acquiring goods that serve higher ends, to serving the purpose of earning money as an end in itself.

From an Aristotelian point of view, the artificial art of acquisition deflects the household's attention from the cultivation of the good life to the acquisition of wealth. As he puts it, households engaged in the artificial art of acquisition "turn all [virtues] into forms of the art of acquisition, as though to make money were the one aim and everything else must contribute to that aim".[12] This is the household that tells Johnny to cultivate fortitude so that he will be able to work hard on the job and make a lot of money. More importantly for our purposes, it corrupts the art of acquisition itself. The physician who heals with the aim of making money is not practicing the same art as the one who heals for the sake of healing.[13] Aristotle himself offers a brief narrative on how the rise of money and commerce generates a widespread shift from the art of natural acquisition to the art of artificial acquisition.[14] Once currency becomes a medium of exchange, it is mistaken as the object of trade, rather than a mere intermediary. Karl Marx characterizes this shift as a transition from thinking of trade as primarily exchanging one commodity for another (C → M → C') to thinking of trade as primarily about buying and selling commodities in order to make money (M → C → M').[15] There are many ways to understand why this shift happens, but the fact of the shift is commonly recognized.[16]

Although the dangers posed by commerce and the associated vice of *pleonexia* were well known in the ancient world, there was a signal change as we entered into modernity and as markets spread: *pleonexia* ceased to be regarded as a vice. Albert O. Hirschman takes up the question of how the vice of what he calls greed was transmuted into the virtue of self-interest in his book *The Passions and the Interests: Political Arguments for Capitalism before Its Triumph*.[17] Hirschman documents the early modern trend toward thinking about regulating the disruptive passions not by urging people to be virtuous but rather by taming the vices by pitting them against each other. Acquisitiveness emerged as the best "passion" to play this role since profit-seeking shopkeepers are less likely to want to go to war.

In a culture that sees the unlimited acquisition of wealth as a good, the value of things come to be measured in money, which in turn can make it difficult to see their real value.[18] With respect to labor, this means that the dollar value of work comes to be seen as paramount, both in terms of its benefit to the worker and its cost to the employer. Because labor is thought of in terms of its role in acquiring money, the subjective dimension of work in which work has meaning in terms of the service it provides other is obscured. Other subjective dimensions of work, like its role in cultivating excellence can be acknowledged, but they drop out of our analysis because they are not quantifiable. The transformation of the economic life of the household has another dimension that poses an independent challenge for our understanding of the meaning of work. In addition to the art of acquisition, the household is also the locus of a type of economic production that must be performed in the household. As the market economy has expanded, that role has been diminished, obscuring the ultimate purposes that economic activity is meant to serve and the relational character of human work. Its decline thus marks the emptying out of an institution that once embodied the essence of meaningful work. To that subject I now turn.

Oikos, virtue, and household production

Both Aristotle and economists distinguish between production and consumption (to use economists' terms). Production entails converting raw materials, labor, and capital into useful goods and services. Consumption entails acquiring those goods and services for use. As economic production shifted from the household to the marketplace, firms or businesses became the locus of economic production understood in this sense. And on the standard modern understanding, the household is the locus of consumption. In any standard introductory economics text, a "circular flow" diagram is depicted illustrating the relationship between households, firms, and markets (Figure 14.1):

Households are conceived of as owning the "factors of production" used to produce goods and services. These include "land" (any raw materials), "labor" (human work effort), "capital" (goods that are of use in the production of economic goods, most easily thought of as machinery, but extending beyond that), and "entrepreneurship" (the creativity and willingness to take risk that firms need).[19] The factors of production are "sold" to businesses

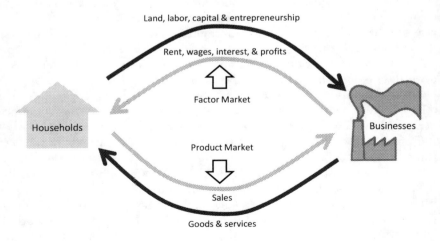

Figure 14.1 Circular flow diagram.

Labor of love: the meaning of work in the household   253

or firms, which use the factors of production in order to produce goods and services. These goods and services are then sold back to households. The income households earn from selling their factors of production to businesses are used to purchase the goods and services the household desires from businesses. For both economists and Aristotle, economic activity is focused on external goods, with a particular focus on external goods that can be exchanged with others. From the household's perspective, economic life is outward facing – we either produce goods and services for sale to others, or we sell our labor or other factors of production to firms that produce goods and services for sale to others. The picture of the economy that undergirds this worldview thus associates economic life with the market and the productive work that takes place in firms.

But that vision obscures two important functions performed by the household. First, it puts consumption into something of a black box. Households go into the market and use their income to purchase goods and services. That purchase is counted as "consumption" and can be mistaken for the end of the economic process. Second, it leaves us with a conundrum about how to handle "household production", economic production that takes place in the home and is performed by members of the household for members of the household. In both cases, we end up overlooking or discounting economic activity that gives labor its deepest meaning.

Virtue and consumption

Beginning first with a closer look at consumption, we find that the art of acquisition for the household includes not just the question of how to acquire the income the household needs, but also the question of how to spend that income wisely. Households need to determine what goods and services they need to run the household well, and to facilitate the flourishing of the household's members. Is our income better spent on a new dishwasher? Or violin lessons for Luisa? Just as the artificial art of acquisition can corrupt productive activity, converting a doctor who pursues his human excellence by healing his patients into a doctor who heals his patients in order to earn money, the artificial art of acquisition corrupts consumption. Aquinas points to the problem by distinguishing between natural wealth and artificial wealth.[20] Natural wealth consists in the actual goods (and services) we need in order to sustain our lives and pursue our goals. As Aquinas observes, our desire for such wealth should be limited. It is an instrumental good, in service of higher ends, and our need for it is measured by the ends it is meant to serve. A household that recognized this would think about its economic problems by first determining what income it needs to provide itself with the material goods it needs, and then deciding how best to secure that level of income. Should one find oneself earning more than that, the excess wealth constitutes an "abundance" that ought, properly, be given to others in need.[21]

254   *Mary L. Hirschfeld*

Our culture as a whole has embraced the artificial art of acquisition. Thus, most households aim to maximize their income. But, in doing so, they deflect attention away from the question of how to spend their income well. If we conceive of our pattern of consumption, which I will refer to as a "standard of living", as something that should be expanded out as income allows, we are not thinking of it as ordered to a proper end. We get trapped in a sequence of purchases, buying one thing, and then another without thinking about how that serves the household's pattern of life. I develop an interest in cooking. I buy new pots and pans and new kitchen gadgets. These take up space. As I buy the next new gadget and the next, I begin to think I need to remodel the kitchen. In the meantime, my transient thought that I might want to do some serious photography means there is a rather expensive camera sitting in a crowded closet somewhere. The clutter that is pervasive in the modern home is what happens when we think in terms of buying the next thing and the next thing. And this pattern can often distract us from what matters. Meanwhile, the ends we intended to pursue get lost in the shuffle. Did I really need a new set of pots and pans to get serious about cooking? Or would it have made more sense to perfect my skill as a cook by actually cooking?

There is an art or virtue to manage the purchases of a household so that they serve a holistic vision of what the family's good is. This would be the family that thinks first about what ends it wants to pursue. Does the family have a collective interest in good cooking? Or music? If so, it will form a household around those ends. It would enter into the market with a clear idea of what goods it needs in order to serve those ends, and would not come back with three random purchases in addition to it. Such homes will have an aesthetic quality to them – everything serves a clear purpose and is arranged into a harmonious whole. The role of making purchases has typically fallen to the wife, and it is possible that economists have never taken up the question of what constitutes a good pattern of life because it is work that is done by women, not men. These women had a small school of consumption economics, but it went into eclipse in the mid-twentieth century. Indeed, it was first stumbling onto these women economists that alerted me to the fact that the economic vision displayed in the circular flow diagram obscures an important component of economic activity. Economists worry about efficient production of goods, but rarely if ever take up the question of the extent to which households spend their money wisely.[22] And to repeat a point, the clutter in our basements, garages, and closets all represent labor that went into producing goods that in the end had no real purpose.

Work within the household

These twentieth-century women economists largely found employment in home economics departments.[23] Two of the most important of them were Hazel Kyrk (1886–1957), who held a joint appointment in economics and

Labor of love: the meaning of work in the household   255

home economics at the University of Chicago and her student Margaret Reid (1896–1991), who spent most of her career in the home economics department at the University of Iowa.[24] In addition to extensively exploring the economic activity of "consumption", Kyrk and Reid also studied household production, or the work that takes place in the home. It is a topic that disrupts the standard economic categories of thinking.

As Margaret Reid suggests, household production is obviously important to economic life, judging from the fact that it is ubiquitous. If we think of production as the process of making goods available for use, the household is the locus of the final chain in the sequence of events that begins in firms. Adam Smith famously said he does not expect to get his dinner from the benevolence of the butcher, the brewer, or the baker, but rather from an appeal to their self-interest.[25] But in point of fact, if Smith relied *only* on the butcher, the brewer, and the baker, he still would not have had his dinner. For that, he required someone to cook it and serve it to him.[26] Economists, thus, from the beginning have been blind to the final stage of production that typically takes place within the household. That invisibility may have something to do with the fact that it was work typically performed by women, but as Reid suggests, the even more important reason household production is overlooked is that it is not *paid* labor.[27] As we have increasingly come to think of economic life in monetary terms, aspects of economic activity that fall outside of the commercial economy is obscured.[28]

The question of what "counts" as economic production has evolved as the discipline of economics evolved. As already suggested, the line between production and consumption is blurry. In addition, if production entails creating value of some sort, one needs to decide what constitutes "value" in order to define "production". If we take Adam Smith as the founder of the discipline of economics, we find that the focus was on producing the kind of "value" that would allow an economy to "grow". He seems to have in mind, specifically, the kind of "value" that allows the accumulation of "capital". For Smith, even paid domestic servants were not "productive".[29]

With the rise of the "marginal revolution", Classical economics gave way to Neoclassical economics, in which market prices just are the value of whatever is being bought and sold, shifting attention away from the goods or services themselves toward their monetary value. On this view, paid labor produces value, because it is paid. Unpaid household labor and volunteer work thus are not counted as productive economic activity.[30] This is the view that underlies the circular flow diagram depicted above, and it entails seeing consumption as something of a black box. Economic analysis focuses on determinates of the level of consumption, measured as household expenditure, but does not inquire further into what goes on within the household.

Or at least that was true until Gary Becker, a Noble laureate economist from the University of Chicago, spearheaded a move to extend the tools of economic analysis to all spheres of human life. Becker and allied economists returned to the question of household production and consumption,

256 *Mary L. Hirschfeld*

developing a "household production function" in which households are modeled as converting purchased goods and services and household labor into the ultimate goods desired (health, prestige, comfort, pleasure, and so on).[31] The household production function is presented as an exercise in maximizing "utility" rather than "profits" but is otherwise of the same form as a firm's production function. But as discussed above, thinking of household decisions as a matter of maximization imports market logic into the realm of the family, and is fundamentally incompatible with wise use of economic wealth. Moreover, in treating the household as a sort of firm, the modern economic approach to household production also obscures the human dimension of productive activity, artificially separating it from the art of living itself.

As St. John Paul II observes in *Laborem Exercens*, work is multidimensional. It is partly instrumental – a way of providing ourselves with the material goods we need, but it is also intrinsically good, an exercise of our human capacities and our way of living out the *imago dei*.[32] In other words the division between consumption and production is not, in fact neat. Work that we would all call "productive" is also an intrinsic aspect of simply living. The role of work as a dimension of simply living is even clearer when we turn to household production. To see the issue, it is instructive to consider how Margaret Reid, trained as an economist, wrestled with the problem of how to think about activities in the home that both produced goods and services, but also embodied the family's relationship and the virtues of mutual care and concern.

Reid begins, naturally enough, by trying to define household production. Her first move is to accept economists' demarcation between market and non-market activity. She thus excludes paid labor, even if it takes place within the home. The paid domestic servant is engaging in market production whether he lives in the household or not; the family member who works from home, say by writing novels, is performing market production even if she does not go to the office to do her work. Reid then considers the problem that there are monetary arrangements within the household. For example, the children might receive an allowance connected with the chores that they do. Reid argues that such "payments" have more to do with the allocation of resources within the household and cannot properly be regarded in the same light as a market transaction.[33]

But in turning to the question of what unpaid labor "counts" as household production, Reid confronts the problem already alluded to in St. John Paul II's discussion of the nature of work: it both aims at "producing" something, but the activity itself is simply part of living. When it comes to household production, the two "sides" of work are even more deeply intermingled. The woman who is planning a birthday party for her 12-year-old daughter is producing something (the party), and her work is part of her developing her own being (as a good mother). In addition, she is doing something that is part of her relationship with her daughter. To take another example, the children who clean up after dinner while joking around are both producing a service

Labor of love: the meaning of work in the household 257

and engaged in the ordinary activities of life. The question becomes how can we disentangle "production" from simply living?

Reid does not take up the problem that the same difficulty pertains to market production, which likewise bundles the production of goods and services with simply living. Arguably, the problem is more acute when one turns to household production. If it all takes place in the household, how do we distinguish planning a birthday party from the care and support spouses offer each other in their conversations? Both "produce" something. Yet, there is more to the give and take between spouses than just "production". Reid concludes that the best way to demarcate productive household activity from that which is simply living by asking whether the activity could, in principle, be replaced by impersonal paid labor. The housewife could hire a party planner. She could not hire out someone to talk through life's issues with her husband, at least not in the way that is proper to her role as his wife.

Accordingly, Reid defines household production as

those unpaid activities which are carried on, by and for the members, which activities might be replaced by market goods, or paid services, if circumstances such as income, market conditions, and personal inclinations permit the service being delegated to someone outside the household group.[34]

The distinction between goods and services is important. As will be discussed in the next section of this chapter, the decline in the production of goods within the home plays an important role in the history of the women's movement and the transformation of the family. But the subject of the "productive" services performed within the home deserves more attention.

We often think of the work of the household as consisting in cooking, cleaning, and childcare. But as Reid and Kyrk both insist, the "service" of making a home is serious business. It is above all things the sort of work associated with the Greek notion of the *oikos*, involving the management of the income the household has earned on the market, transforming money into a valuable pattern of living. Decisions have to be made about what goods and services to purchase in the market. The goods themselves must then be fine-tuned to meet the specific needs of the family. The material conditions of family life depend on the wisdom with which money is spent and the purchased goods deployed. A well-run household is a comfortable place to live. The food consumed by the family members and the clothes they wear are well suited to their particular tastes and needs. Purchased goods will often be modified to better serve those particular tastes and needs. The hem of a dress might be let out; or an accent pillow placed to bring out the color scheme of a couch. The primary work of household production, in short, is to bring to fruition the "good" that can be had from the goods we purchase.

Thinking about household production and the way it differs from market production highlights two ways in which the market economy obscures

258   *Mary L. Hirschfeld*

elements of meaningful work. First, good homemaking requires thinking about the purpose of things, with an emphasis on arranging goods into a pattern that conduces to a harmonious and commodious manner of living. That well-defined *telos* in turn gives meaning to the labor we engage in to achieve that *telos*. By contrast, the logic of the market encourages us to buy goods piecemeal, weighing up the costs and benefits of each decision as it is made along a string of decisions. It is part of a life that does not have a coherent *telos*. Second, household production is bound up in the relationships within the family. The catering is an expression of love. The form of the good embodied in the household's manner of living expresses the household's shared conception of the good. The family with a taste for the outdoors will have a different manner of living than the family with a taste for music. That orientation to some common good, and the cultivation of the relationships within the family are the essence of realizing the fullness of human life, even more so if the family has a shared orientation toward God.

The fragmentation of the good that is embodied in the rational choice model is mirrored in the fragmentation in the family, which has increasingly moved from being a community to being a collection of individuals pursuing their respective ends. In his essay, "Reclaiming the Household", John Cuddeback observes that "the decline of the family has roots in the demise of the *household*", a distinction which is important if "we are to understand and renew family life".[35] By attending to the household, we focus on the domestic community rather than the social ties that bind people together into a "family". For Cuddeback, the key thing to notice is that in modern life, we spend little time in the household, whereas in the past, the household was the locus of most of daily life. Cuddeback has in mind the ongoing activities of family life like sharing meals or activities. But the activities that constitute "household" production are integral to the activities of a shared common life. Children raised in households with little common life lose the chance to understand the deepest meaning and purpose of labor.

An economy in which household production was still important would thus have a natural resistance to the encroachments of the habits of thought inculcated by a commercial society. It embodies the form of the virtues, at least so long as we are willing to think about the art of homemaking. Moreover, the practice of homemaking creates a household that is more naturally oriented toward formation of virtue in its members. Household production is the locus in which the goods available through market production become joined to the ongoing community life of the family. It is in the household that the human ends of economic life are fully realized, and where the deepest meaning of labor is most clearly seen. Yet, household production has been steadily declining since the rise of commercial society, a decline that has accelerated in the last several decades. Thus, we need to attend to the declining status of household production. To that subject we now turn.

Labor of love: the meaning of work in the household   259

The transition from oikos to economy: second take

The story of the rise of the modern economy takes on an extra dimension if we think through the corresponding transition in household production that accompanied it. It is a story about the shift of income-generating activities from the household to the workplace, the substitution of goods produced in the home for goods produced by the market, the impact of public utilities on the work that had to be performed in the home, and the rise and fall of domestic servants in helping families who could afford to keep up with the challenge of running a household. The value of the work of Hazel Kyrk and Margaret Reid lies in their extensive documentation of the development of household production in all of its nuances. It is beyond the scope of this chapter to do justice to the complex story they tell.[36]

For our purposes it is worth highlighting two features of the transition. The first has to do with the change of the character of goods that accompanies the shift from domestic to commercial production. The second has to do with the impact the dramatic changes to household production had on the perception of women's work and the resulting breakdown in the traditional division of labor between the sexes. To highlight both of these features, it is worth considering economics of a peasant household in the Middle Ages, one which offers the strongest contrast with the economics of a modern middle-class family in the developed world.

The changing character of commodities

In the Middle Ages, economic life was organized around manors, or clusters of peasants (serfs) who held land in their own right, and who offered labor or rent to the lords of the manor. There was little trade in the early Middle Ages; so most households were relatively self-sufficient, though there might have been some craftsmen in the village. In addition to supplying its own needs for food through farming, the household produced most of the goods it consumed – clothing, furniture, candles, soaps, medicines, and so on. Both husband and wife were vital to the economic viability of the household. Women's work had little to do with cleaning and child care. Cleaning involved replacing the straw on the floor once a year (spring cleaning), and infants were swaddled until age two. Rather, women worked raising vegetables and tending small animals, hauling water and wood, making clothing and all other goods used by the household, harvesting, and cooking. Men worked primarily in the fields. As the old rhyme put it, "a man works from sun to sun, a woman's work is never done". Indeed, not only was the wife's labor essential to the survival of the household, children were generally "assets", able to contribute to the work necessary to sustain life from young ages.

Economic development can be understood as the replacement of much household production by work done by others. At first, this would typically be done by hiring domestic servants, but later by simply buying products

260   *Mary L. Hirschfeld*

from businesses.[37] The transition through the early modern period was slow. As towns and commerce rose, it would have been more typical to purchase cloth, bread, and other basic supplies. But most of these purchases were not nearly ready for final use. The cloth must be sewn into articles of clothing. Cooking from scratch is time consuming. In addition, without the public utilities of gas/electricity and water, the work involved in heating the home, washing the clothes, and cooking the food was considerably more time-consuming than modern people are typically able to conceive of. Consider that Dorothy Day reports arranging lodging for herself in the 1920s in exchange for doing the family's laundry, work that would take up an entire day each week.[38] In the wake of the Industrial Revolution, the transition accelerated. We can see the impact of advancing capitalism by considering the shift from households that purchased flour (in the nineteenth century) to households that purchased sifted flour (early twentieth century) to households that purchased cake mixes (mid-twentieth century) to households that purchase "customized" birthday cakes at the grocery store (late twentieth century) to households that have these cakes delivered to them by grub hub (early twenty-first century).

As Hazel Kyrk observes, there are many trade-offs involved in substituting commercial products for goods that were once produced in the home.[39] On the one hand, market production avails itself of the productivity of the specialization of labor celebrated by Adam Smith. In addition, it makes more intensive use of capital equipment. The industrial oven is in continuous use, whereas the household oven is used at most a few hours a day. And market production is more amenable to continuous technological improvements. On the other hand, goods produced in the home are tailormade, and are or at least can be expressions of the relationships within the family. When I was growing up, my mother purchased most of my clothes. But every new school year, I had one outfit she had made herself, just for me. Although Kyrk herself does not discuss it, the issues raised by John Cuddeback are salient. To the extent that the family makes goods for its own use, more of family life occurs within the household. The shift to commercial production also involves a shift in the center of gravity of life away from the home and toward the market. It thus arguably contributes to the increasing atomization of human life.

There thus seems to be something of a trade-off involved. The transition to market production substantially increases the standard of living, allowing households to enjoy more and better food, clothing, and other goods. But it erodes a form of production that is more personal.

The changing status of women

But it is the second feature of the transition from *oikos* to economy that highlights the difficulty of retrieving a deeper understanding of the meaning and purpose of work. The economic transitions involved in the ever-expanding role of the market materially impacted the relative status of men and women.

Labor of love: the meaning of work in the household 261

Both Kyrk and Reid, observing the rapid transitions occurring in the early to mid-twentieth century, devote whole chapters to the status of the housewife, clearly anticipating what would become "second wave" feminism.

The problem, in a nutshell, is that as the decline in household production accelerated, the "occupation" of being a housewife became less viable. The shift away from the production of goods necessary for the household and the reduction in the labor required to do basic household work like cooking (due to the spread of electricity and gas), meant that the work of household production became less than a full time job, especially for urban families that did not have small children.[40] The transition in the nature of homemaking unfolded steadily over the decades in the wake of the Industrial Revolution. The employment of domestic servants fell dramatically. At the same time, the allocation of the time of housewives shifted. In part, the decrease in time spent producing goods and services was offset by a rise in the managerial tasks involved with running a household in a commercial society: budgeting, book keeping, and shopping. But the decline in "necessary" work also led to a shift toward more "secondary" work. Standards of living became more elaborate. Fancier meals were served, more time was spent on crafts aimed at decorating the house, and attention to child care increased (more piano lessons for Johnny). Finally, as Christopher Lasch points out, women used some of the newly freed time for volunteer work, though this movement declined as families moved out to the more atomistic suburbs.[41]

Both Kyrk and Reid observe the rising discontent with the situation, which in retrospect was a foreshadowing of the concerns that animated second-wave feminism. We often think that it was only with the rise of feminism that women began to "work". This is a misconception. As the brief history sketched here should make obvious, women have always worked. Household production was essential to the survival of the family, and it was largely undertaken by women. But as household production was increasingly displaced by the market and by the spread of public utilities, it became less clear what value to attach to the work women were doing in the home.

In part, this is due to the fact that the shift in the nature of homemaking was toward activities centered on judiciously using goods purchased in the market to make a beautiful home. I have tried to argue that if we were attuned to the virtues associated with *oikos*, it would be clear that the transition of women's works toward managing the household represented a turn toward work that was crucial to economic flourishing. The spread of markets raised our ability to generate wealth in abundance, but the economic process is not complete unless that wealth is well spent. But unfortunately for women, an economy that is focused on producing wealth does not seem to attach much value to the art of spending that wealth well. Accordingly, the important function of managing household finances, and deploying income artfully has been rendered invisible, and is therefore likely to be undervalued. A similar observation could be made about the shift in time toward improving the quality of household life. Fancier meals, more elaborate entertainments, and

262 *Mary L. Hirschfeld*

so on could all arguably be construed as part of the art of living well. But while such work could contribute to the art of living "well", it is not strictly speaking "necessary", and as Hazel Kyrk suggests, this undermines the status of women:

> The division of labor between men and women today takes the form of a concentration of the former upon gainful employment and of the latter upon non gainful. The result is an economic status for the latter that in many ways is in marked contrast to that of other workers. Here is a group producing for use and not for profit, whose incentive to efficiency and effort is not financial reward, and whose returns are largely the health and happiness of others. In a world engaged in creating exchange values these workers are creating use values. From this flows the fact previously noted that no financial value can be placed upon their services. As a consequence also the wife may be considered a dependent of the husband without a claim to money income independent of his discretion. The propriety of such a status may well be questioned. It is obviously out of harmony with our accepted ideas in regard to the appropriate relation between adults.[42]

From this perspective, the migration of married women to the paid labor force in the second half of the twentieth century is a symptom of the eclipse of our culture's sense of the importance of ordering our economic activities to a life well-lived. The very idea that married women are working only now makes sense if the work involved in producing use values is entirely invisible. The ubiquity of the idea that women only recently started to work is a measure of the force of the headwinds we face if we want to recover a richer understanding of the meaning and purpose of work. The migration of married women to the paid labor force also contributes to the fragmentation of the family.

As Gary Becker observes, as women move into the paid labor force, their contribution to the household becomes more similar to the contribution made by men.[43] The spouses become less complementary. In a traditional marriage, the spouses provide different forms of labor and thus depend on each other. But as they both become capable of providing the same thing (a paycheck), that interdependence diminishes, and we would expect, as a result, that divorce would increase. Moreover, as divorce becomes a more common outcome, women have an increased incentive to make sure they can compete in the paid labor market, so that they can support themselves in the event of a divorce. But that very effort to raise their earning power in turn reduces spousal complementarity, making divorce a more likely eventuality. At the same time, the decline in household production along with a transition away from agriculture changes the economic role of children. To use economists' perhaps unpleasant jargon, children in pre-modern society are valuable as producer goods (i.e. they can work on the farm), but in modern

Labor of love: the meaning of work in the household   263

commercial societies, they are only valuable as consumer goods (i.e. parents view children as an "expense", which is worth bearing to the extent that parents enjoy having children). The result is a decline in the number of children in the household, which in turn makes divorce less costly.

In other words, the economic transition from *oikos* to economy plays an important role in the breakdown of the family. And if the family is necessary for cultivating virtue, then there are even fewer resources available to slow down the ethos of a culture that is formed around the values of commerce.

Conclusion

The rise of commerce and the corresponding decline in household production is a crucial backdrop for thinking about the meaning and purpose of labor today. Labor in the household can never be reduced to its monetary value. Moreover, it is the form of labor that gives meaning to all of the labor leading up to it – it is the work in the household that converts the goods and services produced into the market into their final uses. Our inability to see the value of that work must have an impact on our ability to see the deepest value of labor done in the market. If we are only working for paychecks in a world that pays little attention to what we do with those paychecks, the meaning of work as a way of producing goods and services for the community is obscured.

The decline of household production also provides a useful lens for thinking through the meaning of work in an increasingly affluent culture. Most of our theological intuitions about the nature and meaning of work rest on the sort of work that must be done to survive. Yet as Reid and Kyrk point out, as women's work shifted away from the kind of work that is necessary to survive to the type of work that is necessary to make a more commodious life for the family, their status as workers declined. But in the economy at large, the share of the workforce engaged in producing the goods that are necessary for life declines as nations become wealthier. We could see this during the Covid pandemic, in which large swaths of the working population in wealthy nations could suspend working for a long period of time without threatening the survival of the nation. As long as these "inessential" occupations command salaries (and often good ones), the status of those workers will not be threatened. But we need to ask whether the fact that these occupations, well-paid though they may be, are not "essential" is not part of the rising sense that work is meaningless. It would seem that reflection on the nature of work in the home is essential if we are to understand the dimensions of work that are obscured in a commercial culture.

Notes

1 Greg Mankiw, *The Principles of Economics*, 4th ed. (Mason, OH: South-Western, 2007), 3.
2 Gary Becker, discussed further below, won a Nobel prize for his pioneering efforts in extending economic research to all areas of economic life. See Gary Becker, *The*

264　*Mary L. Hirschfeld*

Economic Approach to Human Behavior (Chicago, IL: University of Chicago Press, 1976), 3–14, for a description of his project. See Gary Becker, *A Treatise on the Family*, enlarged edition (Cambridge, MA: Harvard University Press, 1991) for an extended account of the economics of the family.

3　St. Pope John Paul II, *Laborem Exercens*, 5–6, 1981.

4　St. Pope John Paul II, *Centesimus Annus*, 36, 1991.

5　William James Booth, *Households: On the Moral Architecture of the Economy* (Ithaca, NY: Cornell University Press, 1993).

6　Aristotle, *Politics*, trans. Ernest Barker (Oxford: Oxford University Press, 1995), III. v., pp. 95–97.

7　Aristotle, *Politics*, trans. Ernest Barker (Oxford: Oxford University Press, 1995), I. viii, 1256b26, pp. 23–24.

8　Aristotle, *Politics*, trans. Ernest Barker (Oxford: Oxford University Press, 1995), I. ix, 1256b40, p. 24.

9　Aristotle, *Politics*, trans. Ernest Barker (Oxford: Oxford University Press, 1995), I. ix, 1257b35, p. 28.

10　Adam Smith, *Wealth of Nations* (New York: Bantam Dell, 2003), I.1, 14–17. As Jacob Viner, *The Role of Providence in the Social Order: An Essay in Intellectual History* (Princeton, NJ: Princeton University Press, 1972), 36–38, observes, the idea that it was part of God's providence that nations should specialize and trade with one another forms an important strand in early Christian thought. Trade creates interdependence and thus is a building block for community. It is not difficult to extend that insight to the providential design behind the economic interdependence that exists within a given community.

11　Aristotle, *Politics*, trans. Ernest Barker (Oxford: Oxford University Press, 1995), I. ix, 1257b23; Mary Hirschfeld, *Aquinas and the Market: Toward a Humane Economy* (Cambridge, MA: Harvard University Press, 2018), 119–132 discusses this distinction at length.

12　Aristotle, *Politics*, trans. Ernest Barker (Oxford: Oxford University Press, 1995), I. ix, 1257b35.

13　Economic competition will ordinarily constrain the physician who heals for the sake of money to practice good medicine. A doctor whose patients are rarely healed would not have many patients. As Aristotle said, the two arts are deceptively similar. But we can see the difference in places where a doctor makes a choice that is not in the patient's interest in order to serve his bottom line, recommending harmless but unnecessary medicines or procedures, for example.

14　Aristotle, *Politics*, trans. Ernest Barker (Oxford: Oxford University Press, 1995), I. ix, 1257a19–1257a41.

15　Karl Marx, *Capital*, Vol. I, in *The Marx-Engels Reader*, 2nd ed., ed. Robert C. Tucker (New York: W.W. Norton & Company, 1978), 329–336.

16　Mary Hirschfeld, *Aquinas and the Market: Toward a Humane Economy* (Cambridge, MA: Harvard University Press, 2018), 139–144.

17　Albert O. Hirschman, *The Passions and the Interests: Political Arguments for Capitalism Before its Triumph* (Princeton, NJ: Princeton University Press, 1977).

18　Michael Sandel, *What Money Can't Buy: The Moral Limits of Markets* (New York: Farrar, Straus and Giroux, 2012).

19　Entrepreneurship is distinguished from labor because the household is paid for labor in the form of wages and paid for entrepreneurship in the form of profits. Notice that the conception here is that the firm is a sort of empty shell that is the locus of productive economic activity. Non-economists might think of "firms" as earning profits, but ultimately, the profits earned by firms form the income of whichever households own those firms.

20　Aquinas, *Summa Theologica*, trans. Father of the English Dominican Province (Allen, TX: Christian Classics, 1948), I–II, 2.1.

Labor of love: the meaning of work in the household   265

21 Aquinas, *Summa Theologica*, trans. Father of the English Dominican Province (Allen, TX: Christian Classics, 1948), II–II, 66.7.

22 Economists assume firms are "efficient" because if nothing else, market pressures drive inefficient firms out of business. Wesley Mitchell, *The Backward Art of Spending Money and Other Essays* (New York: A.M. Kelley, 1950) observes that there is no corresponding mechanism for households. Hazel Kyrk cites him as an influence. Juliet Schor, *The Overspent American: Upscaling, Downshifting, and the New Consumer* (New York: Basic Books, 1998) is a modern economist who has turned back to the question. There are others, but the subject of "efficient" consumption is still radically underdeveloped.

23 In the early twentieth century, women with PhDs were often only able to find academic employment in home economics departments. Chemists focused on sanitation, biologists on nutrition, and economists on household production and consumption. *Rethinking Home Economics: Women and the History of a Profession*, eds. Sarah Stage and Virginia B. Vincenti (Ithica, NY: Cornell University Press, 1997).

24 Margaret Reid was named a Distinguished Fellow by the American Economic Association in 1980. Her empirical work on consumption inspired the development of important models of consumption developed by Milton Friedman and others, though those models do not pick up on the insights about consumption developed by Kyrk and Reid discussed in this chapter.

25 Adam Smith, *The Wealth of Nations*, ed. Edwin Cannan (New York: Bantam Dell, 2003), Book I, Chapter 2, 23.

26 Smith himself was a bachelor. Presumably the person whose work is made invisible by Smith's formulation was a domestic servant. As we will see, Smith did not regard any sort of domestic service, whether paid or unpaid as "productive" labor.

27 Margaret Reid, *Economics of Household Production* (New York: John Wiley & Sons, Inc., 1934), 3.

28 The same phenomenon causes us to fail to see that voluntary work contributes to the material flourishing of society, just as does paid work. See Christopher Lasch, *Women and the Common Life: Love, Marriage, and Feminism*, ed. Elisabeth Lasch-Quinn (New York: W.W. Norton & Company, 1997); for a narrative of the shift in women's economic activity that places a greater spotlight on their voluntary work.

29 Adam Smith, *The Wealth of Nations*, ed. Edwin Cannan (New York: Bantam Dell, 2003), Book II, chapter 3, 422.

30 GDP accounts do retain some sense of moral accounting. For example, black market goods are excluded, even though they are bought and sold.

31 Kelvin Lancaster arguably first developed this line of inquiry (Kelvin J. Lancaster, "A New Approach to Consumer Theory" *Journal of Political Economy* 74, no. 2 (1966): 132–157). But Becker is the one who extended and popularized it. See George Stigler and Gary Becker, "De Gustibus Non Est Disputandum" *American Economic Review* 67, no. 2: 7–90.

32 St. John Paul II, *Laborem Exercens* (1981). In *Centesimus Annus*, (1991, 36) St. John Paul II makes the crucial distinction between thinking of progress as advancement in "having" rather than advancement in "being". Work allows us to have more. But more importantly it allows us to "be" more.

33 Margaret Reid, *The Economics of Household Production*, 4–6. Viviana Zelizer, *The Social Meaning of Money: Pin Money, Paychecks, Poor Relief, and Other Currencies* (Princeton, NJ: Princeton University Press, 1997) and *The Purchase of Intimacy* (Princeton, NJ: Princeton University Press, 2005) offers a modern reflection on the difficulty of disentangling personal relationships and economic transactions.

266 *Mary L. Hirschfeld*

34 Margaret Reid, *The Economics of Household Production* (Princeton, NJ: Princeton University Press, 1997), 11.
35 John Cuddeback, "Reclaiming the Household," *First Things*, November, 2018.
36 For Hazel Kyrk's Contribution, see Hazel Kyrk, *Economic Problems of the Family* (New York: Harper & Brothers Publishers, 1929).
37 Adam Smith's dismissal of domestic service notwithstanding, domestic servants were a significant part of the labor force up until the early twentieth century. They were employed not only by the leisured aristocracy, but also by upper middle class and even lower middle class households. In Jane Austen's *Mansfield Park* (1814), for example, the "poor" sister, Mrs. Fanny Price of Portsmouth employed one servant girl.
38 Dorothy Day, *The Long Loneliness: The Autobiography of the Legendary Catholic Social Activist Dorothy Day* (New York: Harper & Row, Publishers, Inc., 1952). That entire day's work of doing the weekly wash was in a world that had running water.
39 Hazel Kyrk, *The Family in the American Economy* (Chicago, IL: University of Chicago Press, 1953), 243–269. Kyrk also reflects on economic aspects like the "waste" of market production that cannot be sold, and the advantage of household production in making productive use of the odd bits of time that emerge between other household chores.
40 Margaret Reid, *The Economics of Household Production* (Princeton, NJ: Princeton University Press, 1997), 77–92.
41 Christopher Lasch, *Women and the Common Life: Love, Marriage, and Feminism*, ed. Elisabeth Lasch-Quinn, (New York: W.W. Norton &Company, 1997).
42 Hazel Kyrk, *The Family in the American Economy* (Chicago, IL: University of Chicago Press, 1953), 275.
43 Gary Becker, *A Treatise on the Family*, enlarged edition (Cambridge, MA: Harvard University Press, 1991), 238–276; 324–361 is well worth reading on the effects of the spread of commerce on the family. For Becker, these transitions are a feature, not a bug, but he is insightful on just how much of a challenge markets pose to traditional family life.

15 Embracing better work

A reply to Jeremy Posadas

David Cloutier

In a collection of essays devoted to broad themes in a Christian theology of work, why devote a chapter to replying to a single scholar's recent essays? Because the essays by Jeremy Posadas are representative of a larger stream of thought which must be engaged; they challenge not particular themes or emphases in a theology of work, but rather the entire premise on which "theology of work" is built: that work is a fundamental aspect of human flourishing, consistent with the divine will. By contrast, Posadas "is suspicious of any claim that work is necessary for human life on any grounds other than purely technological" and "places the burden of proof on those who wish to maintain the moral or ontological necessity of work, to demonstrate how such a position is not simply a rationalization of the work-society's governing ethic".[1]

In this essay, I will engage Posadas' specific arguments, but I also contextualize those arguments within a broader stream of thought which his work may be said to represent. Similar arguments from Christian theology and ethics have been made recently by Kathryn Tanner, and it connects to themes found in some secular writers.[2] One could call this the "anti-work" position, although "less work" or "minimizing work" might be a more accurate representation of their claims. I will argue that the "less work" position is comprehensible against the historical background of achieving what I call "good-enough work" for large segments of the population, while compromising the further goal of "good work". As such a compromise frays, proponents of "less work" constitute a powerful alternative to theologies of good work. In responding to them, I first examine Posadas' definition of "work", suggesting that his implied target is either too narrow or too comprehensive – his argument for less work is really about (1) less work *for a certain set of workers* or it is about (2) less work *because it defines all work as a form of wage enslavement* to capital. Since the latter argument seems most decisive in his work, I then articulate why and how this is an unconvincing description of the actual work done by large numbers of people, even in today's economy (which, like Posadas, I think also needs substantial improvement). I then suggest that anti-work arguments ultimately rest on an anthropology of spontaneous freedom that fails to understand the *distinction* between

DOI: 10.4324/9781003508212-18

268   *David Cloutier*

work and play, but also implicitly *dichotomizes* the two things, disabling a proper understanding of the ways adult work integrates play in order to exhibit a human freedom that discovers deeper joy in and through the finitude that makes necessary the focus, cooperation, and discipline involved in work within a system of market exchange.

The historical background for the anti-work position

Discussions of work in the modern world implicitly assume a certain background, that of the "dark satanic mills" of early industrial England, the brutal steel mills and slaughterhouses of late nineteenth-century Chicago, or (more recently) the Third-world "sweatshops" making First-world fashion or electronics.[3] It remains the case that sub-human conditions, exploitative and unjust compensation, and even forms of enslavement are realities in today's world. In an earlier essay, I write about these struggles in terms of achieving "good-enough" work.[4]

But what then? Particularly in developed societies with widespread (if incomplete) enforcement of labor laws, the answer has not always been clear. This juncture – where to go with the ethical analysis of work in situations where good-enough work has been achieved – is where the conversation with anti-work needs to start. In my prior essay, I make a distinction between achieving "good-enough" work and truly "good" work, work that is truly humanizing.[5] The idea of "good work" is most prominent for Catholics in John Paul II's *Laborem Exercens* – work that is "for man", in which the subject "decides about himself" and "fulfill[s] the calling to be a person that is his by reason of his very humanity".[6] The idea of improving the *quality* of work is also found in many secular commentators. Moreover, many common choices people make in effect focus on work *quality*: they may accept lower pay to stay at a firm where they have more autonomy or better co-workers, they may support their children's education so they can have a job that is more fulfilling (and not just more lucrative), etc.

Yet, as my previous essay argues, this attempt to move forward toward "good work" has far less traction in our social discussions. In many parts of the world (even in formerly impoverished countries, like China), there has been great progress in achieving good-enough work; the further development of truly good work, especially on a society-wide level, has not gotten nearly as far. Why?

In a very illuminating and characteristically wide-ranging essay from the early 1980s, Charles Taylor describes a key answer to this problem. He notes that much modern work is "dull, monotonous, without meaning", and that work structures do not put the wage worker in a position of autonomy and equality, but subordinates him or her to orders determined from above.[7] In this description, Taylor captures something of the conundrum of stopping at "good-enough work" – if the factory worker of the 1970s had enough legal and union protection to ensure basic safety and solid

Embracing better work   269

compensation ("good-enough"), he or she was under no illusion that the work was actually good.[8]

Taylor suggests the situation is poorly analyzed by Marxist tools, since what has happened is a compromise: "the compromise consists in accepting alienated labour in return for consumer affluence".[9] Postwar workers were more or less willing participants in the bargain, trading off any sense of full citizenship at work in favor of enough compensation and time off (including, at that time, retirement on a pension) to pursue private ends, primarily of consumption. However, the labor unrest of the late 1960s and 1970s (which under-1950s are apt to forget) questioned this bargain, which suggests to Taylor that consumerism "is a victim of its own success".[10] He explains that it may have seemed like a worthwhile bargain to make for those "still struggling to make decent housing and basic consumer durables" widely available – and it should not be forgotten that the original participants in the postwar bargain had experienced decades of upheaval from the Depression and World War II. But the basic vision of suburban prosperity, especially for a generation that grew up with it, increasingly did *not* seem like a worthwhile trade-off, especially if (as Taylor points out) the work just produces more and more frills and embellishments. Moreover, he adds that the fragmentation of the family, the increased congestion, the cost crises produced by infla-tion, and alienation from government accompanying mass urbanization all increase the discontent. Microwave ovens and VCRs were not nearly enough to compensate.

Despite the fragility of the 1970s, I suggest that the basic bargain or compromise – good-enough but "alienated" work in exchange for private security and increasing affluence – was never really rethought. The alienated work of the 1990s might have been in office cubicles rather than factories; today, it may be getting stuck in endless email chains and zoom meetings. But people endured it for what Juliet Schor, in her "less-work" bestseller of the early 1990s, *The Overworked American*, called the "work-and-spend cycle".[11] Meanwhile, gradually, those who remained in blue-collar or low-level service jobs – still necessary for the economy, but less of a force than were the working middle-class of the postwar age – saw their lives as increasingly precarious, their communities as decaying, and the lives of their children as less and less likely to even reach the level of their parents, much less rising to someplace "better". Oren Cass' late 2010s book, *The Once and Future Worker*, suggests that, beneath working-class political anger, is a long-term set of economic trade-offs in which the United States imple-mented policies favorable to ever-increasing upper-middle-class consumption at the expense of meaningful, remunerative, and above all stable jobs for the working class.[12] In complementary ways at different times in recent eco-nomic history, Schor and Cass depict the decades-long fragile state of the "alienated-work-for-increasing affluence" compromise.

Today, especially amidst the 2010s, discussions about "the end of work" in the face of new technologies and the fundamental disruptions of work

270 David Cloutier

structure during the pandemic, the anti-work approach has found some new, albeit still limited, energy. A 2022 BBC feature article explains the position:

Anti-work, which has roots in anarchist and socialist economic critique, argues that the bulk of today's jobs aren't necessary; instead, they enforce wage slavery and deprive workers of the full value of their output. That doesn't mean there would be no work, however. Supporters of the anti-work movement believe people should self-organize and labor only as much as needed, rather than working longer hours to create excess capital or goods.[13]

However, the article's examples also display a less radical position: workers in better bargaining positions simply seek improved conditions or, failing that, better jobs with other employers. The contentious arguments over work-from-home are a microcosm of this approach. Work-from-home obviously produces significant non-work benefits for many – in effect, it is a kind of "less work" position, although the actual productivity and even work hours of any individual vary. At the same time, employers have increasingly pushed back, as evidence mounts about the decrease in productivity, especially in terms of coordination problems and in the lack of informal wisdom-sharing characteristic of in-person workplaces.

This historical narrative is the backdrop against which the anti-work position makes sense. As is clear in Posadas' article, despite the provocative title of the "refusal" of work, his position is really one that seeks to move from the achievement of "good-enough" work to a further goal of "less" work. Thus, it can be seen as the alternative to a position (which I defend, and which I take to be the standard Catholic position) that our society must move beyond "good-enough" work toward "good work" – that is, not toward *less* work, but higher-quality work, work that truly humanizes the worker.

Less work vs. good work: contending views

I turn to Posadas' actual argument with this narrative in mind, because he explicitly objects to the approach of trying to make work "good". His essays criticize numerous Christian authors of the past two decades that extol work, and then seek to improve work that falls short of the ideal they propose. He dubs this the project of "redeeming work".[14] The project identifies some "work-in-its-essence" that is fundamentally good, and then explains how actual work is corrupted by various factors and must be reformed (332).

As with many disagreements about the ethics of work, the most important starting point is to examine more closely what "work" means. Posadas makes clear he is not against activity. He says he is "pro-productive activity and creativity, but anti-work as a way of organizing them". (349) Thus, in his denying the claim that God or Christ "works", he does not mean to deny divine activity.

Rather, he says that, "God makes concentrated efforts, pursues planned action, persists, creates, produces, distributes, cares, provides, sacrifices, struggles against difficulties, and does many other activities that workers

Embracing better work   271

do", but "if one wishes to say, in addition, that God is a worker or that work is part of God's nature, one must justify why it is accurate to understand these divine activities *in terms of the earning of wages*", as opposed to some other characterization of the activity (355; italics added).

Anti-work: two (distinguishable) targets

What does he mean? In the prior remark, I think we can start to discern and distinguish two targets in his overall critique. The first pages of his essay hint at one target: the "work" he is critiquing is work for wages that offer little or no economic flexibility and tied directly to the number of hours worked. Throughout the paper, he criticizes the connection between work and "daily necessities", a connection most visible for those with little cushion, living paycheck to paycheck, always in fear of an unexpected major expense that will wreck everything. At one point, he indicates he wants to "denaturalize" the idea that humans all have to and should have to work for necessities. His favored social theorist explains that something like wage work may remain a "technological necessity", but it "should be limited as much as possible" such that we are "no longer so thoroughly and relentlessly dependent on work" (350).

In light of this, it is perhaps not surprising that, without much elaboration, he announces that the preferred policy paths for this anti-work vision are a version of universal basic income and an immediate reduction to a 30-hour work week, but with no wage reduction. In both cases, the goal here is to reduce the extent to which work – and long hours of work – is a *necessity* for people to make ends meet. At this point, his proposal looks more reformist than it did at the outset. In effect, the position is: don't worry about jobs beyond "good-enough" for this group, just give people more time off and (crucially) allow them to opt-out. He writes,

> From the standpoint of the refusal of work, it is not self-evident why Christian theology and ethics should accept any system in which people cannot, unless they work, have access to the things necessary for living with basic human dignity.
>
> (352)

There is a sense in which this claim about the non-necessity of work is accepted by moral theology: basic human dignity is owed to all, even those who can't work. To care for the biblical "widows and orphans" is to care for those who do not have a head of household to care for them – and who presumably can't or shouldn't work. The early church example in Acts, where possessions are distributed "according to need" (see Acts 2:45; 4:35), emphasizes the distribution specifically to widows (Acts 6:1). But "widows and orphans" are evidently understood as "dependents".[15] The claim of the impoverished relies on the idea that *most* wives and children are supported

272   *David Cloutier*

by the work of the head of household – it is his absence that calls forth generosity. The biblical teaching presumes what would *have* to be presumed in the ancient world – namely, (most) people had to work. While ancient Israel's history does not reveal a classless society, it does suggest norms that are clearly more egalitarian than most societies of the time and frequently threatens the wealthy if they do not exercise generosity. But the background presumption is that most people can and should work. In the great Psalm 104 praising the order of God's creation by describing the different lives of plants and animals, the psalmist writes of the human animal: "People go out to their work, to their labor till evening falls" (v. 23). The Hebrew *Bible* throughout is the product of an agrarian society of work, one that goes wrong whenever it seeks excessive wealth or military power.

A "good work" position would address Posadas' concerns in a different way. At the heart of his first targeted concern are workers who are "trapped" in situations where they are more or less forced to take poor, irregular hours in insecure positions that pay a wage barely equal to or less than their expenses.[16] Such workers, as they age, do not find advancement, but instead find that they are increasingly expendable. What such workers lack most of all is even the *hope* of finding a longer-term path to security and stability. The early encyclicals pay serious attention to this problem (Pius XI calls it "the lot of the proletarian"), but they consistently suggest that the response is to (1) pay better wages, so that (2) workers can be "freed from hand-to-mouth uncertainty", and eventually (3) "acquire a certain moderate ownership", including through creative forms of organization like partnerships.[17] We may today look at the wealth-building potential in retirement investment plans or long-term homeownership as very imperfect substitutes for the kind of thing Leo XIII sought when he said that "the law should favor ownership and its policy should be to induce as many people as possible to become owners".[18] But they are a form of economic security for necessities. Perhaps better are the forms of mutualism, like cooperatives, praised by Benedict XVI,[19] and movements like the Economy of Communion.[20] Further, that the economy should be "human in scale"[21] is an idea that has received too little attention in Catholic social thought. It seems evident that, while "small business" can be romanticized, there are scale questions that can even be applied to large employers, and they are also certainly relevant to overcoming a sense of malaise and disempowerment, as well as better taking account of ecological responsibilities at the root level.[22] All these paths aim at removing the marginality and fragility of the workers in the position Posadas describes, but by moving actual working conditions in the direction of more ownership, participation, control, and security – that is, better work. There is no doubt that Posadas is right that there are very powerful "defaults" in the capitalist system that work against these paths, but he neglects the fact that these paths are "realistic" in the sense that we can point to many examples of them.

Of course, this image of "good work" means increasing responsibility and perhaps "more" work – as an early twentieth-century Catholic social teaching text pointed out, there are also advantages to what it calls "the labor contract or salariate" – namely, that the worker is somewhat sheltered from overall responsibility for all aspects of the firm and can leave freely, among other things.[23] The wage worker can just "do her job" – the *partner* must pay more attention to the overall health of the enterprise.

That greater investment in the work, however, is the target of Posadas' second, more sweeping understanding of the "work" that he is against. He states his position as "rejecting capitalism's demand that people be integrated as fully as possible into the profit-generating modern-day work structure" (348–49). He criticizes Esther Reed's reformist proposals, which otherwise he views as the strongest of the writers he surveys, insofar as they concede "that work should continue playing the dominant role it has in structuring human life today" (342). Claims about the intrinsic goodness of work, he says at another point, "are nearly always used to justify the kind of work that capital needs in order to maximize its profit" (353).

This critique, as I see it, has two prongs: one, the extent to which work becomes life-defining and identity-defining, and two, the fact that making work central to one's identity in this way ultimately (in our structures) serves the interests of capital.[24] Such a claim, of course, could be applied as easily to harried Uber drivers and poorly paid medical assistants as to exhausted (if salaried) Wall Street traders and Walmart store managers. That is, the critique of work's centrality for life applies both to the lower-wage, strapped wage workers and to those who do not have the same kind of constraints. If you make the conditions of work better but allow it to continue to have the place in life that we have given it, Posadas wants to claim, you still do not serve "life".[25] The refusal of work, he says, aims ultimately at making "work less present and less necessary in everyone's life, in order to make more time and capacity available for collectively experimenting with new ways of being and being-together" (350).

The moral force of these claims hinges, I think, mostly on the latter prong. Presumably, if our activity is *not* ultimately in service to capital, it might be understood as a form of "collectively experimenting" – and that such activity could be central to our lives. Indeed, this prong is fundamental to understanding the less work/good work debate. Advocates of good work simply do not make the assumption that Posadas does about a "work ethic" always ultimately serving capital. Good work advocates admit that work-centrality can function in this way, but that this is not a necessity. For example, John Paul makes it clear that a fundamental component (if not *the* fundamental component) of Catholic social teaching on work is "the principle of the priority of labor over capital" in which "the only legitimate title to [the] possession [of capital goods] … is that they should serve labor", and not the other way around.[26] This is so central because it is a form of the deeper moral claim "of the primacy of man in the production process, the primacy of man over things".[27] The error of "economism" – to assume "the opposition of labor and capital" – is common to both laissez-faire capitalists and doctrinaire

274   David Cloutier

socialists. There is here a fundamental conflict between the pope's hope and Posadas' account – who is right?

Can capital serve labor? Some responses

I want to argue first and foremost that Posadas' abstract description unfairly reduces work to a caricature, creating a spurious dichotomy between "work" that is in fact a quasi-enslavement to employers and "life" that involves spontaneous, satisfying activity with others – a dichotomy that finds its plausibility against the backdrop of the earlier-described postwar compromise. But this is not how many people understand their work. Many people's experience of work – and perhaps especially a work to which one is devoted over a long period of time – is of activity that is intrinsically satisfying.[28] A recent feature article offered a number of stories about professional workers who said they would "never" retire.[29] The primary reasons are neither about dutifulness nor money, but rather about how much satisfaction they get from the work they do. While a number of them tellingly suggest that, freed from monetary necessity, they have shifted the *shape* of their work – for example, one attorney moved from a practice to an independent operation to enable her to take only the cases she found most interesting – most do not describe this primarily in terms of "less" work. Most of these anecdotes reinforce both the goodness of work and also the need to think *strategically* about how to "make work good" that is the hallmark of the "good work" position.

It is wrong to imagine that this only applies to "professional" workers – rather, what we need to be doing is asking structural questions about why some workers and professions seem more able to do this than others. It's certainly the case that many people in skilled manufacturing and trades view their work in this manner. Michael Naughton's outstanding book *Getting Work Right* – perhaps the best single volume out there describing the Catholic imaginary on work – outlines how providing good work is ultimately about "gift recognition", that this gift recognition is encapsulated in the principle of subsidiarity, and that "businesses can coordinate the gifts of their workers by doing three things: (1) designing work well, (2) educating and equipping employees, and (3) trusting that those employees will do their work well".[30] Naughton isn't naive about the forces that distract and distort ownership decisions away from these objectives, but he also provides many examples of workplaces in which they serve both workers and the business, and he quips, "despite what Dilbert says, businesses have made a lot of progress in humanizing work".[31] Proponents of "good work" should aim at pushing these questions about job design, training, and opportunities for creativity in *all* types of jobs.

Views like Posadas' – perhaps unintentionally – denigrate all the efforts Naughton describes. Naughton is no apologist for neoliberal capitalism, any more than is John Paul II! Rather, Naughton enables us to look more carefully and with much more attentiveness to how the economy actually

Embracing better work 275

works, to see both real successes and abject failures – and better explain both. Ironically, it is descriptions of the economy like Posadas' that mirror the sweeping generalizations of the very pro-market fundamentalists they oppose. For example, waged employment is "performed for the purpose of making a profit for the employer, and the ultimate purpose of profits is to expand the privately owned wealth of employers",[32] and capitalism itself "is a parasite that infests human communities and forces their webs of care to produce the workforce it needs in order to generate the profits it craves".[33] Recent decades are characterized as the "period of neoliberal capitalism's vicious war on the working class" and reformist attempts to improve work are dismissed as lying "within capitalism's conceptual death grip".[34] These framing claims paint the world in black-and-white, either-or terms. They are sweeping cartoons whose real truth in critiquing capitalism is undermined by the lack of any attention to the complexities of real economies and real practice. A further irony is that Posadas is critical of positive theologies of work for being "abstract", insisting that any adequate theological treatment of work must recognize that work "only exists in concrete forms, not in the abstract" (354) – but then himself gives extraordinarily abstract and theoretical macroeconomic accounts!

As important as the sense of self-satisfaction and personal development that is present in many people's work (and is possible for all, though never without periods of toil in a fallen world) is the further satisfaction arising from understanding one's work as a service that does good for others. Posadas' description neglects the way in which our work does not simply serve an employer, but rather serves *others*. It is widely understood that to describe a job as "paper-pushing" and to be unclear about how one's work "matters" are intuitive ways of wanting to understand our work as serving others. As Darby Ray puts it, "service is not something we are summoned to do on the side. Rather, it should be the center of our activity".[35]

Oliver O'Donovan offers a helpful description along these lines: "work is the point at which our exertions are *depended on* by others". Thus, he says, "in work, we spin a thread tough enough for others to weave with".[36] He uses as an example the difference between a host who invites some friends over for dinner from a chef who runs a restaurant; crucially, both the other workers and the customers *depend on* the chef in a way that does not apply to the former activity (which is of course also good). This description is valuable insofar as it helps us see that the importance of reliable, sustained work *commitments* in people's lives is not just a matter of the "needs" of capital; instead, it makes possible an economy in which we can count on open restaurants, fully staffed flights, and stocked grocery shelves, among hundreds of other things. A key reason to work hard and diligently is because the work serves the needs of others. The times when I am most cynical about my job are surely when I feel like I'm doing it "for the University" – but at best, I am regularly reminded that I am working for others, and above all for my students.

276   *David Cloutier*

It is simply wrong to assume that an emphasis on service is merely a smokescreen for getting more profits. Such service is possible in so many positions. While anecdotes are always just anecdotes, my university recently named the main dining room in the new dining hall after Willie Joyner. "Ms. Willie", as she is known, has worked for dining service at Catholic University since 1974, and is beloved by generations of students for her unfailingly warm and generous presence in various positions throughout the changing years. Remarkably, many alums described Ms. Willie's work in terms of "mentorship", so much more than a friendly hello. She knew countless students by name, called them her "babies", and keeps up with many through texts and emails. In a *Washington Post* feature piece on her life, Joyner herself described her work: "It was all about love. It was all about respect".[37] It is safe to say that Joyner consistently saw her work as something more than the utilitarian functions for which she received a paycheck. She made of it as much of a service as she could, and happily, she was repaid in countless ways for that. It is lamentable that, in many workplaces, there cannot be "Ms. Willies" because employers do not value such service, or even give workers the sort of autonomy that's needed for them to be able to give this time. Ms. Willie says about the honor of the naming that "It lets me know I am doing the right thing at Catholic and in God's name".[38] The problem with Posadas' account is that it cannot make sense of these descriptions, except as either deep self-deception or a rare exception to the rule. I reject the first, and the second ignores the fact that there are many such stories about a life of good work. The "good work" position wants more and more of them – and insists that, insofar as this is *not* the experience of many workers, we must work to change that. This desire to improve work is not an abstract argument from "work-in-its-essence", but from examples like Willie Joyner's concrete lifetime of service.

The fact that non-paid work can serve in this essential way also does not invalidate the point. It is correct that non-paid work, especially in the family, and especially by women, is devalued by an economic system that puts a premium (literally) on paid work. This point should certainly strengthen the need for a family wage or other social structures that visibly "compensate" work in the home and indicate its value to the society. At the same time, there are good reasons why we expect parents to do the work of child-rearing primarily out of love, just as we expect some social activity to exclude monetary exchange.[39]

More importantly on this point, Posadas does not really make clear what alternative structure of committed and coordinated mutual service would be as or more effective in meeting people's needs. A recent biography indicates that he is "formulating the concept of the 'cogenerative commonwealth', an eco-queer economic framework that offers an alternative to capitalism".[40] Any such proposal faces the paradoxical challenge well-characterized by Yves Simon in his analysis of the idea of "work made attractive" in early socialists like Fourier and Marx: a necessarily very highly organized collectivist account of production married with a suggestion that people will be able

Embracing better work 277

to do fully and precisely what they want to do. Simon quotes Marx's famous statement that

> society regulates the general production and thus makes it possible for me to do one thing today and another tomorrow, to hunt in the morning, fish in the afternoon, rear cattle in the evening, criticize after dinner, just as I have a mind, without ever becoming hunter, fisherman, shepherd, or critic.[41]

In such a vision, it seems inevitable that either the collectivization will in fact be quite destructive to human freedom *or* the "just-as-I-have-a-mind" free action will result in a failure to produce necessary goods and services. To argue, as Weeks seems to do, that we need to open up space to imagine alternatives overlooks the fact that we have a history of attempts to conceive and implement practical alternatives, and neither Weeks nor Posadas seems to give any account of why these efforts fail or peter out. Ownership and market exchange may be characterized as the "least bad" way of organizing large-scale service of needs – rather than extolling it – but at the same time, it has developed a track record at the point. When implemented in "inclusive" rather than "extractive" ways, the typical features of capitalist economics do enable economic development that is widely beneficial.[42]

A deeper anthropological problem: the fascination with spontaneous activity

This practical lacuna in fact opens up an even deeper problem at the level of anthropology, one which is brought out by understanding the importance of human dependence and interdependence in the previous discussion. Posadas' work rests on a normative fascination with human freedom as autonomy. It is not a coincidence that, in another essay, he emphasizes the importance of "reproductive justice", in which persons "enjoy liveliness and living with joy" freed from the necessity of wage labor, and with "unconditional self-determination" of everything related to their body and sexuality, so that "all pregnancy-capacitated persons have access to the full spectrum of procreative justice".[43] This normative picture of the human person and human flourishing places self-determination above everything else, and resists any notion of "dependence" that is not continually open to one's free choice.[44] Such an imaginary suggests the best activity is spontaneous and authentic. It is activity that is not determined in any way by political obligations, by familial responsibilities, or by economic authorities. At one point, questioning the image of God as worker, he says, "On what grounds is it better to conceptualize God's activities as God's work rather than as (for example) God's art, God's *eros*, or even God's hobby?" (333).

Such a description leads straight to the concept of "play". What Posadas is describing is a world with less work… and more play.[45] Posadas unfortunately

278   *David Cloutier*

does not theorize the work/play distinction. The theoretical discussion of "play" is complicated and contested;[46] that said, one consistent element in it is the identification of play with a kind of autonomy and free activity that opposes the "compulsion" of work.[47] Any "anti-work" approach is going to run quickly into the problem that, in consumer societies, "play" is most often tied up with activities of expensive consumption; a further difficulty would be, at least in the American context, the increasingly "play-less" character of highly structured and supervised childhood, in which children are never given the opportunity to just go out with other kids and "play".[48] Thus, if anti-work advocates want to encourage more skillful, cooperative ways of being together, they will have to vigorously oppose the commercialization of play and helicopter parenting, both of which disable agents from the kind of "good play" that Posadas wants to encourage.

Yet the real problem here is to identify human flourishing so strongly with completely autonomous and spontaneous activities. Indeed, one of the difficulties with the work/play distinction is that "play" itself is often highly structured and makes demands on its participants (e.g. "fair play" or sportsmanship). In many cases, children "play" by mimicking adult work, and even animal playthings replicate the natural "work" the creatures do.[49] Posadas' appeal to a social order in which all people can "live with joy and enjoy liveliness" seems to neglect this point. By contrast, if we look at MacIntyre's account of practices, we see that – while he is just as relentlessly critical of capitalist distortions – his alternative does not look like a spontaneous, self-organized (though government-supported) commune-like commonwealth. MacIntyre thinks one must learn right desire (=virtue) over time in lasting cooperative activity, and his examples have a hard-nosed realism that is lacking in anti-work accounts. His most recent work includes examples that are drawn from competitive business – he cites at some length the writings of the management consultant W. Edwards Deming and how they transformed auto manufacturing in Japan in a way that both empowered workers and vastly improved the quality of Japanese cars in a competitive marketplace.[50] MacIntyre's examples are animated by the sense that St. Josemaría Escrivá focused on in discussing the holiness of work: that it be "well done and lovingly completed" with "a careful concern for the quality of ...everyday work".[51] A shared commitment to well-done work is necessary for true cooperation; it is not an accident that MacIntyre's fundamental anthropology rests on what he calls "virtues of acknowledged dependence", in which the self-determination of the individual is in fact a matter of belonging and membership with and for others.[52] Capitalism in MacIntyre distorts work via pleonexia, but this distortion is ultimately rooted in an anthropology and an account of practical reason that portrays happiness in terms of preference maximization – suspiciously similar to the hobby-like activity Posadas seems to favor. This approach matches the insightful (and still neglected) account of "superdevelopment" in John Paul II's *Sollicitudo Rei Socialis* and *Centesimus Annus*, in which he affirms the need to continue to seek "good-enough" work

Embracing better work   279

in underdeveloped economies, but astutely recognizes that the challenges in developed economies are different.[52] Thus, the problems of pleonexia and preference satisfaction (and, I would add, the underlying vice of luxury)[54] are left largely unaddressed in Posadas.

By contrast with an approach that insists on spontaneous play-like activity *over* work, the "good work" approach insists, as Burke does, that "both [play and work] are equally free and intrinsically motivated, apart from false economic conditions which tend to make play into idle excitement for the well to do and work into uncongenial labor for the poor".[55] This suggests not a collapsing of the distinction, but rather a sense that work has possibilities of "being playful" (and play has possibilities of being "good work") that resists what Michael Naughton characterizes as "the divided life".[56] Posadas, insofar as he does not eliminate work (and what would that mean?), continues to endorse a divided life, one in which toil and joy, obligation and spontaneity, self-emptying and self-realization are *separated* into two opposing spheres. I'm suggesting here that he needs to think more deeply about play, and in particular whether he is captivated by an unrealistic (and ultimately consumerist) view of spontaneity, autonomy, and preference satisfaction that leads him to be unable to see the real possibilities for transformation in the world of work that still retains a formal economic structure involving imperatives like market incentives and efficiency trade-offs.[57]

This affirmation of the importance of work is associated with what Vatican II termed "the universal call to holiness". I do not think the Catholic intellectual tradition has yet come to terms with this; it surely means some re-thinking of the hierarchical distinction of the active and contemplative lives, and of the analogous hierarchy borrowed from classical philosophy between work and leisure. When I say "re-thinking", I do not mean rejection. As John Hughes argues, using Josef Pieper's classic book, the importance of defending leisure in the modern world is to resist the "totalitarian claims" of the "realm of utility".[58] Hughes notes that for Pieper, the problem is turning all of life into "utility… so those other realms of non-utility are either abolished or forced to conform to this alien logic".[59] Philosophy becomes about "production" and time off is not sabbath but merely a recuperative "break from work". Like Pieper and Hughes, Posadas' argument can be understood as attempting to minimize the dominance of a utility-maximizing approach to human activity.

The resistance to the tyranny of "utility" is in principle correct, but the line between some activity as "useful" and some activity as being "of service" is hard to draw – just as a well-made object or well-tended farm can be both beautiful and useful. The continued presence of the work/leisure or work/play hierarchies obscure the real promise of a theology of work: that a true "marriage" of nature and grace, of human and divine, can open up possibilities of deeply human living beyond a work/play dichotomy that open us up to the infinite *through* our finitude and mutual dependence. This is surely what Benedict XVI is aiming at when he insists that "quotas of gratuitousness"

280 David Cloutier

must be present "within" and not simply "after" economic activity. This is what Catholic marriage theology has aimed at after the Council. It is the promise that nature – in this case, the work of our hands that provides sustenance and beauty for our earthly life together – can be transformed by grace.

Posadas resists the "grammar of creation" as a guide for true freedom in finitude; this guide requires both a certain sort of work (which, it is true, capitalism can distort) and a certain kind of sexual relationship (which is also distorted by capitalism, especially insofar as its consumeristic ethic of self-determination and enjoyment comes to apply to sexual relations). Indeed, as I argue more fully in my other essay, we find a strange bedfellow for the anti-work fascination with maximizing autonomy: the consumerist eschatology of standard economic treatment of labor as a disvalue to be minimized.[60] Far from a challenge to consumerist capitalism, Posadas' view rests on the same vision of human flourishing as maximum individual autonomy, with the proviso that workers should be able to consume more of the productivity gains – another version of the postwar compromise described at the beginning of my essay. By contrast, if a cogenerative commonwealth looks like MacIntyre's communities of shared practice, it will *not* be because those communities maximize autonomy or overall "productivity" ordered to maximum (but re-allocated) consumption. Rather, these communities will ask critical questions about how work can be organized in ways that preserve productivity, but better allow for joy *in* the work itself. They will explore how the "first principle" of the whole order, the universal destination of goods, can be achieved "through labor", as John Paul insists it must.[61]

Conclusion: beyond the postwar compromise

Capital serves labor, but labor serves people, whose good work then serves the truly common good. This is the alternative to the postwar compromise, which was unable to conceive of this common good except in terms of ever-growing private consumption. Catholic Social Teaching from *Rerum Novarum* to *The Vocation of the Business Leader* has developed a consistent position: all people must receive the rights and protections for "good-enough work", and that societies should move toward an "integral human development" in which "every life is a vocation"[62] and every worker realizes themselves in their work. Ultimately, this self-realization is found in understanding one's whole life as a gift. Such an approach is not merely a romanticized vision, but a practical social project that (with many problems and setbacks) is the road forward for Catholic social ethics.

In this paper, I have tried to show what assumptions and deeper narratives animate the alternative social project: the one, represented by Posadas, promising to move us toward "less work". While the "less work" and "good work" visions share many of the critiques of the present order, the "less work" vision misunderstands both the human person and the real economy – in both cases, the misunderstanding is ultimately an oversimplification – and so

Embracing better work 281

presents a vision that is mistaken. In practice, the anti-work position requires a highly bureaucratized state economy (which is unlikely to present us with good work) or an economy that simply gives us more "play time" – a position that ultimately remains within the postwar compromise. Instead, we must both work with and shape market economic activity such that it aimed at its real end: persons, and their giving of themselves to one another. This is not only *possible* through truly adult work; it can be a cause of great joy and celebration in living our lives here and now in the reciprocal self-giving of finite creatures in ways that point toward God's transformation of those gifts in eternity.

Notes

1 Jeremy Posadas, "The Refusal of Work in Christian Ethics and Thelogy: Interpreting Work from an Anti-work Perspective," *Journal of Religious Ethics* 45, no. 2 (2017): 330–361, here 353. Further citations in text.
2 Kathryn Tanner, *Christianity and the New Spirit of Capitalism* (New Haven, CT: Yale University Press, 2019), I engage her argument in relation to Joseph Ratzinger's Christology in "(Christ's) Work Is the Key to the Social Question", *Modern Theology* 36, no. 2, (2020): 378–390.
3 For an excellent recent study of the history of this struggle, especially how it expands to become more inclusive of various social groups, see Christine Firer Hinze, *Radical Sufficiency: Work, Livelihood, and a US Catholic Economic Ethic* (Washington, DC: Georgetown University Press, 2021).
4 David Cloutier, "The Worker's Paradise: Eternal Life, Economic Eschatology, and Good Work as the Keys to Social Ethics", *Plenary Address, Catholic Theological Society of America*, June 2021; published in *Proceedings of 75th Annual Meeting of the Catholic Theological Society of America* 75 (2021): 37–55, https:// ejournals.bc.edu/index.php/ctsa/issue/view/1211.
5 David Cloutier, "The Worker's Paradise: Eternal Life, Economic Eschatology, and Good Work as the Keys to Social Ethics", *Plenary Address, Catholic Theological Society of America*, June 2021; published in *Proceedings of 75th Annual Meeting of the Catholic Theological Society of America* 75 (2021):, 41–42, https:// ejournals.bc.edu/index.php/ctsa/issue/view/1211.
6 *Laborem Exercens*, #6.
7 Charles Taylor, "Legitimation Crisis?," *Philosophy and the Human Sciences: Philosophical Papers 2* (New York: Cambridge University Press, 1985), 248–288, at 278.
8 See, for example, the descriptions of his work offered by Mike Lefevre, a steelworker, in Studs Terkel's classic *Working* (New York: Pantheon Books, 1974), xxxi–xxxviii.
9 Charles Taylor, "Legitimation Crisis?", *Philosophy and the Human Sciences: Philosophical Papers 2* (New York: Cambridge University Press, 1985), 279.
10 Charles Taylor, "Legitimation Crisis?", *Philosophy and the Human Sciences: Philosophical Papers 2* (New York: Cambridge University Press, 1985), 282.
11 Schor's book, from a different era, provides an interesting comparison to Posadas: while critical of structural incentives that favor employers to push longer hours, she also recognizes the "pull" that many workers have toward the increased consumption possible by more work. Posadas has nothing to say about the "work-and-spend" dynamic that is central to her account. Perhaps most interesting in her study (for suggesting that it is not capitalism per se that is the problem) is her recognition that from 1948 to 1969, there was little rise in overall working

282 David Cloutier

hours, whereas from 1969 to the early 1990s, there has been a steady increase in hours – and that multiple factors contribute to the difference. See *The Overworked American* (New York: Basic Books, 1992), 79–81.

12 See Oren Cass, *The Once and Future Worker* (New York: Encounter: 2018), 1–6.

13 Brian O'Connor, "The Rise of the Anti-work Movement", https://www.bbc.com/worklife/article/20220126-the-rise-of-the-anti-work-movement.

14 He especially criticizes three typical claims of these projects: the idea that work is intrinsic to our humanity, that work is essentially "imago Dei" in the sense that God works, and that economically degrading work can be transformed into something worthwhile. The first and third points, as I will describe later, ignore the experience of many who find work intrinsically humanizing and satisfying, and who have made efforts to transform work in the current economy into something good. On the second point, Scripture itself seems to attribute to God in creation the fact of "work", it sanctions work in part because of the commandment for sabbath rest (which even God takes, and is explicitly cited as the analogy for the human sabbath [Ex 20:8–11]), and (perhaps more importantly, but ignored by Posadas) it seems clear that Christ, as the imago of both God and humanity, worked, both in the (more peripheral) carpenter sense and in the (more central) sense of his work of ministry.

15 Obviously, whom we judge to be "dependent" and in need of such support can and does vary.

16 For a book important in my own formation, see Barbara Ehrenreich, *Nickeled and Dimed* (New York: Metropolitan Books, 2001).

17 For all this, see Pius XI, *Quadragesimo Anno*, #59–65.

18 *Rerum Novarum*, #46.

19 *Caritas in Veritate*, #38, #66.

20 For the activities of the North American branch of this international movement, see their website: https://eocnoam.org/. For theoretical perspectives on the movement, see *The Economy of Communion: Toward a Multi-Dimensional Economic Culture*, ed. Luigino Bruni (New York: New City Press, 2002).

21 *Caritas in Veritate*, #41.

22 For one extended example of this thinking, which raises lots of questions, but ones we should consider more, see Kirkpatrick Sale, *Human Scale Revisited* (White River Junction, VT: Chelsea Green, 2017).

23 Valere Fallon, S.J., *Principles of Social Economy*, trans. Rev. John McNulty (New York: Benziger Brothers, 1934), 245–247.

24 Kathryn Tanner's targeting of what she calls "Finance-Dominated Capitalism" (New Spirit, 9–25) amplifies this criticism; indeed Tanner's book is somewhat more helpful in engaging the specific problem of how the dominance of the *Financial* sector is a problem.

25 The contrast between "work" and "life" comes from theorist Kathi Weeks, *The Problem with Work: Feminism, Marxism, Antiwork Politics, and Postwork Imaginaries* (Durham, NC: Duke University Press, 2011). Posadas relies heavily on Weeks for his own argument, calling it "the most comprehensive articulation to date of an anti-work perspective in relation to late capitalism". (344) Weeks provides the basic deconstruction of how hard work becomes naturalized such that "the moral goodness of work is politically constructed rather than entailed in its very nature, Weeks aims to open a space where it is possible to imagine different relations among and configurations of human work, material production, and creativity".(345)

26 *Laborem Exercens*, #12, 14.

27 *Laborem Exercens*, #12.

Embracing better work 283

28 For an exemplary summary of this argument, see Barry Schwartz, *Why We Work* (London: Simon & Schuster/TED Books, 2015).

29 Demetria Gallegos, "When Will I Retire? How About Never," *Wall Street Journal*, April 20, 2023, https://www.wsj.com/articles/when-will-i-retire-e3750715?mod=hp_lead_pos11.

30 Michael Naughton, *Getting Work Right: Labor and Leisure in a Fragmented World* (Steubenville, OH: Emmaus Road Publishing, 2019), 90.

31 Michael Naughton, *Getting Work Right: Labor and Leisure in a Fragmented World* (Steubenville, OH: Emmaus Road Publishing, 2019), 77–78.

32 Jeremy Posadas, "Reproductive Justice Re-constructs Christian Ethics of Work," *Journal of the Society of Christian Ethics* 40 (2020): 109–126, at 110.

33 Jeremy Posadas, "Reproductive Justice Re-constructs Christian Ethics of Work," *Journal of the Society of Christian Ethics* 40 (2020): 121.

34 Jeremy Posadas, "Reproductive Justice Re-constructs Christian Ethics of Work," *Journal of the Society of Christian Ethics* 40 (2020): 110.

35 Darby Kathleen Ray, *Working* (Minneapolis: Fortress, 2011), 123.

36 Oliver O'Donovan, *Entering into Rest* (Grand Rapids, MI: Eerdmans, 2017), 114, italics added.

37 "*Washington Post* spotlights Catholic University's beloved 'Ms. Willie'" December 8, 2022, https://communications.catholic.edu/news/2022/12/washington-post-spotlights-catholic-universitys-beloved-ms.-willie.html.

38 Given the context, this is not a corporate manipulation of an employee's religious faith. For a seminal exploration of a more complicated example of low-wage service work infused with Christianity, see Bethany Moreton, *To Serve God and Wal-Mart* (Cambridge, MA: Harvard University Press, 2009).

39 On the importance of excluding things from the system of monetary exchanges, see Michael Sandel, *What Money Can't Buy: The Moral Limits of Markets* (New York: Farrar Straus Giroux, 2013).

40 https://www.religionandjustice.org/interventions-forum-reproductive-and-economic-justice; No further details are offered on what these terms indicate. An online search for the term "cogenerative commonwealth" does not yield clues.

41 Letter to Mrs. Florence Kelley Wischnewetzky, February 25, 1886, in *Marx and Engels: Basic Writings on Politics and Philosophy*, ed. Lewis S. Feuer (New York: Doubleday, 1959), 254; quoted from Yves Simon, *Work, Society and Culture* (New York: Fordham University Press, 1971), 30.

42 Daron Acemoglu and James A. Robinson, *Why Nations Fail* (New York: Random House, 2012).

43 Jeremy Posadas, "Reproductive Justice Re-constructs Christian Ethics of Work", *Journal of the Society of Christian Ethics* 40 (2020): 122–125.

44 And, as already noted, hides the extraordinarily large dependence on the state.

45 And of course this is also exactly compatible with a sexual ethic that requires abortion for reproductive justice, since without it, one's sexual life will not be free in this "play" way. But this is another essay.

46 For an accessible and thoughtful philosophical account on which I generally rely here, see Richard Burke, "'Work' and 'Play'", *Ethics in the Conflicts of Modernity* 82, no. 1 (1971): 33–47.

47 Richard Burke, "'Work' and 'Play'", *Ethics in the Conflicts of Modernity* 82, no. 1 (1971): 38, makes this point, although his examples of compulsion are either biological instinct or physical compulsion. He later suggests that for someone who is a professional athlete or gambler, the "pay" is (or should be) extrinsic to the original enjoyment of the "play" that enticed the person to become good at the activity. But this ability to be paid for activities that one finds intrinsically enjoyable is

284 *David Cloutier*

key to Burke's fundamental claim that the best human activity combines aspects of work and play.

48 An exceptional example from my own neighborhood: a group of high school and junior high school girls put on a front-porch version of Shakespeare's *The Comedy of Errors*, with weeks of rehearsal and no adult supervision or direction. It was actually a full and credible performance that was a remarkable exhibition of creative play.

49 I thank Mary Hirschfeld for drawing my attention to this point.

50 See Richard Burke, "'Work' and 'Play'", *Ethics in the Conflicts of Modernity* 82, no. 1 (1971): 130, 170. In addition, note his use of the Cummins Engine Company of Indiana (172), as well as his use of the obligatory fishing village (178–180) – though this time a real one in contemporary Denmark that organized a cooperative approach to respond to EU fishing quotas!

51 St. Josemaría Escrivá, "Working for God", *Homily Posted* February 6, 2015, https://stjosemaria.org/working-for-god/.

52 See Alasdair MacIntyre, *Dependent Rational Animals* (La Salle, IL: Open Court, 1999), 120f.

53 See *Sollicitudo Rei Socialis*, #28, and *Centesimus Annus*, #36, the latter of which leads into a critique of resource use that is quite consonant with *Laudato Si*'s criticism (#106f.) of the "technocratic paradigm".

54 David Cloutier, *The Vice of Luxury* (Washington D.C.: Georgetown University Press, 2015). In that book, I argue extensively that the real problem we face in affluent cultures is the loss of a sense that luxury is a vice to be avoided, an argument that coheres with the basic history of developed economies I outlined above in Taylor. In my previous essay on work, I describe how economics itself assumes a negative attitude toward labor, such that it is simply to be aimed at maximizing one's consumption.

55 John Dewey, *Democracy and Education* (New York: Macmillan Co., 1916), 205–206, quoted in Richard Burke, "'Work' and 'Play'", *Ethics in the Conflicts of Modernity* 82, no. 1 (1971): 33.

56 Michael Naughton, *Getting Work Right: Labor and Leisure in a Fragmented World* (Steubenville, OH: Emmaus Road Publishing, 2019), 3.

57 More deeply, this problem seems to be a fundamental one that goes back to Rousseau, in which social structures of obligation and duty and individual free human flourishing are defined as *opposed* to one another, but the effect is to imagine a social order where people are "forced to be free" by a collective "general will". It is not an accident that a key problem is Rousseau is the imaginary shift in which sin and evil, rather than being identified with persons, comes to be identified as solely with malign structures. The opposite problem (all individual sin, no structural sin) is also a problem, but Posadas' proposal relies on an implied anthropology that leans very strongly in the Rousseauian direction.

58 John Hughes, *The End of Work: Theological Critiques of Capitalism* (Malden, MA: Blackwell, 2007), 163–164.

59 John Hughes, *The End of Work: Theological Critiques of Capitalism* (Malden, MA: Blackwell, 2007), 164.

60 For the more detailed argument, see David Cloutier, "The Worker's Paradise: Eternal Life, Economic Eschatology, and Good Work as the Keys to Social Ethics", *Plenary Address, Catholic Theological Society of America*, June 2021, 45–49.

61 *Laborem Exercens*, #14.

62 Paul VI, *Populorum Progressio*, #15.

16 Work, hope, and secularity

Ana Marta González

When people periodically speak of a "job crisis", they generally think of the disappearance of certain forms of work and their replacement by new ones. This was the case in the 1990s debate on the future of work,[1] which is still open, due to the transformations brought about by artificial intelligence, employment platforms, and the expansion of teleworking in many sectors. Yet, all these changes not only force us to rethink the technical and legal aspects of work, but also to reflect on its meaning.

Indeed, the world of work is experiencing a period of redefinition that affects not only the spaces, modes, and rhythms of work, but also how it is organized and integrated into human life. In this sense, more recent phenomena, such as "the great resignation", which has not yet been studied in depth, or more common – and quiet – acts of "quitting", are pointing toward a more general crisis related to the meaning of work.

In this contribution, I propose an interpretation of this crisis in terms of a disconnect between individual and social expectations around work. While, from a structural or economic point of view, individual work is mostly seen as an objective contribution to social production, from a cultural point of view, work is increasingly seen in terms of individual satisfaction. In my opinion, such disconnect can be considered as one more consequence of the collapse of modern utopian thought, which attempted to think both dimensions together, suggesting that the introduction of structural changes in the social division of work would bring about the cultural ideal of social freedom. From this perspective, the crisis of work could be easily reinterpreted as a crisis of hope and reframed in theological terms. Indeed, the collapse of the particular hope that utopian thought placed upon work does not necessarily mean the collapse of work as a site for ordinary human hopes, as well as for theological hope, whose exact nature has to be clarified.

Yet, before walking that path, it is important to reflect on the way work itself provides the basic structure for human existence in this world. In this regard, the modern reflection on work provides us with relevant insights to understand the manifold ways in which work articulates the internal dynamics of the secular world, thus contributing to a positive conception of this world. By a "positive conception of secular world", I mean one that

DOI: 10.4324/9781003508212-19

286　*Ana Marta González*

articulates its internal logic, rather than primarily presenting this world in opposition to a sacred world. Indeed, in my view, exploring the historical changes of work not only represents a key to illustrate the internal dynamics of the secular realm; it also shows how this secular realm is demanding a new source of meaning: not so much through the relationship to any utopia, but rather through the relationship to the sacred, in terms of theological fulfillment of a possibility inherent to ordinary human life.

Work as a site for hope

While particular events in the world of work can make its crisis of meaning more manifest, like any cultural crisis, it began to take shape decades ago. Already in the 1980s, Habermas summarily spoke of the "end of a utopia"[2] to indicate that, while work had constituted the epicenter of social causes for decades, at the time he wrote this was no longer the case. Instead, the work experience was becoming individualized, privatized, aestheticized, to which Bauman eloquently referred years later:

> Work has claimed the privileged place [it had in modernity], its status as the axis around which all efforts to constitute itself and build an identity revolved. But, as the path chosen for moral improvement, repentance and redemption, work has also ceased to be a focus of ethical attention of notable intensity. Like other activities in life, it now comes under the scrutiny of aesthetics first and foremost. It is judged according to its ability to generate pleasurable experiences. Work that does not have that capacity – that does not offer 'intrinsic satisfactions' – lacks value. Other criteria (among them his old moralizing influence) do not support the competition of aesthetics nor can they save the work from being condemned as useless, and even degrading, for the collector of aesthetic sensations.[3]

Today it is taken for granted that people work for only as long as they need or feel like. As soon as they have satisfied their individual expectations, of a useful or an aesthetic nature, they would no longer have a relevant reason to work and would be justified in dedicating themselves to other activities that, in the meantime, have been gaining weight in the shaping of one's social identity.

Indeed, while one can be intellectually persuaded that one's work represents an objective contribution to social production, from a subjective point of view, it is easy to lose sight of its objective dimension of service to one's own family, to society in general, and see it merely in utilitarian or hedonistic terms. Thus, in the minds of many people, work has lost its privileged place in the shaping of one's own identity, and has been separated from of its contribution to social development such that, in many cases, work itself is stripped of its status as an honest good, and is instead seen only as a pleasant or useful good.

Other times, however, it is not so much a question of a moral devaluation of work as of a more adjusted consideration of its place in the general context of human life. This is because the modernization process, boosted in part by the very division of work, not only has privileged a reductively economic view of work, but also has given rise to new social spaces, creating unprecedented forms of leisure and interaction in which modern individuals discover intra-mundane possibilities of self-realization that were previously only accessible to a small minority.

In this latter case, we might not be facing a crisis of the moral dimension of work as such, but rather a crisis of the modern way of organizing it, i.e., a context in which human beings are unilaterally subordinated to the production process. Phenomena like "the great resignation" precisely highlight the crisis of such a mode. From this perspective, it would not be work as such, but rather the underlying reductively economic view of work that puts aside its most specific human dimensions – its creative and social dimensions – which would have entered into crisis. As a result, people escape from work toward those other activities that are still experienced as humanly enriching, basically leisure activities.

If this analysis is correct, underlining the human dimensions of work would represent a way of rediscovering the internal relationship between work and leisure, no longer in terms of non-human and human activities, but rather in terms of two different dimensions of human life – a vision that again makes room for experiencing work as an ordinary site of human hope.

Relating work and hope makes sense because work is closely linked to the human condition itself, to our condition as precarious and temporary beings, to the fact that we have desires and needs. The satisfaction thereof, in addition to involving others and thus demanding a certain level of solidarity, requires a sustained effort over time, which is only possible when there is hope.

Yet, the mention of hope is also one of the reasons why work enters in its own right not only the realm of philosophical but also theological reflection: insofar as work is at the core of what it means to live in the world, *in hoc saeculo*, its ultimate meaning only becomes clear with reference to the "future world". As Charles Taylor has highlighted in his magnum opus, *A Secular Age*, the contrast between the present and future worlds appears within the framework of the axial and post-axial traditions to designate the temporal and immanent as opposed to an eternal and transcendent realm. The idea of secularity would originally spring from the contrast between the temporal and the eternal, which makes sense by reference to the idea of a future century not subject to movement and necessity. Yet, unlike a purely Platonic view of the contrast between the temporal and the eternal, which sees the descent of the eternal into the temporal in terms of degradation, Augustine articulated a positive view of time, which echoes a typically Christian assumption of the temporal by the eternal[4] in which the temporal and secular are revalued, and, in a certain way, "sacralized". Indeed, the pair

288   *Ana Marta González*

secular–sacred acquires an entirely new dimension once Christ himself has assumed a human nature forever.

Against this background, I would like to suggest that, if work provides the key to articulating the positive content of the secular world, the fact that the human reality of work has been assumed by Christ changes the way we should think about the relationship between the secular and the sacred. Instead of thinking about this relationship in terms of different times or spaces, we should consider the possibility that the work itself, in its structure and dynamism, demands a fullness of meaning that can only be granted by a sacred source.

My approach to this relationship, however, will be mainly philosophical, and nourished by the classics of social thought.[5] I am, above all, interested in understanding, with the help of these authors, how and why the dynamics of work contribute to positively configuring the different historical, social, and cultural forms that our world adopts, and that modulate our secular existence.

Secularity and the paradoxical nature of human work

Indeed, precisely because of its link with movement and change, the idea of secularity contains a reference to the specific historical ways in which human beings socially satisfy our needs and desires; hence the intrinsic connection, underlined by Marx, between the course of history and the transformation of the modes of production and work.[6]

The latter, however, does not mean that the direction of that history, from necessity to freedom, needs being thought in the utopian way pointed out by Marx. Before taking the general direction of history upon our shoulders in those terms, we should approach the practical meaning of freedom in the realm of work by considering more carefully what Aristotle meant, when he criticized salaried jobs arguing that they "deprive one's mind of leisure making it vile",[7] for, while with those words Aristotle was not denying the necessity or the hardships associated with work, his main interest was warning us against mercenary work, i.e. work done merely for the money and deprived of intrinsic meaning.

Indeed, the reference to meaning is implicit in the mention of preserving some leisure, and thus of freedom, in the midst of work itself. In other words: the world of work need not be just the world of necessity; it can also be the world of creativity. From this perspective, rather than restoring any sort of modern utopia, we are invited to consider how to reframe labor practices so that they make room for nourishing ordinary human hope in the integral development of human beings.

"Is not the life of man on earth a militia, and his days like those of a hired hand?" Job wondered (7:1) and thereby confirmed a simple fact – that human life is inseparable from work. But interpreting this fact is not easy: in Job's words, the affliction and harshness that accompany the laborer's work

Work, hope, and secularity   289

stands out above all, which he takes as a metaphor for human life in general. However, understanding this metaphor requires understanding the paradoxical nature of human work, i.e., an activity through which one earns a living, but, at the same time, wears it out.

This paradox admits different approaches. Simone Weil spoke of "the law of work" to designate this condition, whereby the satisfaction of any desire entails work, which postpones the gratification of that desire,[8] and, in this sense, involves asceticism and effort, although it can also be joyful, as the Holy Scripture suggests at other times.[9]

Both aspects are fused in our experience and in that repository of human experience that are human languages. Thus, in the action of work two meanings come together for which the classical languages had two different terms: _ponos/ergaszomai_; _labor/opus_: ponos and labor allude to the effort that accompanies earning a living; ergon and opus emphasize the creative, often joyous, dimension of human work.

Something similar occurs in other cultural traditions. As Richard Madsen pointed out to me, in modern Chinese there are also three words that translate as "work". One of them, (_gongzuo_) refers to work collectively oriented toward a common purpose, which includes, for example, academic work, but also, under the current communist system, work carried out within state-owned companies that are not usually very productive; another word (_laodong_) literally means strenuous exertion, and is often used to describe work in the workshops or factories of the modern industrial sector; another (_ganhuo_, "do what you have to do to live") refers to the brutal work that peasants have to do to survive amidst intensive agriculture.[10]

The latter two terms mainly touch on the effort and fatigue that accompany productive tasks. On the contrary, the former (_gongzuo_) touches on a more creative and, in that sense, joyful aspect of work, although it does so in a way that is far from contemporary Western sensibility. In contrast with emphasis on the individual that characterizes the modern West, the Chinese tradition stresses the communal orientation of work, the fact that one does not simply work for oneself, but for a community. It should be noted, however, that, before Adam Smith described the operation of the market as exclusively based on the usefulness of self-interest – something that was compatible with bourgeois virtues – the traditional vision in Western Europe was based on the integration of individual work with the common good.[11]

Both the joyful and the painful dimensions of work are present in the Genesis account that shapes the Judeo-Christian vision of work: the joyful aspect is prefigured in the Garden of Eden, where Yahweh placed man "to keep it and protect it" (Gn 2:15); while the painful, and even penal, dimension appears after the fall, when Adam is told of the fatigue that will accompany his work outside of paradise (Gn 2:17–19). The Genesis story also prefigures in the first couple the communal dimension of work, even if the possibility of conflict is announced very early on.

290 *Ana Marta González*

Division of work, alienation, and solidarity

In the first account of creation, the first couple jointly received the mandate to multiply and dominate the earth (Gn 1:28), after the fall, and therefore not without a certain penal dimension, they are addressed separately: the woman is told that she will suffer labor pains; the man is told that he will earn his bread with the sweat of his brow.

The division of labor also has a negative connotation in the story of Cain and Abel, where a primitive division of labor between farmers and herdsmen is seen as a potential source of conflict between brothers. But it is also made clear in the story of Babel that not just any union of forces is valid to generate authentic human fraternity. Indeed: while these texts suggest that there is a relationship between work and human fraternity, they also indicate that this relationship is not easily forged. On the one hand, the work necessary for getting ahead in life cannot be done in isolation; it must be divided and reciprocally exchanged, and this itself can be a source of solidarity. However, the division of labor is also an occasion for conflict.

It is not surprising, therefore, that, in modern economic history, the division of labor also has diverse readings: on the one hand, as Adam Smith stressed, it constitutes the main source of economic progress; on the other – as the authors of the nineteenth century highlighted – it is also the beginning of numerous personal and social forms of alienation.

Marx, in particular, questioned the goodness of the spontaneous division of labor, which results from natural differences based on sex, aptitude, etc. In his opinion, this kind of division led very early on to the difference between freemen and slaves. In fact, it can explain the ancient division of tasks into free and servile ones, which is responsible for the negative view of work that has prevailed in the West for centuries. Indeed, Aristotle thought of work itself in terms of "limited servitude".[12] Even when recognizing its necessity, it was considered an impairment of human freedom, which shines brightest in philosophy or politics. In his *The Theory of the Leisure Class*, Thorstein Veblen observed that, from very early on, the division of labor was associated with the appearance of a working class, made up of women and slaves, who performed routine tasks, and a leisure class, made up of men, who dedicated themselves to feats and competed with each other to see who could achieve the greatest feat.[13]

The naturalness with which ancient societies accepted the institution of slavery, including the idea that there are slaves by nature, makes it possible to understand why Marx saw in the progressive mechanization of work an opportunity to replace that "natural" division with another one dictated by the human will: precisely because the mechanical nature of tasks would make natural differences irrelevant. According to Marx, in communist society, the socially necessary work would be distributed equitably, and everyone could then dedicate themselves to the activities they deemed appropriate, without being confined to a single task.

Marx thought this way because he had previously reduced labor to pure, formally undifferentiated "work force". The truth, however, is that human work, as a concrete and personal action, is neither brute force, nor mere technique, for it is always embedded in a social practice and, as such, can be more or less qualified, yet is always inseparable from a broader exercise of practical reason. In fact, neither the mechanization of many tasks nor the appearance of computers and the development of artificial intelligence have canceled the need to specialize in other tasks that emphasize the more human and social dimensions of work, such as communication, empathy, criteria, judgment, and an integrative vision, qualities that are particularly evident in the professional field of care, which continues to grow and employ an increasing number of workers.[14]

In fact, care itself could be taken as paradigmatic of all professional practices to the extent that they involve dealing with human beings. Not only that: to the extent that care assumes the fragility of the human condition, and its dependence on nature, considering work from the perspective of care also implies reviewing the way in which our work both impacts nature and sustains social ties. It is clear, moreover, that in relation to the latter, the way in which we organize care work, which is currently divided between families, the market and the state, is of particular importance.[15] In this sense, working under the care paradigm requires delving into the nature of social solidarity.

While the division of labor can be read as leading to different kinds of alienations, it can also be interpreted as a call to greater solidarity. Indeed, as Durkheim famously observed,[16] increasing specialization makes us more interdependent, thereby making room for a type of cooperative solidarity that is not based on similarities of tribe, nation, etc.), but rather on differences, even if the moral activation of this solidarity still requires a certain feeling of community. According to Durkheim, in modern, deeply individualized societies, this feeling of community draws its strength precisely from a shared awareness of the incomparable dignity of the individual, beyond and despite any differences.[17]

Both insights are in tune with our times: we find ourselves in a moment of social evolution that is leading us to pay attention, on the one hand, to everything related to communication practices, and, on the other, to the division and organization of care. An opportunity lies ahead to recover the genuinely communal and moral sense of the division of labor. Indeed, if communication is part of an adequate organization of human work that engenders solidarity, awareness of the dignity of each person makes it possible to illuminate the challenges posed by the division of labor involved in information management and care. In this way, it is possible to recover the genuinely communal and moral sense of the division of labor.

In fact, throughout history, economic development has led us to ever greater and progressive specialization, which also promotes the moral solidarity outlined in the functional structure of divided work. Now, solidarity articulated around functional interdependence does not typically operate

292   *Ana Marta González*

solely among peers – for example, only among workers or only among managers. For this reason, to the extent that awareness of working on a common project is present, the human organization of work requires considering the ways in which carrying out a task provides relevant information to direct it, and, therefore, attaching importance to information flowing in both directions: from managers to workers and vice versa. As noted, communication is related to an adequate organization of human work, which is always more than pure undifferentiated force: it is an active and conscious contribution to a cooperative action, deliberately oriented toward a goal known and shared by all, with which it contributes to satisfying some human need.

In this horizon, human work clearly emerges as something more than pure undifferentiated force: it emerges as a conscious contribution to a cooperative action, deliberately oriented toward a clear human need, a goal shareable by all of us, to which each can contribute in a significant way. In other words, it clearly emerges as a service.

Service and professionalism

Precisely because it is oriented to satisfy some type of need, all work objectively constitutes a service, and, as Weber points out, represents a type of "economically oriented action".[18] We should consider that the word "service" can be regarded from an objective and a subjective point of view. From an objective point of view, every work, structurally inserted into the economy, contributes to the creation of utility, and thus objectively represents a service, even if this is not usually perceived by the worker, because of the division of work. Precisely, one of the goals of corporations is to make their workers more aware of their contribution to society, so that they can really develop a subjective attitude of service.

The connection of economy, and thus of work, and human needs is nothing new. It must be borne in mind that, in its original meaning, "economy" means administration of scarce resources to satisfy human needs. Undoubtedly, these needs are varied and open, since the division of labor itself, which multiplies with social density, also multiplies the needs that must be satisfied.[19] The job of businessmen and women is precisely to perceive those needs, and to find ways to satisfy them, for which they have to be deeply involved in the dynamics of the world, which also explains the close relationship between the market and the world.

This very fact shows to what extent economic relations have a prominent place in the configuration of the human world, and why work and market relationships are at the center of that worldliness. In each historical moment, the goods or services that each person produces with their work constitute their particular way of contributing to the common good and, where society is sufficiently broad, the market is where we go to exchange the goods or services that each one of us needs. To facilitate this exchange, we use money. For this reason, in principle, the money that we have – and that we have obtained in exchange for our services – is nothing other than our way of participating in the circulating wealth.

It should be kept in mind, however, that neither the human world nor society is completely identified with the market, nor is money the only measure of exchange; in fact, the market economy, which is governed by an exchange of goods whose value we estimate equivalent and measure with money, comes after a family economy governed by another kind of reciprocity of goods and services, with which we satisfy daily needs. And, as we well know, domestic economy also requires work. Likewise, in the midst of civil society, the market economy coexists with other types of economy that do not rely on exchange of equivalents, and also involve work. In fact, the very word economy comes from *oikos*, meaning house, home, and family. Now, there is no doubt that the goods and services that are produced inside the household also involve work, even if that work does not use money as a measure of exchange value: what a father or mother does for their child is not paid with money; nor would it be accurate to say that the child "pays" for the care received in childhood by taking care of his elderly parents. Although family life requires a certain justice and reciprocity, it does not take the form of the exchange of equivalents, which is typical of commutative justice. And although it is characterized by a certain benevolent and friendly interaction, it does not involve friendship based on interest, which, according to Aristotle, is friendly in the postponement of the payment of a debt.[20] In reality, the reciprocity proper to the family responds to the logic of gratuitousness and donation.

As cultural anthropologists who study the gift economy[21] have highlighted, the main difference between the latter and the market economy resides in the dual and simultaneous structure that market exchange adopts, as opposed to the triangular and deferred structure that the gift economy adopts. Compared to the giving–returning typical of the market, the exchange of a gift is a triangular structure, characterized by giving–receiving–returning. In this experience, in fact, the acceptance of the gift, we would say, the moment of gratitude, is decisive. The satisfaction of the need is important, but it is even more so the fact that this satisfaction responds to a liberal act, an act of love, which does not contravene, but rather exceeds the reasons of justice.[22] This is what justifies that, in matters of human relations, there is a presumption in favor of the family; because it is understood that, in general, the family takes better care of people, not worse. Certainly, the penetration of the market economy in all spheres of life can lead to the blurring of the logic of family life, but usually it never completely annuls it. Importantly, that dynamics is not alien to ordinary social life beyond family life. I consider Kant's insistence on the sacredness of the duty of gratitude significant in this regard.[23] Gratitude is not, in fact, a minor duty. It reminds us that not everything in human life, both inside and outside the family, is subject to the logic of the market.

Thus, noting the plurality of meanings of "economy" allows us to understand why defining work as an "economically oriented action" encompasses both the work inside and outside the home. What this definition does not

294 *Ana Marta González*

cover is what the ancients called "skhole", and which we have translated as "leisure", understood as free activities that are significant to us by themselves, and not because of the consequences derived from them. In our time, the word "leisure" – which should also be distinguished from the word "rest" – evokes a wide variety of activities. Of note, for the Greeks, it also included activities such as study, which, in contrast with economic work, we could refer to as "formative work". This is reflected, moreover, by the closeness between the Greek word *skhole* and our word "school".[24] In a similar way, what the Romans later called "otium" (*leisure*) was undoubtedly opposed to "nec-otium" (business), to occupations imposed by economic or political responsibilities, but not necessarily to study, to intellectual work, which is governed by its own internal logic: understanding a problem, composition, etc.

From another point of view, however, it is worth noting that studying itself could also, in a broad sense, be considered "economic work" to the extent that it is integrated into a praxis at the service of the community, that is, when it is ordered to a useful purpose. Thus, the medieval religious exempted those dedicated to the choir from manual labor. Here we must recall that, as Thomas Aquinas explains, manual work does not simply mean work that is done with the hands, but work ordered to the general utility.[25] This observation also makes it possible to understand – by the way – why both productive work, which we associate with the private sector, and the work associated with the so-called public service, count as economic work; it is because everything that has an objective dimension of service is counted as work. For this reason, people in the Middle Ages could refer to university teaching as "manual work".[26] And something similar could be said today of so-called "civic work",[27] with which a person voluntarily puts his professional competence at the service of the community.

What I would like to stress in this context, however, is that work born out of gratuitousness, be it domestic or civic work, needs not be less professional than work subject to the contractual logic of the market. But, also, that, in order to account for the reality of social life and arrive at a positive characterization of secularity, all types of work need to be taken into consideration.

As Weber notes, three features are implicit in the notion of profession: (a) the first is the idea of *dedication*, which evokes the religious origins of the term and explains the need for specialized knowledge as well as its ethical code; for this reason, Weber's text "Politikals Beruf" is sometimes translated interchangeably as "Politics as a vocation or profession". Simmel also speaks of "professional vocation", an expression that connotes the idea of a dynamic adjustment between personal qualities and social needs.[28] (b) The second is the *probability* of a lucrative opportunity, even if for whatever reason it doesn't materialize for a while. (c) The third is the specific training or preparation needed to carry out a socially relevant task.[29]

Work's reference to the satisfaction of needs, and, therefore, to the economy, explains why the configuration of the professions varies according to economic needs. It also explains why the allocation of professions is influenced by the socio-economic regime. Thus, in a feudal society, with a predominantly agrarian economy, the tasks that each one had to carry out were predefined by their position, and, therefore, the assignment of profession was not free. In a market economy, working under a free contract regime, in principle one chooses one's profession, which also fosters greater social mobility. This feature, in turn, accentuates the individuality of the professional *career* – one goes where there is work – and explains the importance that the concepts of training and "professional competence" acquire, which make us "competitive" in the market.

As advanced above, reflection on these distinctive facts, which emerge from the very dynamics of work, is central to articulating a positive definition of secularity, which encompasses the idea of economic work, culture (or formative work), and rest. Indeed, in this approach, work emerges not only as the ordinary site for hope, but also as the key element articulating the different dimensions of human life.

Professional work as the keystone of secular existence

The various reasons why work shapes secular existence should be clear by now: (a) for economic reasons, since we owe our subsistence and material prosperity to it; (b) for social reasons, because it gives us a position, a social identity, as well as the possibility of establishing bonds of solidarity beyond the family; (c) for practical reasons, because it compromises our reason and our freedom in an activity through which we objectively provide a service to others and in which we can grow personally; (d) for existential reasons, because, ultimately, the jobs we do throughout our lives – our work history – shape our peculiar way of being in the world, a vision of things that lasts beyond retirement.

Undoubtedly, all these reasons refer to our condition as needy creatures whose needs and desires, however, are not satisfied simply by nature, but by making use of reason and freedom, i.e. through work. Thus, it makes sense to maintain that the entire life of man is work, which is obviously a deeper category than formal employment.

The latter does not mean that everything in our life constitutes economic work. To the extent that human reason and freedom can be applied to activities that have meaning in themselves, we also speak of leisure – which also encompasses the broad world of education and culture. But, to the extent that these activities are also grafted onto an existence conditioned by space and time, even leisure or cultural activities are accompanied by some form of work; this is why we can call it formative work.

In addition, to the extent that every kind of work is accompanied by fatigue, rest itself becomes a necessity for us. In Aristotle's view, the meaning of rest would be none other than to restore the strength necessary to return to work. The idea that rest can have a deeper meaning, however, emerges

296   *Ana Marta González*

from Augustine's analysis of the "rest of God" in his *Literal Commentary on Genesis.*[30]

Indeed, as Augustine argues, the work of creation, which God carries out through his Word, does not involve any fatigue for Him; accordingly, the rest to which he consecrates the Seventh day, which knows no sunset, does not point back to any precedent fatigue; rather, it points at the plenitude of life of God himself. In this way, a fuller meaning for man's rest is also suggested, beyond simply restoring strength to return to work, namely, entering and sharing in God's rest through knowledge and love; something that will only take place fully "in the future world", not so much because there "we do nothing" but because "God will be all in all" (1 Co 15, 28). Compared to this perfect rest, any other rest that we can experience *in hoc saeculo* is nothing more than a momentary interruption of work, and therefore always relative rest, although it is all the more real the more it participates in God's rest.

Indeed, to the extent that work is sanctified, or performed in God, it participates in the very joy of God. And that is also why, to the extent that personality, economy, social ties, and cultural progress are tied to the reality of human work, the sanctification of work constitutes the foundation of the sanctification of secular realities. This is how Saint Josemaría Escrivá summed it up:

> Work is the vehicle through which man is inserted into society, the means by which he is assembled in the set of human relationships, the instrument that assigns him a place, a place, in the coexistence of men. Professional work and existence in the world are two sides of the same coin, they are two realities that require each other, without it being possible to understand one apart from the other.[31]

We know that in Escrivá's work and preaching, work does not appear solely as the natural enclave of human existence, but rather acquires a specific theological dimension, as a sanctifying and sanctifying reality. But it can acquire such a dimension only because it is regarded as a noble human reality:

> I have never been able to understand – he wrote – how for centuries Christians have come to think – and to practice it in this way – that work degrades. Work ennobles, because it is the fulfillment of a mandate from God, of a service done to God, and we have to serve him with joy.[32]

Indeed, throughout most European history, work has been undervalued due to the lasting prestige and influence of the lordly vision of life that, justified in Greece, lasted until well into the modern age. Still in 1930s Spain, when Escrivá began to speak of the sanctification of work, his words contrasted with the aristocratic vision of holiness that "had dominated the life of the Church for centuries. They sounded more aligned with the revaluation of the ordinary life" which, according to Taylor, we largely owe to the Protestant Reformation.[33]

In this sense, from a sociological point of view, Escrivá's appreciation for work might seem to place him, in line with the reformers. Yet, in addition to viewing work as man's obedient response to a divine mandate, or as a human way of serving others, in imitation of Christ, Escrivá invited to see it as a way of cooperating with God in the work of creation, and as a vehicle of his redeeming grace.[34] Along these lines, he used to speak of "sanctifying work, sanctifying oneself with work and sanctifying others with work", meaning that the grace of Christ, which Christians participate in through Baptism, heals and elevates the actions that they carry out, and with them all worldly realities, which, for this very reason, can no longer be considered as simply profane realities: "Strictly speaking", he writes,

> it cannot be said that there are noble realities that are exclusively profane, once the Word has deigned to assume an integral human nature and consecrate the earth with his presence and with the work of his hands. The great mission that we receive, in Baptism, is co-redemption.[35]

Installed in the logic of Incarnation that brings the eternal into the temporal, Christian's participation in Christ through Baptism also means that all secular realities, including ordinary human labor, can be interpreted in light of the redemption operated by Christ. Insofar as Christians work and rest in Christ, their ordinary work and rest are no longer just profane activities, but rather have a sacred dimension: they may be seen as having a real, although mysterious, efficacy in the configuration of the new heavens and the new earth, which God will bring out at the end of time. With this, a higher hope for human work emerges, a hope deeply rooted in human nature and yet of a theological source; a hope capable of welcoming and giving fuller meaning to the ideal of progress that inspired modern history.

That modern ideal, which now seems to have lost steam in the face of an individualist vision of work, could recover a deeply social dimension in light of a transcendent horizon, which, although it only appears as such to those who share in the same faith, does not cease to have an impact on this secular world, insofar as that very faith commits one to recover the full meaning of work, without reducing it to its productive and monetary value. Hence, I would like to conclude by relating the reflection on work to the issue of development, in all its dimensions, incorporating the cultural contributions with which modern times have enriched our experience of work.

Development around a human concept of work

In the eighteenth century, political economists, such as Smith, mainly addressed work as the only measure of value and the basic engine of improvement; by contrast, during the nineteenth century, perceptive observers of

298 *Ana Marta González*

social dynamics, such as Tocqueville or Marx, and the entire sociological tradition, warned of the dangers involved in a purely economic vision of work. Picking up Smith's own distinction of use and exchange value, Marx, in particular, warned against subordinating human development to increased production and, ultimately, to capital.

In the twentieth century, the evolution of organizational theory, from Taylorist schemes to more human schemes, as well as the social models that sought to balance work and capital, managed to reduce tensions and established a model of economic and social progress, the so-called "standard model of work". However, the globalization of markets at the end of the century once again altered this balance, favoring the financialization of the economy and the precariousness/progressive informalization of work. Despite the Pandemic and more recent geopolitical events, this is the context we are still in; and, precisely in this context, recovering the human sense of economic development becomes an urgent, not delayable goal.

Undoubtedly, the economy is in function of man, not the other way around. But the economy is put at the service of man by putting man himself at the center of the economy, not only as a passive consumer of goods and services, but as an active producer of those same goods and services; not only as an anonymous piece in a productive machine, but also as source of moral and relational goods that, through sustaining family and civic life ultimately sustain the market and the state. Promoting a human economy means promoting the creation of good jobs that give everyone a place and a recognizable identity, from which they can actively contribute to the society of which they are a part; it also means recognizing the specific contribution of third sector professionals to the wellbeing of our societies. Both pathways represent different forms of what we could describe as "meaningful work".

Ultimately, to talk about meaningful work is to talk about each person coming to see their own work as an integral part of a broader action, organized to serve some human need and with which we can feel solidarity, because of our common humanity. In our time, it is increasingly clear that this kind of service cannot be separated from attention to the natural and social environment, on which human development itself depends. This is related to the need to move from a linear development model, based on increasing production, to a sustainable development model, articulated around a human concept of work.

Indeed, one practical way of advancing toward a sustainable development model involves paying attention to the more human dimensions of work, for which it is essential to stop seeing it in purely abstract terms, as a pure factor of production, and to see it in contextual terms. This means putting the specific person of the worker first, who is never just an autonomous and individual producer, but a relational and dependent being who can go to work every day only because she is supported by her family, by her community. Under this view, a worker is comfortable working not just because of the economic incentives that she receives as an individual, but, to a large

Work, hope, and secularity   299

extent, because of the environmental and social conditions that accompany her work; and because, beyond the strict scope of work, she finds opportunities for rest and enjoyment in nature and in culture that simply have nothing to do with profit.[36]

Ultimately, an integral approach to the issue of development involves noticing the multiple ways in which the productive system depends on natural, ethical, and social factors that the economy cannot generate by itself, and that can only be appreciated and promoted when we make room in our lives – including our working life – for the non-utilitarian dimensions of our secular existence.

Notes

1 Jeremy Rifkin, *The End of Work: The Decline of the Global Labor Force and the Dawn of the Post-Market Era* (New York: G. P. Putnam's Sons, 1996).
2 See Jürgen Habermas, *El fin de una utopía*, El País, 1984.
3 See Zygmunt Bauman, *Trabajo, consumismo y nuevos pobres* (Barcelona: Gedisa, 2005), 57.
4 Cf. Charles Taylor, *A Secular Age* (Cambridge MA; London: The Belknap Press of Harvard University Press), 57. According to Taylor, Augustine articulated a positive view of time, which condenses the sheer flux of time into an instant, and which we can access by participating in divine life.
5 See Ana Marta González, *Trabajo, sentido y desarrollo. Inflexiones de la cultura moderna* (Madrid: Dykinson, 2023).
6 Karl Marx, *Early Political Writings* (Cambridge: Cambridge University Press, 1994), 145 fw.
7 Aristotle, *Politics*, VIII, 2, 1337b 15 (Chicago; London: The University of Chicago Press, 2013).
8 See Simone Weil, "El trabajo y el derecho," *Primeros escritos filosóficos* (Madrid: Trotta, 2018).
9 See *Qoh*, 3, 9–13.
10 Richard Madsen, *Personal Email*, Tuesday, January 25, 2022.
11 "It is not from the benevolence of the butcher, the brewer, or the baker that we expect our dinner, but from their regard to their own self-interest. We address ourselves not to their humanity but to their self-love, and never talk to them of our own necessities, but of their advantages". A. Smith, *The Wealth of Nations* (Harmondsworth, Middlesex: Penguin Books, 1982), Chapter 2.
12 Aristotle, *Politics* (Chicago, London: The University of Chicago Press, 2013), I, 13, 1260 b.
13 See Thorstein Veblen, *The Theory of the Leisure Class*, (New York: Oxford University Press, 2007), 11. See also p. 9.
14 See Dani Rodrik, "An Industrial Policy for Good Jobs", *Hamilton Project*, September 2022. https://drodrik.scholar.harvard.edu/files/dani-rodrik/files/rodrik_-_an_industrial_policy_for_good_jobs.pdf
15 Ana Marta González and Craig Iffland, "The Challenges of Care," *Care Professions and Globalization. Theoretical and Practical Perspectives*, eds. Ana Marta González and Craig Iffland (New York: Palgrave MacMillan, 2014), 1–29.
16 See Emile Durkheim, *The Division of Labour in Society* (New York: McMillan Press, 1984.
17 See Emile Durkheim, *Moral Education* (Mineola: Dover Publications, 2002), 12–13; 72–74.

300   *Ana Marta González*

18   Max Weber, *Economy and Society* (Cambridge: Harvard University Press, 2019), 210, §15.
19   For this reason, Durkheim considered that the purpose of civilization is not happiness: because civilization indefinitely multiplies the needs. See Durkheim, *The Division of Labour in Society* (New York: McMillan Press, 1984), 182 fw.
20   See Aristotle, *Nicomachean Ethics,* VIII, 13 (Cambridge: Cambridge University Press, 2013).
21   See Marcel Mauss, *The Gift: The Form and Reason for Exchange in Archaic Societies* (New York, London: W.W. Norton, 2000).
22   See Seneca, *On Benefits* (S.l.: The Floating Press, 2009).
23   See Immanuel Kant, *Metaphysics of Morals* (Cambridge: Cambridge University Press, 1998), 6: 455.
24   See Nicolás Grimaldi, *El trabajo. Comunión y excomunicación* (Pamplona: Eunsa, 2000).
25   "It must, however, be observed that under manual labor are comprised all those human occupations whereby man can lawfully gain a livelihood, whether by using his hands, his feet, or his tongue. For watchmen, couriers, and such like who live by their labor, are understood to live by their handiwork: because, since the hand is 'the organ of organs' [*De Anima* iii, 8], handiwork denotes all kinds of work, whereby a man may lawfully gain a livelihood". Thomas Aquinas, *S. Th.* II. II. q. 187, a.3
26   Cf. Jacques Le Goff, *Les intellectuels au Moyen Âge* (Paris: Seuil, 1985).
27   Cf. Ulrich Beck, *The Brave New World of Work* (Cambridge, Malden, MA: Polity Press, 2000).
28   See Georg Simmel, *Sociology: Inquiries into the Construction of Social Forms* (Boston: Brill; 2009).
29   Max Weber, *Economy and Society* (Cambridge: Harvard University Press, 2019), 248, §24.
30   Cf, St. Agustine, *De Genesi ad litteram libri duodecim, Opera Omnia,* XV (Madrid: BAC, 1969).
31   St. Josemaría Escrivá, *Carta 6-V-1945,* n. 13. Yet unpublished.
32   St. Josemaría Escrivá, *Instrucción sobre la Obra de San Miguel,* n. 26. Yet unpublished.
33   See Charles Taylor, *Sources of the Self. The Making of the Modern Identity* (Cambridge: Cambridge University Press, 1989).
34   Although the reformers assumed these ordinary realities from the perspective of the "Obedience of Faith", they continued to consider them affected by sin. See José Luis Illanes, *Tratado de teología espiritual* (Pamplona: Eunsa, 2007).
35   St. Josemaría Escrivá, *Christ Is Passing By* (New York: Scepter; 2002), n. 120. See also n. 112.
36   See Ana Marta González, *Trabajo, sentido y desarrollo. Inflexiones de la cultura moderna* (Madrid: Dykinson, 2023), Chapter 8.

Index

Note: Page numbers followed by "n" refer to end notes.

access to basic food needs 158, 159, 164
angels 30, 82, 210, 211, 213, 215, 216, 218, 222n54, 230
anthropocentric 204, 205, 208, 210, 212
anthropocentrism 86, 203, 206, 208, 210, 211
anti-work 40, 267, 268, 270, 271, 278, 280, 281, 282n25
"antiwork ethic" 11
antiwork theory 30
Aquinas, St. Thomas 10, 20, 25, 37n84, 201, 209–213, 217, 221, 222, 223n69, 224n95, 253, 264n20, 265n21, 294, 300n25
Aranda, Antonio xi, xvii, 8, 95, 107n2
Aristotle 83, 94n50, 179, 185n31, 245n41, 248–253, 264, 288, 290, 293, 295, 299, 300n20
Arocena, Félix María xi, 10, 169, 182n6, 183n8, 184n22
Atkinson, Tyler 134, 143, 145, 149n34–36
Athonite the Silouan, St. 51
Athonite the Sophrony, St. 45, 56n8–10, 57n27
Augustine, St. 31, 37n86, 38n92, 81, 82, 92n28, 181, 184n22, 200n13, 224n85, 287, 296

Barth, Karl 182n3, 230
Basil of Caesarea, St. 48–50, 54, 55, 57, 58n33–35, 180
Baxter, Richard 231
Beale, Gregory K. 214, 223n72–74
Beauchamp, Paul 136, 145n13
Becker, Gary 262, 263n1, 264n2, 265n31, 266n43

Benedict of Nursia, St. 79, 171, 174
Benedict XVI (Joseph Ratzinger) 100, 101, 103, 109n22–27, 110n28–31, 185n25, 186n37, 189, 200n14, 207, 219n16, 220n29, 272, 279
Berdyaev, Nikolai 8, 60, 66–72, 75–76
Bergsma, John 21, 32n12–14, 166, 223n74
Bible, The xv, 20–22, 78, 81, 88, 131, 136, 145n9, 147n24, 150, 155, 180, 183n9, 206, 236
biocentrism 204, 205, 207
Bonaventure, St. 8, 77, 78, 81–8, 91n22, 92–94, 132–135, 143, 145n3
Brentano, Lujo 232, 233
Brown, Wendy 240, 245n54
Brugarolas, Miguel xvii
Buckley, William 241
Bugnini, Annibale 176, 185n26
Bulgakov, Sergey 8, 60, 62–72, 72n4–5, 73–75
Burke, Richard 279, 283n46–47, 284
burnout 1

Caballero, Juan Luis xi, 8, 14n12, 112, 126–127, 144n1
Cabasilas, St Nicholas 51, 57n26, 184n22
care of the planet 161, 162
career 53, 229, 295
Caritas in Veritate (Encyclical) 282
Casper, Bernhard 96, 97, 107n6–7
Cass, Oren 269, 282n12
Catholic social thought 10, 13n10, 203, 206, 207, 272, 273, 280
celebration 79, 88, 156, 158, 179, 183n7; and celebration of creation

302 Index

214, 281; and celebration of Mass
177; and Eucharistic celebration
175, 178, 185n23; and liturgical
celebration 169–175, 181
Centesimus Annus (Encyclical) 187,
265n32, 278, 284n53
Cerfaux, Lucien 118, 126n4, 127n27
Chenu, Marie-Dominique 13n2, 30,
31n2, 37n82, 89n2, 90n5
Chesterton, G. K. 237
Ciulla, Joanne 3, 14n18, 197, 202n41
civic work 294
Cloutier, David xi, 11, 267, 281n4–5, 284
co-creationality 208
Comblin, Joseph 3
common good 9, 11, 54, 80, 81, 88,
162, 165, 183n9, 189, 195, 196, 198,
199, 217, 236, 258, 280–289, 292
consequences of technological
innovation 165; technological
progress 47, 69, 71
Constantine 133
contemplation 9, 10, 89, 97, 133, 134,
140, 143, 203, 207, 209–211, 213,
216–218
contemplation of God 30, 37n86, 204,
205, 211, 218
context of work 6–8, 10, 12, 48, 112,
122, 123, 150, 151, 199
Cosden, Darrell 4, 5, 9, 10, 15, 19, 24,
26, 27, 29–31, 32n3, 34–37
cosmic liturgy 213–216, 218
Crenshaw, James 140
Cuddeback, John 258, 260, 266n35

Day, Dorothy 260, 266n38
decent work 72, 163, 164
definition of work 2–7, 41, 63, 112,
117, 122, 123, 198
Deming, W. Edwards 278
development xv, xvi, 3, 11, 12, 13n1,
24, 40, 47, 60, 70–72, 86, 87, 96;
and development of creation 5, 41,
84, 112, 198; and development of
nature 78, 84; and development of
the cosmos 5; and development of the
spirit 71; and human development
108n17, 112, 113, 115, 117, 119,
120, 152, 163, 180, 189, 195, 198,
207, 232–234, 244n26, 248, 249,
259, 268, 275, 277, 280, 286, 288,
291, 297–299

disabled and vulnerable (protection of
the) 159, 164
divine filiation/children of God 12,
99, 106, 119, 124, 180, 184n16,
222n51, 224n93
division of labor 228, 250, 259, 262,
290–292
division of work (labor) 285, 287,
290, 292
domestic economy (family economy)
247–249, 258–260, 263, 293
Domingo, Rafael xvii, 224n94
Douglas, Mary 151, 157, 159, 166n6,
167n37–39, 168
Durkheim, Emile 291, 299, 300n19

Eagleton, Terry 239
Ecclesiastes 9, 47, 131–133, 138,
140–144, 145n12, 147n21, 147n24
Eck, J. 234
ecocentrism 204, 205, 207–209, 218
ecojustice 206, 208
ecology 203, 206
ecospirituality 206, 209, 220
ecotheology 204, 206, 220n30
Ellingson, Stephen 206, 220
employment (as distinct from work)
1, 4, 37n86, 44, 45, 49, 51, 57n21,
163, 254, 261, 262, 265n3, 275,
285, 295
equity 52, 162
Escrivá, St Josemaría 10, 12, 16n41,
37n85, 87, 94n67, 98, 107, 111n38,
181, 186, 224n96, 278, 284n51,
296, 297, 300
Eucharist 9, 10, 45, 133, 175–182,
185n23, 216–218, 223n71, 236, 237

faith and work 1, 4, 8–10, 43–7, 49, 88,
96, 97, 171, 180, 181, 229–231, 240,
283n38, 297
Firer Hinze, Christine i, 14, 281
Florovsky, Georgy 59, 61
Fourier, Charles 276
Francis of Assis, St 81, 209
Francis (Pope) 203, 207–210, 218n2,
219n3–12, 221n33, 221n34, 221n36,
221n39, 239n40
Friedman, Milton 232, 233, 244n29,
265n24
Fyodorov, Nikolai 8, 60–62, 66–69,
71, 72

Gaudí, Antoni 180
Gaudium et spes 27, 98, 205, 220n17
Gautier, Christine 30, 37n81
genetic manipulation 160, 164
Genung, John Franklin 140, 147n20
gift economy 293
Gnilka, Joachim 101, 109n19, 109n20
God, the owner of the earth 162, 165
God, the owner of time 161
God's plan 4, 117, 120, 127n30, 138, 145n14, 178
Golitzin, Alexander 212, 223n62
González, Ana Marta xi, xvi, xvii, 11, 12, 14n11–13, 15n26, 20, 31n1, 32, 40, 41, 56n2, 56n3, 89n1, 125n2, 144n1, 166n5, 202n42, 285, 299, 300n36
González de Cardedal, Olegario 105, 111n35–37, 111n38
good of human life 6, 80, 89, 164, 258
Good, Edwin M. 140
Gordis, Robert 140, 147n23, 148n26
Granada, Daniel 10, 15n37, 201n25, 202n39
Green Thomism 209
Gregory, Brad 232, 233, 236, 243n14–17, 244n29
Guardini, Romano 98, 107n10, 127n44, 179, 182n4, 185n30
Guitián, Gregorio xi, xv, 1, 13n3, 14, 15n26–27, 20, 31n1, 32, 40, 41, 56n2–3, 89n1, 125n2, 144n1, 166n5, 202n42

Habermas, Jürgen 286, 299n2
Hamesse, Jacqueline 81, 91
Hanson, Jeffrey 4, 14n21
Hauerwas, Stanley 238, 239, 241, 245n50–51
Hayek, Fiedrich 232, 233, 244n29
Headlam, Stewart 227, 233, 237, 245n43–49, 246n56
Hebrew Bible 21, 32n13, 132, 151, 152, 272
Hélio, Luciano 10, 14, 144n1, 187, 200n10
Henry VIII 208
hierarchy 4, 6, 9, 44, 79, 134, 210–213, 216, 279; and "hierarchy of creativity" 68
Hirschfeld, Mary L. xii, 11, 243n18, 247, 264, 284n49

Hirschman, Albert O. 251, 264n17
homo œconomicus 232
honesty in transactions 159, 164
Hughes, John 279, 284n58–59
human action 5, 77, 80, 86, 119, 138, 141, 189, 190, 192, 193, 197, 199, 230
human dimensions of work 287, 298
human economy 298
human work and trinitarian creation xv, xvi, 3, 4, 7, 8, 10–12, 14n22, 15n32, 19–25, 27, 28, 30, 33n18, 34n44, 36n75, 42, 44–47, 52, 55, 60, 62, 63, 65, 77, 78, 82, 85–89, 97, 99, 102, 106, 109n19, 119, 121, 122, 125, 154, 170, 173, 175, 176, 190, 193, 197, 198, 203–206, 209, 212, 213, 215, 218, 252, 282n25, 288, 289, 291, 292, 296, 297

image and likeness 4, 7, 8, 119, 152
incarnation 8, 27, 39, 40, 42, 43, 52, 55, 78, 79, 89n2, 95, 96, 98, 213, 215, 218, 236, 297
integral ecology 203
integration (of work) 1, 2, 8–10, 12, 129, 169, 189, 193–195, 197–199, 289
integrity of the moral subject–unity of life 181
intentional dimension of prudence 190–192, 195, 200n21, 201n22
intervention in the economy 162
Izquierdo, César xvii, 14n12, 144n1

Jardine, Lisa 232, 243n13
Jensen, David H. 20, 32n7
Jerome, St. 133, 145n3
Jesus Christ (Jesus) 7–10, 12, 13, 21–23, 25–31, 32n11, 34n44, 39, 40, 42–44, 46, 47, 49, 52–54, 56, 57n20, 61, 78, 79, 84, 88, 95–106, 107n12–13, 108n14, 109, 110n31–32, 111–119, 122–125, 126n18, 127n29, 139, 142, 169, 170, 173–182, 184n17–18, 185n23, 188, 189, 192–196, 200n13, 213, 215–218, 224n93, 230, 231, 235–237, 270, 281n2, 282n14, 288, 297
John Paul II, St. 3, 4, 10, 14n17, 15n35, 21, 24, 25, 32n10, 46, 74n50, 90n4, 188, 189, 200, 209, 221n39,

304 *Index*

223n71, 248, 256, 264n3–4, 265n32, 268, 273, 274, 278, 280
Johnston, Robert K. 142, 147n21–23, 148n27
Joubert, Callie 141, 147n24, 148n25

Kant, Immanuel 63, 293, 300n23
Keynes, John (Maynard) 229, 244n34
Kyrk, Hazel 254, 255, 257, 259–263, 265, 266

labor relations 198
Laborem Exercens (Encyclical) 3, 10, 21, 24, 46, 187, 188, 194, 201n37, 256, 268
Lange, Rocio de xvii
Lasch, Christopher 261, 265n28, 266n41
Laudato Si' (Encyclical) 92, 207, 208, 218n2, 219, 221, 284n53
learning (formative work) 294, 295
LeFebvre, Michael 214, 223n75–80
Leo XIII 1, 13n4, 200n1, 201n34–35, 272
León-Sanz, Isabel, M. xii, 8, 77, 92n23, 93n36, 94
Lille, Alain de 81
lineal versus sustainable development model 298
liturgy (and work) 45, 56n11, 166n9, 169–181, 183n15, 184n20, 185n30, 213–216, 218, 236
Lohfink, Norbert 140
Long, Duane Stephen 11, 15n25, 227
Long, Steven A. 209, 221n37
Lossky, Vladimir 59
Lubac, Henri de 28, 37n78, 201n24
Ludlow, John 233, 235, 236
Luther, Martin 14n12, 23, 34n27, 132, 134, 135, 143, 144n1, 145n3, 231, 234

Macarius the Great, St 54, 57n31, 58n32
Machiavelli, Niccolò 234
MacIntyre, Alasdair 278, 280, 284n52
Madsen, Richard 289, 299n10
Mankiw, Greg 247, 248, 263n1
man's vocation to work 12, 153, 166n16, 176
manual and intellectual work 78, 79, 81, 294
Maomed, Carola xvii
market economy 252, 253, 257, 293, 295

Marx, Karl 63, 67, 196, 233, 240, 243n19, 246n56, 251, 264n15, 276, 277, 288, 290, 291, 298, 299n6
Massaro, Thomas 207, 221n31
Mattison III, William C. xvii
Maurice, F. D. 227, 233, 235–239, 241, 244n33, 244n34, 245n36–40
Maximus the Confessor, St. 42, 43, 56n4–6, 59, 223n71
McLaughlin, Ryan Patrick 210, 211, 222n47–48
meaning of work xv, 2, 4, 6, 20, 39, 40, 43, 56, 65, 72, 78, 103, 105, 106, 131, 187, 189, 193–199, 247, 249, 252, 263, 285, 297
"Meaning of Work in Recent Theology, The" (project) xv, 2, 89n1, 131
meaningful work 1, 3, 6, 45, 67, 71, 196, 197, 252, 258, 298
mediation of man in the universe 78, 83
migrants (attention to) 163–164
Milgrom, Jacob 159, 167n33, 168
Mitchell, Hinckley G. 140, 147n19
Moltmann, Jürgen 24, 26, 27, 29, 31, 33n25, 37n87, 38n89
moral dimension of affections 190–193, 195–197, 199, 201n22
Murphy, R. 140
mystical language 209
mystical vision 217
mysticism 203

Nash, James A. 204, 219n14
Nash, Roderick 206, 220n19
Naughton, Michael J. i, 9, 15n33, 274, 279, 283n30–31, 284n56
New Testament 21, 22, 49–51, 53, 78, 100, 105, 111n38, 112, 142, 144n1, 145n9, 174, 179, 215
Nichols, John 240, 245n55, 246n57
Nocke, Franz Joseph 28, 36n76, 37n77
normative or moral dimension (of work) 5, 6, 99, 198

objective dimension of work 4, 71, 187–190, 193, 196–199, 249
O'Donovan, Oliver 26, 275, 283n36
oikos 248, 249, 252, 257, 259–261, 263, 293
Old Testament 68, 79, 103, 109n19, 111n38, 114, 128n52, 145n9, 183n9, 214, 215
Opus Dei 16n40, 107n9, 187

ordo amoris 189–193, 195, 197–199, 201n25
Origen 132, 133, 143, 145n2
Orthodox perspective xv, 7, 8, 39, 40, 42–47, 49, 51, 53, 55, 56n12, 57n21, 59, 61, 62, 64, 67, 245n41
otiari–negotiari 179

Pannenberg, Wolfhart 31, 37n83, 38n88
paradoxical nature of work (labor and work) 80, 81, 256, 288–292
Paul, St. 8, 54, 55, 98, 112–123, 126n24, 184n17, 215, 236
Pérez Gondar, Diego 9, 14n12, 15n34, 131, 144n1, 145n2, 166, 167n35
Pérez-Soba, Juan José 190, 200, 201
Persidok, Andrezj xii, 7, 8, 59
Peterson, Eric 215, 218, 223n82, 223n84, 224
Pieper, Josef 170, 182n4, 185n31, 279
Piketty, Thomas 229, 242n4
Piper, Otto 2, 14n14
Pirke de Rabbi Eliezer 154, 167n21
Pius XI 27, 200n2, 272, 282n17
Posadas, Jeremy 16n39, 21, 30, 32n9, 267, 270, 272–283, 284n57
profession xvi, 22, 41, 49, 107n9, 112, 114, 204, 274, 294, 295
professional life and family life 2, 144, 163, 181, 185n23, 257, 258, 260, 266n43, 274, 283n47, 291, 293–296, 298
Protestant perspective xv, 7, 11, 19, 20, 24, 29–31, 227–238, 241, 243n22, 244n29, 297
Pseudo Dionysius (the Areopagite) 25, 59, 87, 212, 216, 222n58, 223n59–61

Rad, Gerhard von 15n29, 140, 147n21
Rahner, Karl 96, 107n3–5
Ray, Darby Kathleen 275, 283n35
redemption 10, 12, 19, 20, 24, 26, 34n44, 35n46, 40, 45, 47, 53, 68, 78, 84, 113, 135, 162, 177, 230, 286, 297
Reed, Esther 273
Reid, Margaret 255–257, 259, 261, 263, 265, 266
relationality 204
Rerum Novarum (Encyclical) 187, 193, 280, 282n18

respect for nature 158, 159, 164
rest xvi, 25, 28–31, 39, 40, 42, 43, 46–48, 55, 56, 56n4, 79, 81, 88, 116, 119, 121, 124, 127n30, 131, 135, 138, 139, 142, 146n15, 160, 161, 163, 164, 179, 188, 215, 242, 294–296, 299
rest (God's rest) 21, 22, 24, 25, 32n14, 42, 161, 179, 215, 282n14, 296
right to property 159, 162, 164, 194
rite 111n38, 148n31, 170, 176
Romeu Dale 194, 200n7, 201n36
Rowlands, Anna 218, 224n97

Sabbath 21, 22, 27, 115, 121, 150, 151, 160, 161, 163, 179, 214, 215, 279, 282n14; and sabbath of the Lord 121, 161, 215
Saint Victor, Hugo of 81, 93n39
sanctification of work 106, 111n38, 187, 204, 205, 218, 296
Sanz Sánchez, Santiago xii, 7, 19, 32n4, 37n83, 38, 126n26
Scheffczyk, Leo 97, 107n8
Scheid, Daniel P. 209, 221n37
Schlag, Martin xii, 10, 13n1, 15n36, 203
Schmaus, Michael 28, 37n79
Schor, Juliet 265n22, 269, 281n11
Scott, R.B.Y. 140
Seidel, Emil 240
Simmel, Georg 294, 300n28
Simon, Yves R. 3, 5, 14n19–20, 276, 277, 283n41
Smith, Adam 228, 233, 234, 250, 255, 260, 264n10, 265, 266n37, 289, 290, 297, 298, 299n11
social dimension (of work) 3, 97, 188, 198, 287, 291, 297
social justice 158, 181, 212
social protection 158, 164
Sollicitudo Rei Socialis (Encyclical) 278, 284n53
Solomon (King) 133–135, 143
Solovyov, Vladimir 8, 60–62, 64, 67, 71, 72
spiritual worship 118, 173–175, 184n17
Stallman, Bob 150, 165n1–2
SteenkampNel, Annalie E. 142, 148n29–32
Steuart, Sir James 228, 234, 240, 242n1–2
stewardship 144, 206–209, 220n22
Stone, Christopher 204, 219n13

306　*Index*

subjective dimension/experience of
　work 1, 9, 10, 88, 94n67, 187–190,
　192–194, 196–199, 201n25, 248,
　251, 297
sustainability xvi, 163–165, 298
"sweatshops" 1, 268
Symeon, St. 50, 57n25
Szrot, Lukas 207, 208, 220n28, 221n35

Tanner, Kathryn 229, 242n3, 267,
　281n2, 282n24
Tawney, R. H. 227, 230, 233–235, 238,
　243n21–23, 244
Taylor, Charles 20, 32n5, 37n85, 268,
　269, 281n7, 281n9–10, 284n54, 287,
　297, 299n4, 300n33
Taylor, Paul 204, 219n15
temple 27, 102, 103, 108n18, 111n38,
　118, 127n29, 152–154, 165, 183n9,
　184n22, 214, 215
terminology on work 20, 22, 80, 81
Theodore the Studite, St. 52, 53, 57n29
theology of work xv, 1–4, 6, 7, 9–11,
　14n22, 19, 23, 25, 28, 30, 33n25,
　36n75, 39–42, 44–47, 51, 54–56, 77,
　81, 89n2, 97, 125, 151, 163, 169,
　174, 175, 267, 279
Thils, Gustave 25, 31n2, 35
Thomas, Joseph 3, 4, 14n15, 14n22
Thompson, Christopher J. 209, 221n37
time for God 121, 161, 215
to till and to keep 9, 10, 78, 146n15,
　153, 154, 289
Tocqueville, Alexis de 298
Toma, Daniel 216, 224n86–90
Torrance, Alexis xii, 5, 7, 56, 57n28–30
Tran, Jonathan 239, 245n52
Trubetskov, Sergey 64
Turner, Phillip 238, 245n50
types of economy 293

unity of moral action 10, 189, 190,
　197, 199
University of Navarra xv–xvii, 2,
　89n1, 131
University of Notre Dame xvii; and
　Department of Theology xvii; and
　Mendoza College of Business xvii
utopian and Christian hope 28, 285, 286

Varo, Francisco xiii, 10, 150, 166n18
Veblen, Thorstein 290, 299n13

virtue 10–12, 30, 41, 51, 181, 192,
　195, 199, 200n13, 201n22, 201n25,
　206, 217, 229, 231, 232, 235, 239,
　240, 248–254, 256, 258, 261, 263,
　278, 289
"Vocational Professions and the
　Organization of Work" xvi
Volf, Miroslav 4, 14n22, 15, 19, 21,
　23–26, 29–32, 33n25, 34n26–35,
　35n50–59

wages 80, 159, 177, 188, 229, 240, 252,
　264n19, 271, 272
Weber, Max 11, 227, 229–234, 242,
　243, 292, 294, 300
Weeks, Kathi 16n39, 32n9, 277,
　282n25
Weil, Simone 289, 299n8
Whewell, William 235
Wolff, Richard 240, 245n53
work and care xvi, 12, 106, 114, 118,
　121, 125, 144, 145n14, 152, 153,
　155, 161, 204, 206, 207, 256, 259,
　271, 275, 278, 291, 293
work and communication 173, 291, 292
work and contemplation 9, 10, 204,
　205, 218
work and creation 4–7, 9, 19–31,
　33n18, 33n25, 36n75, 37n85, 41, 62,
　63, 65, 79, 82, 84, 85, 87, 88, 89n2,
　94, 97, 105, 106, 112, 113, 118, 144,
　147n21, 152, 153, 161, 165, 166n16,
　169, 179, 182, 187, 194, 198, 205,
　206, 213, 214, 216–218, 241, 280,
　292, 296, 297
work and creativity 2, 8, 22, 31, 47, 68,
　78, 87–89, 91n20, 113, 119, 135,
　160, 164, 252, 270, 274, 282n25, 288
work and family 9, 11, 131, 144, 152,
　153, 157, 163, 185n23, 230, 256–263,
　276, 286, 293, 295, 298
work and human dignity 4, 28, 68, 88,
　143, 164, 271
work and leisure xvi, 9, 80, 170, 179,
　279, 287, 288, 290, 294, 295
work and love 8, 10–12, 20, 22, 28, 29,
　33n18, 34n44, 44, 54, 55, 84, 85,
　87, 89, 94n67, 98, 114, 121, 182,
　184n16, 197, 199, 217, 218, 229,
　239, 241, 242, 247, 276, 296
work and play 147n21, 268, 277–279,
　281, 283n47

work and rest 9, 21, 22, 25, 27, 32n14, 39, 48, 49, 80, 88, 121, 150, 151, 161, 163, 174, 214, 282n14, 296, 297

work and service 1–3, 5, 6, 8, 9, 11, 12, 15n27, 26, 46, 54, 79–81, 83, 88, 89, 106, 113, 121, 161, 175, 181, 196, 198, 248, 251, 252, 257, 262, 265n26, 266n37, 269, 273, 275, 276, 279, 283n38, 286, 292–296, 298

work and solidarity 10, 88, 121, 170, 177, 189, 195, 199, 290, 291, 298

work and tension 9, 10, 40, 63, 97, 113, 136, 189, 199, 298

work and the common good 9, 11, 54, 80, 81, 88, 183n9, 189, 195, 196, 198, 199, 217, 280, 289, 292

work and the Cross 12, 24, 34n44, 47, 70, 97, 174, 182, 217, 218

work and the glory of God 54, 87, 180

work and the image of God in man 20, 77, 78, 81, 82, 87, 88, 97, 144, 188, 277

work and worship 9, 10, 26, 113, 151–155, 157, 163, 164, 165n3, 166n16, 169–175, 181, 183, 213, 214

"Work as a Human Vector of Sustainable Development" xvi

work as art 8, 31, 50, 65, 66, 70, 77–79, 81, 84–87, 90n5, 91n20, 105, 108n17, 248–254, 256, 261, 262, 264n13

work as key for understanding the dynamics of the secular world 11, 204, 285, 286, 288, 295–297

"Work, Care, and Development" xvi

worship and livestock activity 30, 155

worship and the processing of agricultural products 156

Zimmerli, W. 140

Printed in the United States
by Baker & Taylor Publisher Services